THE OXFORD HISTORY
OF ENGLISH ART

Edited by T. S. R. BOASE

THE OXFORD HISTORY OF ENGLISH ART

Edited by T. S. R. BOASE
President of Magdalen College, Oxford

Plan of Volumes

SIR FRANCIS CHANTREY: MRS. BOULTON (DETAIL). Great Tew, Oxon

ENGLISH ART
1800–1870

T. S. R. BOASE

OXFORD
AT THE CLARENDON PRESS
1959

Oxford University Press, Amen House, London E.C.4

GLASGOW   NEW YORK   TORONTO   MELBOURNE   WELLINGTON
BOMBAY   CALCUTTA   MADRAS   KARACHI   KUALA LUMPUR
CAPE TOWN   IBADAN   NAIROBI   ACCRA

PRINTED IN GREAT BRITAIN
AT THE UNIVERSITY PRESS, OXFORD
BY VIVIAN RIDLER
PRINTER TO THE UNIVERSITY

PREFACE

NO one can hope, or I think wish, to have read all that contemporaries wrote about art in the first three-quarters of the nineteenth century. I have seen much of the painting, sculpture, and architecture, but cannot claim that the survey is in any way complete. Many paintings, famous in their day, I have failed to trace, and the quest is none the easier from the changes that have taken place in their titles, the long Academy inscriptions being too lengthy for convenient reference. For this prolific and voluble period there are fortunately many guides. Since 1928, when Sir Kenneth Clark in his *Gothic Revival* blazed a new trail through what he described as 'these unmapped regions', nineteenth-century architecture has had many exponents and the names of Goodhart-Rendel, B. F. L. Clarke, Summerson, Betjeman, Pevsner, Colvin, and Hitchcock must be constantly had in grateful remembrance by any worker in this field. Mr. Rupert Gunnis in his *Dictionary of Sculptors* has made possible a reassessment of much that has been long forgotten. In painting the great names, Blake, Constable, Turner, the Pre-Raphaelites, have received detailed and often distinguished treatment: others await reinterpretation after the neglect into which they have too completely fallen.

Her Majesty the Queen has graciously permitted me to reproduce works in the Royal Collection. I trust that the Deans and Chapters, Trustees and Gallery Directors, corporate bodies and private owners who have allowed me to reproduce works in their possession will accept the acknowledgements in the list of plates as an expression of my most sincere thanks. Many of them have added to their kindness by sending photographs and information, allowing me most ready access, and bringing out from storage paintings not generally on exhibition. In particular the staffs of the Courtauld Institute, the National Buildings Record, the Bodleian Library, the Ashmolean Museum, the Print Room of the British Museum, and the Tate Gallery have shown the most kindly tolerance of the trouble I have constantly caused them. Over less

protracted periods the galleries of Australia, Canada, and the United States have been most generous in facilities, and I have a particular debt to the National Gallery of Victoria and the Department of Fine Art in the University of Melbourne. It would be pleasant to set down the long list of those who have answered questions, sought out facts, taken me on expeditions, and encouraged me with their interest, but it would indeed be a lengthy list, and no doubt in the end an incomplete one. I hope they will realize how grateful I am without more public acknowledgement. Miss Rhoda Welsford and Mr. John Woodward have each read the text in typescript and greatly assisted me with their comments: and constantly in writing I have been aware how my thoughts go back to conversations, over many years, with Sir Kenneth Clark, whose chance phrases have a germinal quality to which this book owes much.

T. S. R. B.

January 1958

CONTENTS

LIST OF PLATES

*(The paintings and sculpture are reproduced by the courtesy of
the Trustees, Curators, Directors, and private owners concerned)*

Frontispiece. SIR FRANCIS CHANTREY: MRS. BOULTON [detail]. 1834. Great Tew,
Oxon.
Photograph by courtesy of Dr. J. R. H. Weaver.

AT END

1. WILLIAM BLAKE: THE GENIUS OF SHAKESPEARE. 1809. Water-colour.
British Museum. [$9\frac{1}{5} \times 6\frac{7}{10}$ in.]

2. BENJAMIN WEST: DEATH ON THE PALE HORSE. 1817. Pennsylvania Academy
of the Fine Arts. [177×312 in.]

3a. SIR JOHN EVERETT MILLAIS: THE RESCUE. 1855. National Gallery of
Victoria, Melbourne. [$46 \times 32\frac{1}{2}$ in.]
Photograph by courtesy of Visual Aids Department, University of Melbourne.
— b. J. H. FUSELI: ALMANSARIS VISITS HUON IN PRISON. *c.* 1802. Kunsthaus,
Zurich. ($24\frac{1}{2} \times 18$ in.)

4a. J. H. FUSELI: HELENA AND THE COUNTESS. Engraved by J. G. Walker for
The Plays of William Shakespeare with a series of engravings from
original designs by Henry Fuseli, Esq., R.A., Professor of Painting.
F. C. and J. Rivington, 1805. [$6\frac{3}{8} \times 3\frac{1}{2}$ in.]
Photograph by courtesy of the Courtauld Institute of Art.
 b. JAMES GILLRAY: DIDO IN DESPAIR [detail]. 1801. Colour print. British
Museum. [$12\frac{3}{4} \times 19\frac{1}{4}$ in.]

5a. HENRY ROSSI: THE BATSMAN. 1819. Coll. the Duke of Bedford. [Marble
statuette: Height 28 in.]
 b. JAMES LOUGH: THOMAS MIDDLETON, BISHOP OF CALCUTTA. 1832.
St. Paul's Cathedral.
Photographs by courtesy of the Courtauld Institute of Art.

6a. SIR THOMAS LAWRENCE: PRINCESS OF WALES AND PRINCESS CHARLOTTE.
1802. Buckingham Palace. [305×206 in.] Reproduced by gracious
permission of Her Majesty the Queen.
Photograph by courtesy of the British Council.
 b. G. H. HARLOW: THE MISSES ANNE AND FANNY LEADER. Philadelphia
Museum of Art. [93×57 in.]

b. ENTRY OF GEORGE IV INTO HOLYROOD HOUSE. 1828. Scottish National Portrait Gallery. [20×34 in.]

60. PORTRAITS OF WILKIE:
  a. SIR WILLIAM BEECHEY. 1808. Scottish National Portrait Gallery. [35½×27½ in.]
  b. JOHN JACKSON. 1807. Pencil drawing. British Museum. [7×5¼ in.]
  c. SELF PORTRAIT. 1813. National Portrait Gallery. [5½×4 in.]
  d. THOMAS PHILLIPS. 1829. Tate Gallery. [39¼×30 in.]

61*a.* SIR FRANCIS CHANTREY: SIR WALTER SCOTT. 1820. Lady Lever Art Gallery, Port Sunlight.
  b. SIR FRANCIS CHANTREY: MRS. JORDAN [detail]. 1834. Coll. the Earl of Munster.
    Photograph by courtesy of the Courtauld Institute of Art.
  c. THOMAS WOOLNER: LORD TENNYSON. Replica made in 1876 of bust of 1857. Westminster Abbey.
    Photograph by courtesy of the Warburg Institute.
  d. SIR JOSEPH EDGAR BOEHM: THOMAS CARLYLE [detail]. 1861. Scottish National Portrait Gallery.

62*a.* WILLIAM ETTY: THE COMBAT: WOMAN PLEADING FOR THE VANQUISHED. 1828. From an engraving by G. T. Doo of the painting in the National Gallery of Scotland. [99¾×134 in.]
  b. SIR GEORGE HAYTER: CIRCASSIAN WOMEN SOLD TO BRIGANDS. 1827. Coll. J. Gold, Esq. [48×72 in.]

63. B. R. HAYDON:
  a. NERO HARPING WHILE ROME BURNED. 1846. Coll. Sir H. Gengoult Smith, Melbourne. [Figure life-size.]
    Photograph by courtesy of Visual Aids Department, University of Melbourne.
  b. CHAIRING THE MEMBER. 1828. Tate Gallery. [60×75½ in.]

64*a.* WILLIAM COLLINS: DISPOSAL OF A FAVOURITE LAMB. 1813. Messrs. Williams &Son, Grafton Street. [39½×31 in.]
  b. E. M. WARD: THE ROYAL FAMILY OF FRANCE IN THE PRISON OF THE TEMPLE. 1850. Harris Museum and Art Gallery, Preston. [40×50 in.]

65*a.* C. R. LESLIE: THE TWO PRINCES IN THE TOWER. Sheepshanks Coll., Victoria and Albert Museum. [13×17 in.]
    Crown copyright.
  b. SIR CHARLES EASTLAKE: THE CHAMPION. 1824. City Art Gallery, Birmingham. [48½×68¾ in.]

66*a.* CLARKSON STANFIELD: THE ABANDONED. 1856. Formerly in the Northbrook Coll. From a collotype. [35⅜×59½ in.]

b. P. F. POOLE: SOLOMON EAGLE. 1843. Mappin Art Gallery, Sheffield.
[61 × 89 in.]

67. C. R. COCKERELL:
a. DESIGN FOR THE ROYAL EXCHANGE: Pen, pencil and wash drawing.
1840. Royal Institute of British Architects.
Photograph by courtesy of the Courtauld Institute of Art.
b. THE ASHMOLEAN MUSEUM AND TAYLOR INSTITUTION, OXFORD. 1841–5.
Photograph by Thomas Photos, Oxford.

68*a.* SIR CHARLES BARRY: ST. PETER'S, BRIGHTON. 1824–8.
Photograph by National Buildings Record.
b. JAMES SAVAGE: ST. LUKE'S, CHELSEA. 1820–4.
Photograph by Mr. A. F. Kersting.

69. A. W. PUGIN: ST. CHAD'S CATHEDRAL, BIRMINGHAM. 1839–41.
a. EXTERIOR FROM THE NORTH.
b. SCREEN AND EAST END.
Photographs by National Buildings Record.

70*a.* A. W. PUGIN: ST. GILES', CHEADLE. 1846.
b. R. D. CHANTRELL: ST. PETER'S, LEEDS. 1837–41.
Photographs by National Buildings Record.

71*a.* R. C. CARPENTER: TOWER OF ST. PAUL'S, BRIGHTON. 1846–8.
b. WILLIAM BUTTERFIELD: ALL SAINTS, MARGARET STREET, LONDON: SOUTH
WALL OF NAVE. 1849–59.
c. WILLIAM BUTTERFIELD: TOWER OF ALL SAINTS, MARGARET STREET.
Photographs by National Buildings Record.

72*a.* SIR CHARLES BARRY: BRIDGEWATER HOUSE. 1847–57.
Photograph by courtesy of the Warburg Institute.
b. ANTHONY SALVIN: HARLAXTON HALL: WEST FRONT. 1831–8.
Photograph by 'Country Life'.

73. A. W. PUGIN:
a. WEST DOORWAY, ST. GILES', CHEADLE.
b. ANGEL FROM CHAPEL IN ALTON TOWERS.
Photographs by National Buildings Record.

c. C. R. COCKERELL: SPANDREL FIGURE, ST. GEORGE'S HALL, LIVERPOOL.
*Photograph by courtesy of the City Engineer and Surveyor's Department,
Liverpool, and Mr. P. Fleetwood-Hesketh.*

74*a.* H. L. ELMES: INTERIOR, ST. GEORGE'S HALL, LIVERPOOL: ORGAN CASE
DESIGNED BY C. R. COCKERELL. 1842–54.
*Photograph by courtesy of the City Engineer and Surveyor's Department,
Liverpool, and Mr. P. Fleetwood-Hesketh.*

90a. JOHN PHILIP: PUGIN, SCOTT, COCKERELL, AND BARRY FROM FRIEZE OF
ALBERT MEMORIAL.
 b. WILLIAM THEED: AFRICA. Albert Memorial.
 Photographs by the author.
 c. EDWARD ARMITAGE: RETRIBUTION. 1858. City Art Gallery, Leeds.
 [114×105 in.]

91. ALFRED STEVENS: THE WELLINGTON MEMORIAL. St. Paul's Cathedral.
 Photograph by Mr. A. F. Kersting.

92a. G. F. WATTS: LADY MARGARET BEAUMONT AND HER DAUGHTER. 1862.
 Coll. Viscount Allendale. [76×45½ in.]
 Photograph by courtesy of the Royal Academy.
 b. SIR JOHN EVERETT MILLAIS: THE BLIND GIRL. 1856. City Art Gallery,
 Birmingham. [32×24½ in.]

93a. ALFRED STEVENS: MRS. COLLMANN. c. 1854. Tate Gallery. [27¾×21¾ in.]
 b. SIR THOMAS LAWRENCE: MRS. WOLFF. 1813–15. W. W. Kimball Coll.,
 Art Institute of Chicago. [50×40¼ in.]
 Photograph by courtesy of the Art Institute of Chicago.

94a. DANTE GABRIEL ROSSETTI: THE MAIDS OF ELFEN-MERE: from William
 Allingham, The Music Master and Day and Night Songs, 1855.
 Engraved by Dalziel. [5×3 in.]
 b. SIR FREDERICK LEIGHTON: SCENE FROM ROMOLA. Cornhill Magazine
 [Dec. 1862]. Engraved by Joseph Swain. [6⅕×4 in.]

95a. SIR JOHN EVERETT MILLAIS: THE UNMERCIFUL SERVANT. Wood engraving
 from Good Words. 1863. [5½×4⅕ in.]
 b. R. REDGRAVE: ILLUSTRATION TO THOMSON'S SEASONS, 'GATHERS HIS
 OVARIOUS FOOD'. Engraved by T. Williams. 1842. [6⅕×4⅕ in.]

96a. THOMAS WEBSTER: A VILLAGE CHOIR. Sheepshanks Coll., Victoria and
 Albert Museum. [24×36 in.]
 Crown copyright.
 b. WILLIAM HOLMAN HUNT: MAY MORNING ON MAGDALEN TOWER. 1890.
 Lady Lever Art Gallery, Port Sunlight. [59½×78 in.]

LIST OF FIGURES

ABBREVIATIONS

Arch. Rev.	*Architectural Review*
Burl. Mag.	*Burlington Magazine*
Christie's	Sale Catalogues of Messrs. Christie, Manson and Woods, Ltd.
C.L.	*Country Life*
D.N.B.	*Dictionary of National Biography*
Faringington, *Diary*	*The Farington Diary*: ed. by James Greig. 8 vols.
I.L.N.	*Illustrated London News*
Journ. R.I.B.A.	*Journal of the Royal Institute of British Architects*
Journ. W.C.I.	*Journal of the Warburg and Courtauld Institutes*
O.H.E.A.	*Oxford History of English Art*
O.W.-C.S.C.	*Old Water-colour Society Club*
P.P.	Parliamentary Papers. (Sessional bound sets, with MS. paging as arranged for the House of Commons)
Q.R.	*Quarterly Review*
Ruskin, *Works*	*The Works of John Ruskin*, ed. by E. T. Cook and A. Wedderburn. 39 vols.
Whitley, i and ii	W. T. Whitley, *Art in England, 1800–1820* and *1821–1837*.

The following abbreviations are used for museums and galleries. Where no reference is given in the text or notes, paintings are in the National Collection of British Art now distributed between the National Gallery and the Tate Gallery: in the case of paintings illustrated by plates, the present location is given in the list of plates: where the reference is only to a reproduction, the painting is untraced.

Ashmolean	Ashmolean Museum, Oxford
Birmingham	City Museum and Art Gallery
B.M.	British Museum
Boston	Museum of Fine Arts, Boston, Mass.
Edinburgh	National Gallery of Scotland
Guildhall	Guildhall Art Gallery, London
Leeds	City Art Gallery
Liverpool	Walker Art Gallery
Manchester	City Art Gallery
Melbourne	National Gallery of Victoria
N.P.G.	National Portrait Gallery, London
Newcastle	Laing Art Gallery
Ottawa	National Gallery of Canada
Philadelphia	Museum of Art
Port Sunlight	Lady Lever Art Gallery
Preston	Harris Museum and Art Gallery
R.A.	Royal Academy
S.N.P.G.	Scottish National Portrait Gallery, Edinburgh

Sheffield	Graves Art Gallery
Stratford	Memorial Theatre Picture Gallery, Stratford-upon-Avon
Sydney	National Art Gallery of New South Wales
V. and A.	Victoria and Albert Museum, London

I

ROMANTICISM

'JACQUES LOUIS DAVID is dead. He died about a year after his bodily demise in 1825. The romanticism killed him. Walter Scott, from his Castle of Abbotsford, sent out a troop of gallant young Scotch adventurers, merry outlaws, valiant knights, and savage Highlanders, who, with trunk hosen and buff jerkins, fierce two-handed swords, and harness on their back, did challenge, combat, and overcome the heroes and demi-gods of Greece and Rome. . . . See! Robin Hood twangs his bow, and the heathen gods fly, howling. *Montjoie Saint Dénis*! down goes Ajax under the mace of Dunois; and yonder are Leonidas and Romulus begging their lives of Rob Roy Macgregor. Classicism is dead.' So wrote Thackeray in his *Paris Sketch Book* of 1840, and his light-hearted approach conveys much of the truth of the matter. The new humanism of the nineteenth century had repeopled the realms of the imagination. The traditional figures, with all their correct postures, attributes, and didactic values were gone. Heroes were to be interesting as individuals, visualized rather than analysed, recognizable rather than significant. New settings, new activities, new characteristics were in demand. New homeliness as well: the range of human emotions was to be studied in the mysterious and the horrific but also in the everyday. Wilkie, from the manse at Cults, was another facet of the power of descriptive characterization that Scotland so generously contributed to the stocking of the European mind.

The Romantic Movement, for all Thackeray's assertion that classicism was dead, is an elusive concept, and particularly so in England where the classical rules had never been unhesitatingly accepted, where above all the name of Shakespeare authorized an emotional gamut full of horror, confusion, and the unpredictable eccentricities of human nature. Scott's heroes sallied out from a fortress that had long been held by far more redoubtable figures,

Hamlet, Macbeth, Othello, and Falstaff, leaders of very anti-classical battalions. Yet it seemed in the opening years of the century that in the visual arts Shakespeare as an inspiration had been tried and failed. In 1805 the Boydell Shakespeare Gallery, following the financial failure and death of its promoter, was dispersed by auction. The '170 items (84 of large size)', painted by all the leading artists of the time from Reynolds downwards, brought in only £6,181. 18s. 6d. These were for the main part paintings that aimed at the grand manner as expounded by Sir Joshua, full of poses borrowed from the great masters, academic in their cult of tradition and in many cases technically deficient.[1] 'The artists after Reynolds', wrote the Redgraves in 1866, 'were like flies in a honey-pot, entangled with viscid and sticky paint.'[2] It is an ever-recurring theme: to Holman Hunt looking back over the century it seemed that by the use of 'this pernicious Dead Sea pitch . . . many admirable works of Wilkie, Hilton, and their contemporaries have been doomed to complete destruction. In another century no one will know what powers of delicacy in manipulation these artists had, for the bitumen, ever dilating and contracting with atmospheric changes, is tearing the paintings to pieces.'[3] More than technique seemed out-dated. 'It is curious', the Redgraves continued, 'in looking over the series of pictures painted at this period and published by Boydell to note not the inaccuracies so much as the glaring inconsistencies of costume which pervade them all . . . the figure painters seem to have had a costume equally applicable to all persons, all periods and all countries.' Thus they wrote, after fifty years in which archaeology had revealed much about distant ages and in which new historical standards had been

[1] For Boydell's Gallery see T. S. R. Boase, 'Illustrations of Shakespeare's Plays in the Seventeenth and Eighteenth Centuries', *Journ. W.C.I.* x (1948), 83.

[2] *A Century of British Painters*, ed. Ruthven Todd (1947), 122. The passage occurs in a discussion of Northcote's paintings, which have in fact lasted well.

[3] *Pre-Raphaelitism and the Pre-Raphaelite Brotherhood* (1905), ii. 454. Bitumen was first brought from Persia to England, but the Dead Sea area was another source. It gave a rich, transparent brown, which soon darkened and was very liable to crack. 'Megilp', mastic dissolved in turpentine with oil added, was another source of the *craquelure anglaise*. There is much information about early nineteenth-century methods in J. C. Ibbetson, *Painting in Oil* (1803), a book which Wilkie copied out because he could not obtain it (Allan Cunningham, *Life of Wilkie* (1843), i. 67).

accepted into the visual imagination. It was not only an accession of knowledge that had intervened, it was a new approach to the past, a desire to understand a period for itself, to relive it as an extension of experience, not merely to learn some precept from it.

Over the period of transition there presided, from the presidential chair of the Royal Academy, an artist who, while susceptible to some of the changes around him, was singularly unapt to understand their meaning and implications. Benjamin West was at the beginning of the new century in his sixty-second year.[1] Born in Pennsylvania in 1738, coming to Rome in 1760 and to England in 1763, the early paintings which won him royal patronage and foundation membership of the Royal Academy had been of a classical correctitude in the manner of Raphael Mengs, the idol of his Roman journey. On the death of Reynolds in 1792 he succeeded him as President of the Royal Academy. For a time it had seemed as though under his leadership American painting might make a real impact upon England. His own *Death of Wolfe* (1771: Ottawa), though classically posed, had been the most famous example of the rendering of a contemporary scene in the actual costume of the time, and his fellow countrymen and pupils, Copley and Trumbull, carried much further this new realistic mode.[2] The presidency of the Royal Academy was, however, a post that did not suit with revolutions. At times tactless, never an Englishman to the manner born, a little unscrupulous in puffing his own works, West was, notwithstanding various attacks on him, respected as an honest, kindly, reliable man. In 1804 there was indeed an attempt at the annual Academy election to substitute James Wyatt for him, and the following year West refused to stand and his rival was elected;[3] but in 1806 the voting once more was for West. Academicians might laugh at his lack of literary polish, at the simplicity and repetitiveness of his Academy discourses, but no one seriously

[1] The main biography is still that of J. Galt, 2 vols. (1850): for the revolution in history painting see E. Wind in *Journ. W.C.I.* ii (1938), 116, and Charles Mitchell ibid. vii (1944), 20.

[2] See L. Einstein, *Divided Loyalties* (1933).

[3] Whitley, i. 94, 115: there are many references in Farington, *Diary* iii and iv. See also W. Dunlap, *A History of the Rise and Progress of the Arts of Design in the United States*, new ed. F. W. Bayley and C. E. Goodspeed (Boston, 1916).

questioned his integrity; and in the period between his re-election and his death in 1820 his great pictures were painted, *Our Saviour healing the Sick* (1811), *Christ rejected by Caiaphas* (1814), and *Death on the Pale Horse* (1817). 'We feel no hesitation in saying', wrote the critic of the *New Monthly Magazine* of the *Christ rejected*,[1] 'that for composition, expression and masterly execution, this epic picture possesses a greater degree of pathos than any painting in the world. . . . We are at a loss to conceive the mighty step that the painter has taken in his approach to the perfection of art, in so short a period, and at so advanced a stage of life.' Many of the periodicals echo this lavish praise, but Hazlitt took a different view of his paintings: 'I doubt whether, in the entire range of Mr. West's production, meritorious and admirable as the design and composition often are, there is to be found one truly fine head. . . . They exhibit the *mask*, not the *soul*, of expression':[2] and to Haydon's remark 'Au moins, il compose bien', Canova replied, 'Non, il met des modèles en groupes.' Haydon himself found the *Healing the Sick* 'hard, red, mean, well composed; nothing can be more despicable than the forms'.[3] Hard they are, with a precision that Haydon never obtained, and, except for the last, the *Pale Horse*, dry and undistinguished in colour; but they are admirably planned. On these vast canvases West knew how to marshal and dispose his forces. Poor Haydon beside him was always to remain an envious incompetent. The *Rejection* and the *Pale Horse* now hang on the staircase of the Pennsylvania Academy of the Fine Arts in Philadelphia, the Academy of which West was the first honorary member. They are decorations in the grand style:[4] the former with its columns and porticoes recalls the earlier period of West's work, more traditional, correct in the sense of Mengs and the Roman School. In other paintings there was a certain slackening of restraint. His *Apotheosis of Nelson*, perhaps the strangest of the

[1] i (1814), 68.

[2] *Criticisms on Art*, i (1843), 218; reprinted *Essays on the Fine Arts* (1873), 262.

[3] Whitley, i. 189, 252; Haydon, *Autobiography* (1926), i. 132; for current distinctions between 'grouping' and 'composition' see E. C. Mason, *The Mind of Henry Fuseli* (1951), 214.

[4] *The Healing of the Sick*, 108 in. by 168 in. (destroyed by flood 1928); *Christ Rejected*, 200 in. by 264 in.; *Death on the Pale Horse*, 177 in. by 312 in.

hero's memorials, though classical in the draped figure and flying putti has a mannerist confusion of figures and action; it belongs to the world of frenzy inhabited by Fuseli and Blake.[1] This is the world of the *Pale Horse* also, where the gleaming charger leaps through storm clouds, lions spring on their victims, and the crowned Rider moves mysteriously from the scene of devastation (Pl. 2). Hazlitt did not care for it: he wrote a furious attack in the *Edinburgh Review*:[2] 'Death is in a great splutter . . . his presence does not make the still air cold.' His indignation had been, very understandably, roused by the ludicrous account of the picture in the catalogue raisonné issued at its exhibition in West's own gallery, where it was hailed as a British triumph comparable to Waterloo, and where Death is described as 'animated almost to ignition with inextinguishable rage'. Hazlitt admits, however, that it is 'the best coloured and most picturesque of all Mr. West's productions'; and in fact the violence of the subject is matched with a new breadth in the painting. It looks forward to Delacroix rather than backward to David. 'It is a wonderful picture', wrote Keats, '. . . but there is nothing to be intense upon.'[3]

On West's death, galleries were built by his sons, designed by John Nash, in the garden of his house at 14 Newman Street, and ninety-four of his paintings were exhibited to large numbers of visitors. 'His reign in fine taste', wrote the *British Press*, 'is now perfectly established':[4] but nine years later the sale of the pictures showed a rapid deterioration in the prices offered. His influence is apparent in much of the painting of the next two decades; then it waned and, save by American patriotism, West was for long forgotten.

[1] Greenwich National Maritime Museum; E. Wind in *Journ. W.C.I.* ii (1939), 120: see *Q.R.* lxxiv (1844), 194.

[2] Dec. 1817. *Centenary Edition of Collected Works*, xviii (1933), 138.

[3] H. B. Forman, *Letters of John Keats*, i (1931), 76. It was a subject which West had long had in mind: Farington in 1815 referred to the design as 'made 20 years ago' (*Diary*, viii. 42). The sketch in the Museum of Art, Philadelphia, dates from *c.* 1787, and there is a later sketch of 1802 in the same gallery.

[4] Quoted Whitley, ii. 11. See for a detailed account of the gallery *European Mag.* lxxix (1824), 524: at the sale many of the paintings were bought by Joseph Neeld, and still decorate the great staircase hall in the Romanesque house later designed for him at Grittleton by James Thomson (*The Builder*, xi, 1853, 279: Pl. 15 *b*).

In 1804, on West's recommendation, the king had appointed Henry Fuseli Keeper of the Royal Academy. 'A very able man . . . distinguished as a Literary Character . . . and known to all Europe.' This was West's description of him. Fuseli's opinion of the President was less flattering.[1] He admitted his technical accomplishment, but complained that 'he has scarcely ever thought, and he hasn't any soul'. Such a comment is as revealing of the critic as the criticized. Fuseli's own technique had many weaknesses. He had little sense of colour, little feeling for brushwork or quality of paint; many of his works today are hopelessly darkened, bituminous wrecks; but there was soul in plenty. Born in Zurich, trained in Rome, he brought to England a Germanic violence and an exaggerated Italian mannerism as a vehicle for representing it. His muscular distortions and elongated figures are a curious phase in English art, but one to which others were receptive. William Hamilton (d. 1801) was early influenced and his paintings for the Boydell Gallery, to which he was the most prolific contributor, show Fuseli's wild forms affectedly applied to an English traditional style. Hamilton was employed by Malton to paint figures in his landscapes,[2] and his long, slender personages passed from here into the works of Turner. Richard Westall, another Boydell contributor, whose exhibition in 1814 at the New Gallery was much praised by some of the journals[3] and marks the culmination of his popularity, shows similar tendencies, and some of the same distortions and fancies disturbed Henry Howard's art, more generally used for pleasant social scenes. Henry Rossi's popular marble statuettes of the bowler and batsman (Pl. 5 a) at cricket have the same close-fitting garments and muscular development as Fuseli's tragic heroes. It was a mannerist elongation that curiously adapted itself to directoire fashions with their breast-high waistline, a fashion with which Fuseli was much obsessed and of which he fully exploited all the sensual attraction. In 1810 he was reappointed Professor of Painting in the Academy, a post that he now held conjointly with the keepership till his death at the age of eighty in 1825. He was much liked and respected by his students, and grateful

[1] E. C. Mason, op. cit. 139. [2] Whitley, i. 75.
[3] *New Monthly Mag.* ii (1814), 141.

references to him are frequent. His lectures can still be read with considerable interest,[1] but it would be difficult to deduce from them the strange, obsessed world that Fuseli frequented in his own paintings. Terror was for him 'the chief ingredient of the sublime';[2] in the coming of romanticism he stands for the agonized search for new emotional stresses in haunted, tortured, unnatural scenes; to an age that gloated over Ambrosio's incestuous crimes, 'fiends, incomprehensible characters, shrieks, murders and subterraneous dungeons',[3] the stock in trade of Fuseli, were readily acceptable. At times the loathsomeness that he repudiated intrudes through strange subconscious channels into his visions. The painter whom above all he recalls, in his grotesque *terribilità*, is Pellegrino Tibaldi, and Fuseli's criticisms of the Bolognese master almost describe his own mannerisms: 'Conglobation and eccentricity, an aggregate of convexities suddenly broken by rectangular, or cut by perpendicular line, composes his system.'[4] Until his death in 1825, Fuseli continued to paint large and striking pictures, for many of which the *Niebelungenlied* and Wieland's *Oberon* (Pl. 3 b)[5] now provided subjects. He at times essayed portraiture, the last stage in his English naturalization, and at Easton Neston there is a group of the Pomfret children (*c.* 1785), whose conventional poses have an odd touch of the bizarre. His Milton gallery, exhibited in 1799 and including forty paintings, some of them of very large dimensions, was his most ambitious undertaking. Financially, however, it was unsuccessful, though there were some distinguished purchasers, amongst them Lawrence and John Julius Angerstein. Contemporary critics such as W. Y. Ottley considered it 'one of the greatest works of painting ever produced'.[6] In 1805 appeared his illustrations to a

[1] J. Knowles, *The Life and Writings of Henry Fuseli*, 3 vols. (1831); see review in *Library of Fine Arts*, ii (1831), 87.   [2] E. C. Mason, op. cit. 216.

[3] The list is from a review of M. G. Lewis's *The Monk: The Critical Rev.* xix (1796), 194. For an attack on Fuseli see E. Dayes, *Works*, ed. by E. W. Brayley (1805), 326, 'the wild effusions of the perturbed imaginations of this inhabitant of Zurich'; no doubt this represented the views of many of the older generation of English artists; Fuseli himself sharply distinguished between 'terror' and 'horror'.

[4] Knowles, op. cit. iii. 31; see ibid. ii. 95; F. Antal, *Fuseli Studies* (1956), 95.

[5] For the second English translation made in 1802; Wieland had lived in Zurich between 1752 and 1759 and had known Fuseli's father.

[6] Knowles, op. cit. i. 426. Ottley's own drawings are in Fuseli's manner. Six of the

ten-volume edition of Shakespeare published by F. C. and J. Rivington.[1] In these engravings, where the whole design is linear, Fuseli's art can be very readily appreciated. Some of them have a powerful and exciting use of distortion, that looks back to the triumphs of Romanesque art and forward to the defiant images of Picasso. In the scene from *All's Well*, Helena's vast arms wind upwards in an insistent rhythm embracing a countess whose modish costume and attitude are disturbingly contemporary, with a peculiarly Fuselian malaise (Pl. 4 a). He was both a marvel and a puzzle to his contemporaries. It was high art beyond question, but Dance and Farington, leaving his studio, talked of how, for all his ability, it was impossible to like his pictures:[2] 'The pathetic and the ridiculous are in a constant struggle for a mastery over the feelings', wrote *Bell's Weekly Messenger*, 'it is much easier to be singular than to be original.'[3] Today his nervous, vivid drawings are returning to favour, and we recognize in him something of the fervour which inspired his contemporary, Blake.[4]

Traces of the same mannerist poses can be found in the early work of Thomas Stothard (1755–1834), one of the most popular and prolific artists of the turn of the century.[5] His book illustrations for Shakespeare, Chaucer, Richardson, Goldsmith, Rogers, and innumerable others prolonged the eighteenth-century tradition of Hayman and Wheatley, while adding a certain fluid rhythm borrowed from his exact contemporary, Flaxman. Famous for his vignettes, his roundels, his head and tail pieces, he was in fact more striking when working on a large scale, painting allegorical scenes on the staircase of Burghley House (1799) or in the cupola of the

Milton paintings were in the Samuel Sale, Christies, 29.3.1927 (photographs in Witt Coll.: several are now in Swiss collections).

[1] T. S. R. Boase, 'Illustrations of Shakespeare's Plays', *Journ. W.C.I.* x (1948), 83; H. A. Hammelmann, 'Henry Fuseli', *The Book Collector* (1957), 350.

[2] Farington, *Diary*, v (1925), 220.   [3] 1811, 149.

[4] There is a stimulating essay on Fuseli by Ruthven Todd in his *Tracks in the Snow* (1946); see also A. Federmann, *Johann Heinrich Füssli, Dichter und Maler* (Zürich, 1922); Paul Ganz, *Die Zeichnungen von Hans Heinrich Füssli* (Bern, 1947), English translation (1949); N. Powell, *The Drawings of Henry Fuseli* (1951); *Catalogue* of Fuseli Exhibition, Kunsthaus, Zürich (1941).

[5] Mrs. Bray, *Life of Thomas Stothard* (1851); A. C. Coxhead, *Thomas Stothard R.A.* (1919); for the Burghley House frescoes see C. Hussey in *C.L.* cxiv (1953), 2104.

Advocates Library at Edinburgh (1822), and large oils such as the *Othello and Desdemona* at Stratford-upon-Avon (Pl. 23 *a*), whose rich colour, poses, and breadth of painting attest the artist's admiration for Rubens. When he painted himself in his rather bleak studio in Newman Street it was with a large allegorical canvas on the easel and a free version of Titian's *Venus and Adonis* hanging on the wall.[1] His was a pervasive influence: sculptors and goldsmiths used his designs and few of his brother painters are without traces of his poses and methods. He was immensely industrious and a speedy worker, and much of his output is repetitive and conventional, but at his best he was a fine and individual artist; a gentle, homely character, tried by misfortune (for one son was accidentally shot by a schoolfellow; another, the gifted archaeologist, Charles,[2] was killed in falling from a church roof where he was sketching), but unembittered, one with whom sweet memories were associated.

The sublime was, it was generally agreed, only to be found in historical painting, but the example, as opposed to the precepts, of Reynolds had commended the view that portrait painting was the only reliable source of profit. At the turn of the century Sir Joshua, eight years dead, was still the dominant influence. Opie was to live till 1807, Hoppner to 1810; Northcote's long life was to stretch out to 1831, and in some of his large paintings, his *Alexander of Russia* (Pl. 7 *a*) on a huge charger supervising the rescue of a peasant lad from drowning and thereby earning the Gold Medal of the Royal Humane Society, he employs the subject-matter and melodrama of the new romanticism. In portraiture he showed 'a just perception of character',[3] but it was his *Life of Reynolds*, published 1813, and his conversation, with its pointed, slightly malicious reminiscenses, that were the main occupations of his later years. Romney, now wandering in his mind, died in 1802. Court and Society for

---

[1] Christies, 23.3.1956, No. 147.

[2] Draughtsman to the Society of Antiquaries, best known for his *Sepulchral Effigies*.

[3] 'Memoir of the late James Northcote Esq., R.A.', *Library of the Fine Arts*, ii (1831), 6; and in the same vol. 'Anecdotes of Northcote', 101; W. Hazlitt, *Conversations of James Northcote* (1830; centenary edition, xi (1932), 185); S. Gwynn, *Memorials of an Eighteenth Century Painter* (1893); E. Fletcher, *Conversations of Northcote with James Ward* (1901); H. Jackson in *C.L.* cxvii (1955), 40.

the moment turned to William Beechey, whose equestrian group of *George III reviewing the 10th Hussars and the 3rd Dragoons* (Windsor) had secured him a knighthood in 1798. Sensible and solid, at times a little crude in colour, a little naïve in pose and expression, Beechey can easily be underrated. He modelled firmly and clearly; he manipulated the eighteenth-century tradition with confidence; his sitters fill their frames with ease and assurance, sometimes hard in outline and stiff about the joints, but individuals and almost certainly very adequate likenesses. No trace of mannerist distortion or fashionable malaise disturbs the work of this Cotswold man, who came to London keeping something of a countryman's old-fashioned ways, swearing a little too much for polite society, but making a very reasonable place for himself.[1]

A new generation of patrons was, however, finding the work of younger men more interesting, and pre-eminently that of Thomas Lawrence. At the opening of the century he was thirty-one years old and at the height of his powers. He had recently (R.A. 1797) essayed a vast canvas in the Fuseli manner, *Satan summoning his Angels* (R.A. Diploma Gallery), in which he had used many of Fuseli's tricks, in particular the figure 'rising upward in moderate foreshortening' and 'commanding the horizon'.[2] To the painter himself, devoted to the teaching of Reynolds and the Grand Style, it seemed 'such as neither Mr. West, nor Sir Joshua, nor Fuseli could have painted':[3] but he was sadly blind in thinking so. There is a ludicrous, inflated quality about this demon which Anthony Pasquin[4] found very easy matter for ridicule. There is none of the disturbing quality which haunts all Fuseli's work, and which, if it often falls short of the horror and grandeur at which it aims, seldom fails to touch some vague disquiet. Lawrence could do none of these things. It was to be in portraits only that he could successfully

---

[1] W. Roberts, *Sir William Beechey* (1907).

[2] E. C. Mason, *The Mind of Fuseli*, 219.

[3] G. S. Layard, *Sir Thomas Lawrence's Letter-Bag* (1906), 85. There is a considerable literature on Lawrence: see D. E. Williams, *The Life and Correspondence of Sir Thomas Lawrence*, 2 vols. (1831); R. Sutherland-Gower, *Sir Thomas Lawrence* (1900); Sir W. Armstrong, *Lawrence* (1913); D. Goldring, *Regency Portrait Painter* (1951); K. Garlick, *Sir Thomas Lawrence* (1954).

[4] John Williams, *Critical Guide to the Present Exhibition at the Royal Academy* (1797).

find himself, but the wider vision was only reluctantly surrendered, and as late as 1815 his friend, Mrs. Wolff (Pl. 93 *b*), seated in her satin dress and modish turban, leans pensively over a volume with plates of Michelangelo's sybils, these great forms of high art. Between Lawrence and Hoppner there was a certain rivalry that many seem to have liked to stimulate, the critics finding them useful comparisons (Lawrence infers that Hoppner managed the critics better), and mutual friends enjoying the game. Hoppner was painting large canvases broadly and firmly, and his gestures are telling, if at times over dramatic. His *Mrs. Jerningham as Hebe* (exhibited 1805), much admired at the time,[1] is an example of the fashionable distortions and overstatement. 'Shee, Lawrence and Hoppner', wrote a critic in 1802,[2] 'are the only competitors of Beechey. The first with all his merits has propensity to make his figures too broad and colossal; Lawrence is too glossy and *petite* for portraits in oil as large as life; and Hoppner too eccentric and gaudy and fluttering for the modest purposes of nature.' Shee, whose administrative career will require frequent notice, was in the next few years to be more talked of as a poet than a painter, and was no serious opponent.[3] Hoppner's death left the field to Lawrence. He was employing many of the exaggerations used by his rival and almost parodied by lesser artists such as Henry Thomson.[4] Painting in 1800–1 the portrait of the Princess of Wales and her daughter Charlotte (Pl. 6 *a*), in some prolonged sittings which Caroline's enemies later tried, unsuccessfully, to exploit in 'the Delicate Investigation' of 1806, Lawrence uses the grand manner to the full. The princess strikes an immense pose; the whirling scarf, the stage-like set are all as remote from actuality as the inspired lady at the harp is remote from the coarse-grained and unhappy Caroline. The *Princess* is the grand manner in decline. In his numerous stage

[1] *Bell's Weekly Messenger* (1805), 141; reproduced W. McKay and W. Roberts, *John Hoppner* (1909), 130; in Lord Michelham's sale, Nov. 1926, No. 299.
[2] Quoted Whitley, i. 36.   [3] Memoir in *European Mag.* lxxxiv (1823), 483.
[4] Henry Thomson (1773–1843), best known for his *Crossing the Brook* (R.A. 1803); see Whitley, i. 52: now coll. R. W. Lloyd, Esq. His *Innocence*, a study of a mother and child, with long distorted curves, was in Christie's: 1.7.1955, No. 137, and his large historical piece *Eurydice hurried back to the Infernal Regions* (79 in. by 86 in.: R.A. 1814) was No. 69 in the sale of 13.12.1957.

portraits Lawrence becomes more nearly a romantic. It was a great period in the London theatre, and painters and actors had much social intercourse. Lawrence himself found in the Siddons family an emotional centre, full of sorrows and distraction; but his great paintings are of the actor Kemble. In the Academy of 1798 he exhibited his portrait of him as Coriolanus (Pl. 7 *b*); this was followed by full-length portraits of the actor as Rolla (1800) and Hamlet (1801). Whether the actor's interpretation lent a new vision to the painter, or whether they met in a congenial appreciation of the *zeitgeist*, these heroic figures, dark cloaked against murky skies, are emotionally far removed from the direct glances of Reynolds or the elegant reticences of Gainsborough. Hamlet's introversion, Coriolanus's humiliated pride, Rolla's desperation, are the symptoms of the Byronic melancholy which was to be a readily accepted revelation to the men of the first quarter of the century. It was a fleeting gloom, more fashionable than profound, and when in 1812 Lawrence once more painted Kemble, the mood has passed. It is as Cato in Addison's classic, reasoned tragedy that the actor is shown, clad in a white Roman tunic and looking up from his rolls of papers with a meditative but thoroughly controlled expression, a prototype of the great world statesmen whom Lawrence was now to be called to portray.[1]

It began in 1814 when Lawrence was commissioned to paint the allied kings and princes then in London, a commission accompanied by his knighthood and completed in 1817–18 at Aix-la-Chapelle and in 1819 at Vienna and Rome. The fruits of these labours are collected in the Waterloo Chamber in Windsor castle, but replicas of them exist in many European capitals, maintaining the fame of their painter. His portrait of Pius VII may be taken as an example of this grand European phase. The frail figure is seated in a large chair with, beyond, a gallery where the *Laocoon* and the *Apollo Belvedere* are vaguely to be seen; the face has an expression of weariness, but the weariness of a strong, resigned man; it is perhaps the most subtle psychological study that Lawrence ever painted, and he himself thought it 'the most interesting and best head' of

[1] *Rolla* untraced; *Cato* Coll. A.B.C. Philips Esq.; *Hamlet* is in the Tate Gallery. All are engraved.

any he had done.[1] In return for sitting to Lawrence, the Pope received (1822) a full-size version of the portrait of George IV in Garter robes, a papal bull being added for this occasion to the crown on the table beside him. The painting was hailed as a masterpiece in Rome, and still hangs in the Vatican Gallery, a surprising conclusion to its display of the great Italians. No English painter had ever before enjoyed such a continental reputation.

In 1820 Lawrence returned from Rome, to find that West had died nine days previously and to be immediately elected President of the Royal Academy, a post that he held till his death in 1830, a few months before the royal master with whom he had been so closely associated. These last years he was busied with his collection of drawings, advising on works of art, the business of the Academy, 'the too numerous Dinner Engagements and Parties to which Persons of High Rank invite me'.[2] Some of his earlier friends had died. Farington, the diarist and Lawrence's most regular correspondent, in 1821 from a fall resulting in a fractured skull;[3] John Julius Angerstein, the collector, in 1823; Mrs. Siddons, her daughters both early dead, was to outlive him, but there is no record of their meeting in these closing years. Charles Stewart, after Castlereagh's suicide Lord Londonderry, the Peels, Mrs. Wolff, W. Y. Ottley, these were now some of his closest contacts; and from these years come some of his best paintings: the *Countess of Blessington* (1822: Wallace Coll.), where the eyes are as limpid,[4] the satin as gleaming as in any of his works, and where some remains of mannerist elongation are kept in skilful bounds; *Master Lambton*, the *Red Boy* (1825: coll. the earl of Durham), the most romantically posed and lit of all his pictures of starry-eyed children;[5] *Lady Peel* (1827: Frick Coll., New York), whose charming feathered hat was

[1] G. S. Layard, *Letter-Bag*, 145.   [2] Ibid. 155.

[3] See F. J. Roe in *Walkers Quarterly*, v (1921).

[4] 'On n'a jamais fait les yeux, des femmes surtout, comme Lawrence, et ces bouches entr'ouvertes d'un charme parfait. Il est inimitable.' *Lettres de Delacroix*, 1 Aug. 1825. A. Joubin, *Correspondance générale de Delacroix*, i (1935), 166.

[5] The boy died when he was thirteen, Sarah Moulton Barrett (*Pinkie*: Huntington Foundation), another of his most popular pieces, when she was twelve. There were some grounds for the gentle, foreboding sadness with which he invests them. His most cheerful infant, Emily Calmady (Metropolitan Museum), survived till 1906.

intended as a rival to a more famous *Chapeau de Paille*;[1] *Lady Robert Manners* (1826: Edinburgh), one of those splendid old ladies, whose time-informed features set to the portrait painters a stronger challenge than the sheen of younger beauties.

The sparkle, the vivid unreality of Lawrence has obscured the merits of a group of painters working beside him.[2] William Owen (d. 1825) was born in the same year as Lawrence. Owen's early work was much in the Reynolds manner, particularly in his paintings of children, and some coy Bacchantes and fancy subjects show his plodding acceptance of the popular line. The turn of the century saw more solid elements in his work. He could give a genuine dignity to his sitters and paint their clothes with swift, lively brush strokes. Lady Beaumont (Pl. 8), mother of the great collector, sits by a window in her Suffolk home of Dunmow; the head is beautifully modelled and expressive; the shimmer of the silk dress, the hairy dog, are textures indicated rather than elaborated. It is a very noble portrait. She was, Owen told Farington, ninety-one, cheerful, and strong.[3] There is here no distortion, no romanticism, but sound, painterly recording. Thomas Phillips (1770–1845) and John Jackson (1778–1831) possessed considerable talents. Jackson's career[4] furnishes a lively commentary on the problems of an artist's profession. Apprenticed to his father's trade of tailor in his native Lastingham, his early drawings attracted the notice of Lord Mulgrave and the earl of Carlisle, and gave him the entrée to the collection at Castle Howard. Lord Mulgrave and Sir George Beaumont bought out the last two years of his apprenticeship and these two patrons maintained him in his early years in London. He soon had regular employment as a portrait painter, and was at his best with the strongly characterized features of older men, Chantrey, Northcote, Sir John Soane. Lawrence makes Soane magnificent; Owen shows him alert and vigorous; in Jackson's

---

[1] At that time in Sir Robert Peel's collection.

[2] See M. H. Spielmann, *British Portrait Painting to the Opening of the Nineteenth Century*, ii (1910).

[3] *Diary*, v (1925), 94.

[4] H. C. Morgan, *The Life and Works of John Jackson*, unpubl. thesis, University of Leeds (1956); Hugh Honour, 'John Jackson R.A.', *The Connoisseur Year Book* (1957), 91; for a contemporary estimate see *Library of Fine Arts*, i (1831), 445.

rendering he is dull-eyed and realistically weary.[1] With women Jackson was less happy; he lacked glamour; but to Haydon and Wilkie his low, sensitive range of tones seemed those of a fine colourist.[2]

Thomas Phillips, coming from an upper middle-class family, had not the same problems. He began as a student under Francis Eginton, the Birmingham glass painter, and his early ambitions were for history painting. When he became a Royal Academician in 1808 his diploma picture was *Venus and Adonis*, treated in a Titianesque manner, with some borrowing of actual poses. As a portrait painter he caught as no other the noble gloom of the romantic pose and the inspired intensity of the creative imagination. His *William Blake* is a prophetic figure appropriate to his work; Byron in Albanian dress is the true portrait of Childe Harold; no one else suggests so vividly the quizzical charm of Samuel Rogers; Humphry Davy and Michael Faraday represent the new interest in science;[3] Beriah Botfield (Pl. 9), 'taken in 1828 aged 21', is the quintessence of stylish youth: he had something of Van Dyck's gift for perpetuating a generation. George Henry Harlow (1787–1819) was for a time a pupil of Lawrence, with a leaning to history painting rather than portraiture, and his two striking portrait groups of the Leader family (Philadelphia) were painted after the original commission, *Hubert and Arthur* (Stratford), had failed to please. The Miss Leaders (Pl. 6 *b*) and the younger children have the poses and rhythms of Fuseli, who took much interest in Harlow and painted a figure into his most celebrated work, *Mrs. Siddons as Queen Katherine in the Trial Scene* (private collection). Despite such influence, there is originality in his work and his early death cut short a career that might have been of some moment.[4]

In 1810 it appeared that these artists might have to face competition from north of the border. Henry Raeburn,[5] who had in

[1] All these portraits are in the Soane Museum.

[2] Haydon, *Autobiography* (1926), i. 23.

[3] All these are in the National Portrait Gallery.

[4] *Library of the Fine Arts*, ii (1831), 24; D. Cook, *Art in England* (1869), 295. There are versions of the *Queen Katherine* at Stratford and the Garrick Club.

[5] There is no satisfactory recent monograph on Raeburn. E. R. Dibdin, *Raeburn*

Edinburgh an acknowledged position as the leading portrait painter, came to London and was invited by the Academicians to a dinner at the Crown and Anchor in honour of the king's birthday. He was back in London in 1812, when his *The Chief of the Macdonells*, the splendid, kilted Colonel Alastair now in the Scottish National Gallery, was No. 1 in the Academy, and in 1813 he was elected A.R.A., defeating Bird, the Bristol painter of anecdote and history, by twenty-two votes to fourteen. Two years later he became a full Academician. Raeburn, however, never settled in London. He remained till his death in 1823 a resident of Edinburgh, of whose citizens, in this its great period, he has left us one of these rare records, where an artist of ability working in some limited milieu, sixteenth-century Venice or the court circles of Caroline England, has caught and fixed not the appearance of his contemporaries, but the moulding character that underlay it. Raeburn's virtues are those of a lonely genius. Had he come south to the world of Lawrence he might well have lost some of that directness which is his chief attraction. Many sitters commented on the decision with which he painted. With no preliminary drawing in chalk, he brushed in the head, painting thickly, now marking the paint with broad sweeps, now with deep indentations from the side of the brush. Compared to English work, these portraits lacked finish; to tell, they must be seen from a correct distance; too near, the heads are flat; but in the Raeburn room in Edinburgh, we become aware of a world for which the right formulas have been found.

Portraits were for profit, historical painting for the high realms of imagination, but in the popular mind landscape was rapidly becoming the main pictorial theme. In 1794 a Herefordshire squire, Sir Uvedale Price, published an *Essay on the Picturesque*.[1] Dissatisfied with Burke's categories of the Beautiful and the Sublime, the former standing for smoothness and gentleness, the latter for terror,

(1925), and J. Greig, *Sir Henry Raeburn R.A.* (1911), give some revision to the story as told by his great-grandson, W. Raeburn Andrew, *Life of Sir Henry Raeburn* (1886); see also Sir Walter Armstrong, *Raeburn* (1901), with catalogue by J. L. Law; and D. Baxandall in *Raeburn Bicentenary Exhibition Catalogue* (Edinburgh, 1956).

[1] The whole question has been brilliantly examined by C. Hussey in *The Picturesque* (1927), a book that opened up new aspects of the history of taste.

vastness, and obscurity,[1] he claimed that there was an intermediate grade, in which objects, of themselves neither beautiful nor sublime, gave pleasure by their very deviation from these qualities, their irregularity, strongly marked contrasts of light and shade, and mellow tints. It was an appeal for the observation of every-day incidents and of the changing shadows and broken lights of the English scene. Capability Brown and his school had done much to give the scenery of England the balanced vistas and well-placed trees of a painting by Claude, but the English weather could not provide a constant golden haze to set them off. 'The forms of clouds, and the tints, with which they are occasionally over spread, ... are so varied, that he, who can imitate all their hues exactly, has attained a high degree of excellence in his art, tho his pictures have little else to recommend them. The sky, in such landscapes, instead of being an appendage becomes principal. If Claude himself had depended more on his skies, and less on his landscape ... his pictures perhaps would have been more valuable.' So, somewhat daringly tilting at the most secure of idols, wrote the Rev. William Gilpin, rector of Boldre, who from 1782 till his death in 1802 published a series of *Observations* on English scenery, *chiefly relative to Picturesque Beauty*.[2] These books are a plea for transient effects in nature, the dark object seen against the setting sun, the colours on a distant mountainside, 'rarely permanent—always in motion—always in harmony—and playing with a thousand changeable varieties into each other'. Gilpin liked mountains, finding in them those fleeting changes which he admired, and also 'terrifick grandeur', horror, fear, and the sublime. He set the amateurs of England on a new pursuit of sketchable material, and his own cunning drawings, reproduced in acquatint, showed how atmospheric effects, particularly if associated with a convenient foreground repertory of shaggy trees, ruined walls, a Gothic arch or two, were more easily accomplished than detailed studies more generally lit. Now Uvedale Price gave a clearer definition of the rector's

---

[1] Burke's *Philosophical Enquiry into the Origin of our Ideas of the Sublime and Beautiful* was first published in 1757.

[2] For Gilpin's publications see Hussey, op. cit. 111. The quotation is from *On Sunsets*, manuscript in private possession.

predilections: 'I am therefore persuaded that the two opposite qualities of roughness and of sudden variation, joined to that of irregularity, are the most efficient causes of the picturesque.'[1]

His views, however, did not go unchallenged. A friend and neighbour, Richard Payne Knight of Ludlow, published in the same year, 1794, a long, didactic poem *The Landscape*, and in a note to the second edition (1795) formulated the opinion, later (1805) worked out in detail in his *Analytical inquiry into the principles of taste*, that objects in themselves were not picturesque, but were only associative.[2] Aesthetic pleasure came from the manner in which they were viewed: 'it must always be remembered in enquiries of this kind, that the eye, unassisted, perceives nothing but light variously graduated and modified'.[3] This was the beauty that the painter intensified, but the trained eye could find it in the most ordinary scenes, the more ordinary, in fact, the better, for then the associative values are less obtrusive. Today Knight's views are recognizable as the precursors of Impressionism, containing much that has been used in defence of modern schools of painting, but at the time, startling enough though they were, they were worked out within the limits of the then known pictorial practice. Price replied in *A Dialogue on the distinct characters of the Picturesque and the Beautiful*, an imaginary tour through northern England. The first scene noted was a 'ruinous hovel on the outskirts of a heathy common. In a dark corner of it, some gipsies were sitting over a half-extinguished fire, which every now and then, as one of them stooped down to blow it, feebly blazed up for an instant, and shewed their sooty faces and black tangled locks.'[4] It was a familiar enough picture: Gainsborough's fancy paintings come at once to mind, but even more the hovels and stables of George

---

[1] *Essays*, 2nd ed. (1810), i. 49.

[2] The theory of association had already been expounded by the Rev. Archibald Alison in his *Essays on the nature and principles of Taste* (Edinburgh, 1790), to which Knight owed much.

[3] *The Landscape*, 2nd ed. (1795), 19. 'The venerable ruin, the retired cottage, the spreading oak, the beetling rock and limpid stream, having charms for the imagination, as well as for the sense ... as far however as they do afford sensual pleasure, it depends ... upon a moderate and varied irritation of the organic nerves' (*Principles of taste* (1805), 63).   [4] *Essays on the Picturesque* (1810), iii. 262.

Morland,[1] who at the time of the *Dialogue* was desperately seeking to avoid debt and to keep himself in liquor by a continuous output of these slick and superficial country pieces which have never lost their hold on the heart of the public. They were the very stuff of picturesque doctrine, and the ready demand for them, and the forgeries and imitations of them, show that Knight, Price, and the others were formulating theories to explain tastes already active.

It was a speedily established cult. Marianne Dashwood wished to have 'every book that tells how to admire an old twisted tree'.[2] Young Ladies were constantly at their sketchbooks, and Ibbetson has shown us the Ladies Elizabeth and Anne Lindsay, sitting above a rocky waterfall on the North Esk, selecting under his instruction some of the features into a landscape.[3] Nothing, however, provided so fascinating an exercise in the picturesque as landscape gardening. The eighteenth century had sought to beautify the country-side by smoothing it out, bending its lines into curves, planting clumps of trees at well-proportioned intervals, and here and there closing the vista with a classical monument or temple. Then the aim had been to reproduce a painting; now it was to find the right treatment to draw out the natural feeling of the spot. Humphry Repton's 'red books' with suggested improvements, the 'before' and 'after', cunningly indicated by drawings with hinged slips, were much in demand, and his schemes sometimes, though by no means always, carried out. Polite, agreeable, a good draughtsman, a little too subservient, Repton tried to keep pace with all the theorizing around him and, anxious to please, fell into inconsistencies, which Price and Knight readily pointed out. He aimed in fact at the patter of the time, rather than the formulation of a system. But he had a keen eye for the possibilities of a site: his dislike of forced and permanent effects such as the avenue closed by an obelisk, his constant aim to 'call forth the charms of natural landscape', brought

[1] *Life* by George Dawe, ed. J. S. Foster (n.d.); cf. an account of Morland's subjects in the *Examiner*, cxl (1816), 553.

[2] Jane Austen, *Sense and Sensibility*, chap. xvii.

[3] In the collection of the earl of Crawford and Balcarres: reproduced R. M. Clay, *J. C. Ibbetson* (1948), pl. 74.

back the 'English Garden' to the haphazard informality which is particularly associated with it.

These theories corresponded to a movement that already was apparent in the field of painting. Artists such as de Loutherbourg (1740–1812)[1] and Julius Caesar Ibbetson (1759–1817) were already employing the picturesque in their delineation of landscape, painting with broad strokes their rugged mountains, woods, and stormy skies. In Ibbetson's *Conway Castle by Moonlight* (Pl. 10 *a*), the picturesque and the romantic meet, and Conway with its uneven circle of towers and surprising silhouette, 'eminently rising sublimely over a noble estuary',[2] was to become the obligatory subject for all romantic painters. Ibbetson shows himself sitting with his easel on the foreshore: he was to have many successors: but how different it is from the clear outline and broad planes, the last sublimation of the topographical style, with which Francis Towne had painted the same subject (Pl. 10 *b*). Philip de Loutherbourg, the Strasbourg artist who settled in England as scene painter to Garrick,[3] became R.A. in 1781, and died in London in 1812, was much addicted to 'blood, calamity and strife'.[4] His *Deluge* (c. 1790) in the Victoria and Albert Museum, his *Tempest* (1793) at Stratford-upon-Avon, his *Avalanche in the Alps* (1804) at Petworth, are instances of themes which were to haunt the minds of some of his younger contem-

---

[1] D. Cook, *Art in England* (1869), 201; H. A. Hammelmann in *Country Life Annual* (1956), 152.

[2] 'Welsh Excursions', *European Mag.* lxxix (1821), 138. Ibbetson's friend William Anderson (1757–1837), for whom see M. H. Grant, *Old English Landscape Painters*, i (1926), 151, iii (1947), 151, also painted a rugged version of Conway (Oxford: coll. of the author). Turner's *Conway Castle* is in the coll. of the duke of Westminster.

[3] De Loutherbourg's stage sets, as far as they can be judged from some *maquettes* in the Victoria and Albert Museum and photographs of drawings, now lost, for *Richard III*, mark a complete break with traditional 'Baroque' stage sets, and reproduce picturesque landscapes with the help of flats arranged in rows, so as to create an uneven and broken acting space. The development of stage scenery, with its use of dioramas and, under Charles Kean in the mid-nineteenth century, its search for historical accuracy in architecture and costume, is immensely important for the progress of visual imagination, but it is a subject that requires reconstruction from very scattered evidence and cannot be dealt with in detail in this book. See G. Rowell, *The Victorian Theatre* (1956).

[4] *The Landscape* (1795), l. 90: Knight is describing a typical landscape by Salvator Rosa.

poraries. His *Survivors of a Shipwreck attacked by Robbers* may be thought perhaps to agonize overmuch.[1]

The greatest exponent of the large imaginary and melodramatic landscape was J. M. W. Turner. Crushing avalanches, burning houses, sinking ships were for him themes of distress played out against the vast background of natural forces. His long life and complex, voracious genius must wait for more detailed treatment. Here the cult of immensity may be illustrated in the work of a more senior and much lesser artist. James Ward was born in 1769, the son of a drunken Thames-side grocer.[2] He and his elder brother, William, became apprentices to the engraver John Raphael Smith, and William proved an apt pupil. James succumbed to another influence, that of his genial, improvident, and drunken brother-in-law, George Morland. Ward's animals, however, had none of the easy charm of the Morland types. Starting as straightforward records, much in demand by sporting and stock-breeding gentry, his animal paintings take on the strange hunted ferocity that was to become one of the marks of romantic art. Stubbs, who died in 1806, and Sawrey Gilpin, who died in 1807, had for some time been painting scenes of fighting horses, chargers with flying manes and tails, fiercely contending, 'beauteous and swift' but 'turned wild in nature'. These horses remained an element of Ward's art from the early years of the century till his death in 1859 at the age of ninety, and in them, in his *Fighting Horses*[3] of 1806, his *Horse and Boa Constrictor*, a life-size painting rejected by the Academy in 1803 and sunk in 1822 in transit to America, or in *Napoleon's Charger, Marengo*, pawing the ground against a stormy sky 'emblematic of his Master's Downfall' (1826: Alnwick castle), he has his place as one of the romantics from whom Géricault and Delacroix learned much. This was one trend of the times, to which this sensation-seeking age was curiously responsive; another inspiration came from the past. In 1803 Lady Beaumont purchased for her husband

[1] Photograph in Southampton Art Gallery; *The Deluge* was engraved for Thomas Macklin's *Bible* (1800); Macklin ranks with Boydell and Bowyer as a commercial patron of high art.

[2] C. R. Grundy, *James Ward, His Life and Works* (1909).

[3] For Ward's various versions of this subject see photographs in Witt Library; *Catalogue*, Ward Exhibition, Roland, Browse, and Delbanco (1952).

Rubens's *Château de Steen*. Sir George sent it to be shown to the interested artists in Benjamin West's studio. Ward 'remained the whole day studying it', returned to his studio and painted, in a passion of concentration, on a panel of similar size, his *Fighting Bulls with St. Donat's Castle in the background*. The wide landscape achieves something of the glowing atmosphere of its great proto-type; Ward's tight, close brushwork is relaxed into unwonted fluency; his imagination has been genuinely stirred; but the hushed, afternoon peace of Rubens's masterpiece, the country quiet, where the hunter stealthily stalks his game and the rumble of the cart is the only sound, is in Ward's painting changed into a strident bellow-ing; the great bulls strain against one another in a violent deadlock; the gnarled trunk across the foreground is twisted into sinister shapes. It was a recipe congenial to contemporary taste and Ward overheard West saying to Beckford that it made Rubens seem 'gross and vulgar'. Such comparisons Ward was only too ready to make for himself. Megalomania seized him, and he became a victim to his own grandiose delusions. He was a strong Irvingite, much moved by the sensationalism of the great preacher, and violent religious ecstasies added to his confusion. In 1815 the British Institution offered a £1,000 prize for a painting 16 ft. by 21 ft. expressing in an allegorical spirit the triumph of Wellington. Ward's sketch (Royal Chelsea Hospital) shows the duke in a car drawn by four white horses driving over prostrate figures amid a riot of emblems and allegories; but his painting, completed in 1821, measured 35 ft. by 22 ft. Not surprisingly the Institution, who wished to present it to the Chelsea Hospital, said they could not accept it, or could only exhibit it by doubling under the excess length, a process that was attempted for a period, after which the painting was removed and has disappeared.[1] Ward's smaller allegorical pieces consist of somewhat florid and floating muses, cousins of Etty's, but more tightly drawn. In *The Deer Stealer* (90 × 44 in.), exhibited in the British Institution in 1823, he could still handle a large Rubenesque landscape, though his melodramatic thief lacks the humour which Ward so badly needed; and his cattle, lean and wrinkled, retain a mannered vitality (Pl. 23 *b*).

[1] C. G. T. Dean, *The Royal Hospital Chelsea* (1950), 265.

His later history was one of continuous quarrels, with the R.A., the British Institution, other artists, and his own family.

Architecture was as susceptible as the other arts to the romantic afflatus, perhaps even more so, for romanticism was a way of life and one that craved new settings for its pursuits. There was much eagerness to demonstrate how many styles were now permitted to the man of taste. Gothic led the way. The middle ages were a new and exciting country from which the cultivated mind had long been debarred, and their architecture, so deeply absorbed into the country-side as to be almost a piece of it, had all the irregularity which the picturesque required. The mid-eighteenth-century Gothic fanciers, such as Horace Walpole, had regarded it as an eccentric and amusing type of ornament, a kind of arabesque applied to shapes of a different age. At Strawberry Hill or at 'light, cheerful and elegant' Sheffield Place,[1] it has a pleasant, humorous domestication, and it is not surprising that it lent itself to garden ornaments and follies. At Shobdon in Herefordshire, when in 1753 the Norman church was replaced by a charming rococo Gothic substitute, the old arches, with their figured pillars and tympana, were erected as a 'terminary' on a nearby hill.[2] The crumbling, overgrown abbeys were gradually evolving from monuments of superstition into sites of elevating melancholy; the fashionable soul was 'associate with the kindred gloom'.[3]

Classicism also claimed its ruins, reinforced by the increase in archaeological journeys, the sketches of fallen columns and moustachioed Turks seated on fragments of vast cornices, drawn by William Pars or others for the Dilettanti Society; and miniature copies of some fractured temple occasionally closed an English vista. Even in ruins there was a battle of the styles, and George IV outdid many Gothic follies by erecting a present of columns from Leptis Magna in the grounds of Virginia Water, recently laid out by Thomas Sandby.[4] As the century drew to a close, as the passions

---

[1] H. A. Tipping, *Engl. Homes*, vi. 1 (1926), xxxix.

[2] M. Whiffen, *Stuart and Georgian Churches* (1947–8), 69; see *O.H.E.A.* iii (1953), 78.

[3] *London: a poem* (1812). For the cult of ruins see R. Macaulay, *Pleasure of Ruins* (1953).

[4] G. E. Chambers, 'The "Ruins" at Virginia Water', *The Berkshire Archaeological Journ.*, liv (1954–5), 39.

as well as the fancies were released from embargoes, the horrific rather than the quaint was demanded. Horace Walpole himself had given the hint when he wrote that Strawberry Hill had inspired the castle of Otranto. By 1795 *The Mysteries of Udolpho* was setting a higher standard of spiral staircases, vaulted dungeons, and battle-mented walls. There was a 'rage for turning comfortable houses into uninhabitable castles'.[1] Even as classical an architect as Sir Robert Smirke designed corner towers lit by arrow slits, pinnacled façades, and battlements at the castles of Lowther, Eastnor (Pl. 15 *a*), and Kinfauns, and William Porden's Eaton Hall (1804–12), known to us in the detailed drawings by John Buckler and his son, John Chessell, provided a vast array of pinnacled buttresses, octagonal turrets, and perpendicular tracery. Within, fan vaulting was moulded in plaster and carved figures stood in canopied niches at the end of the dining room. The Eaton Hall of today reflects quite other tastes in its rebuilding by Waterhouse in 1870. In Wales, whose castles were a recognized source of romantic inspira-tion, the new cult took easy root. Cyfarthfa Castle in Glamorgan-shire, built for William Crawshay, close to his great ironworks at Merthyr Tydfil, and Maesllwch Castle in Radnorshire, built for Walter Wilkins, who changed his name to the more romantically appropriate de Winton, were designed by Robert Lugar, one of the great popularizers of the style in his various books of designs.[2] His embossed stonework makes the smooth ashlar of most of his contemporaries seem timidly unreal (Pl. 15 *c*). On the north Welsh coast Penrhyn Castle still stands little altered since Thomas Hopper rebuilt it for the slate magnate, George Dawkins-Pennant.[3] Hopper had been employed at Carlton House in 1807 and had, therefore, experience of elaborate designs. At Penrhyn, between

[1] Maria Edgeworth, *Tales of Fashionable Life*, iv (1814), 48.

[2] Cyfarthfa is illustrated in his *Villa Architecture* (1828), pls. 41–42; a design of Maesllwch was exhibited in the Academy of 1841, the building was begun in 1829 by Walter Wilkins II and completed by his son Walter Wilkins III in 1839, when the name de Winton was adopted; see *The Silurian*, 18 May 1839, and S. Lewis, *Topographical Dictionary of Wales* (1845), i. 376. I am much indebted to Mr. and Mrs. Gerald de Winton for information and assistance.

[3] Douglas Hague and Christopher Hussey, 'Penrhyn Castle', *C.L.* cxviii (1955), 80, 140, 192; R. Fedden, *Arch. Rev.* cxvi (1954), 381; cf. the remarkable 'Design for a Villa in the Norman Style' by E. B. Lamb in *The Architectural Mag.* i (1834), 333.

1827 and 1846, he created a great keep, modelled largely on that of Rochester (Pl. 14), his native town, and from this central feature carried the Romanesque idiom throughout the whole building. The chevroned pillars of Durham are everywhere apparent, freely mixed with the neater geometric patterns of the later period of the style: on the tympana of the great stairway arches, the Welsh craftsmen seem to have reverted through Romanesque back into traditional Celtic patterns; the stained glass, wonderfully able pastiche by Willement, shows the Signs of the Zodiac and the Labours of the Months. To walk through these vast rooms, still with their original furniture, to scale in size and fantasy, is to experience one of the fullest expressions of Regency unchastened exuberance, and to wonder at the confidence of a generation who could deck out its daily life in such lavish appurtenances of past greatness.

Medievalism, however, reached its climax in the building of Fonthill abbey. It brought together two striking and controversial characters, William Beckford, the owner, and James Wyatt, the architect. The Beckford money came from the plantations, but the family was an ancient one of Gloucestershire. Thoughts of medieval grandeur mingled in the mind of the young millionaire with dreams of oriental voluptuousness: the latter were embodied in *Vathek*, a strange, exotic masterpiece which he published when he was twenty-one, the former in the building, on his father's estate at Fonthill, first of a great ornamental ruin, then in stone of a vast Gothic palace. James Wyatt,[1] born in 1746, the son of a Staffordshire builder, five of whose sons became architects, had had some years' study in Italy, returned to England in 1768, and suddenly sprang into fame by building the Pantheon in Oxford Street. This fashionable pleasure house became the admiration of the town: it was a domed building with a coffered roof; scagliola columns (imitation marble), the first use of the compound in England, supported a double colonnade, the upper story with Corinthian capitals, the lower with Ionic; outside a simple classical portico showed the restraint which, rather surprisingly in view of his dark reputation, characterizes so much of Wyatt's work. Inside, it was

[1] See A. Dale, *James Wyatt* (revised ed. 1956).

lively, elegant, distinguished, and thoroughly 'Roman' in the Adam sense.[1] Wyatt's finest works are in the classic style: Heaton House, Lancashire (1772), with its connecting colonnades and central pilastered apse; the great hall and staircase at Liverpool Town Hall (1789–1811); Heveningham Hall, Suffolk (in the nineties), with fine examples of decoration by Biagio Rebecca, his favourite collaborator; and Dodington Park, Gloucestershire (1796–1817).[2] As early, however, as 1776 he had been appointed surveyor to Westminster Abbey, and this position made him the natural authority and consultant on all questions of restoration. At Lee Priory in Kent he had experimented (1782–90) with domestic Gothic;[3] in 1790 a new opportunity came in the fantastic schemes of William Beckford.

The story of Fonthill has often been told; its thin octagonal tower, 230 feet high to the top of its pinnacles, rises like a mirage over all accounts of early romanticism. Innumerable artists painted it, mainly from the one particular viewpoint from which the building looked a completed and effective whole. Inside, the great hall, 120 feet high, with its flight of steps leading to a high lancet opening, was immensely sublime and singularly difficult to heat. The deep-red carpet and curtains, the wall hangings of crimson silk, the 'characteristic' chimney pieces of Purbeck marble, the gilded fan-vaulted or coffered ceilings struck a note of more modern luxury, and provided a setting for some important works of art, and many pieces of fairly dubious authenticity: an inlaid table of *pietre commesse*, 9 feet long, from the Borghese Palace; six carved ebony chairs belonging formerly to Cardinal Wolsey; a very large coffer of Japan, once the property of Cardinal Mazarin; the Japanese idol Armida, and other such rarities. With this profusion of place, period, and style, it is little surprising that the Gothic framework itself was not of the purest, and ranged freely from lancet to flamboyant, with the visual readiness that characterizes all Wyatt's work (Pl. 12 a). Begun in 1796 as a 'folly',

[1] Completed 1772; in 1792 the young Turner was to paint its smouldering ruins.
[2] For Heaton and Heveningham see H. A. Tipping, *Engl. Homes*, vi. 1 (1926), 199 and 347; for Dodington Park see C. Hussey in *C.L.* cxx (1956), 1176 and 1230.
[3] Demolished 1954; a room is preserved in the Victoria and Albert Museum.

a mere ornament for picnics, the first tower, a flimsy business of lath, canvas, and cement, was soon blown over; then the owner decided to make this extraordinary elongated cross of buildings his residence (Fig. 1): it was never really completed. In September

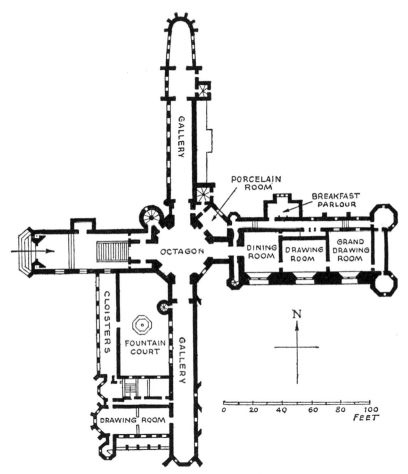

FIG. 1. *Plan of Fonthill*

1813 Wyatt was killed when his carriage overturned: in 1822 Beckford sold Fonthill and built himself a mansion at Bath in the classical style; in 1825 the great tower collapsed. In several copies of John Rutter's *Delineations of Fonthill* (1823),[1] a lithograph by William Westall from John Buckler's drawing of *The Ruins of*

[1] See also J. Storer's *Description of Fonthill Abbey* (1812); J. Britton, *Illustrations,*

Fonthill is fastened into the end pages. The great hall still stands, but the lower and southern arm lies in ruins, a confusion of broken masonry. Rumour said that the clerk of the works confessed on his death-bed that the foundations had been skimped through pressure of haste. Extravagant, spectacular, disastrous, and shocking in its irresponsibility, it summed up in a fantasy of excess much that was stirring as the century opened.

Graphic and Literary, of Fonthill Abbey (1823); Boyd Alexander, *Life at Fonthill* (1957); H. A. N. Brockman, *The Caliph of Fonthill* (1956).

II

PAINTERS IN WATER-COLOUR

'THE dewy freshness of a spring morning—the passing shower,—the half-dispelled mist—the gay partial gleam of April sunshine—the rainbow—the threatening storm—the smiles and frowns of our changeful sky, or their infinite effects upon the character of the landscape—the unsubstantial brightness of the grey horizon—and the fresh vivid colouring of the broken foreground—all these features in the ever-varying face of Nature can be represented by the painter in water-colours, with . . . a day-like brightness and truth, which we will not say *cannot* be produced in oil-painting, but which we at least have never yet witnessed. . . . All that we have yet seen inclines us to think, that, in the representation of land, sea, and sky, the art of water-colour painting which has so recently begun to be cultivated, and is probably so little advanced towards its possible perfection, is superior to the long-established art of painting in oil.' Thus, perceptively, wrote a critic in the *Edinburgh Review* in 1834.[1] We would today question his view of the greater perfections in store, for water-colour had already reached some of its rarest achievements, but there were unquestionably new potentialities for the rendering of weather, of the haziness, dampness, and glistening of the English country-side. Translucent washes of colour on an unprepared ground could catch hints of the sky which had been denied to thicker paint, and blots of colour, stroked in by the brush with no defining lines, gave a sense of fleetingness that realized peculiarly English qualities and were, or so contemporaries believed, methods largely of English origin.

It was only gradually that these changes came about. Teachers such as Edward Dayes still at the turn of the century assumed that there would be a drawn outline, with the shadows blocked out in neutral tints before colour was applied,[2] the 'tinted drawings' of

[1] lxix. 59.
[2] *Instructions for Drawing and Colouring Landscapes* in *Works*, ed. E. W. Brayley

the eighteenth-century topographical tradition. As long as water-colours were largely used as a basis for engravings, especially engravings of Gothic buildings for which there seemed to be an insatiable demand, this method was well suited to provide the necessary sharpness of detail for the engraver's plate. Not that the tinted drawing lacked its poetic creations, for at the turn of the century it was reaching its greatest maturity. The landscapes of Francis Towne (d. 1816)[1] employ brown outlines enclosing flat washes that suggest foliage, distant mountain slopes, the surface of water, with a telling economy of means (Pl. 10 *b*): in figure subjects the tinted outline was at the same time serving for the most fervid visual imaginings England had ever known, the drawings of William Blake. The growing prestige of water-colours as works of art began to invest studies, made only as notes or records of places, with virtues in their own rights, and the formation of the Society of Painters in Water-colours was a protest against the Royal Academy's treatment of the medium as a subordinate branch. The aim now was to produce 'gallery' pictures, which in heavy gilt frames, as large as could be glazed, would 'bear out in effect' as powerfully as their oil rivals—a dangerous rivalry which often led to the overstraining of water-colour resources.

The new vogue was largely due to developments in the production of the materials.[2] In 1821 Messrs. Thomas and William Reeves had been awarded a silver palette by the Society of Arts for the progress they had made in the manufacture of paints, and at the same period Mr. Whatman had been experimenting with paper, producing a surface that would bear washing and sponging, and that, unbleached by any acid, had no injurious action upon the colouring. Effects thus made possible roused the ambitions of

(1805). See 'Historical Sketch of Painting in Water-colours', *Library of the Fine Arts*, i (1831), 403.

[1] A. P. Oppé in *Walpole Soc.* viii (1920), 95; H. Lemaitre in *La Revue des Arts*, iii (1953), 171. Towne stated that he 'never exhibited a *drawing*', and his oils attracted little attention. His repute and his disciples, such as John White Abbot (see Oppé, *Walpole Soc.* xiii (1925), 67), were localized in the West Country. He is an example of an artist coming to fame after 100 years of obscurity.

[2] See *Cat. of Exhibition of Society of Painters in Water Colour* (1821), quoted H. M. Cundall, *A History of Water-Colour Painting* (1929), 51.

many amateurs, for the new breadth seemed, misleadingly, an easier undertaking than the old precise delineation. The even focus of the topographical drawing was disregarded for more atmospheric impressions, where the middle distance might be sharply indicated but the foreground roughly sketched. The elder Cozens had been the great experimenter with blots of paint, using them particularly for the suggestion of foliage, always a problem that required some conventionalized solution. Now a whole generation of artists were experimenting with the fluid shapes that water-colour could produce and the fascination of this new approach was expounded in practice and handbooks by many teachers. At the opening of the century William Payne[1] was one of the most popular of them, and under his influence the use of pen outlines went out of fashion, texture was achieved by variations of brush work, and the highlights were secured by washing or rubbing out patches of colour. At his best, as in the skating scene in the British Museum (Pl. 16 a), Payne is an attractive artist, but his dexterity easily degenerated into tricks, and his forms, though created with the brush, are still laid in with Indian ink or lamp-black and then coloured, in his later work with heavy body paint and sometimes finished with a yellow wash or varnish. John (Warwick) Smith (1749–1831) is another to whom new developments in technique, in particular the use of a grey ground, are attributed.[2] The use of colour directly on the white paper, without any preliminary grey ground or brushing in the shapes in black, was traditionally attributed to Girtin and Turner,[3] but that is merely the attraction of great names. The scope of water-colour was being discovered in the general practice of a wide group of painters.

If teaching was the great provider for the needy artist, encouragement and even instruction were provided by the discerning patron. Of such Dr. Thomas Monro, John Henderson his neighbour in

[1] Payne's dates are uncertain, c. 1760–c. 1830. See Redgrave's *Century of British Painters* (1947), 152, and B. S. Long, *Walker's Quarterly*, vi (1922).

[2] B. S. Long in *Walker's Quarterly*, xxiv (1927).

[3] This originates in a statement by W. H. Pyne in *The Somerset House Gazette*, i (1824), 67. The articles in this brief-lived journal on 'The Rise and Progress of Water-colour Painting in England' represent the views current among artists in the first quarter of the century.

Adelphi Terrace, James Moore, and Sir George Beaumont were the most influential on the early water-colourists. Dr. Monro[1] was an authority on mental diseases of sufficient eminence to be consultant to the king; he was also an accomplished draughtsman, whose numerous wash and charcoal sketches still give much pleasure. In his rooms in the Adelphi or at his house at Bushey he collected young painters, paying them small sums for copying drawings in his collection and giving them advice and supper. Among these drawings were some by J. R. Cozens, who had been the doctor's patient. Cozens had died in 1797, but through these drawings he became an influence on his successors, admitted by both Turner and Girtin, who copied his works for Dr. Monro; in particular his sense of atmospheric distance, his power of suggesting the vastness of the mountains revealed a new range of scenic imagination, the substitution as a mountain symbol of the Alps to the hills of the Campagna.[2]

The English artists, Cozens, Pars, and Towne, who were attempting to delineate mountain immensity, had contact with a school of water-colour painters that, though mainly composed of French, Swiss, and German artists, had its centre in Rome. Its immediate object was the sketching of classical remains, but the neo-classical mood is always close to the romantic, and painters such as Ducroz (1748–1810) and Clérisseau (1722–1820) were facing problems, amongst them that of rendering mountains, similar to those of their English confrères, and finding many English patrons for their works. Swiss colour prints of mountain scenery, generally with foreground details of happy peasant life, were already by 1800 popular throughout Western Europe.[3] The English development was not so isolated as it is traditionally represented, a tradition formulated by the early nineteenth century; but it remains true that there was much ferment of ideas in the evenings at Dr. Monro's and in the sketching club formed by Girtin,

[1] C. E. Coode, 'Turner's First Patron', *Art Journ.* n.s. i (1901), 133, and W. Foxley Norris in *O.W.-C.S.C.* ii (1925), 1.

[2] See A. Bury, 'Some Mountains in Water-Colour', *O.W.-C.S.C.* xxiii (1945), 3. For the Cozens, see A. P. Oppé, *Alexander and John Robert Cozens* (1952).

[3] See C. F. Bell in *Walpole Soc.* v (1917), 57; W. R. Schweizer, 'The Swiss Print, 1760–1840', *The Connoisseur*, cxxx (1952), 85.

Francia, Cotman, Ker Porter, Callcott, and others,[1] ideas which can best be illustrated in the brief, ill-fated career of Thomas Girtin.

Born in 1775 in Southwark, of Huguenot stock like others who have done much for art in England, he had only twenty-seven years of life in which to establish his fame.[2] His early drawings when he was apprenticed (1789) to Edward Dayes are mainly architectural and the outline is drawn with the pen, though from the first Girtin could convey qualities of shape by broken strokes that are quite unlike the more precise drawing of elder artists. By the time that he was twenty, he could, without any or little drawn outline, show clumps of trees, distant clouds, the shifting colours of the view in a manner that Cozens, Canaletto, Wilson, or any of his models had never surpassed. Some of these water-colours were shown in the Academy in the last years of the nineties; his only recorded oil painting, *Bolton Bridge*, was shown in 1801; his largest work, possibly in tempera, was a panorama of London, the *Eidometropolis* as he called it, which was exhibited at Spring Gardens in 1802.

These topographical paintings, generally stretched on canvas cylinders so as to surround the spectator, had been popularized at the close of the eighteenth century by the Edinburgh artist, Robert Barker (1739–1806). Their painting was, as an alternative to scene painting, to employ many young artists, and a friend of Girtin's, the young Ker Porter, had recently (1799) achieved success with his panorama of the taking of Seringapatam. Some drawings for Girtin's panorama survive in the British Museum and the Whitworth Art Gallery; and the sketches he made in Paris may have had another panorama in view. In 1800 he married, but his strength was rapidly deteriorating from some pulmonary complaint. It may

---

[1] The membership was a fluctuating one: see F. H. H. Guillemard, 'Girtin's Sketching Club', *Connoisseur*, lxiii (1922), 189, and A. P. Oppé, *Connoisseur*, lxvii (1923), 189.

[2] The basic account of his career is an anonymous article 'Recollections of the late Thomas Girtin', *Library of the Fine Arts*, iii (1832), 307; see also J. L. Roget, *History of the Old Water-Colour Society* (1891), i. 83; R. Davies, *Thomas Girtin's Water-Colours* (1924); J. Mayne, *Thomas Girtin* (1949); T. Girtin and D. Loshak, *The Art of Thomas Girtin* (1954).

have been in search of health that he went to Paris in October 1801, but Paris in winter with the Peace of Amiens not yet finally signed was a strange place for recuperation, and there is a certain mystery about this visit, for which special permits must have been necessary. Perhaps it was the desire to press on with new subjects in the short time left him, rather than any hopeful quest for health. He died in 1802.

Time has dealt unkindly with much of Girtin's work. He had a liking for warm, golden tints and often bathed his whole landscape, sky and earth alike, in them, using a rough yellow cartridge paper and heavy washes of lake, indigo, and Indian red in his skies; but in many cases, where fading has taken place, that which was golden has become hot: the yellow paper shows through too darkly, the indigos have gone from the skies leaving only the lake.[1] Of all the great water-colourists Girtin fades with least charm. In his latest sketches, those in Paris, he uses a clearer, greyer range of colour, with a wonderful subtlety in the tones of the masonry, and he is as happy in town streets as in his windswept country fields. He is the most calligraphic of them all; small blots of paint, squiggles with the brush, minute heightenings with the pen build up the surface texture of his ancient buildings or the foliage of his trees. He could see, with a new release from older conventions, the movement of the sky, the wind sweeping the trees, the varying shadows on the ridge: and in his greatest moments he could build up a design of impressive finality, the slope of Lulworth Cove (Leeds) or Kirkstall abbey across the meadows (Pl. 17 a).

After brief promise, ripe fulfilment. Turner was born in the same year as Girtin. They had met as boys; Turner's father, a barber, lived in Maiden Lane, Girtin was brought up by his mother at St. Martin's-le-Grand; both worked at colouring prints for John Raphael Smith and both were patronized by Dr. Monro and by his neighbour in Adelphi Terrace, John Henderson. As early as 1790 Turner exhibited at the Royal Academy, and his energy and prolific genius from the first carried him into some measure of repute. These drawings of the nineties are mainly architectural

[1] See M. Hardie, 'Thomas Girtin, the Technical Aspect of his Work', *O.W.-C.S.C.* xi (1934), 1.

and have the engraver's requirements strictly in view: they are more accurate, less personal and inventive than those of Girtin; the architectural detail is more closely studied; but there is already a sense of scale, of rendering the relationship in space by a treatment of atmosphere; now and then, even in this early period, a storm on the sea coast or the glow of an iron foundry releases his passionate interest in light and he breaks away from the limitations of architectural drawing. He was also occupying himself with paintings in oil, and to them was due his surprisingly early recognition by the Academy (A.R.A. 1799, R.A. 1802). He was to be equally at home in both mediums. To him an Academy picture could as well be a water-colour as an oil, and in the former medium he painted large canvases as ambitious as any that he undertook. His art is governed by this ambivalence, and, once he leaves the early architectural records behind him, it would be a false dichotomy to attempt to separate his stylistic progress. He transcends the scope of other water-colour painters, and lies outside the limits of the history of their technique. His art must be treated as a whole.

Individual and unmistakable as is his style, John Sell Cotman stands more in the direct line of development. The flat expanses, rolling outlines, wide skies, and luxuriant canal banks of East Anglia have had a curiously powerful hold on the English creative intellect and have been a striking stimulus to it. Here a local individuality was established strong enough to resist the dominance of London tastes and forms. Norwich itself, cut off from the main traffic routes, was still a great centre of industry, proud of its trade secrets and unaware that its smooth-running waters could not vie with the quicker streams of the Pennines in the new demand for power and that the seams of coal were not to enrich East Anglia; the most confident of English provincial capitals, it was the right setting for and the explanation of its artists. Cotman's senior by fourteen years, John Crome is the most typical and influential figure of the local school. In his rare water-colours he shows a keen understanding of the medium and builds up with broad washes on rough paper scenes of the country-side as intensely felt as anything he achieved in oil. *The Shadowed Road* (Pl. 18 *a*) is unfortunately not dated and it cannot therefore be known whether its breadth of treatment was borrowed from Cotman, or whether the younger artist's style, so surprisingly certain of itself in his earliest pictures, owed something to his fellow citizen. Certainly no others were at this time painting water-colours with such a rich and structural sense of pattern masses.[1]

Cotman,[2] born in 1782, the son of a barber turned draper, was brought up to assist his father, but in 1798 went off to London, with little money and no security, to become an artist. Working for a year or so with Rudolph Ackerman at the latter's Depository of Arts in the Strand, he became known to Dr. Monro and joined his band of copyists. In July of 1800 he was in Wales and at Conway castle, where a group of young painters were collected round Sir George Beaumont, no doubt at his expense. It is a moment on which it is tempting to pause, the great patron before the most popular symbol of the picturesque.[3] Sir George was now in his forty-ninth year; himself a talented painter who had received lessons at Eton from Alexander Cozens, he was recognized as the most discerning collector in the country. His kindness to young artists, Constable and Girtin among them, was both considerable and sensitive. He could be opinionated and impatient, and certainly was often given cause to be the latter; but there are too many recorded instances of his imaginative friendliness at critical moments for there to be any doubt of his unusual gift for sympathy and understanding. His name will recur constantly in these pages. Acceptance into the Beaumont circle was a great opportunity for the young Cotman, and he seems to have availed himself of it, for in the following year he was a member of Girtin's sketching club in London, and it has been said that Jane Ker Porter, whose brother was another member, borrowed some details of Cotman's early struggles to sell his drawings for her hero, Thaddeus of

---

[1] For Crome see monographs by C. H. Collins Baker (1921), S. C. Kaines-Smith (1923), and R. H. Mottram (1931).

[2] Monographs by S. D. Kitson (1937), A. P. Oppé (Studio Special Number 1923), and V. Reinaker (Leigh-on-Sea, 1953).

[3] Some years later (1808) Sir George speaking to Farington (*Diary*, v. 71) 'reprobated the rage for Water Colour drawings': for his influence see *Memorials of Coleorton*, ed. W. Knight, 2 vols. (Edinburgh, 1887): Sir George's *Entrance to Conway Castle* was in the Stafford Coll., *Catalogue* by W. Y. Ottley (1818), ii. 142.

Warsaw, in that once so famous and now perhaps unduly neglected novel. But if for Cotman this first Welsh visit was peculiarly momentous, Sir George's approach to the picturesque and Girtin's emphatic style did not overwhelm him. His handling of the famous castle, as shown in two soft ground etchings[1] based on sketches of this period, was characteristic, for, neglecting the famous silhouette of walls and towers, he drew one round tower rising up cylindrically and solidly, and a vista of arches seen from the ruins, those round shapes that he always particularly loved.

The summer of 1802 saw Cotman once more in Wales. Some of the material collected on this tour was later worked up by him with notable effect, in particular the drawing of the new aqueduct recently completed by Telford at Chirk, Llangollen (Pl. 18 *b*), whose round, shadowed openings, contrasting with the sunlight on the flat surface, admirably provided him with his favourite shapes. More important, however, than the two Welsh tours were the visits to Yorkshire in 1803, 1804, and 1805 and his meeting with the Cholmeley family. Those new friendships open the most vividly creative period of his art. Mrs. Cholmeley arranged sketching tours of the Yorkshire abbeys; Cotman wandered by himself in the woods round Helmsley or went with Francis Cholmeley to stay at Rokeby Park, where the Greta runs through the grounds. He began to use large flat washes, where form is indicated by slight flecks or even by the broken roughness of the paper, building up with it wonderfully decorative patterns. Hackneyed a little by imperfect colour reproduction, *Greta Bridge* (B.M.) remains the symbol of Cotman's achievement, of that particular perception which he alone brought to English art.

Something perhaps was owed to the discipline of an archaeological passion which existed side by side with this intense feeling for the massed effects of foliage, the wide tilth of fields, the sheen of water and the distant Yorkshire hills. It is customary to deplore the time spent by Cotman on architectural studies for engravings, to pity him for the close adherence to detail that this entailed, to regret the antiquarian interests of his second patron, Dawson Turner. Everything, however, suggests that the friendship between

[1] *Liber Studiorum*, publ. by H. G. Bohn: 5th ser. (1838).

Turner and Cotman was one of shared interests. 'Warmly partaking in the admiration of them', Turner wrote of Cotman's interest in the Norman doorways of Norfolk;[1] and, if further evidence is needed, there are the plates themselves, records which could only have been made by someone of real architectural knowledge and stylistic sympathy. He was, too, a romantic of his time: costume, colour, oddity were essential to him: 'Everything is picturesque. On our road to Chateau d'arques we met the Peasants coming to Market. I want words to express my delight. Women, Men, Horses, Mules and carriages with such attire, harness etc., better seen than described; the Head dresses of y women are like to y Icelandic.'[2] He was, because he was romantic, eclectic; the rules of pure taste were overthrown in a new liberty; when he sketched the Yorkshire harvest, he borrowed a group of figures from some engraving of Giorgione's country fête (Giorgione had borrowed it from Raphael) and set down the poses in his English field (Pl. 22 a).

In 1806 Cotman left London and settled in Norwich, buying a house there, holding an exhibition of his paintings and marrying a local girl, Ann Miles, a farmer's daughter. At Norwich in 1804 John Crome and Robert Ladbrooke had founded their society of artists and amateurs, and it seemed a promising centre for an artist's career. Mercurial in temper, either enthusiastic or depressed, Cotman, tired of the city life of London or drawn by some old attachment to his home, returned to a life at Norwich and at Yarmouth, where drawing lessons, etching, portrait studies, rubbing brasses and then making drawings from the rubbings, were to fill much of his time and were not always adequate to provide for his family needs.

In this period of his life, the decisive figure is Dawson Turner, a Yarmouth banker, botanist, bibliophil, and antiquarian. It was through him that Cotman moved to Yarmouth and became drawing master to the family, not on the close, easy terms that he had enjoyed with the Cholmeleys, but on a solid enough basis of mutual

[1] *Introduction to Architectural Antiquities of Normandy* (1822), iii.
[2] 'J. S. Cotman's Letters from Normandy', ed. by H. Isherwood Kay, *Walpole Soc.* xiv (1926), 97.

understanding and liking; and it was for Dawson Turner's *Architectural Antiquities of Normandy* (1822) and *Tour in Normandy* (1820) that Cotman went to Normandy in 1817, 1818, and 1819 and found new inspiration. Never entirely at home in etching, Cotman can always be better enjoyed in water-colour, in sepia wash, or in his rarer oil paintings than in any reproductive process; but his own etchings of Château Gaillard, of the round towers at Tancarville, of the castle of Falaise are grand and memorable pieces. In wash, there is a searching analysis of form in rock and building which looks onward to Cézanne.

In 1834, through the good offices of Dawson Turner's daughter, Lady Palgrave, he was appointed Professor of Drawing at King's College, London, though the titles Professor and College were as yet somewhat grander than either the post or institution warranted. He died in London in 1842. He had tried in his last years to catch public fancy with large brightly coloured and dramatic water-colours; *Lee Shore with the Wreck of the Houghton Pictures, Books etc. sold to the Empress Catherine of Russia, including the celebrated and gorgeous Landscape of the Waggoner, by Rubens*, is typical of this phase; pictures and objects of vertu lie in a pile on the shore, while sailors drag the dead bodies of their comrades out of the waves and the ship overturns in the background. It is a fashionable horror piece, and the fantastic incident is an imagined one. It was very large, 2 ft. 3 in. by 3 ft., 'which I consider a whacker', Cotman wrote of it.[1] It was not sold. For himself, as notes for paintings or in sheer, final response to the thing seen, he did a series of chalk drawings on grey paper; bending trees and branches, the wind across the Norfolk flats, one or two old churches, the waters of a flood; these were his final utterance.

Lincoln also found a genius to interpret its atmospheric mood, though not a native son or permanent resident. Peter de Wint was born in Staffordshire in 1784 and most of his working life he lived in London,[2] but his close friendship with the historical painter

---

[1] Kitson, op. cit. 344. It is now in the Fitzwilliam Museum, Cambridge. The Houghton pictures were sold to Catherine in 1779, but arrived safely, and Rubens's *Charrette Embourbée* is now in the Hermitage.

[2] R. Davies, 'Peter de Wint', *O.W.-C.S.C.* i (1924), 5.

William Hilton, a Lincolnshire man, whose sister he married and whose memorial[1] in the cathedral he shares, brought him often to Lincoln, and he had many friends and patrons in the county. De Wint recalls Cotman in his use of broad blocks of colour, but his paint is far thicker, his brushwork broader. He could give a mysterious rich depth to the 'intelligent shapes' of his dark clumps of trees,[2] a translucent shimmer to his water—'The murmuring undulations of quiet streams'[3]—and his haystacks or cornfields come to a crisp, crackling life of individual straws though shown by broad washes, with highlights only here and there scraped out. He liked long panoramas, sticking the pages of his sketchbooks horizontally together. Today his skies have often faded, and his dark shadows are too strongly contrasted, but there are certain mid-day lights on the English scene which will always bring him to mind. His was a successful career; pious, businesslike, healthy, happily married, he was much in demand as a teacher and, though his oil paintings did not sell, impressive enough as they seem today, his water-colours had a fairly steady market at twenty to thirty guineas.

In London the Old Water-Colour Society had been the first focus of the art. It had been founded in 1804 and held its first exhibition in 1805. The moving spirit ('*Promoter, Originator* and chief *Corner Stone*') had been William Wells,[4] author of a *Compendious Treatise of Anatomy . . . adapted to the Arts of Designing* (1796), and, though some years his elder, a friend of Turner and the proposer of the *Liber Studiorum*. His water-colours are conventional pieces of little note, but he had it appears great belief in the medium, and gathered round him a group of friends, Sawrey Gilpin, George Barrett, Samuel Shelley, Francis Nicholson, Nicholas Pocock, Robert Hills, and William Pyne. These were the first members, to whom very shortly eight others were added, Joshua Cristall, John Glover, William Havell, James Holworthy,

[1] It is carved by J. Forsyth with subjects from Hilton's pictures and with de Wint's *Lincoln Cathedral from the West* and was erected by de Wint's widow in 1864.

[2] 'Try something like the solid blocks of sober colour in de Wint' (Samuel Palmer): quoted M. Hardie, *Peter de Wint* (Studio Special Number, 1922), 3.

[3] Thackeray writing of de Wint in *The Landscape Painters of England* (1850), quoted in *O.W.-C.S.C.* i. 13.   [4] Basil Long, *O.W.-C.S.C.* xiii (1936), 1.

J. C. Nattes, S. Rigaud, John and Cornelius Varley.[1] The first exhibition of the Society was held in 1805 and met with considerable success, nearly twelve thousand people paying for admission in the course of the seven weeks for which it was open. This initial prestige led the Royal Academy in 1810 to repeal the clause excluding water-colour painters from membership, but, though the Academy was now open to them, Academicians, until 1863, were not allowed to be members of other exhibiting societies, a situation which caused much heart searching and confusion of loyalties. The first years of the Old Water-Colour Society were troubled ones, with many rivalries and secessions. Its founders were mostly men already established in their particular fields. Samuel Shelley (1750–1808) was a pleasant painter of miniature portraits and fashionable, trivial subject pieces, with an occasional hint of Fuseli.[2] Nicholas Pocock, probably the oldest of them all (c. 1741–1821), a Bristol sea captain, had made a name for himself as a marine painter, using the conventional formulas for representing waves as a setting for the battle pieces which the war had brought into considerable demand. When he died at the age of eighty, 'the last representative, in the Society, of the old school of tinters passed away'.[3] Francis Nicholson's (1753–1844) water-colours are now mostly faded and sombre, and the rocks and waterfalls in which he delighted have lost their sparkle, but in his day he was regarded as an experimental artist, using the new practice of stopping out the highlights, and important as a teacher.[4] As early as 1821 he was producing

[1] Clara Wheeler (daughter of W. F. Wells), 'A Sketch of the formation of the Old Water-Colour Society', *O.W.-C.S.C.* xi (1934), 53. J. L. Roget, *History of the Old Water-Colour Society*, 2 vols. (1891), remains the authoritative account of English water-colour painting in the first half of the nineteenth century; see also A. J. Finberg, *English Water Colour Painters* (1906); H. M. Cundall, *A History of British Water Colour Painting* (1929); L. Binyon, *English Water-colours* (1933); C. E. Hughes, *Early English Water Colour*, ed. by J. Mayne (1950); I. A. Williams, *Early English Water-colours* (1952); H. Lemaitre, *Le Paysage anglais à l'aquarelle* (Paris, 1954). For J. L. Roget, see A. Bury, *O.W.-C.S.C.* xxvi (1948), 32.

[2] R. Davies in *O.W.-C.S.C.* xi (1934), 21.

[3] J. L. Roget, op. cit. i. 143, 297, 146; R. Davies in *O.W.-C.S.C.* v (1928), 1.

[4] He published *The Practice of Drawing and Painting Landscape, from Nature, in Water Colours* (2nd ed. 1823). See *Somerset House Gazette*, i (1824), 30; B. S. Long, *Walker's Quarterly*, xiv (1924); R. Davies, *O.W.-C.S.C.* viii (1931), 1.

lithographs and was one of the first of the water-colourists to realize the possibilities of this medium. 'To the honourable labours of a few artists', wrote the *Foreign Review* in 1829, '. . . England is indebted for the advances which the art (of lithography) has hither-to made . . . at the head of these artists is Francis Nicholson.'[1] John Glover (1767–1849), on the other hand, was a reactionary, making his finished drawing in indigo, India red, or Indian ink, and then applying colour. Methodical and industrious, his output enjoyed great popularity, and of the early water-colourists he for a time had the most general recognition and most numerous imitators.[2] He became, however, repetitive and his large landscapes (52 in. by 36 in. was a common size) were more and more loosely constructed and vaguely delineated. In 1831, possibly realizing that his vogue was passing, he emigrated to Australia and settled in Tasmania, where with extraordinary vitality in a man of his age and consider-able corpulence he set himself, both in oil and water-colour, to tackle trees that were unrelated to any traditional formulas. His renderings of the contorted branches of gum trees, the setting for aboriginal dances, were a real approach to a new world, and a release to his own creative gifts (Pl. 16 *b*). In his seventies, he could paint his Tasmanian garden with a sense of detail and solid form that suggests the art of Stanley Spencer.[3] W. H. Pyne (1769–1843)[4] painted pleasant, picturesque cottages and in his *Microcosm, or a Picturesque Delineation of the Arts, Agriculture, Manufactures, etc. of Great Britain in a series of above a thousand groups of small figures for the embellishment of landscape* (1802–7) provided a generation of artists with examples of appropriate foreground scenes. It is, how-ever, as the gossip of the movement, in the pages of the periodicals or of his *Wine and Walnuts* (1824) that Pyne matters most to us: much of what we know and think of early English water-colours depends on him.

Of the founder members, Robert Hills (1769–1844),[5] Pyne's

---

[1] *O.W.-C.S.C.* viii. 10, from manuscript notes by the Nicholson family.

[2] For comments on Glover see *Somerset House Gazette*, i (1824), 132; Farington, *Diary*, iii. 87, and v. 53: B. S. Long in *Walker's Quarterly*, xv (1924).

[3] National Gallery of S. Australia, Adelaide.

[4] A. Bury in *O.W.-C.S.C.* xxviii (1950), 1.

[5] Martin Hardie in *O.W.-C.S.C.* xxv (1947), 38.

exact contemporary, was the most closely connected with the fortunes of the Society, for between its founding and his death he is said to have exhibited 600 paintings. His work reflects a trend in the use of the medium; his early fluid washes give place to an opaque body colour employed to give a brilliant but unreal effect. In 1817 he was still painting 'gallery' water-colours, where stags roam among misty mountains, the noble beasts on the whole dominating their heavy gilt frames and devotedly observed (Pl. 24 b). Later he only painted the beasts ('Mr. Hills has lived upon the same piece of venison for the last twenty years')[1] and the landscapes are often by a younger painter, G. F. Robson (1788–1833), who exploited the romanticism of the Scottish mountains or the hill-top cathedral of his native Durham (Pl. 22 b). Robson's heavy paint, often purple in tint, mars some of his effects, but his *Loch Coruisk and the Mountains of Skye* (V. and A.), with its 'purple mass of mountains far removed',[2] breathes the very atmosphere of *The Lady of the Lake*, and never, said the *Quarterly Review*, 'has the analogy between poetry and painting been more strikingly exemplified than in the writings of Mr. Scott'.[3] 'Ut pictura poesis' was still sound, accepted doctrine.

The Varley brothers, John (1778–1842) and Cornelius (1781–1873), were sons of a Lincolnshire man, Richard Varley, settled in Hackney.[4] They had through their mother descent from Oliver Cromwell, and Cromwell remained a family name. It was a rich and vigorous stock: John divided his energy between painting, teaching, where his pungent admonitions became traditional aphorisms, and astrology: Cornelius, a lesser but competent artist, had considerable scientific attainments. John's style is somewhat too pondered; his paintings tend to be over-organized, and at times his interest in range of colour led him to overload his paint and lose something of the essential virtues of his medium; his violent contrasts of warm browns with vivid streaks of sunset or deep purple hills are over-stated in search of strength. His

---

[1] *Fraser's Mag.* i (1830), 535.

[2] Ruskin, *Works*, iii (*Modern Painters*, i, chap. vii), 193; for Robson see *O.W.-C.S.C.* xvi (1938), 37.   [3] iii (1810), 512.

[4] R. Davies, 'John Varley', *O.W.-C.S.C.* ii (1925), and B. S. Long, 'Cornelius Varley', xiv (1937); A. Bury, *John Varley* (Leigh-on-Sea, 1946).

Landscape Design (1816) with its detailed instructions for composition was a work that had a beneficial and steadying effect on the
practice of others, but as so often with great teachers, his own
precepts absorbed some of his vitality.

To the artists at the time the pre-eminence of landscape, particularly as studied from nature, was not as incontrovertibly accepted
as the main function of water-colour as it is today. The Sketching
Society, formed in 1808 largely on the instigation of the Chalon
brothers, themselves essentially figure painters, had as its original
aim the Study of Epic and Pastoral Design;[1] and many of the
practitioners of the first half of the century never abandoned the
tradition of Poussin and the classical piece. Of these, George Barret
(1767/8–1842) is perhaps the most typical.[2] Son of another George,
a foundation member of the Royal Academy, he carried on an
older tradition of landscape painting, and though, like all his contemporaries, he made his Welsh journeys, his water-colours more
and more tended to arranged pieces, sylvan scenes with pastoral
accessories: in some of these sun-bathed fantasies, with distant
temples and pensive shepherd-boys, he caught and rendered the
classic, eclogue note, less powerfully and inventively than his
contemporary Palmer, but with genuine period charm. The classic
inspiration was, however, wearing thin. Some newer settings were
required. G. F. Robson's Scottish mountains were one answer.
Francis Oliver Finch (1802–62)[3] also painted them, but his most
characteristic scenes are woodland vistas with groups of figures, a
pair of lovers as often as not, in the foreground. He himself was a
poet of some merit, a gentle, gifted creature, whose water-colours
sometimes have a fine poetic intensity; they are a reinterpretation
of classical pastorals in romantic terms; where we half expect a
temple we find a castle, and the forest glades are English where
those of Barret had still remembered Greece.

Joshua Cristall (1767–1847)[4] summed up these classical, literary

[1] H. Hubbard in *O.W.-C.S.C.* xxiv (1946), 19.

[2] A. Bury in *Connoisseur*, cv (1940), 237.

[3] A. Bury in *Connoisseur*, ciii (1939), 254; Eliza Finch, *Memorials of Francis Oliver
Finch* (1865); Samuel Palmer in Gilchrist's *Life of Blake* (2nd ed. 1880), ii. 354.

[4] R. Davies in *O.W.-C.S.C.* iv (1927), 1.

trends and brought to them a broader, more spacious sense of form
and design. Three times President of the Society, the last period
(1821–31) being for ten years, he had considerable influence on its
policy, and it was under him that in 1822 the Society leased its
premises in Pall Mall East. When success began to come to him in
London, his health, also perhaps his inclination, forced him to seek
a country life, at Goodrich on the Wye. His scenes of peasant life,
natural and everyday in clothes and movement, were admired by
contemporaries and deserve perhaps more reputation than they
have today. 'Mr. Cristall', wrote a critic in the *Magazine of Fine
Arts*,[1] 'has been extremely happy in seizing the leading features
which characterise a form, and omitting all that is unimportant or
injurious to that general character. His figures of peasants . . . are
valuable examples of the grand style in art' (Pl. 19 *a*). Some of his
classical fancy subjects, products often of sketching club problems,
either in London or Hereford, are equally broadly and effectively
treated.

It was an age of prolific genius, and also of remarkable longevity
amongst the practitioners of the art. Septuagenarians are common,
octogenarians not infrequent in the list of the early English water-
colourists. Girtin's early death is a rare instance which invests his
brief but brilliant achievement with a peculiar potency. One other
gifted youth, dying like Girtin at twenty-seven, left his impress on
the work of his successors. Richard Parkes Bonington was born at
Nottingham in 1802, but in 1817 or 1818 his father moved to
Calais.[2] There the young Richard came under the influence of
Louis Francia, who had returned to his native town in 1816, and
through him received something of the tradition of Girtin. Shortly
afterwards, Bonington was in Paris, where he formed a friendship
with the young Delacroix, and became a pupil in the studio of
Gros. In 1822 he exhibited two water-colours, both of Norman
scenes, in the Salon, and from then on his reputation steadily grew.
After the great 'English' Salon of 1824, where he along with

---

[1] i (1821), 452.
[2] 'Memoir of Richard Parkes Bonington', *Library of Fine Arts*, iii (1832), 301; see
also monographs by A. Dubuisson and C. E. Hughes (1924), A. Shirley (1940), and
G. S. Sandilands (Studio Special Number, 1929).

Constable and Copley Fielding received gold medals, he came to England with Delacroix. In 1826 he went to Italy: in 1828 he died in London of consumption, an end that for some time had seemed inevitable. 'Il y a terriblement à gagner', Delacroix wrote, 'dans la société de ce lieron-là.'[1] Bonington's work is almost equally divided between oils and water-colours. In the latter medium he owes his fluid use of paint to the teaching of Francia, and his early success in France was partially that of a representative of the new English school. Many of his subjects also belong to an English tradition, though in others, particularly the historical or pseudo-oriental scenes, the atmosphere of the young Parisian romantics predominates. As a technician, he was no innovator, and the fine brush strokes with which he sketched his buildings have many English parallels; but he was a great colourist. He could sum up red-brown Italy as few others, and his flecks of brilliant scarlet could bring the sparkle of sunlight. His water-colour of the Colleoni statue (Louvre), only 9½ in. by 7 in., has an interpretive force, a grasp of essentials which few of his English fellows could equal.

His use of colour was not unnoted, to judge from his practice, by a landscape painter whose career could hardly have run along more different lines. David Cox[2] was born in 1783 in Birmingham, the son of a smith still practising a variety of crafts in what was little more than a country village; he died in 1859 at Harborne, the village suburb of a great city. His early training came, as with so many of his brother artists, in scene painting, and his friendship with the Macreadys was one of the many links between studio and stage: again like many others, he owed much to the generously given instruction of John Varley. He himself became a teacher and published his *Treatise on Landscape Painting and Effect in Watercolour* (1814–15) at the request of his pupils. Like Cristall he settled for a time at Hereford (1814–27) and like all of them found in the Welsh mountains his earliest inspiration. The paintings that endeared his name to the later nineteenth century and fetched auction prices

---

[1] A. Joubin, *Correspondance générale de Delacroix*, i (1935), 173.

[2] Monographs by N. N. Solly (1873), W. Hall (1881), A. J. Finberg (1906), F. Gordon Roe (1946), Trenchard Cox (1947); B. S. Long, *O.W.-C.S.C.* x (1933), 1.

between two and three thousand pounds were the windswept fields and heaths, peopled with harvesters, shepherds, or rain-caught travellers. Cox had a neat gift of anecdote that pleased: under his lowering skies, his men and women are cosily cloaked, seldom without umbrellas. Simple, good-hearted, industrious, and very variable, he remains elusive; when a certain repetitive facility begins to tire us, he suddenly rouses interest by a broad vigorous sketch, as penetrating in its response to natural phenomena as a piece by Constable. Many attempts have been made to reduce this variety to periods of development, and no doubt his greater pieces, more sombre, broadened by his contact with William Müller whose bravura he much admired, come from the last twenty years of his life, painted on rough Scotch wrapping paper so that the surface itself has form and variety; but at any time in his career he can surprise by some intensity of observation. The wild night sky, the stampeding horses, the wind in the grass, the new magic monster with its trail of smoke, *The Night Train*, may serve as an example of Cox in one of his profounder moods (Pl. 17 *b*). Across the sensible advice of his manuals, his conventional platitudes about treatment of subjects, comes suddenly his reply to the Committee of the Water-Colour Society, commenting on the roughness of his painting, 'these are the work of the mind, which I consider very far before portraits of places'.[1]

While the country-side was thus interpreted, there continued to be a vast demand for more architectural subjects. John Buckler (1770–1851), whose early career as a surveyor's clerk was patronized by the Fisher family, the friends of Constable, and whose later career was in the service of Magdalen College and its venerable President, Martin Routh, calculated at the end of his long life that he had drawn and etched 'the whole of the English cathedrals and many of the abbey and collegiate churches . . . more than two thousand parish churches and chapels . . . with respect to the sketches I have made I think I may estimate the number of more than thirteen thousand'.[2] In 1805 John Britton began the publica-

[1] Trenchard Cox, *David Cox* (1947), 105.
[2] For Buckler see T. S. R. Boase, 'An Oxford College and the Gothic Revival', *Journ. W.C.I.* xix (1956).

tion of his *Architectural Antiquities of Great Britain*. Britton had come to London in 1787 as apprentice to a wine dealer. His varied career had included recitations and songs at the exhibition of de Loutherbourg's *Eidophusikon*. Then in 1801 he and E. W. Brayley published the first volume of their *Beauties of England and Wales*. Picturesque tours were now common enough; in succession to Gilpin, Samuel Ireland had in the nineties been publishing his *Picturesque Views*; but Britton combined the picturesque approach with careful scholarship.[1] As opposed to Ireland's aquatints from his own drawings, Britton remained faithful to line engraving on copper, employing the brothers John and Henry Le Keux, and the designs were provided by a team of artists, among whom were Augustus Pugin,[2] George and Richard Cattermole, Frederick Mackenzie, W. H. Bartlett, and R. W. Billings. Mackenzie's sepia drawings are at their best distinguished works. Auguste Charles de Pugin, a French refugee from the Revolution, was much employed by John Nash and also by Rudolph Ackermann,[3] a German who had come to London in 1779, founded a printseller's business there, and done much to popularize the aquatint process. His *Repository of Arts, Literature and Fashions* (1809–29) is an essential guide to the Regency period, and, begun in 1825, his *Forget-me-not Annuals* were to create a new vogue. His *Microcosm of London* (1805) was in its illustration a co-operation between Pugin and Thomas Rowlandson, whose rare abilities must have later consideration. Here, as in all these works, posterity owes much to these preservers of vanished views. Apart from these professional architectural draughtsmen, the demand for book illustration gave a livelihood to many a young artist, from Turner and Girtin downwards.

The opening of Europe after the war led to an interest in architecture other than English and a spate of volumes dispersed archaeological studies into wider fields: Dawson Turner's *Architectural Antiquities of Normandy* (1822), Henry Gally Knight's *Architectural Tour in Normandy* (1836) and its sequel *The Normans in Sicily*

---

[1] For the Irelands, father and son, and the Shakespeare forgeries see the very full notice in the *D.N.B.* For Britton, see *Gentleman's Mag.* (Feb. 1857), 185, and P. Ferriday in *Arch. Rev.* cxxii (1957), 403.

[2] F. G. Roe in *O.W.-C.S.C.* xxxi (1956), 18.

[3] See S. T. Prideaux, *Aquatint Engraving* (1909), 110 ff.

(1838), William Whewell's *Architectural Notes on German Churches* (1830), George Vivian's *Spanish Scenery* (1838) and *Views from Gardens of Rome* (1848) are only some examples of the many tomes that appeared: *Childe Harold* and Rogers's *Italy*[1] portrayed in verse the new zest for travel. Most of these volumes were illustrated with numerous plates, and Cotman, Turner, Harding, and others supplied them. But the chief purveyor of drawings and prints of medieval Europe, displaying an architecture often more picturesque than exact, appealing to a wider public than the pundits of the *Gentleman's Magazine*, was Samuel Prout.[2] Born at Plymouth in 1783 he served an apprenticeship with Britton, but his early repute was mainly for seascapes and his studies of ships. Then in 1819 he went abroad. Rouen with its 'grotesque labyrinths of Norman streets' won him, and from now on, in repeated travels, 'every corner of France, Germany, the Netherlands and Italy was ransacked for its fragments of carved stone'.[3] In 1830 Robert Jennings published his first *Landscape Annual, The Tourist in Switzerland and Italy*, with engravings after Prout and letterpress by Thomas Roscoe, son of the great Liverpool magnate. These annuals appeared regularly throughout the thirties[4] and did much to stimulate the cult of picturesque Europe, and to provide employment for the artists who rendered it. Prout from his youth had uncertain health, and this, though it never broke his kindly good temper, probably explains the unevenness of his output. He worked largely with ochre or cobalt washes over the designs laid on in brown or grey, and his best drawings are in this already old-fashioned method: but at times the browns come through too hotly, and when he applies bright colours in his lively crowds, whose manners and costumes are a marked feature of his sketches, the result can be garish and commonplace. Ruskin admired him immensely and he has suffered from his overpraise, but he was a great popularizer; his vision of romantic Europe strongly affected

[1] See J. R. Hale, 'Samuel Rogers and the Italy of *Italy*', *Italian Studies*, x (1955), 43.

[2] E. G. Halton, *Sketches by Samuel Prout* (Special Studio Number, 1915); J. Quigley, *Prout and Roberts* (1926); C. E. Hughes in *O.W.-C.S.C.* v (1929), 1; F. Gordon Roe in *O.W.-C.S.C.* xxiv (1946), 41.   [3] Ruskin, *Works*, xii. 310.

[4] *Italy*, Prout, 1831; *Italy*, Harding, 1832 and 1833; *France*, Harding, 1834; *Spain*, Roberts, 1835, 1836, 1837, and 1838; *Portugal*, James Holland, 1839.

the English mental image of the Continent and few have rendered so skilfully the texture of elaborate stonework (Pl. 20 *b*).

J. D. Harding had his training in the office of P. F. Robinson, whose *Rural Architecture, Ornamental Villas, Tudor Style*, and so forth were being published in the twenties and thirties. He was therefore from the first familiar with the book trade, and his work was largely designed for it. 'Scarcely', he writes in the preface to his *Lessons on Art* (1849), 'a publication is now issued and not illustrated . . . we breathe an atmosphere of art.' In particular he became one of the great English exponents of lithography. His *Sketches at Home and Abroad*, a set of fifty lithographs published in 1836, showed many new refinements in the process, among them lithotint, the application of the ink to the stone with a brush, a process invented by Charles Hullmandel, a Londoner of German origin, with whom Harding, Cattermole, Nash, Roberts, and others worked in close collaboration.[1] His water-colours, brightly coloured Swiss and Rhine views, reinforced the Proutian tradition with less archaeology and even more picturesqueness; and at times his monochrome sketches, on the tinted paper he used for his lithographs, the highlights painted with opaque white, have a charm that is all his own.

A group of painters, of whom George Cattermole and Joseph Nash were the leaders, produced a long series of semi-historical pieces, costume scenes set against the background of old English mansions, treated with accuracy but for picturesque rather than archaeological effect. Nash's *Mansions of England in the Olden Time*, which appeared in four series between 1839 and 1849, showing the stately homes of England[2] 'enlivened with the presence of their inmates and guests',[3] did much to establish the Elizabethan period as the most correct example for domestic building. Cattermole

[1] See R. M. Burch, *Colour Printing and Colour Printers* (1910); for lithography, *Library of the Fine Arts*, i (1831), 44, 201. The inventor of lithography, Aloys Senefelder, visited England in 1800 and his book was published in English in 1819. The title-page of Harding's *Sketches* has enchanting vignettes of the troubles of sketching abroad.

[2] This famous phrase had been recently coined by Mrs. Hemans.

[3] *Description of the Plates*, by Joseph Nash (1849): these are brilliant examples of chromo-lithography, though the four series (100 plates in all) become a trifle monotonous. See Charles Holme, *Old English Mansions* (Special Studio Number, 1915).

enjoyed great contemporary popularity, and his historical inventions suffer today from having had many and inferior followers.[1] Brought up in the school of Britton's *Cathedral Antiquities*, he began in the twenties to paint subject pieces, some of which suggest that works by Bonington may have influenced him. He worked with light, broken outlines, but his thin brushwork is sometimes unpleasantly streaky. He moved in the circle of Dickens, Macready, Maclise, and Landseer, and was socially as successful and popular as were his paintings.

Amongst the travel artists, David Roberts has a place of his own through the great interest of his subject-matter, the sketches of Egypt and Palestine. He was trained as a scene painter, and it was at the Pantheon in Edinburgh, his native city, that Roberts first met Clarkson Stanfield, working at the same tasks, and formed a life-long friendship with him.[2] Both artists were to be distinguished in oils and water-colours; both were R.A.s and therefore not members of the Water-Colour Society, but, while Clarkson must wait for a discussion of oil paintings, Roberts lives in his sketches and in the reproductions of them. Tough and courageous, he was an admirable traveller, and his tours in Spain and Morocco (1832–3), undertaken on the advice of Wilkie, and in Egypt and Palestine (1838–9) were no light enterprises. Things seen are methodically noted in his diaries[3] and his sketches are all named and dated. There is in fact a prosaic rather than a romantic approach, though the groups of figures are often lively enough and Roberts, who lived for two years in Eastern dress as an Arab, understood the swing and fall of galabiehs and abayas at first-hand experience. His technique is serviceable rather than distinguished; but his designs are lucid, his architecture accurate, and, where the subjects were of such general interest, these were considerable virtues.[4] Of

[1] R. Davies in *O.W.-C.S.C.* ix (1932); see *Fraser's Mag.* i (1830), 537.

[2] See *Art Journ.* iii (1857), 209. Each presented one of their finest oils to the Garrick Club, where they still hang, facing each other, in the smoking-room.

[3] Considerable extracts are published in J. Ballantine, *Life of David Roberts* (Edinburgh, 1866). See also M. Hardie in *O.W.-C.S.C.* xxv (1947), 10.

[4] For Roberts's successor in Near Eastern sketches, J. F. Lewis, see below, p. 293; Edward Lear's sketches, a few years later in date, have a much liked place in the series (A. Davidson, *Edward Lear* (1938)).

all the great book undertakings the volumes of *Views in the Holy Land, Syria, Idumea, Arabia, Egypt and Nubia* (1849–9) was one of the most costly and most successful. Reproduced by lithography, it was less advanced in process than some other contemporary works, and the coloured edition had only two-process printing and was then completed by hand. Louis Haghe, himself a talented artist, worked on the stone, and devoted seven years to the task.

India was another new source of visual inspirations, of which the two Daniells were the chief interpreters.[1] Their *Picturesque Voyage to India* appeared in 1810 and the title describes aptly enough their aims. Their drawings had considerable influence on the Regency taste for Hindu art; but the nabobs of the East India Company were more ready to commission portraits than landscapes, and it was as portrait painters that most English artists sought their luck in the East. 'Chinnery himself', said Colonel Newcome, 'could not hit off a likeness better.' That artist had known Richmond Thackeray, the novelist's father, in Calcutta and in 1814 had drawn a family group of Mr. and Mrs. Thackeray, with the young William Makepeace aged three.[2] It is not, however, for his portraits that he is remembered today, but for his landscapes, the rare oils, such as that on the easel in his own self-portrait (N.P.G.), luminous, atmospheric works that seem to belong to later developments of the art; and for his vast numbers of line and wash sketches. Born in 1774 and dying in 1852, the greater part of his vagrant, extravagant, and cheerful life was spent in India or China, painting portraits of rajahs, instructing English officials and above all constantly sketching the scenes around him. In his early years his drawings belong to the romantic school of Fuseli and Romney; later in the East, he developed rapid, calligraphic methods of his own. Of all the artists who journeyed eastward he was the most visually perceptive, though the scattered, fragmentary nature of

[1] See Sir William Foster, 'British Artists in India' *Walpole Soc.* xix (1930–1); M. and W. G. Archer, *Indian Painting for the British* (Oxford, 1955), 11; and M. Hardie and M. Clayton, 'Thomas and William Daniell', *Walkers Quarterly*, xxxv–xxxvi (1932).

[2] Preston; reproduced in G. W. Ray, *Letters and Private Papers of W. M. Thackeray* (Oxford, 1945). For Chinnery see E. J. J. Cotton in *Bengal Past and Present*, xxiv (1922), 98, xxvii (1924), 85, 113, and *Catalogue*, Arts Council Exhibition of his works (1957).

his work, much of which remained in the Far East, has lessened the fame which is his due.

A group of younger men carried on the tradition of foreign views. Thomas Shotter Boys (1803–74),[1] trained as an engraver, had known Bonington in Paris in the last years, 1825–8, and derived many of his merits from his example, though these are grafted on to the older English topographical tradition of Malton and others. In 1839 Boys issued in London a collection of his own work, 'drawn from nature on stone', *Picturesque Architecture in Paris, Ghent, Antwerp, Rouen, etc.* Printed by, and dedicated to, Charles Hullmandel, this production, with Nash's *Mansions*, marks the definite transition from lithography tinted by hand to chromo-lithography.[2] The preface to the volume claimed that the process was entirely new and that 'the drawings . . . are produced entirely by means of lithography: they are printed with oil colours, and come from the press precisely as they now appear. It was expressly stipulated by the Publisher that not a touch should be added after-wards.' It is the proud statement of an age of invention: none of it is, directly, by hand, all is 'Machine made'. There are naturally enough crudities: the bright flecks of colour in the manner of Bonington are a little too marked; but Boys had a good sense of design and selection, and his figure groups are lively and appro-priate. In his *Original Views of London as it is, 1842*, he has left us a splendid topographical record of the Regency's achievement. He remains, however, a subsidiary artist, working for a wide, popular market without expressing any strong individuality of his own. The same is largely true of James Holland (1800–70)[3] and William Callow (1812–1908). The former came from the Potteries, where his father was a manufacturer of 'Black and Red China Ware', that popular Regency product, and was trained as a flower painter. In 1835 he made his first Italian journey, and from then onwards

[1] Hugh Stokes in *Walker's Quarterly*, xviii (1926); see the reissues by E. B. Chan-cellor of *Original Views of London 1842* (1926) and *Picturesque Architecture in Paris, Ghent, Antwerp, Rouen, etc. 1839* (1928).

[2] See R. M. Burch, *Colour Printing and Colour Printers* (1910), and Basil Gray, *The English Print* (1937).

[3] Hugh Stokes in *Walker's Quarterly*, xxiii (1927), and R. Davies in *O.W.-C.S.C.* vii (1930), 37.

he became a painter of romantic architecture, mainly Italian, though the *Landscape Annual* for 1839 has records of his Portuguese journey. In particular Venice charmed him: he saw it with Bonington's eyes, but with a colour sense heightened by Turner. He had talent and taste, but his rivals were too great for him. William Callow lived on till 1908, walking five or six miles each morning, a magnificent, nobly bearded Victorian, until his last illness, an attack of influenza, at the age of ninety-six. He left an account of his early years[1] which admirably depicts the life of these English landscape artists in Paris, though it has little that illuminates the artistic intentions of the time. Taught by the Fieldings, a close friend of Shotter Boys and of the marine painters, Charles Bentley and E. W. Cooke, his allegiance remained faithful to the technique of freely handled water-colour, with no body colour and no ground work. In the choice and arrangement of his subjects he owed much to Prout and Harding, but worked with a smoother finish. Popular, prosperous, and estimable, his works have a solid sincerity and competence, which will always commend them.

In 1787 a Yorkshire portrait painter, Theodore Fielding, gave to his second son the resounding names of Anthony Vandyke Copley.[2] The child's genius was to lie in very different subjects from those of the great Fleming, but he was to come to wide popularity and from 1831 till his death in 1855 was to be President of the Water-Colour Society. His three brothers were all painters, and one of them, Thales (their father had an odd fancy in names), makes some appearance in art history as the friend of Bonington and Delacroix. Wales and the Lakes were Copley's earliest interest, but gradually these gave way to seascapes. His quick brush strokes could give the texture of mist or the restless surface of the sea with surprising effect and, at his best, he had a keen sense of colour, dun-coloured earth or milky sea under a cloudy sky, or vivid patches in the sunlight, but his immense dexterity undid him. His works had a wide market and the speed with which he met the demand led to repetition. More and more he worked out old themes in the

---

[1] Edited by H. M. Cundall, *William Callow, an Autobiography* (1908); see also F. L. Emanuel in *Walker's Quarterly*, xxii (1927), and Martin Hardie in *O.W.-C.S.C.* xxii (1944), 12.   [2] S. C. Kaines Smith, *O.W.-C.S.C.* iii (1926), 8.

studio, lacking the outdoor, immediate contact with the thing seen. His fame and his market value have never altogether declined, and his colours have faded surprisingly little: but in his vast output (it is said that between 1821 and 1831 he exhibited 522 drawings in the Society's gallery) there is much that is unworthy of him. As President he did much for the Society, and for his weakness as an artist, administrative virtues should bear some of the blame.

The great epoch was passing; already in Fielding's later works it is in decay. Water-colours at the beginning of the century were matters for a patron's portfolio, for the selection that Dr. Monro kept at hand in a special case in his carriage. Now new patrons wished for wall decoration[1] and water-colours had once more to compete with paintings in oil. Ruskin's teaching, his discussions of various artists in *Modern Painters*, had stressed exact observation and the analytical approach to the subject. It was easy to quote his authority, not always correctly, in condemnation of experiments and impressionism. Earlier subtleties were at a discount and instead the sentiment was overstressed. The book trade continued its demands, but here too a more facile approach was demanded. Myles Birket Foster (1825–99)[2] became the most popular of land-scape water-colourists, his drawings as 'negotiable as five pound Bank of England notes',[3] and his carefully pretty vignettes appeared in many books and journals, while his gaily coloured paintings set a standard for later coloured prints and postcards, which was long and too loosely followed.

The use of water-colour is so deeply associated with the inter-pretation of landscape, that it is hard to remember that, as sketches for book illustration or as preliminary studies for oil paintings, the output of figure subjects in this medium was almost as large. These subject pieces, however, more rarely attain standing of their own. They remain subordinate to the finished oil or the engraving. Some

[1] In Mr. Yorke's house (Charlotte Brontë, *Shirley*, chap. iii) 'the matted hall was lined almost to the ceiling with pictures. . . . There was no splendour, but there was taste everywhere. . . . A series of Italian views decked the walls; each of these was a specimen of true art; a connoisseur had selected them; they were genuine and valu-able. . . . The subjects were all pastoral.'

[2] L. Glasson in *O.W.-C.S.C.* xi (1934), 34.

[3] W. Matthew Hale in *O.W.-C.S.C.* iv (1927), 52.

of Fuseli's strange, forbidding female figures, half sorceress, half fashion plate, are inventions in their own right, with no intention of translation to another medium: Romney's wash drawings have a sweep and intensity of movement that were never transferred to canvas: Flaxman's drawings belong to a genus of their own: Robert Ker Porter (1777–1842),[1] a restless figure, whose Russian journeys and marriage and Eastern travels were as romantic as the adventures of the heroes in his sister's novels, occasionally surprises by the vigour of his sketches of literary or historic themes. Thomas Heaphy (1775–1835)[2] was elected an associate of the Water-Colour Society and in 1809 exhibited there his *Fish Market* (coll. the earl of Yarborough) which sold for 400 guineas, at that time a record price for a water-colour. In 1812, however, he resigned from the Society, went out to Spain, and painted a remarkable series of small water-colours of English officers in the Peninsular War. His equestrian portrait of the duke of Wellington on a white charger against a stormy sky (N.P.G.) is in the full romantic manner. Very different in character was William Henry Hunt (1790–1864).[3] A weakly, partially crippled man, he was much helped by Dr. Monro, and he and Henry Edridge (1769–1821), who painted pleasant water-colour portraits and also romantic landscapes, often stayed with the doctor at Bushey. Hunt painted humorous or sentimental figure scenes, banal in choice though skilfully rendered, and portraits such as the young James Holland at his easel, debonair in a long white painting smock (Pl. 21 *b*); but his popularity rested largely on his studies of birds' nests among flowers and foliage. These he worked up to a wonderfully detailed finish, and his bright opaque colours have lasted remarkably well. Ruskin was fascinated by his close observation of detail and at times ranked him as 'the greatest of all'. But it was perfection in a most narrowly limited field.

Meanwhile, the general public received much of their visual stimulus not from water-colour drawings, aquatints, or lithographs of the picturesque, but from the coarse, vigorous, and remarkable sheets of the English political and social satirists, or caricaturists as

[1] See *Athenaeum* (1842), 479, and (1843), 290.
[2] W. T. Whitley, *Thomas Heaphy* (1933); H. Hubbard, *O.W.-C.S.C.* xxvi (1948), 19.
[3] F. G. Stephens in *O.W.-C.S.C.* xii (1935), 17.

they were beginning to be called.[1] The ordinary process used was line or stipple engraving or etching, and colour was frequently applied by block printing or in some cases by hand. The tradition of Hogarth had in its scope of comment been enlarged by James Gillray (1757–1815), whose work covers the Napoleonic war and who produced some of his most famous plates in the first decade of the century, till in 1811 madness brought a sad close to his activities.[2] His fertile imagination was rich in horror images as striking as those of Fuseli, and he could preserve a likeness through the wildest extremes of travesty. Where Hogarth had been general in his comment, Gillray was personal and it is with him that the leading figures of the day become more and more familiar in their distorted roles of butt. The patriotic satirist of Napoleon's aggrandizement, his drawings were often bloody and violent; his protests against the sensual licence of society were often lewd; coarseness was his partiality and method, but it was always witty. His *Connoisseurs examining a collection of George Morland's* had to await a worthy successor in Max Beerbohm. His *Dido in Despair* (Lady Hamilton)[3] is most inventively scurrilous, but the vast ungainly limbs have the monumental forms of Picasso's neo-classical phase (Pl. 4 *b*). His more flowing, baroque lines have at times great delicacy and his print (1792) of the prince, *A Voluptuary under the horrors of Digestion*, is perhaps the most striking and convincing rendering of the central figure of the Regency.[4]

Thomas Rowlandson (1757–1827) was less passionate in his political views, content to mock rather than to convert; bawdy, at times cruel, he chronicles the passing scene, using the tinted

[1] The great source of information is M. D. George's *Catalogue of Political and Personal Satires . . . in the British Museum*, one of the great achievements of scholarship: vols. vii (1942), viii (1947), ix (1949) cover the period 1793–1819. F. D. Klingender, *Hogarth and English Caricature* (1944), is a useful introduction to the subject and David Low's *British Cartoonists, Caricaturists and Comic Artists* (1932), though brief, is full of penetrating comment. See also G. Everitt, *English Caricaturists and Graphic Humorists of the nineteenth century* (1893).

[2] T. Wright and R. H. Evans, *Historical and Descriptive Account of the Caricatures of James Gillray* (1851).

[3] 'He's gone to fight the Frenchmen, to lose t'other arm and eye,
And left me with the Old Antique, to lay me down and cry.'

[4] See David Piper, *The English Face* (1957), 248.

drawings of the topographical convention and in his groups of small figures inventive and complete. At his best he creates memorable images. In *The Exhibition Stare-case* (Pl. 21 *a*), the famous comment on the narrow, spiral approach to the Academy galleries in Somerset House, the delicacy of the drawing is delightedly used to enhance the indelicacy of the subject.[1]

In Gillray's decline, Mrs. Humphrey, his publisher, had employed two brothers, Robert and George Cruikshank, to finish some of Gillray's incompleted plates.[2] In 1820 the brothers combined in illustrating *Life in London*, a novel published in monthly parts with three plates a part. This new scheme had immense success, and from now on George's work was mainly for the publishers. *Robinson Crusoe, Oliver Twist*, and Harrison Ainsworth's *Old St. Paul's* are among his finest successes, but his thin, wiry lines, close hatching, and over-formalized faces have something scant about them, and are a poor substitute for Gillray's robustness. It was Hablot Knight Browne ('Phiz') who was to figure out Dickens's fancies, though he and many others owed much to Cruikshank's manner. In his last years, and he did not die till 1878, the latter devoted himself to temperance campaigns, painting a vast canvas in oils with Victorian scenes, a morality on the evils of alcohol, which, at least in some of its details, deserves better than the permanent storage in the Tate Gallery, to which its size and its oddity have condemned it.[3]

The one man of outstanding genius who combined water-colour with figure subjects for some of his profoundest utterances was William Blake. Since Alexander Gilchrist's enthusiastic biography was edited and published by his widow and the two Rossetti brothers in 1863, there has been a steadily increasing stream of Blake publications, which of recent years has taken the proportions of a flood. The man and his works are sometimes nearly

---

[1] There is a considerable literature on Rowlandson: J. Grego, *Rowlandson the Caricaturist*, 2 vols. (1880); F. G. Stephens in *The Portfolio*, xxii (1891); A. P. Oppé, *Thomas Rowlandson: His Drawings and Water-Colours* (1923); F. G. Roe, *Rowlandson* (Leigh-on-Sands, 1947); A. Bury, *Rowlandson Drawings* (1949); B. Falk, *Thomas Rowlandson* (1949).

[2] B. Jerrold, *Life of George Cruikshank* (1883); R. McLean, *George Cruikshank* (1948).   [3] Reproduced in S. Sitwell, *Narrative Paintings* (1937).

submerged beneath the commentary, and, with new psychological techniques, with the infinite pains of modern scholarship, we know the stray emblem, the chance engraving, the underlying complexes, the whole interior history of the disturbing final work far better than Blake himself or any of his friends could ever have known it.[1] Born in 1757, the son of a London hosier, he was apprenticed at fourteen to the engraver James Basire, for whom he drew and engraved much medieval sculpture, particularly at Westminster, and the Gothic furnishing of his mind dates from this early period.[2] In 1782 Blake married and in 1784 opened with a fellow apprentice, Parker, a print shop in Broad Street, where his youngest brother Robert lived with him and Catherine, his wife. Robert's death in 1787 was a great emotional blow, and Blake left the Broad Street shop, where he had been engraving some of Flaxman's designs for the *Iliad* and enjoying his friendship and help. His own creative urge was now too strong for him to be content with other men's designs. He had always been a seer of visions, one whose visual, symbolic imaginings had a transcendent actuality. His dead brother appeared to him, and communing together, Blake's mind was attuned to his first great creative period, the production of the *Songs of Innocence* and the *Prophetic Books*. The characteristic feature of this phase is the combination of text and illustration by a process of relief etching. Only by this duality of purpose could Blake's fullness of imagination be released and the reactions of his sensitive mind find an outlet. In his always experimental hands, the process itself varied, and the exact method of writing on the metal still remains a secret today. Once the page had been printed, sometimes in three or four colours, sometimes in outline only, it was coloured by hand.[3] It could hardly be described as publishing; twenty-five copies of *Songs of Innocence* are known: of his last illuminated book, *Jerusalem* (c. 1820), there are five complete copies, only one of which is coloured.[4] It was perhaps as well for their author that they

[1] See Bibliography in Ruthven Todd's edition of Gilchrist's *Life* (revised ed. 1945).

[2] See A. Blunt, 'Blake's Pictorial Imagination', *Journ. W.C.I.* vi (1943), 190.

[3] The whole question of Blake's methods is explored at length by Laurence Binyon in his *Engraved Designs of William Blake* (1926).

[4] See the magnificent facsimile edition published for the William Blake Trust, ed. J. Wicksteed (1951).

appeared in this limited form, for into them Blake poured all his revolutionary fervour, his unrestrained joy in sensual impulses, his protests against conventional religion. It was a time when such thoughts were dangerous, and several of those who met in the shop of Joseph Johnson, bookseller of St. Paul's churchyard, the set to which Blake now belonged, were to experience the repressive force of the law. Even, however, had the engraved books been more widely accessible, it is doubtful if they would have been very fully understood. Blake invents a mythology of his own, with perhaps Ossianic echoes more strongly marked than any others, and he interprets it in visual forms where there are memories of Michelangelo, Raphael, Gothic sculpture, Flaxman's drawings, scenes earlier engraved by him,[1] and, pervasively, the forms, proportions, and gestures which were being used by Fuseli. 'When Flaxman', Blake wrote, 'was taken to Italy, Fuseli was given to me for a season.'[2] Much of the disquieting horror of some of Blake's work has in fact the same recipe as that of the Swiss painter, exaggerated muscular development, disproportionate length of limb, hard profiles with receding foreheads. Elsewhere he is obsessed by more Gothic imagery, a huge bearded figure, often squatting on the ground, seen in strange perspectives, a figure which produced the colour prints of the Ancient of Days and Nebuchadnezzar. These prints, which are mainly associated with the year 1795, represent another of Blake's discoveries, printing his background colours from mill board and filling in or completing the figures by hand.[3] Work was also done for other publishers: in 1796 the vast undertaking of border designs for Young's *Night Thoughts*, where the formalized, dancing nudes have an ecstatic rhythm that was not to be equalled till Matisse, and the almost stranger drawings, never engraved, for Gray's poems.[4]

[1] Such as those for Capt. J. G. Stedman's *Expedition against the Revolted Negroes of Surinam*, 2 vols. (1796). For the influence of this book, in itself a document of romanticism, on Blake see D. V. Erdman, 'Blake's Vision of Slavery', *Journ. W.C.I.* xv (1952), 242.   [2] *Blake's Illustrations to Gray's Poems*, ed. H. J. C. Grierson (1922), 17.
[3] See Darrell Figgis, *The Paintings of William Blake* (1925), 24.
[4] G. Keynes, *Illustrations to Young's Night Thoughts done in Water Colour by William Blake* (1927); the original drawings are in the British Museum: for the drawings for Gray's poems see H. J. C. Grierson, op. cit.

The turn of the century brought a change in Blake's circumstances. Flaxman had introduced him to William Hayley, then in high repute as a poet, the friend of Romney and Cowper. Hayley invited Blake to design engravings for his life of Cowper, and Blake and his wife moved to a cottage in Sussex, at Felpham near Hayley's 'turreted marine cottage', where they remained for three years, a closer contact with country life than Blake had at any other period. Amongst works done for Hayley were the engravings for his *Ballads founded on Anecdotes relating to Animal Life* and nowhere is Blake's invention more bizarre than when trying to render the jingling rhymes that tell of Fido's self-immolation to save his master from the crocodile or Jessey's rescue of her child from the eagle's nest (Pl. 20 *a*). For the frieze of Hayley's library he painted in tempera the series of heads of poets, set between scenes from their writings, which are now in the City Art Gallery at Manchester.[1] It was not, however, possible for Blake to work in prolonged co-operation with anyone. The sense of gratitude in itself irked him:

> Thy friendship oft has made my heart to ache,
> So be my enemy—for friendship's sake.

At the end of 1803 he returned to London, but the years had been fruitful, and he brought with him, partially completed or moving in his mind, the designs for *Milton* and *Jerusalem*. The former is one of the strangest, most brooding of his series; the latter, not completed before 1818, contains in *Albion before the Crucified Christ* and *The Soul embraced by God* two of his most haunting images.

From 1803 till his death in August 1827 Blake resided in London. It was a period that saw many disappointments, the ill-planned exhibition of 1809, with its defiant preface: 'Real art, as it was left us by Raphael and Albert Dürer, Michael Angelo, and Julio Romano, stripped from the ignorances of Rubens and Rembrandt, Titian and Correggio, by William Blake';[2] the publication by

---

[1] See M. Bishop, *Blake's Hayley* (1851), 265.

[2] R. Todd ed. of Gilchrist's *Life* (1945), 406. See *The Examiner* (1809), 605, for an attack on this 'unfortunate lunatic', offspring of the muse of Fuseli: R. Davies, *O.W.-C.S.C.* xxii (1944), 1.

Cromek of his designs for Blair's *The Grave* engraved by another hand; the quarrel with Stothard over *The Canterbury Pilgrims*, another of Cromek's ventures, in which the guileless Stothard's part was probably an innocent one. From 1809 dates the joyous aspiration of the soaring horse, the symbol of Shakespeare's genius, which he drew for the Rev. Joseph Thomas's extra-illustrated second folio (Pl. 1).[1] The years that followed were characterized by Gilchrist as 'of deepening neglect'. They passed gradually, however, into a happier phase, surrounded by a new band of friends, some of them young enough to be disciples. In 1818 Blake first met John Linnell, who was then twenty-six: his house at Hampstead became a meeting place where a group of painters, Samuel Palmer, Edward Calvert, Francis Oliver Finch, the two Varley brothers, Cornelius and John, George Richmond, and the sculptor Frederick Tatham, collected and where Blake became the presiding genius. These artists were for the most part landscape painters, and it is in a special approach to landscape, a subject he hardly touched, that Blake's influence was to find its chief perpetuation: hardly, but with a notable exception, the woodcuts to *The Pastorals of Virgil*. These appeared in 1821. It was to Blake a new untried medium. They were the first wood blocks he had cut and seemed so rough and unfinished to the printers that some of the blocks were recut by them. They have in fact many crudities in execution, but a directness and vigour of imagination which has been concentrated by the limitation imposed on it. 'They are', Samuel Palmer wrote of them, 'visions of little dells, and nooks, and corners of Paradise; models of the exquisitest pitch of intense poetry.'[2] And this new sunset world of contrasted lights, peopled with thickly mysterious figures, filled Palmer's mind, till he became an inhabitant of it in his own right, able to extend its boundaries, imagining its colours, disposed in circular forms, great drifts of blossom or the glow of ripe corn. Calvert and Linnell borrowed Blake's idiom, and his mannerist figures stalk through their landscapes, but, though something of his intensity was transmitted into this unfamiliar theme, it is only with Palmer that it endows a

[1] See *British Museum Quarterly*, xx (1955), 4.
[2] *Life and Letters of Samuel Palmer*, ed. A. H. Palmer (1892), 15.

new, lasting and individual creation, one that has awakened many responses in the more abstract, formalized paintings of the present century.

It was Linnell who at this time (1823) was responsible for the best known and in some ways most mature and complete of all Blake's achievements, the engravings for *The Book of Job*, commissioned from him by his friend, partially as a means of making, during their production, some weekly addition to the scanty finances of the Blake household. In these designs, compactly formed, monumental in their shapes, Blake used a statement direct beyond his wont, but including a whole inner world of significant gesture, in which he conveyed his final messages about the struggle between good and evil in the human soul.[1] These completed, Linnell suggested that he should next illustrate the *Divina Commedia*. This undertaking was unfinished at the time of Blake's death; between him and the Florentine there were conflicts as well as sympathies, but in these last drawings there is a lyrical note hardly touched before. The landscape of Limbo is rendered with an economy of means as yet beyond the dreams of the Water-Colour Society (Pl. 26 *a*), and the piercing tragedy of Paolo and Francesca passes in a great circle of spirits, in which the serpentine coils he had so long imagined reach a final solution (Pl. 27 *a*).[2] He was greater than he had been, even in the terrible themes of the Inferno: on 12 August 1827 he 'sang loudly and with true ecstatic energy, and seemed so happy that he had finished his course'[3] and at six of the evening he died.

The group of young artists who had gathered at Linnell's Hampstead house felt for a time the magic inspiration, and their paintings are touched with a poetic quality that they could not, by themselves, maintain. Four paintings hanging in the Ashmolean Museum show the use they made of Blake's example. Calvert's goat girl, walking through a gold brown landscape, has the elongated forms to which Fuseli had given such influential fascination

[1] J. Wicksteed, *Vision of the Book of Job*.
[2] A. S. Roe, *Blake's Illustrations to the Divine Comedy* (Princeton, 1953), and M. Butlin and A. Blunt, *A Catalogue of the Works of Blake in the Tate Gallery* (1958).
[3] F. Tatham, 'Life of Blake', in A. G. B. Russell, *Letters of William Blake* (1906), 35.

(Pl. 37 *b*): Richmond's lovers entwine in curving lines under the evening star: more forcefully Linnell's three figures press on with strained, tense faces on the road to Emmaus: Palmer's *Repose of the Holy Family*, painted in oil and tempera, has, for all its glowing depth of quality, a visionary sense of other worlds. For a time, they foregathered at Shoreham, and there Palmer found an outlet for his deeply religious, passionate temperament, in a series of water-colours and sepia drawings, reconciling in his own whirling words, that he poured out in letters to Linnell and Richmond, 'the leafy lightness, the thousand repetitions of little forms' with 'the ponderous globosity of Art' (Pl. 26 *b*).[1] It was a pitch of creative ardour that perhaps could not be expected to endure. In 1837, at the age of thirty-two, he married Linnell's daughter, Hannah, and with her visited Italy. Then he returned to settle in London, bullied by his father-in-law, whose autocratic nature was becoming soured and crusted. Italy and marriage seem to have quelled something in him: he had still forty-five years before him and painted in them many golden landscapes, echoes of Claude, never without some touch of distinction, but records of nature seen at second-hand. Calvert, a man of true if lesser talent, lost himself in a vague pagan worship of what he took to be the Platonic Ideal. George Richmond became a successful portrait painter, particularly in the medium of crayon drawings,[2] and at his death left to his son, William Blake Richmond, a well-established practice and a numerous clientele.

[1] A. H. Palmer, *Life and Letters of Samuel Palmer* (1892), 173. See G. Grigson, *Samuel Palmer* (1947), and M. Hardie in *O.W.-C.S.C.* iv (1927), 25; L. Binyon, *The Followers of William Blake* (1925).

[2] The nearest rival to Richmond is Thomas Wainewright, transported for forgery and suspected of murder, who, as a convict, drew many portraits which are still much prized in Tasmania. See R. Crossland, *Wainewright in Tasmania* (1957).

III

THE REGENCY STYLE

FROM 1811 to 1820 George, Prince of Wales, was regent for his insane father. Later times took this period as the most significant of his career, when his ebullient personality was at its most colourful, his extravagances and wantonness deprecated but also admired. Already in 1789 on the first hint of the King's derangement the Regency had become matter of high politics, and in the circles that set the often dubious tone of society, it remained an intriguing possibility until it actually took place. As a stylistic term it refers in fact to the first quarter of the century, naturally enough for no stylistic term can be narrowed to a decade. Even then it is vague in definition, a trend rather than a period, and as such it recalls the elements of fantasy and excess in the career of its name giver.

The Prince Regent had some of the qualities of a connoisseur. Both the British Museum and the National Gallery owe something to his gifts, advice, and promptings. The friend of Lawrence and Sheridan, he had a genuine appreciation of quality and a sense of responsibility towards the arts. Jane Austen dedicated *Emma* to him; he sent £200 to relieve the wants of Beethoven. Like the strict classical revival which is the basis of Regency style, there was some genuine taste beneath the luxurious trappings of his life; but there is no consistency of purpose in his over indulgent career, and it is the florid waywardness, the misjudged contrasts, the exotic hints which the term Regency first brings to mind, the looped drapings of Carlton House, the Indian domes of the Pavilion, belly-rounded bow-windows, sphinx terminals on chairs, Gothic arches on cottages, elaborate bonnets surmounting the décolleté simplicity of high-waisted Grecian dresses.[1]

---

[1] D. Pilcher, *The Regency Style* (1947), is a useful general summary: see also John Steegmann, *The Rule of Taste* (1936); for an appreciation of his artistic contacts see Shane Leslie, *George IV* (1926), 170 ff.

It is in architecture, furniture, plate, and costume that the name is applicable. In painting there is no clearly marked Regency style. A certain bravura in Lawrence's portraits, an excess of the horrific in Fuseli, of the vast and portentous in John Martin; an over-stressed sweetness in Stothard, a shade too much of sentiment in Wilkie's brilliant variations on Dutch themes. But in architecture the flavour is distinct.[1] Nash's London is a new invention, and its stucco facings[2] made possible a gayer, more irresponsible approach to classical forms. When Samuel Wyatt at Shugborough (Staffs.) built an Ionic colonnade out of the trunks of oak trees, encased in slate with Coade stone capitals, he was exemplifying a new cult of ingenuity.[3]

While Fonthill was being built and falling down, scholars were at work on the actual facts and principles of the Gothic style. Much of the early scholarship went into problems of terminology; there was an attempt to substitute 'English' for the 'opprobrious term of Gothic', 'for if this style of architecture had not its origin in this country, it certainly arrived at maturity here'.[4] There was, too, a sharply contested debate on the origins of the pointed arch, a fascinating topic which has had many revivals. In 1819 Thomas Rickman, the architect of the Gothic buildings of St. John's College, Cambridge,[5] published his *Attempt to Discriminate the Styles of English Architecture from the Conquest to the Reformation*, and his discrimination of 'Early English', 'Decorated', and 'Perpendicular' quickly passed into common currency. In the following year was published another book, *Ivanhoe*, that did even more to

[1] A. E. Richardson, *Monumental Classic Architecture in Great Britain and Ireland* (1914); P. Reilly, *An Introduction to Regency Architecture* (1948); John Summerson, *Georgian London* (1948) and *Architecture in Britain 1530–1830* (1953).

[2] For the development of stucco from the first patent in 1677 to Keen's cement in 1838 see M. B. Adams in *Journ. of R.I.B.A.* xix (1912), 598.

[3] C. Hussey in *C.L.* cxv (1954), 676. Samuel was as good an architect as his younger brother James.

[4] *Essays on Gothic Architecture*, by T. Warton, J. Bentham, Capt. Grose, and J. Milner, 2nd ed. (1808), 2; see for the controversy *Q.R.* ii (1809), 126, and xxvii (1822), 308.

[5] M. Whiffen, 'Rickman and Cambridge', *Arch. Rev.* xcviii (1945), 160. The *Attempt* had appeared earlier in Smith's *Panorama of Arts and Sciences* (1812–15): there were many later and enlarged editions.

endear the Gothic style to the heart of the English public. Scott's architectural descriptions seem to us haphazard enough: *Ivanhoe* is set in a period when Gothic building, except in its earliest transitional forms, was not yet in use; but, even if his dating is uncertain, Scott describes buildings as he had observed them, as structures built for defence and habitation, and a clear visual picture supervenes on the vague architectural mysteries of the earlier 'Gothic' novels.

Regency architects remained a little detached from these antiquarian struggles. They would probably have been just as ready as their predecessors in the eighteenth century to use medieval detail fantastically, but antiquarian pressure made it impossible for them to do so. What they required were rules. Classical architecture was based on the orders and on a body of recognized examples; Gothic had no orders, though Batty Langley had tried to find them and many writers referred to them. It was this search for guiding standards which lay behind the constant attempts to analyse Gothic into clearly defined stylistic divisions: whereas Italian Renaissance, Roman, or Greek models belonged to a coherent, known system, a system of ornament not of construction, Gothic had no recognized corpus of rules. Nor was one such to be found; the rules for revival Gothic that were finally to be established were to be based on the purposes for which the buildings were needed and the constructional problems involved. Regency Gothic, with its shallow mouldings, ogival arches, flat, cusped panels, and balanced design is, however, a style in its own right. Downton Castle, near Ludlow, designed for himself in 1774 by no less an authority than Richard Payne Knight, is perhaps the prototype of the irregular, castellated exterior,[1] but it was Wyatt who successively exploited this new fashion. At Belvoir Castle he began in 1800 a rebuilding which aimed at a great picturesque effect from the viewpoint that gives the castle its name. Some of his work was destroyed by fire in 1816, but his round keep still recalls the Norman origins of the Rutland family (Pl. 13 *a*).[2] Ashridge Park, built

[1] J. Summerson, *Architecture in Britain* (1953), 292; H. A. Tipping in *C.L.* xlii (1917), 36.
[2] C. Hussey in *C.L.* cxx (1956), 1284, 1402, 1456, 1500.

by him for the seventh earl of Bridgwater[1] and the most complete of Wyatt's extant Gothic buildings, is in marked contrast to the rococo elegancies of Strawberry Hill. It is a solid, classical design in which the bow-windows are occasionally converted into oriels, pediments and cornices are replaced by battlements, and the main blocks of the building are firmly indicated by octagonal towers (Pl. 13 b). Within, a lofty hall goes up to a timber roof, and on the staircase ceiling and chapel plaster vault there are clear recollections of Wyatt's long surveillance of Henry VII's chapel. Fenestration is naturally one of the most difficult problems, fenestration and chimneys. At Ashridge the latter are masked where possible inside battlemented turrets, the windows are mullioned Tudor openings. Regency Gothic is largely an infusion of earlier Gothic motifs into the Elizabethan style. Hakewill's north front at Rugby School, with its small octagonal towers, its battlements, its low projection, its mullioned but evenly spaced windows, and its low-pitched roofs is late domestic Gothic in intention, but could never be mistaken for anything but an early nineteenth-century building.[2] The main block was completed in the year of Waterloo.

The Regency style had, however, many ingredients, of which romantic Gothic was but one. To the eighteenth century an alternative to Gothic was Chinese: soon there were ventures in the Indian and Egyptian: but its great rival remained the Grecian. Humphry Repton uses the term for any type of classical Georgian architecture and in Regency parlance its use is emotional rather than precise, a testimony to the end of the long domination of the Roman style, with its wave of fashion in the elegancies of Robert Adam, a fashion that to the eighteen-twenties had all the staleness of a vogue but recently spent. Doric columns, Ionic capitals, hexastyles, cellas, the Tower of the Winds, the Monument of Lysicrates, went into the repertory, but the predominant feature of Regency style is its eclecticism not its exactness: it borrowed readily, and confused its borrowings together; even in the use of Grecian a new romantic liberty was at play.

[1] It was begun in 1806 and completed by Jeffry Wyatville after his uncle's death: see A. T. Bolton in *C.L.* l (1921), 160, 192; H. A. Tipping, *Engl. Homes*, vi. 1 (1926), 339.   [2] G. H. Bettinson, *Rugby School* (1929).

In the Prince Regent's two most celebrated buildings, Carlton House and the Brighton Pavilion, the original designs were those of Henry Holland.[1] In carrying them out he employed a team of French assistants, and his particular blend of Roman and Grecian, his Corinthian portico at Carlton House behind an Ionic screen, was much influenced by French models. Holland, however, died in 1806, and had already been replaced for some two years in the prince's favour, first of all by Thomas Hopper, who added the great Gothic conservatory, modelled on Henry VII's chapel, a piece of full-fledged pastiche on the wildest scale, and then, when Holland's interiors were already submerged by prolific and ostentatious décors, by John Nash who was to become the leading figure of the Regency style.

It is probable that Nash first attracted the prince's notice when, between 1797 and 1802, he was working as an assistant to Humphry Repton.[2] In the Academy of 1798 he had exhibited *A Conservatory for His Royal Highness the Prince of Wales* and this may have been connected with Repton's schemes for the Pavilion. Nash was then forty-six. He had served some form of apprenticeship in the office of Sir Robert Taylor (1714–88), an architect with a large practice, now chiefly remembered by his benefaction for the study of modern languages at Oxford; then he had speculated in building in London, been declared bankrupt, and retreated to Carmarthen, where in 1789 he was building the jail, that popular architectural occupation of the time, when John Howard's writings were awakening the public conscience to the sorry state of the prisons.[3] In Wales and the West Country he prospered and in 1796 returned to London and joined in an informal partnership with Repton, designing 'alterations' and new country houses, either as one of Repton's team or on his own.[4] In 1798, the year of the conservatory design, Nash married the beautiful Mary Anne Bradley, and many have thought she as well as her husband had been or was on intimate

---

[1] D. Stroud, *Henry Holland* (1950).

[2] For Nash see J. Summerson, *John Nash* (2nd ed. 1949).

[3] Howard's *State of the Prisons* was first published in 1777.

[4] The exact nature of the Nash–Repton agreement is uncertain and was probably never very clearly defined: for an instance of their work see T. S. R. Boase, 'An Oxford College and the Gothic Revival', *Journ. W.C.I.* xviii (1955), 145.

terms with the Prince. Certainly from now on Nash grew increasingly in royal favour, detached himself from Repton, and busied himself with a considerable practice of his own. Much of this consisted in designing villas to meet the new vogue, largely created by the improvements in the roads, for small country residences, and for cottages that had the double function of housing labour and forming picturesque incidents. Nash seems to have enjoyed considerable favour as a cottage architect, and built one for Uvedale Price himself. His larger houses were widely scattered throughout England and Ireland. He liked to add Gothic details in the windows and had a great partiality for round towers. His own house in the Isle of Wight, East Cowes castle, formed a splendid archaeologically inaccurate group on its conspicuous height above the bay.[1] He was in the first decade of the century a busily employed man, who was in 1806 appointed architect to the Department of Woods and Forests, and in 1813 was a possible choice, given the Prince's personal intervention, as Wyatt's successor at the Board of Works. The post of Surveyor-General, in which Wyatt had been both authoritarian and negligent, was in fact speedily modified, so that Nash became only one of three attached architects and deputy surveyors. He was, however, palace builder in chief. At Carlton House he remodelled the 'basement' storey, opening onto the garden, into a series of gilded rooms, Corinthian or Gothic or sometimes both, in a genuinely Regency and profuse indifference.[2]

Carlton House has gone, the Brighton Pavilion remains. In 1783 George, Prince of Wales, paid his first visit to Brighthelmston. Bathing was said to be good for the swollen glands from which he suffered. Five years later in 1787 he purchased a site on the open space known as the Steine, and Holland designed for him a long, low building, with a flat central dome between two-storeyed wings, each with two bow-windows and fine iron balconies. Mrs. Fitz-

---

[1] To Summerson writing in 1934 East Cowes castle was still inhabited and cared for: now (1957) it is a gutted ruin, and the house that welcomed so many visitors has a forbidding notice that trespassers enter the ruins at their own risk.

[2] See W. H. Pyne, *The History of the Royal Residences*, 3 vols. (1819), and the splendid coloured engravings that illustrate it. The ormolu clock (1809) with figures copied from David's *Oath of the Horatii* admirably exemplifies Regency taste (Reproduced H. Clifford Smith, *Buckingham Palace*, pl. 145).

herbert, whom, already twice widowed, the Prince had in 1785 secretly married, was generally in Brighton with him, occupying a nearby house, and in 1804 William Porden built one for her, in which she resided in later life. On her tomb, carved by John Carew in 1837, in St. John the Baptist's Catholic church near by, she kneels in high relief before a prie-dieu, the three wedding rings upon her fingers mutely protesting the validity of the third marriage. It is with this, the most genuine affection of his life, that Brighton was associated, becoming thereby the town of the Prince's most personal predilection. In 1804, when Porden was building for Mrs. Fitzherbert, Holland added two large oval rooms set as projecting wings at an obtuse angle to the east front of the Pavilion. Inside Messrs. John Crace and Sons were busy providing Chinese furnishings, on the advice, it is said,[1] of P. F. Robinson, the Prince's superintendent of works, who wished to utilize a fine Chinese paper that had been presented to the Prince. Robinson was a great connoisseur of styles, and in 1812 his Egyptian Hall in Piccadilly was to be one of the most exotic of Regency buildings,[2] but his ready inspiration was hardly needed at the Pavilion, for chinoiserie was a well-established fashion, in which the Prince had already indulged at Carlton House. In 1803 William Porden, who was employing Gothic with great liberality at Eaton Hall, produced a design for a Chinese exterior to the Pavilion,[3] with green pagoda roofs and dragon terminals, but instead of carrying it out he was set to building an immense domed stable. These buildings, impressive in scale, for the central dome (now a concert hall) had a diameter of 80 feet and the riding school (now the Corn Exchange) was 178 feet long and 58 feet wide, were also surprising in style, for they were definitely Indian in their ornamental detail (Pl. 28 a). 'Although', Humphry Repton reported to the Prince, 'the outline

---

[1] E. W. Brayley, *Her Majesty's Palace at Brighton* (1838).

[2] The Egyptian Hall was demolished in 1904: it is shown in the lithograph of Piccadilly in T. Shotter Boys, *Original Views of London as it is* (1842). Another of Robinson's foreign fancies, the Swiss Cottage at Hampstead, though much altered, has proved a more lasting landmark.

[3] The original drawing is in the Royal Pavilion: on the various schemes and outside influences upon them see C. Musgrave, *Royal Pavilion* (1951). For a photograph of the interior of the dome before reconstruction see H. D. Roberts, *The Royal Pavilion* (1939), fig. 94.

of the Dome resembles rather a Turkish mosque than the buildings of Hindûstan, yet its general character is distinct from either Grecian or Gothic, and must both please and surprise everyone not bigoted to the forms of either.'[1]

Repton had recently been dealing with the Hindu style in the gardens of Sir Charles Cockerell's house at Sezincote in Gloucestershire. This retired East India Company man employed his brother, S. P. Cockerell, advised by Thomas Daniell, and Sezincote, with its green copper domes, its chattris, its long, curving orangery, its temple pool and Wellington memorial pillar (serving also as a chimney for the orangery) is full of eccentric and period charm, and wonderfully surprising buried in the Cotswold country-side. John Martin did a series of aquatints of it, but even he cannot suppress the gaiety of the place.[2] Brighton, it was now determined, must see these charms on an even larger scale.

The Regent in 1812 had entrusted James Wyatt with further schemes for the Pavilion, but it is uncertain in what style the designer of Fonthill was to carry them out. Wyatt's fatal accident in 1813 brought John Nash on the scene. His first move was to rebuild Holland's oblique wings as rectangles, with lancet windows of no clearly known provenance, surmounted by tent-shaped spires, between which Holland's flat dome and bow windows look, in contemporary prints, curiously uneasy. By 1818, however, both the western and eastern fronts had been remodelled. A great bulbous dome crowned the centre, echoed by smaller domes; numerous small columns crowned by chattris variegated the skyline and the outer walls were masked by colonnades of horseshoe arches and masharabi open work (Pl. 28 b). The result is undoubtedly bizarre. 'The outside', Croker thought, 'is said to be taken from the Kremlin at Moscow.'[3] Inside the decorative motifs

---

[1] H. Repton, 'Designs for the Pavilion at Brighton' (1808), in J. C. Loudon, *The Landscape Gardens and Landscape Architecture of the late Humphry Repton Esq.* (1840), 368. At Hope End, near Ledbury, Edward Moulton Barrett, 'a West Indian of considerable property', better known through his daughter, Elizabeth, was also building in the Moorish style: A. C. Sewter in *Connoisseur*, cxxxvii (1956), 179.

[2] J. Betjeman in *Arch. Rev.* lxix (1931), 161.

[3] *The Croker Papers*, ed. L. J. Jennings (1884), i. 125. Croker thought it would be 'a ruin in half a century or sooner'.

were mainly Chinese, immense dragons, pagodas, lanterns, panels of painted or embroidered birds and flowering branches, with vast crystal chandeliers as a more contemporary note. Augustus Pugin's drawings, peopling the brilliant, voluptuous décor with contemporary figures,[1] capture and perpetuate this curious world. It was laughed at, admired, caricatured, and disapproved of. 'I do not believe', wrote the Princess Lieven, 'that, since the days of Heliogabalus, there have been such magnificence and such luxury. There is something effeminate in it which is disgusting.'[2] Much of it was also shoddy. The mastic ceilings were soon in need of repair. Behind the extravagance were constant battles about payments and funds, questions in Parliament, courts of inquiry, quarrels between the royal patron and his architect.[3] The ageing King tired of his toy, became less mobile and in the last three years of his life never visited Brighton.

The opportunity which was to give a more lasting and reputable fame to the name of Nash was outlined in a letter from John Fordyce, Surveyor General of His Majesty's Land Revenue, appended to his first report presented to the Treasury in 1797. The main lease of the tract of crown land known as Marylebone Park had been held by the duke of Portland since 1789, but would revert to the crown in 1811. Fordyce argued that it was time to draw up plans for the development of this site, and that there was urgent need for a great street linking it with Charing Cross. Fordyce himself died in 1809, and finally in July 1811 the whole scheme was entrusted to John Nash. Certainly the influence of the Prince Regent stood for much in this decision. He is said to have exclaimed that Nash's plan would 'quite eclipse Napoleon'. A scheme which involved the demolition of some 700 houses, the linking of the Grand Junction canal to the Thames by a continuation, the Regent canal, and the creation of new residential and commercial areas

[1] *The Royal Pavilion at Brighton*, published by the command of and dedicated by permission to the King by His Majesty's dutiful subject and servant John Nash (1826). The original drawings, by various artists under Pugin's supervision, are in the Municipal Library at Brighton.

[2] *Private Letters of Princess Lieven to Prince Metternich 1820–26*, ed. P. Quennell (1937), 150.

[3] H. D. Roberts (op. cit. 126) estimates the expenditure at £502,797. 6s. 10d.

was not likely, then as now, to pass without fierce criticism. Nash's design for the Park itself included a framework of terraces and crescents, and at the centre, 'the grandest apex possible to the whole scenery', a 'Valhalla'; this was early abandoned and the Park left as an open space with but few buildings in it; but a surprising amount of the plan, the outer ring of terraces, Park Square and Park Crescent (originally planned as one huge circus terminating the earlier Portland Place) and the great street itself were largely completed by 1830, and the Quadrant, the largest single unit, was built in 1819–20. This, in a period prone to discussion and procrastination, is in itself remarkable enough. Nash had the enthusiasm, the toughness, the readiness of wit to see it through. He himself took up many of the building sites and speculated in them. His own financial commitments were throughout such as would have distracted most men, and it seemed to many of his contemporaries that they must involve some measure of sharp practice. There are indeed curious gaps in all Nash's transactions; sometimes money is there, sometimes not, often in each case it is contrary to expectation. But no fault was ever proved against him, and his friends throughout all his career numbered men of integrity, who would not have countenanced a shady practitioner. Ebullient, shrewd, and opportunist, he had the gifts for getting on with the job. As he himself said in a statement published at the time of an attack on him in 1829: 'Anxiety to complete my designs . . . has induced me at various times to incur an uncalled-for degree of personal responsibility.'[1] This was a sound analysis. He was driven on by the desire to see his plans in being; quick methods, quick materials appealed to him; he thought in terms of stucco, cast iron, 'musaic gold', or any new substitute product available. There is something rough and ready about all his work, a lack of exactness in measurement and proportion, a lack of pondered judgement in his conjunctions of details, sometimes hidden by a certain freshness of imagination, sometimes provoking in its carelessness.

Of the great design little, apart from the Park Terraces, remains as he left it. Waterloo Place was originally planned as an approach

[1] Summerson, *Nash*, 250.

to Carlton House, which would give the latter, with a series of Ionic porticoes and screens, the setting of a palace rather than a private dwelling.[1] When in 1825 it was decided to pull down Carlton House, Nash with his ever-ready invention came forward with the scheme for a great terrace facing St. James's Park, to surpass in its elaboration even the terraces at the northern end of the thoroughfare. The two blocks were completed by his adopted son, James Pennethorne, but the design is Nash's own, characteristic in its treatment of a row of houses as one great façade, crowned by a central pediment with strongly emphatic attics rising at either end of each block, characteristic too in its haphazard use of orders, where the fluted Corinthian columns rise from a terrace that is buttressed by squat Ionic columns in cast iron. Freshly painted, with constant play of light and shade along its pillared colonnades, Carlton House Terrace has that curious mingling of the dignified and the gay, which is Nash's individual note. There is something vaguely unreal about it, something essentially scenic rather than functional, well calculated to displease the mid-century moralists, but it has become part of the flavour of London and has had merits enough to withstand the fluctuations of fashion.

Nash had planned to link the two blocks with a fountain under a cupola supported on columns from Carlton House, columns which were eventually used in the portico of the National Gallery. The fountain, as explained by Nash to the Select Committee of 1828, was to be a picturesque feature: 'Speaking as a painter', he rather surprisingly said, 'it will improve the view': but there was by then general alarm about Nash's lavish schemes: the fountain was cancelled, and five years later Benjamin Dean Wyatt filled the space with his 124-feet-high column, crowned by Westmacott's statue of the duke of York, a not very memorable figure, most strikingly commemorated (Pl. 30 a).

Lower Regent Street had considerable variety in its elevations. The last of them (No. 11) survived till 1938, probably designed by G. S. Repton, who was responsible for St. Philip's chapel next door, with a Palladian portico and surmounted by a copy of the Tower of the Winds. At No. 2, on the corner of Charles Street,

[1] C. H. Reilly in *C.L.* li (1922), 691, 777.

was the United Service Club designed by Robert Smirke: farther up the street much of the building was by James Burton. Over all these various workers, Nash exercised a somewhat vaguely defined control. His own house, combined with that of his old friend and ally John Edwards,[1] was at Nos. 14–16 and included on the first floor a gallery, 70 feet long, ornamented with full-scale copies of Raphael's loggia arabesques, specially painted for Nash, copies from Titian, Caravaggio, Guido, and Guercino, and casts of antique sculpture. Painted in ultramarine, shining with musaic gold, there was 'for flutter, multiplicity of mouldings, filagrain, and leaf gold' nothing, or so thought Elmes,[2] in Paris to equal it and no doubt Nash's interiors reflected contemporary Parisian fashion, though externally his architectural fancies were his own.

Piccadilly Circus, then truly circular in form and much smaller in area than now, had a general scheme of fluted pilasters over Ionic columns, such as those Nash used in Carlton Terrace. Leading from it was the Quadrant, whose romantic curve was perhaps the most striking feature of the ground plan. Nash himself quoted the bend of Oxford High Street as his precedent and Mr. Summerson has very cogently suggested[3] that not only the curve but the variations of mass and height throughout Regent Street echo a medieval tradition, a romantic element in the lively patchwork of Nash's invention. The progress northwards was full of incident. The Quadrant's colonnades provided shelter for pedestrians, too great obscurity for the shops, a balcony for the eligible apartments of the first floor, and a range of Doric columns 'worthy of a Roman amphitheatre'. Farther up, the dome and curved façade of the Harmonic Institute (designed by Nash) confronted the Ionic portico, the Bath stone, and careful classical detail of C. R. Cockerell's Hanover Chapel, and so the vista continued till it was closed by the highly controversial and still surviving All Souls' church, with its pointed spire rising out of its peristyle. There is a nonsensical air

[1] For Edwards see Summerson, *Nash*, 90. Nash made Edwards's son his heir, but there seems to have been no relationship. Nash's secretiveness about his personal affairs probably makes them appear more mysterious than in fact they were.

[2] *Metropolitan Improvements, or London in the 19th Century* (1827), 149. The gallery was after Nash's death taken down and re-erected at East Cowes castle.

[3] Op. cit. 202. For views of Regent Street see *Repository of Arts*, xiii (1822).

about All Souls'; the great scheme could never be kept quite serious; it had many elements of the grand manner, but it lacked respectful conviction. George IV presented as an altarpiece (led by the universities, altarpieces were coming back into favour) a large *Ecce Homo* by Richard Westall and its halting use of the grand manner fits well enough.

Today it is the Park terraces that retain most of their original appearance and can still be seen in isolation and therefore in their true scale. There has, however, been one general change in them, for Nash's own instructions are clear enough and the plaster work was meant to be 'rejointed in imitation of Bath Stone', a fiction that later theorists rejected in disgust. Cumberland Terrace is the grandest of the designs (Pl. 33 *b*), for it was meant to face the Guinguette, the King's private lodge that was in fact never built; but everyone has his own particular favourite among them.

Nash's last great commission from his royal patron was the rebuilding of Buckingham House and its conversion into Buckingham Palace. In January 1820 the Prince Regent became King George IV. His coronation was one of the most magnificent and lavish spectacles of the time, as though to gloss over the sordid business of the Queen's trial, and once crowned the King looked for new splendours. He was tired of Carlton House. The structure threatened to prove insecure and its associations were not all now acceptable. He decided to rebuild Windsor, but here, though there was some show of competition, he never seems to have intended to employ Nash but turned instead to Jeffry Wyatt, nephew and pupil of the famous James, and now one of the main practitioners in the Gothic style. In 1824 when the first stone was laid, Jeffry took the name of Wyatville, and in 1828 he was knighted. Much of the work at Windsor is hard and unconvincing; the wide bands of mortar, which are even simulated on some of the pre-existing work, make a too strident pattern in contrast to the darkened small rag-work, and the yellow ashlar of the quoins and Gothic windows completes a colouristic effect which is certainly unusual but undoubtedly too pronounced; the raising of the Round Tower by an additional 33 feet is more successful, and created a romantic silhouette that familiarity never stales. The cost far exceeded all the original estimates and as soon as the King died, on 26 June 1830, there was a committee of inquiry: but Wyatville was acquitted of any blame and the work on the castle was continued.[1] At Buckingham Palace it was a different matter. Nash's elaborate design, with its central dome and its side wings, where columned ground storeys carried lofty pavilions, was attacked even during the King's lifetime, though George defended his favourite and sought, unsuccessfully, to obtain for him a baronetcy, a higher honour than any as yet conferred on an architect. George dead, Nash's commission was suspended, a further committee appointed, and the task eventually transferred to Edward Blore, a Gothic architect, who had built the Pitt Press at Cambridge in an ecclesiastical style that is still curiously misleading, and Abbotsford, the dream Gothic house, for Sir Walter Scott. Faced with the remains of Nash's designs and the problems of the Grecian style, he produced an uneasy compromise, a flat eastern façade, built in Caen stone, which had perished so badly by the close of the century that it was replaced in 1913 by the present Portland stone restoration.[2]

Nash was now an old man, ailing and feeble. He died in 1835 at his Gothic castle in the Isle of Wight, and with his death the 'Regency' was finally over. For it is in his architecture that it had found its expression, though a certain superficiality, well enough in keeping with some aspects of the taste of the time, held Nash back from any intellectual grasp of the synthesis of motifs and the new freedom from rules which underlay the style he practised. In this sense, his rival, generally unsuccessful rival, John Soane, differing from him in every way, is more truly the interpreter of the period, informed of all its details, applying Hellenistic idioms with memories of the language of Piranesi. In 1802 Soane,[3] already for seven years an Associate, was admitted a full member of the Royal Academy. Since 1788 he had been surveyor of the Bank of England and had built for them the Bank Stock Office and the

[1] W. H. St. John Hope, *Windsor Castle*, i (1913), chap. xviii, and Sir Owen Morshead, *Windsor Castle* (1951).

[2] H. Clifford Smith, *Buckingham Palace* (1931). Blore worked on the palace 1831–7, converted the conservatory into a chapel in 1843, and added the east front 1846–7.

[3] For Soane see H. J. Birnstingl, *Sir John Soane* (1925); A. T. Bolton, *The Portrait of Sir John Soane* (1927); A. T. Bolton and John Summerson, *Sir John Soane* (1952).

Rotunda.[1] These buildings already showed the dramatic sense, the pleasure in unexpected effects which were to characterize Soane's work. They owe much to George Dance, in whose office Soane had worked and whom he continued to consult. Dance, however, who died at the age of eighty-four in 1825, was in his later buildings, such as Stratton Park (1803–6) and the College of Surgeons in Lincoln's Inn Fields (1806–13), to turn more and more to the neoclassicism of post-Revolutionary France, rendered accessible in L. A. Dubut's *Maisons de ville et de campagne* (1803). His Doric portico at Stratton sets the tone for the grim severity of much English building in the first half of the century. Soane also had a liking for the plain and the primitive, but contrasted it with emphatic and striking detail. The house which he built for himself at Ealing *c.* 1802,[2] Pitzhanger Manor, has a central façade, where the flatness is emphasized by a rectangular pediment, rising above the straight line of the balustrade, but counteracted by four large Ionic columns carrying free standing statues of heroic scale (Pl. 35 *b*). The entablature is made to break forward to cover the columns. The entrance hall and staircase are contrived in a narrow compass to give an elaborate and almost monumental effect. The columns and statues, the rectangular pediment, the round arched windows are found again in the entrance to the Bank from Lothbury Court, but here, as in the immensely fanciful Tivoli corner of the same building, the columns are Corinthian and there is an added richness in the ornament, though there is the same angularity that characterizes so many of his designs and reaches its climax in the mausoleum of the Dulwich Art Gallery, where the straight lines of the tower are emphasized by his favourite incised mouldings and the square brick pilasters have sharp, clean edges. The rounded urns which top the tower serve by their very incongruity to bring out the squareness of the whole. This is neither classical nor Gothic in feeling, but an individual statement. Many of his most important buildings no longer exist: the Bank was largely rebuilt in 1927; his

[1] See H. Rooksby Steele and F. R. Yerbury, *The Old Bank of England*, London (1930).

[2] It was sold in 1810 and Soane then concentrated on 13 Lincoln's Inn Fields (1812); see A. T. Bolton, *Pitzhanger Manor* (Publications of Sir John Soane Museum, No. 4).

State Paper Office, his Regent Street block of houses, the sculpture gallery for Chantrey in Belgrave Place, the Law Courts at Westminster, were all demolished or completely altered in the course of the nineteenth century. Dulwich itself, destroyed by a flying bomb in 1944, is now only a replica. His œuvre has come down to us curtailed of its grandest pieces; but in his house at 13 Lincoln's Inn can still be seen the picturesque ingenuity with which he provided varying vistas, his delight in sharp contrasts of forms, his use of mirrors to give non-existent depth, his constant sense of the effect of light and shade. Here, in the museum he bequeathed to the nation, his collection with its Turners, Hogarths, classical sculpture, Egyptian coffins, medieval manuscripts, is as it were a frozen piece of Regency taste in all its catholicity, its contented jumble, its vague romantic yearnings, its liking for the exotic and the strange.

In its range of interests, the career of one architect, John B. Papworth, may be taken as peculiarly illustrative of the times. His father was the chief stuccoist employed by the Office of Works and in fact controlled all its decorative plastering, no meagre occupation at this period of embellishments. John, the second of his six sons, was first drawn to architecture by his admiration for Michael Angelo Rooker's classical drop scene at the Haymarket Theatre, or so he himself wrote in an autobiographical fragment, but such early anecdotes had since Vasari been part of the necessary recipe for an artist's life.[1] Perhaps the name Michael Angelo made its first indirect impact in this way, and later, in some gathering of artist friends, he added Buonarotti to his own name, not apparently as an act of homage to the giant order, the Farnese Palace or the Laurentian staircase, but to the heroic painter whose forms he had been copying in a drawing, *A Trophaeum*, commemorating Waterloo, much admired by his friends but rejected by the Academy. Papworth in fact had many and varied ambitions. He was always busy with the minor arts, designs for glass, silver, furniture, and textiles. His oblong lustres for glass chandeliers created an instantaneous change of fashion:[2] at Claremont he designed a Gothic

[1] See Wyatt Papworth, *John B. Papworth* (privately printed, 1879).
[2] R. P. Ross Williams in *Arch. Rev.* lxxix (1936), 279.

garden seat for Princess Charlotte and later turned it into a Gothic memorial cenotaph, carried out in Bernasconi's cement; there was a glass chair for the shah of Persia; a memorial column on the field of Waterloo to Colonel Gordon, a severed column broken at the top, a motif then new, 'since', as his biographer puts it, 'overdone in all cemeteries'. When he visited France in 1824, he wrote back: 'In Paris there are a great many things copied from my designs.'[1]

It was, however, on a broader field, that of street and town planning, that Papworth was to leave his most permanent mark. Between 1823 and 1830 he was engaged on St. Bride's Avenue, a new street opening from Fleet Street to give a vista of St. Bride's church; and in 1825 he was invited by Pearson Thompson to lay out as a new spa his Montpellier estate at Cheltenham. The great rise of such spas, several of which might be grouped together in one resort, was a characteristic feature of the close of the eighteenth and early years of the nineteenth century.[2] When George III came for a month's cure in the summer of 1788, Cheltenham was a village of one wide street, with a fine medieval church, some good brick houses, and a population of about 400.[3] By the turn of the century, the population had increased to 1,800, and the town was steadily growing in fashion and repute. The original spa was the Royal Old Wells. The Montpellier Spa in the twenties began to supersede it, and in 1826 Papworth designed his great rotunda, 52 feet in diameter and 54 feet high, with a ribbed dome, 'on the principle of Philibert de l'Orme', which was thought to have no rival in England except Soane's rotunda at the Bank. Before the Rotunda was completed, however, another speculator, Joseph Pitt, was laying out a hundred acres to the north of the town, and there, though the scheme had some setbacks, was opened in 1830 another pump room, from the designs of John Forbes, a somewhat Soanian building with large statues on the parapet (now removed), a long Ionic colonnade, and a dome rising from a raised rectangular base (Pl. 32 b). Meanwhile Papworth, Forbes, and others, such as

[1] Wyatt Papworth, op. cit. 39 and 127.
[2] See A. B. Granville, *The Spas of England*, 2 vols. (1841); W. Addison, *English Spas* (1951).
[3] See H. Davies, *A View of Cheltenham in its past and present state* (Cheltenham, 1843); B. Little, *Cheltenham* (1952).

R. W. Jearrad, were busy with villas, laid out in garden settings, and with churches, some with Ionic columns, some in the Gothic style that they were all prepared to use if asked to do so. The local stone-carvers, the Lewis family, provided a series of monuments for retired Anglo-Indians, favouring a mourning woman by a column whose capital is toppling from it.

Near by, at Leamington, an analysis of the water was published in 1794, and a spa was founded, patronized first by northern industrialists, then by a more fashionable society. But it remained small in scale, with a parade leading up to P. F. Robinson's Norman revival church (1825), with its Augusta Place, Adelaide Bridge, Charlotte Street, Clarence Street, and, of course, Regent Street, a town pleasantly provided with classical façades and some very rounded bow-windows. William Thomas became the chief builder, and designed Lansdowne Crescent on the very shallowest of curves. Then in the mid-century the villa owners took to Gothic and the roads into Leamington are lined with surprising and often successful experiments in the style.[1]

'The form of a crescent', wrote Jane Austen, 'always takes.'[2] The fashion set at Bath by the King's Circus (1754–8) and the Royal Crescent (1767–71) had many successors. Any rising fashionable resort required its curving lines as well as the straight vistas of its parades or drives.[3] At Brighton, Royal Crescent was completed in 1807, a new experiment, for it was the first group of houses to face the sea; with its black tiles, bow windows, sunblinds, and iron balconies, it set a type for the new seaside resort; its central feature, the giant statue by Rossi in synthetic stone of the Prince Regent, proved less lasting and soon disintegrated.[4] Lewes Crescent, 200 feet wider than the Royal Crescent at Bath, opening in the centre

[1] R. P. Ross Williams in *Arch. Rev.* xci (1942), 103.

[2] *Sanditon*, chap. iv.

[3] Everyone will have his particular favourite: Walsingham Place, Truro, with its simple decoration of incised lines has a particular charm; but my own vote would go, I think, to the Paragon at Clifton.

[4] See A. Dale, *The History and Architecture of Brighton* (Brighton, 1950); E. W. Gilbert, 'The Growth of Brighton', *Geographical Journ.* cxiv (1949), 30. E. W. Brayley, *Topographical Sketches of Brighthelmston* (1825), illustrated with twelve engravings by R. Havell, Jun., is an interesting contemporary account.

into a square, was the main feature of Brighton's greatest single piece of town planning, the Kemp estate, in its original scheme never fully carried out, second only in size to Nash's Regent Park and its approaches. Its architects were C. A. Busby and Amon Wilds, the former a London architect who had come to Brighton after a bitter controversy over his iron roofs, which had been rejected by the Commissioners for Building New Churches; the latter a Lewes builder, who had been working in Brighton and now formed a partnership with Busby, a partnership to which Brighton owes much of its architectural character, the projecting porch balconies of Lewes Crescent, the long Corinthian façade, a modest variant from Nash, of Brunswick Terrace, contrasting with the giant Ionic columns and rounded bays of Brunswick Square. Along the coast other sea-side resorts caught a reflection of Brighton's fashion and prosperity. Princess Amelia's patronage brought Worthing into favour[1] and Amon Wilds built Park Crescent there in 1829, giving it as entrance to its varied and scenic Regency curve a dramatic archway supported by large bearded herms (Pl. 32 c), a wonderful piece of impropriety: but Wilds had a weakness for odd details, and his ammonite volutes, modelled on fossils and a pun on his own name, became almost a signature motif. At St. Leonard's, James Burton from 1828 onwards, with his son Decimus to assist him, planned another building estate which soon became popular. As these new favourites drew the public, older spas declined. Tunbridge Wells,[2] though occasionally visited by the duchess of Kent and the young Princess Victoria, was losing its eighteenth-century celebrity and was becoming more and more a residential town in easy reach of London. Here Decimus Burton was called in to design, in the local stone that blackens with age, the Calverley Estate, a plain, now rather sombre group, with a shopping centre, a parade, a crescent, and a Gothic church.

[1] *Worthing by Local Writers*, ed. F. W. H. Migeod (Brighton, 1938), 57.
[2] John Britton, *Descriptive sketches of Tunbridge Wells and the Calverley Estate* (1832); J. C. M. Given, *Royal Tunbridge Wells Past and Present* (Tunbridge Wells, 1946), 43. For St. Leonard's see P. Clarke, 'James Burton', *Arch. Rev.* xc (1941), 93. For Hastings, where similar development took place, see J. M. Baines, *Historic Hastings* (1955). Malvern, Droitwich, Harrogate, and Scarborough had considerable development as resorts in the middle years of the century.

The spas, catering for a fashionable concourse, illustrate the more elegant architecture of their time, and in many cases have retained their original appearance, undisturbed by great industrial changes; but everywhere building was in progress, and the close of the war led to an increase of activity. Bristol, the second port of the kingdom, with its own spas at Hotwells and at Clifton, employed one or two outside architects for its civic buildings. C. A. Busby, before his Brighton period, built in 1810–11 the Commercial Rooms in Corn Street, with a deep portico where four giant Ionic columns support a pediment surmounted by a Britannia-like figure of Bristol, the work of J. G. Bubb, the most pedestrian of Regency sculptors but none the less much employed. Farther up the street Smirke's Council House (1824–5), with its flat pilasters, engaged columns, delicately carved frieze of classical motifs, and rectangular attic, where, in the central recess, E. H. Baily's *Justice* hardly breaks the skyline, is a weightier, more severe design.[1] For domestic buildings, however, local builders were employed, and the Paragon, the crescent standing on the higher ground of Clifton, was begun in 1812 by John Drew, and completed after his bankruptcy by Stephen Hunter.[2] Built on a close radius, the narrow houses are themselves straight, but the doorways have a swelling convex curve of their own, strikingly accentuating the concave curve of the crescent. With its varied assembly of buildings from the first half of the century, its spacious layout above its deep gorge, its balconies and its speciality of stone trellis fencing, Clifton can stand comparison with Bath and Cheltenham.

[1] See W. Ison, *The Georgian Buildings of Bristol* (1952).

[2] Bankruptcy was an all too common feature in the building of Clifton. 'It is to be lamented that those beautiful ranges of buildings, the Prince of Wales's and the Lower Crescent, should remain in their present unfinished state. They were begun in an unfortunate moment by some speculators, who imagined that they should thereby reap a golden harvest but the project failed owing to the late war, and they were ruined' (R. Phillips, *Guide to all the Watering and Sea Bathing Places*, 1806–7, 107). One of these ruined speculators was Francis Greenway, who was driven by the stress of the times to forge a contract and was transported, to become the dominant and turbulent figure in the building of Sydney, where his three churches of St. James', St. Matthew's, Windsor, and St. Luke's, Liverpool, recall the Regency style as practised at Clifton, with, in the mouldings and urns of St. Matthew's, a hint of the influence of Sir John Soane. See M. H. Ellis, *Francis Greenway* (Sydney and London, 1953); M. Herman, *The Early Australian Architects* (Sydney and London, 1954).

To the south-west there was a regional school characterized by a dependence on good masonry rather than decorative motifs. John Nash built in the West Country, and Stonelands at Dawlish has his Doric portico opening into a hall with a coved ceiling, marbled Ionic columns, and a graceful ironwork staircase;[1] a house which soon after its completion was occupied by Sir John Rennie, son of the builder of Waterloo Bridge, himself an engineer and architect of repute, whose Royal William Victualling Yard, Stonehouse, Plymouth (1825–30) is one of the great architectural triumphs of the period. Severe in design, built of large blocks of stone, relief is given by a subtle contrast of materials, grey stone and yellow granite, and by a contrast in the window pediments, curved in the bottom and top storeys, straight in the centre. The main tower is set between two tall chimneys on the advanced sections of the building, and the entrance, leading to a colonnade along the main façade, is through an elaborate gateway, on which stands a statue of William IV, out of scale and slightly absurd, the one concession, in this faultlessly grave ensemble, to contemporary over-statement (Pl. 30 b). Rennie, however, mainly occupied with the great Plymouth breakwater, designed few buildings, and it was John Foulston who was to leave the greatest mark on early nineteenth-century Plymouth and the surrounding country.[2] In 1811 he won the competition for a large central block to include the Royal Hotel, the Assembly Rooms, and the Theatre. This finely reticent stucco building, with a columned Ionic portico and some hints from Soane in the lighting of the great ballroom, lost its unity when the theatre was replaced by a cinema and now, like so much of Foulston's work, it has disappeared in the bombing of Plymouth. Foulston had not only the problem of civic buildings but also of linking Devonport, Stonehouse, and Plymouth by streets and terraces. The small central square of Devonport, where the town hall closes the vista up Ker Street, is still today, declined somewhat from its original estate, one of the most suggestive of

[1] A. E. Richardson and C. Lovett Gill, *Regional Architecture of the West of England* (1924), 133; the attribution to Nash is queried by Summerson.
[2] Ibid. 62 and *passim* for Foulston. Foulston's buildings are shown in lithographs in his *Public Buildings erected in the West of England* (1838).

Regency groups. The street has kept its simple, classical house fronts, with some fine ironwork: it ends with a remarkable Egyptian building, now Oddfellows Hall, in marked contrast with the four plain Doric columns of the town hall porch: over all towers the Naval Column, erected on Foulston's design in 1824 (Pl. 34 *b*).

At the other end of England town planning was being carried out on an even larger scale. 'A citizen of Newcastle', so runs the memorial in St. John's church, 'does not need to be reminded of Richard Grainger.' In 1826 this great speculative builder began his career with the building of Eldon Square. Newcastle, with its riverside, its denes and hills already crowned by the castle, St. Nicholas with its steeple and All Saints with its spire, was as striking a site as could be desired.[1] Grainger turned for advice to an architect, eleven years his senior, John Dobson, who had earlier put forward his own scheme for the expansion of the city. Dobson,[2] a local man born at North Shields, had studied drawing under Boniface Moss, an Italian refugee, and had had John Martin as his fellow pupil. Then in London he had worked, as so many others, under John Varley, and the shy, sensitive, capable north countryman had made many friends. Robert Smirke, whose son Sydney was to become Dobson's son-in-law, urged him to remain in London, but he returned to the north, and there found employment in designing country houses, making some reputation as an excluder of draughts and a man who understood the new standards of comfort; restorations, too, occupied him, Hexham priory, Newcastle Keep, St. Nicholas's church, and others. For Newcastle he built a panopticon jail on the approved Benthamite pattern, which already had been followed by Thomas Harrison in his Doric reconstruction of Chester castle. Grainger had enterprise, push, and a powerful mathematical brain; Dobson 'the fastidiousness of a retiring nature, without that certain something that brings a man to gain all'. The curved streets, still with their sober classical buildings, end in vistas where may be seen the Royal

[1] See Turner's drawing engraved in *River Scenery by Turner and Girtin* (1823–7); and F. D. Klingender, *Art and the Industrial Revolution*, 85.

[2] M. J. Dobson, *Memoir of John Dobson* (1885); see also E. Mackenzie, *A Descriptive and Historical Account of Newcastle on Tyne*, 2 vols. (Newcastle, 1827).

Arcade with its pillared entrance, the ground floor order Doric, the second with capitals more Renaissance than Corinthian, topped by a frieze of coiling foliage; or the Grey column set up in 1837 in honour of the reformer, with his statue upon it by E. H. Baily, a first essay which was to have Nelson in Trafalgar Square as its successor (Pl. 29 *b*). Grey Street has the Theatre Royal with its great pillared portico, designed in the style of the Pantheon by John Green and his son Benjamin, local architects working for Grainger; opposite it is the Turk's Head Hotel, a simple façade with carefully arranged window spacing and unemphatic cornices. The central railway station, designed by Dobson in the later forties, was eventually completed with a great stone portico in the Grecian style, but Dobson could also handle Gothic, and his church of St. Thomas (1828–9) with its spare, narrow pinnacles and thin tower is one of the most arresting of early Gothic revival silhouettes, where classical restraint gives a curiously individual effect to the use of Gothic forms. 'Modern Newcastle', wrote Granville in 1841, 'would surprise every Englishman . . . even though he may have seen and admired the only two other provincial cities that can be compared to it—Edinburgh and Bath.'[1]

In Regency Brighton one of the most familiar and characteristic features was the Chain Pier (Pl. 45). Designed by Sir Samuel Brown and opened in 1823, it was a suspension bridge hung from cast-iron towers. It is a typical example of the Regency delight in ironwork, 'the dandy jetty' as Constable called it.[2] The foundation in 1759 of the Carron ironworks in Stirlingshire had led to a new skill in light castings for domestic purposes, particularly in the first instance for grates. Cast iron lent itself to the simple lines of Greek ornament, and its comparative cheapness made it available for a large variety of uses. Lamp brackets, railings, verandas, and balconies in this material are a constant feature of Regency buildings, one unfortunately that suffered much in the scrapping of iron ornaments during the second world war. L. N. Cottingham

[1] A. B. Granville, *The Spas of England: Northern Spas* (1841), 272. I deprecate the application of the term 'provincial' to Edinburgh.

[2] A. Dale, *History and Architecture of Brighton* (Brighton, 1950), 78; C. R. Leslie, *Constable*, ed. Shirley (1937), 172.

published in 1823 his *Smith and Founders Dictionary*, a great repertory of models which both chronicled existing achievements and provided examples for future work (Fig. 2).

FIG. 2. *Ornamental ironwork: L. N. Cottingham*

Cast iron was used also for much grander projects. In 1779 John Wilkinson and Abraham Darby spanned the Severn in Shropshire, at the place known since as Ironbridge, with a semicircular arch of 100 feet span made of cast-iron ribs. It was the first iron bridge ever built, and still stands today, though limited to foot traffic. In 1802 the engineer architect, Thomas Telford, published proposals for replacing London Bridge by an iron bridge of 600 feet span and a central clearance of 65 feet at high water. In the drawing of it the sweeping curve rises very nobly with the dome of St. Paul's seen above it and below a framed vista of the river.[1] It was a statement of new aesthetic as well as new technical possibilities. But the moment of peace which had encouraged the opening years of the century vanished, and with it the great project of a new London Bridge; it was not till 1819, with the completion of John Rennie's Southwark Bridge, that London saw iron used for this purpose. Rennie had already designed an iron bridge to span the Goomtee at Lucknow (1814), but his ironwork could not hold its place in public esteem with his stone Waterloo Bridge, opened by the Regent in 1817, an event which deeply struck popular imagination and which Constable has immortalized in one of his most arresting paintings.[2]

[1] Reproduced A. Gibb, *The Story of Telford* (1935), 48.
[2] See below p. 113. For J. L. Bond's share in the designing of the bridge, see H. S. Goodhart-Rendel, *English Architecture since the Regency* (1953), 48.

Waterloo Bridge, demolished after much controversy in 1938, was architecturally the most famous of Regency bridges, but Thomas Telford was as notable a bridge builder as Rennie. Many that he put up were in stone, but his two iron suspension bridges, both completed in the same year, 1826, were regarded as amongst his most remarkable achievements:

> Structures of more ambitious enterprise
> Than minstrels in the age of old romance
> To their own Merlin's magic lore ascribed.[1]

Both were on the Holyhead route, one over the Menai Straits, the other over the ferry at Conway castle. This latter brought the most modern and functional of inventions into close proximity to the most favoured of romantic ruins. The bridge was hung from supports built as towers and closely modelled on those of the castle. Telford had already used similar medieval towers, complete with cross arrow slits, at his iron bridge at Craigellachie on the river Spey; there this medievalism seemed no doubt to accord with the Highland country-side: at Conway far more elaborate precautions were taken to bring the new work into accord with the old, but the contiguity defeats the attempt.[2] The ruined towers are still impressive defence works: those supporting the cables are an unhappy masquerade. The problem, one that was to have many successors, was deeply felt but was not solved.

Two other of Telford's works formed happier landscape features, the aqueducts at Pont-y-Cysyllte and at Chirk on the Ellesmere canal. In both iron was largely employed and the long row of arches, with their memories of the distant aqueducts of a Claude painting, were much admired. Sir Walter Scott found the Pont-y-Cysyllte aqueduct 'the most impressive work of art he had ever seen'.[3]

[1] From lines by Southey inscribed on Telford's memorial on the Caledonian canal.

[2] Telford opened his biography, *The Life of Thomas Telford, written by himself* (ed. J. Rickman, 1838), with an account of the border castles largely taken from Scott's *Antiquities*: for Conway see p. 233. For early discussions of the scheme see *Impartial Thoughts on the Intended Bridges over the Menai and the Conway* by A Country Gentleman (1802); and for an engraving by F. J. Havell, *Atlas to the Life of Thomas Telford* (1838), pl. 78; see also L. T. C. Rolt, *Thomas Telford* (1958).

[3] Quoted A. Gibb, op. cit. 35: the aqueduct appears in the background of Samuel Lane's portrait of Telford (Institute of Civil Engineers: R.A. 1822).

It was the age of canals, and not only the aqueducts carrying them over intervening valleys but also the smaller round arched bridges across them became a new and often lovely feature of the country-side.

Such were the triumphs of the new techniques. The Regency was also associated with more domestic matters. In interior decoration and furnishings it was the early years of Carlton House, with Henry Holland as designer, that set the tone, not the later unrestrained fancies of Nash. Holland had borrowed the classic designs of Percier and Fontaine, with their winged victories, sphinxes, and emblems of ancient virtues, motifs echoing the new vigour and sobriety of revolutionary France, and, working in dark woods, mainly rosewood or mahogany, with much inlay and brass mounting, had used them for his royal and profligate master.[1] A new emphasis, that of archaeological exactitude, was stressed by Thomas Hope in his *Household Furniture and Interior Decoration* (1807), the elaborate publication of a wealthy and learned connoisseur, which somewhat unexpectedly proved to have considerable influence. For his Adam house in Portland Place, Hope had carried out, largely from his own designs, a solid, careful selection of neo-Greek furniture (Fig. 3), with here and there an essay in the Egyptian, Indian, or Chinese, though Hope warned the furniture maker to be cautious in using these Eastern and rarely suitable models. What he sought to execute he describes in a rhetorical passage of his preface, namely

that prodigious variety of details and embellishments, which, under the various characters and combinations of imitative and of symbolic personages, of attributes and of insignia of gods and of men, of instruments and of trophies, of terms, caryatides, griffins, chimaeras, scenic masks, sacrificial implements, civil and military emblems, etc. once gave to every piece of Grecian and Roman furniture so much grace, variety, movement, expression and physiognomy; so much wherewithal to afford to the eye and the mind the most luxuriant and uncloying treat.

Some of the furniture that survives is less portentous than the

[1] M. Jourdain and F. Rose, *English Furniture: 1750–1830* (1953); Lord Gerald Wellesley, 'Regency Furniture', *Burl. Mag.* lxx (1937), 233.

description suggests: two tables in the Ashmolean Museum, from the drawing-room at Deepdene, his house at Dorking, are heavy but not unduly elaborated, and a set of rosewood chairs in the same museum are both stylish and elegant.[1] The book, however, received a considerable trouncing from Sydney Smith in the *Quarterly Review*.[2] 'We do not know that we have ever met with anything,

FIG. 3. *Chair and table end: Thomas Hope*

out of a newspaper, so exquisitely bombastic, pedantic, and trashy, as the composition of this volume.' Everyone, however, did not share this contempt. Hope was recognized as an authority, and the hard hitting in vogue seems sometimes to have left hardly a dint. In the genesis of Regency furniture his book is a turning-point. We have many accounts of Regency décor:

The room is admirably painted to represent verde antique columns of the Ionic order, upon a ground of Sienna marble. The chimney-piece, of white marble, is handsomely wrought; and the stove, of a new and elegant form, in bronze, with appropriate Grecian ornaments, together with the rich gilt fender, screens, etc. are strikingly beautiful.... The curtains, ottomans, chaises longues, and chairs, are covered with a

[1] For other examples from Deepdene, formerly in the possession of Mr. E. Knoblock, Beach House, Worthing, see *C.L.* xlix (1921), 126, and R. W. Symonds in *Connoisseur*, cxl (1957), 226. See also J. P. Neale, *An Account of the Deep-dene in Surrey, the seat of T. Hope, Esq.* (1826). [2] xix (1807), 478.

gold and silver India chintz. . . . Tables, with books and drawings, complete the air of polished luxury and refined enjoyment, which seems to reign in this classical apartment.

So Mrs. Hofland,[1] with her fluent pen, rambles on about White-Knights, the Berkshire home of the marquess of Blandford.

Such was a room of the nobility. Perhaps the most celebrated of smaller Regency interiors was that of the poet Samuel Rogers's house in St. James's, with bow windows looking out over the Green Park. It was the meeting place of all the intelligentsia of London, the most exclusive and artistically most influential salon of the first half of the nineteenth century. Endowed with considerable private means from his father's bank, in which he was a partner, Rogers represented the new self-made class in London society, but at the same time achieved recognition as the arbiter of refinement. His biting witticisms, his generous acts, his small, slightly wizened face are everywhere in the literary memoirs of the time. His house was built in 1803: 'the chimney-pieces', Macaulay wrote in 1831, 'are carved by Flaxman into the most beautiful Grecian forms. The bookcase is painted by Stothard, in his very best manner, with groups from Chaucer, Shakespeare, and Boccaccio.'[2] The sideboard in the dining room had been carved by Chantrey while still an unknown journeyman worker. Everywhere were Greek vases, and round the staircase ran a copy of part of the Parthenon frieze.

The characteristics of the opening years of the century, at their most balanced, are summed up in the two editions of Thomas Sheraton's *Cabinet-Maker and Upholsterers Drawing Book*. First brought out in quarto parts, 1791–4, he republished it with additional plates in 1802, and in the posthumous *Designs for Household*

---

[1] *A Descriptive Account of the Mansion and Gardens of White-Knights*, by Mrs. Hofland, illustrated with twenty-three engravings, from pictures [four of which are in the Northwick Park collection] taken on the spot by T. C. Hofland (1819). Barbara Hofland was a well-known novelist; her husband, the landscape painter, took a prominent part in founding the Society of British Artists. Worries over the publication of the White-Knights volume for which he found himself left financially responsible are said (F. M. O'Donoghue in *D.N.B.*) permanently to have affected his health.

[2] P. W. Clayden, *Rogers and his Contemporaries* (1889), ii. 63, and *Early Life of Samuel Rogers* (1887), 448.

Furniture published in 1812. Sheraton himself, born in Stockton-on-Tees in 1751, only came to London in 1790, where he practised as a cabinet maker for six years and then concentrated on publishing and running a small stationer's shop. Poor, pious, a Baptist preacher and pamphleteer, 'looking like a worn out Methodist minister with a threadbare black coat',[1] his influence was through his drawings not through his own work or business. To Sheraton the designs of his great predecessor Chippendale seemed 'wholly antiquated and laid aside, though possessed of great merit, according to the times in which they were executed'. If the 'Ribband-back chairs' of the first plate of Chippendale's *Cabinet-Makers Director* (1754) are compared with Sheraton's examples of Drawing-Room Chairs and Sofas, the remark can be interpreted.[2] The light elegance and curving lines of Chippendale's backs, the

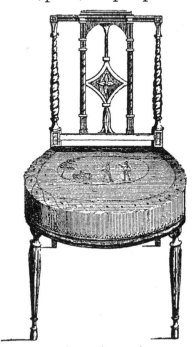

FIG. 4. *Chair: Thomas Sheraton*

bowed out legs, the curved feet, are replaced by legs fluted or slightly rounded but rising from a narrow base, now sometimes supported on the newly invented castor, and continuing in straight lines to the bend of the arm rest. The back is mainly a pattern of strong vertical lines: it is the difference between French flamboyant and English perpendicular (Fig. 4). The sofa itself was a new form of seat,[3] and one that Sheraton's designs did much to popularize. He was in fact singularly inventive and his knee hole or kidney tables, his writing desks, sideboards, and dressing tables brought

[1] *Memoirs of Adam Black*, ed. A. Nicolson (1885), 32.

[2] Both series of plates are given in J. M. Bell and A. Hayden, *Chippendale, Sheraton and Hepplewhite Furniture Designs* (1938).

[3] 'To lounge away the time as they could with sofas, and chit-chat, and Quarterly Reviews.' Jane Austen, *Mansfield Park*, chap. x.

new standards of elegant convenience to the English upper classes, standards and designs many of them based on patterns in vogue in the last ill-fated days of the French court. The *Designs* of 1812 show a remarkable change. Hope has come between: the sofas are replaced by Grecian couches. Rams, lions, griffins, and coiling snakes appear upon chair backs and terminals which have now lost their vertical emphasis in favour of the flat Regency curve; side tables have Greek key patterns and herms as legs. The Grecian has for the moment conquered.

In the field of the applied arts, England had a recognized position in ceramics. Of the famous firms of the eighteenth century, that of the Wedgwoods continued to produce the various types of earthenware that had made them famous, and many of the most charming Regency classical designs still came from Etruria, or were directly due to their influence. The painting of English views, so notably employed in their great dinner service for Catherine II (1774),[1] was also a pleasant feature of some of their table services. The new 'bone-china', a soft paste containing calcinated bone, was used by them, though the perfecting of this technique was carried out in the Spode factory, perhaps the most representative of all Regency producers, whose richly painted porcelain, often with heavy gilt borders, was adapted to the splendours of the décor in which it was to be used.[2] Derby under William Duesbury III (for these were great trade dynasties) and Robert Bloor retained a high level, and was particularly noted for its elaborately painted vases and 'biscuit' figures. Rockingham was another centre of Regency fashions. At Worcester Messrs. Flight and Barr (with the Chamberlains as a competing firm) carried on the traditions of Dr. Wall, and their work was still notable for the richness of its colour and the skill of its painted scenes. Coalport came in the thirties to be noted for its applied decoration: flowers in high relief mingle with those painted on the surface, and mark

[1] See G. C. Williamson, *The Imperial Russian Dinner Service* (1909); W. B. Honey, *Wedgwood Ware* (1948), contains a bibliography.

[2] L. Jewitt, *The Ceramic Art of Great Britain*, ii (1878), is still the fullest account of nineteenth-century products: for a more recent summary see G. Bemrose, *Nineteenth-Century English Pottery and Porcelain* (1952); F. A. Barrett, *Worcester Porcelain* (1953); Compton Mackenzie, *The House of Coalport, 1750–1950* (1951).

the beginning of an ingenuity, a delight in technical skill, that was to run to its full excess in the exhibits of 1851. In Staffordshire the firm of the Mintons was producing porcelain tea sets with elegant spray designs, and in 1836 Herbert Minton began the experiments with encaustic tiles that were to be the especial fame of his business. Meanwhile popular demand was being met by C. J. Mason's Ironstone China, 'relatively cheap and well-nigh indestructible',[1] and it is in remaining pieces of the huge Ironstone dinner services that Regency china is still sometimes found in use. As a whole, though some fine pastes were employed, the general standard of design had declined from that of the eighteenth century. There was less originality; foreign models were closely copied, particularly those of Sèvres. New vigour came in the later thirties and the forties, but it was applied with a virtuosity which was too much at variance with the character of the medium.

It is in the work of the silversmiths that the whims and stylish extravagances of the time are most attractively registered, and here one name stands out pre-eminently, that of Paul Storr. Born in 1771 and apprenticed to a Swede, Andrew Fogelberg, working in Soho, he was trained in the Adam style, but his earliest independent work showed a liking for simple, solider forms.[2] Decisive in this trend in Storr's work was the publication in 1806 of C. H. Tatham's *Designs for Ornamental Plate*, from which Storr's later work borrows freely. 'Massiveness', wrote Tatham, 'is the principal characteristic of good Plate. . . . Good Chasing may be considered a branch of Sculpture . . . it is constant application to Modelling alone that will form a good Chaser.' It was such application that made Storr a craftsman who could render the figures of Flaxman or the elder Theed with a certainty which gives to a piece 21 inches high, such as the Nymphs and Faun candelabra at Windsor, the vitality of a major work, and within the 2 ft. 10 in. of the Anglesey trophy can produce a real sense of monumentality. It is in the royal plate that the greatest collection of his work is still

[1] G. Bemrose, op. cit. 18.

[2] See N. M. Penzer, *Paul Storr* (1954), where the pieces mentioned are all illustrated. For a general summary see G. Taylor, *Silver* (1956), 185; *Regency Domestic Silver* and *Royal Plate* (V. and A. Picture Books, 33 and 37; 1952 and 1954); Charles Oman in *C.L.* cxv (1954), 945.

to be found. The firm of Messrs. Rundell, Bridge and Rundell, of which Storr was for a time a partner, combined business acumen in Philip Rundell with adroit address in John Bridge, and with Storr as their chief craftsman they were the main recipients of royal patronage, and the centre of fashion in an age when there was much demand for lavish table services. Storr retired in 1838 and died in 1844. Many of his later pieces are more elaborately rocaille than anything in his earlier work, and far removed in their deep undercutting, shell patterns, and accumulation of detail from the Theocritus cup (1812–13) at Windsor (Pl. 36 *b*) or the Wellington cup (1817–18) with its enchanting dream idyll of the butterfly, works where Flaxman's reticent influence was to the fore. The Goodwood cup (1829–30), with its lions' masks and chariot race, may serve as an example of a racing trophy, for which silversmiths were now being much employed, and also, with its palmettes and acanthus, as a typical example of the neo-classic epoch.

IV

TURNER AND CONSTABLE

'THEN we all fell to talking about Turner', wrote T. S. Cooper,[1] recalling a dinner at the Athenaeum, 'and of his consummate knowledge of effect and colour, which, as we said, must stamp him amongst all artists and connoisseurs as one of the most original and finest painters that has lived in any age.' Maclise and Charles Turner, the engraver, were of the party: this was the estimate of brother artists and contemporaries, men who remembered the short, paunched, generally unkempt figure, preserved for us in many sketches, half truth, half caricature. He had a few friends, Fawkes of Farnley Hall, William Wells and his daughter Clara, George Jones, Munro of Novar, with whom he could relax into affectionate intimacy: he shared with Chantrey a liking for bluff humour and there was a bawdy streak that shocked Ruskin into the destruction of some of his franker drawings:[2] but at the Ruskin's dinner table at Denmark Hill, at Petworth, or talking to Lady Eastlake he could be unaffectedly at ease and good company. Much of his life, however, was closely hidden: by a mistress, Sarah Danby, widow of a musician, he had a son and two daughters, and a Danby niece, Hannah, was the grim, slatternly, and loyal caretaker of his house in Queen Anne Street. At Ramsgate and later at Chelsea, Mrs. Booth looked after him, and he often passed as her husband. Mean and generous, loyal and secretive, his character was full of contradictions, and his vast, transforming imagination needed a certain animal squalor as part of its diet. Music and poetry meant much to him, he seems to have read widely and indiscriminately, but we have to disentangle his sources from the paintings themselves and the notes or verses he appended to them.[3] Few artists have revealed so little about

[1] *My Life* (1891), 220.

[2] W. M. Rossetti, *Rossetti Papers, 1862–70* (1903), 383.

[3] For a discussion of the seamier side of Turner's life see Bernard Falk, *Turner the Painter: His Hidden Life* (1938), where there is some new material in a book that aims

themselves. 'He possesses', it was said of his lectures at the Academy, 'few of the communicative qualities',[1] and in fact in his tenure of the Royal Academy Chair of Perspective there is a long history of notes left in hackney coaches, sudden postponements, muddled statements, 'a vulgarity of pronunciation astonishing in an artist of his rank and respectability',[2] and finally a prolonged discontinuance when, as Sir Martin Archer Shee told the Parliamentary Committee, 'The Academy have forborne to press on the Professor of Perspective the execution of his duties ... from a delicacy which cannot perhaps be perfectly justified, but which arises from the respect they feel for one of the greatest artists of the age in which we live.'[3]

Turner,[4] it has been already stated, was elected a full member of the Academy in 1802, when he was twenty-seven years old. From contemporary newspaper comment it is clear that he was already recognized as introducing a new approach in landscape and in marine painting:[5] a water-colour such as *Pembroke Castle, Thunderstorm approaching*, exhibited in 1801 (Pl. 11 *a*), has for its subject one of the Welsh castles that were already firmly fixed as essential items in the romantic repertory, but the wild sky has a luminosity that no other painter could have given it, and the whole scene is broadly painted, with a unity of atmosphere, of the particular moment, which is far beyond any mere topographical account. It is romantic too in its melodramatic quality, the conjunction of

at being 'a frank and revealing biography'. For Turner's appearance see Cosmo Monkhouse, 'Some Portraits of J. M. W. Turner', *Scribner's Mag.* xx (1869), 89; for his musical and literary tastes two important articles by A. L. Livermore in *Music and Letters*, xxxviii (1957), 170, and *The Connoisseur Year Book* (1957), 78.

[1] *Library of Fine Art*, i (1831), 239.

[2] *New Monthly Mag.* (1816), 2.

[3] See D. S. MacColl, 'Turner's Lectures at the Academy', *Burl. Mag.* xii (1907), 343, and W. F. Whitley, *Burl. Mag.* xxii (1913), 202 and 255.

[4] The bibliography of Turner is a large one: there is a select list in A. J. Finberg, *Life of J. M. W. Turner* (1939), which is the authoritative account of Turner's career, and which treats fully of the many problems connected with the first biography, W. Thornbury's inaccurate and rambling *Life of J. M. W. Turner*, 2 vols. (1862). I am most grateful to Mrs. A. J. Finberg for information on various points.

[5] Josiah Boydell in 1801 (*Plan for the encouragement of the Arts*, 11) speaks of 'the daring and supernatural efforts of Turner', and couples him with 'the truly original genius of Fuzeli'.

ruin and storm and tossing sea, a melodrama here controlled by a passionate inquiry into the realities of light and reflection. The water is, however, less fully realized than the sky. Turner had already been experimenting with marine pieces in oil. In 1797 his *Fishermen coming ashore at sunset previous to a Gale*, a picture not now known, had been hailed by the critics as giving to the sea 'a transparency and undulation more perfect than is usually seen on canvas'.[1] Actually in these early sea pieces, the undulation is more surely captured than the transparency. In *Calais Pier* (1803) the water is still hard and brittle, as Sir George Beaumont rightly said 'like veins in a marble slab', but the boats really toss, the wind really blows, the small figures, vividly created by blots of colour, are really exposed to the risks of the elements. Two years later in *The Shipwreck* Turner has unleashed the full horror and fury of the waves, and is beginning to add a sense of their depth and fluidity to their restless movement (Pl. 46). Shipwreck was the most possessive nightmare of the time, one that we have replaced with horrors from and in the air. Sir John Graham Dalyell in his *Shipwrecks and Disasters at Sea* (Edinburgh, 1812) calculated that 'perhaps not less than 5000 natives of these islands perish yearly at sea'. Such themes of agony, so close to contemporary and personal fears, were apt subjects for the break with classical restraint and moderation. Géricault's *Raft of the Medusa* was to be one of the manifestations of romanticism in France,[2] but already, some years before, Turner was exploiting the fearful contemplation of disasters in the deep. His *Wreck of the Minotaur*[3] (1810) is an even more complex and alarming interpretation of humanity at the mercy of the elements, and later in his career, when his genius had evolved new forms of expression, the same tortured imaginings were present to him.

It was not only the sea: the mountains also roused in him a desire to render, even in the small compass of a water-colour sheet, some

[1] Anthony Pasquin in *Morning Post*, quoted W. T. Whitley, *Artists and their Friends in England 1700–1799*, ii (1928), 215.

[2] See B. Nicolson, '"The Raft" from the point of view of subject matter', *Burl. Mag.* xcvi (1954), 241.

[3] Now in the Gulbenkian Coll., formerly in that of the earl of Yarborough: for variants see *Preview*, x (City of York Art Gallery, 1957), 384.

of the immensity of nature. In 1802, in that break in the Napoleonic wars that meant so much to English contacts with Europe, Turner paid his first visit to the Continent. We can trace his journey down through France to Savoy, over the Col du Bonhomme to the Val d'Aosta, back by the St. Gothard. The notebooks are full of pencil sketches, sometimes two or three to a page, shorthand outline notes, but so precise in their selection that on the spot the position can be readily identified. Throughout his life Turner made these pencil jottings, topographically exact, here and there names written in his haphazard spelling.[1] He memorized sites in this way; then afterwards, sometimes many years afterwards, the imaginative vision matured; the pencil outlines became the basis of some study of sunlight or storm, of deeply experienced atmospheric conditions, which no notebook contained and which were in fact by his own admission a combination of various experiences, sometimes quite unconnected with the notebook that provided the basis for their setting.

It was in water-colour that Turner most frequently attempted his interpretation of the Alps. The muleteers cling in human insignificance to the narrow causeway between cloud and precipice across *The Devil's Bridge* (Pl. 40 *a*), and we share their awe of the surrounding vastness. In 1812 he painted in oils a work that used some of these mountain memories and transformed them into a visual image such as he had not yet created. This is the painting of *Hannibal crossing the Alps* (Pl. 39 *a*), a theme already treated in an oil painting by John Cozens, not now known but which showed the Carthaginians' first view of Italy, not Turner's violent scene of battle in the mountains. It was not, however, composed from Alpine memories only: one day at Farnley, Turner was enthralled by a thunderstorm sweeping across the moors. 'In two years', he exclaimed, 'you will see this again and call it Hannibal crossing the Alps.' It is a vivid account of a moment of crystallization, of the coming together of odd pieces of information, emotional reactions

[1] See A. J. Finberg, *Complete Inventory of the Drawings of the Turner Bequest*, 2 vols. (1909). For studies of Turner's sketches, see A. J. Finberg, *Turner's Sketches and Drawings* (1910) and *In Venice with Turner* (1930); T. Ashby, *Turner's Visions of Rome* (1925); T. S. R. Boase, 'English Artists in the Val d'Aosta', *Journ. W.C.I.* xix (1956), 283.

to tales of excitement, and super-sensitivity to transient natural phenomena. The Yorkshire thundercloud, split by a great silver radiance as the sun pierces through it, moves amid huge mountains whose presence is mysteriously felt though they are hardly seen, immeasurably dwarfing the struggling figures in the foreground, the man crushed by a rock, the mountaineers quarrelling over two fainting women, and even the elephant waving its trunk behind the soldiers. Recently cleaned, the *Hannibal* is a masterpiece of surprising intensity. Little more than a ray of light against dark clouds, it achieves by the simplest means an overpowering effect of luminous space. Turner clearly regarded it with pride and attached to it a long and incoherent quotation from *The Fallacies of Hope*, a poem of his own writing which probably never existed apart from the numerous verses he appended to the titles of his pictures. It is poor stuff, but two lines stand out with something of the obscure splendour of the painting itself:

> While the fierce archer of the downward year
> Stains Italy's blanched barriers with storms.

This strange, almost abstract work seems surprisingly to have presented no great difficulty to the connoisseurs of the time.

Meanwhile Turner was also exhibiting pictures painted in a more conventional manner, real 'Academy' pictures where Poussin and Claude were his chief models. In 1800 he showed, perhaps as befitting a newly elected Associate, *The Fifth Plague of Egypt*,[1] a solemn, dark landscape, carefully balanced, with a pyramid in the central distance. In 1801 his historical painting, *The Army of the Medes destroyed in the desert by a whirlwind, foretold by Jeremiah, chap. XV, ver. 32 and 33*, 'astounded the connoisseurs'. This is a fine Turneresque subject and seems to have, in its turn, foretold some of his later feats, for a contemporary critic describes it as showing 'the whole army buried in the sand with a single flourish of his brush';[2] but *The Army of the Medes* has long since disappeared;

---

[1] Now in the Herron Art Museum, Indianapolis: see *Cat. Turner in America* (Indianapolis, 1955). Actually, with characteristic inaccuracy of title, it is the Seventh Plague.

[2] Whitley, i. 20, and *The Reflector*, i (1810–11), 230: characteristically the reference is wrong and should be chap. xxv.

should it one day be found it may well be a key-piece in Turner's development. In 1803 he returned to the Plagues, the Tenth, another Poussinesque landscape. To the balanced, firm designs of his example, he was in some of his paintings adding a mellow light, a more pastoral tone. For the next ten years rivalry with Claude was apparent in many of his works, most triumphantly so in *Crossing the Brook* (1815: Pl. 42 *a*), a classical composition in the fashionable taste, but with an atmospheric glow, a sense of summer sun, that never fails of its effect. It has hardly any subject—a girl fords the stream followed by a dog carrying her basket, but they are mere foreground incidental notes—the river Tamar winds its way to the sea, spanned by the Gunnislake Bridge, a Claudian aqueduct. It is an actual spot, sketched originally with all Turner's accuracy, but now worked up into an idealized version, fed from many memories of art as well as nature.[1] It is perhaps the most complete and secure of all Turner's works, with the kind of final simplicity that belongs to Raphael.

The Shipwreck of 1805, besides its expression of romantic melo-drama and power of delineating waves, had marked another stage in Turner's career. Charles Turner, two years senior to the painter and apparently no relation, applied for the engraving rights, reproducing it in aquatint. He was already well known as an exponent of mezzotint, and his interest in *The Shipwreck* opened a new field to the painter. William Wells, of the Old Water-Colour Society, urged him to embark on a larger project, and in collaboration with Charles Turner the *Liber Studiorum* was undertaken in 1806. The long, at times quarrelsome story cannot be told here.[2] Turner himself, on most of the plates, executed the preliminary etching and at times intervened in the later process also. By 1823 when the scheme was virtually abandoned, twenty-one plates had been published and another twenty were well advanced. It had not been unprofitable, but the artist was turning to other things. Since 1814 he had been producing water-colours for line engraving in W. B. Cooke's *Southern England*, *Views in Sussex*, and (from

[1] A. Cornwell-Clyne in *C.L.* cxvii (1955), 974.
[2] See A. J. Finberg, *The History of Turner's Liber Studiorum* (1924), for a very full account.

1823) *Rivers of England*. Here he had learned a mastery over the new process of steel engraving as great as that over mezzotint and seemed attracted by the more lasting and productive method. Certainly in the plates supervised by him, of which the vignettes to Roger's *Italy* (1830) are amongst the finest, steel engraving reached standards of excellence that it was rarely to reach again. They have a brilliance which is a parallel to the light in the oil paintings of his middle period. The mezzotints of the *Liber*, divided into Pastoral, Marine, Mountainous, Historical, and Architectural, reflect in their deeper richness the romanticism of the earlier years.

For much of Turner's work there was now an admiring public, but there was one dissenting voice, the powerful one of Sir George Beaumont, who had for some years professed a poor opinion of it. *Crossing the Brook* seemed to Sir George 'all of pea green insipidity'.[1] The splendour of imagination constantly breaking through in Turner's work, transforming even his most academic designs, appeared outrageous to the sensitive but traditional patron, and it is clear from Sir George's statements that he felt the denunciation of Turner to be a pious duty. The artist's friends rallied to him: the portrait painters Lawrence, Thomas Phillips, Owen (all of them fine colourists) were strongly for him. He had also secured a disciple. Augustus Wall Callcott was only four years Turner's junior; his first intention had been to devote himself to music, where his brother was already a well-known figure, and he obtained a place in the choir of Westminster abbey. Turning, however, to landscape painting he had a rapid success and by 1810 was a full member of the Academy. The silvers and grey-greens of his large, placid landscapes in the Dutch manner have turned leaden and dull; his figures are heavy and often faulty in placing.[2] It is difficult today to understand the popularity that he enjoyed. Callcott's admiration for Turner was profound and belligerent and it is probably to him that is due the authorship of the catalogue raisonné of the British Institution which keenly attacked the pretensions of the leading patrons such as Beaumont,

---

[1] Farington, *Diary*, v. 5.

[2] See J. Dafforne, *Pictures by Sir A. W. Callcott* (n.d.); a collection of his Italian and English landscapes lithographed by T. C. Dibdin was published in 1847.

Holwell Carr and Payne Knight, ridiculing their 'determination to deprive the first genius of the day of encouragement'. The catalogue caused much talk: Sir George thought of prosecuting, but nothing was done.

Other patrons did not share Sir George's views: Sir John Leicester (later Lord de Tabley), 'the munificent patron and encourager of native genius',[1] had early been buying Turner's works, and at the sale following his death in 1827 Turner bought several of them back, for by then he was already hoarding many of his own paintings, stacked inadequately in his gallery in Queen Anne Street. More lasting and closer were Turner's relations with the earl of Egremont. At Petworth, where the pleasant and cultivated 'Mrs. Wyndham' did not enjoy married status till a late stage of her union with the earl, there was an informal and slightly eccentric régime with which he seems to have felt at ease. It was there in the thirties that his art was to find one of its most complete moments of release, but from his first visit in 1809 there is a view of the house from across the lake, whose academy title (exhibited 1810) includes the best of both worlds, *Petworth, Sussex, the seat of the Earl of Egremont: Dewy Morning* (Pl. 44 a). It is light seen through mist: the trees are dark masses whose edges dissolve into the surrounding atmosphere. A critic found that 'manifestly his design is to express the peculiar hue and pellucidness of objects seen through a medium of air'.[2] Obviously the writer was at a loss for the right phrases to describe this new rendering. Turner's preoccupation from now on was with the relation of shapes to light and the creation of distance by gradation of tone; there was a constant avoidance of any linear treatment that was clear cut. His journey, with whatever temporary diversions, was to be towards a blinding light in which no exactly defined forms could have appropriate existence.

In 1813 Turner exhibited two very dissimilar paintings, *Frosty Morning* and *The Deluge*. The former has always been one of his most generally popular works. In its analysis of the road surface and in its flat, open country-side, where the thin tree and the cart

---

[1] Letter from Raeburn, quoted Whitley, ii. 133.
[2] *Bell's Weekly Messenger* (1810), 157.

give the centralizing feature, it recalls some of Crome's designs; but the clear, cold sky and the shimmer of frost on the ground, the real subject of the picture, are Turner's own. Much of the sparkle that amazed critics at the time has gone out of it, probably beyond the skill of even the most judicious cleaning, but it still remains a masterpiece of the open air. 'It is', wrote John Constable to Archdeacon Fisher, 'a picture of pictures'.[1] The simple, naturalistic group is curiously at variance with the other work of the same year, *The Deluge* (Pl. 38 *b*). This somewhat turgid piece with its sombre colours and its contorted, elongated figures belongs to a quite different sphere of the imagination, but one that had much contemporary popularity. Three years later John Martin's *Joshua staying the Sun and Moon* was to arrest public attention and create a new vogue for the sublime and the terrible. It was a vein Turner had already been exploiting and was never entirely to desert, but Martin, and Danby who was to rival him in the twenties, provided an easier approach to the vast and awe-inspiring, expressing it in terms easily understood by everyone and thus more surely purveying what was wanted at the time and for which later ages easily found substitutes. Turner was never at his best in such subjects, disturbed perhaps by the popular demand for them, but painting them answered some need, provided some release, for himself. His creative ferment could leave nothing untried, and his long career requires constant surveys of the surrounding scene.

Born in 1789 in Northumberland, in a farm cottage in Haydon Bridge, John Martin[2] came to London in 1806 as an apprentice to a glass painter: the contrasted enamelled colours of this technique remained with him through all his career, and in the large canvases for which he became famous he never mastered the richness and

---

[1] R. B. Beckett, *John Constable and the Fishers* (1952), 26.

[2] M. L. Pendred, *John Martin, Painter: His Life and Times* (1923); T. Balston, *John Martin: His Life and Works* (1947). Martin was preceded in his 'scenes of magnificence and terror' by J. M. Gandy, Soane's assistant, whose large water-colour of *Pandemonium or Part of the High Capital of Satan* (R.I.B.A.) was in the R.A. of 1805; see J. Summerson in *Arch. Rev.* lxxxix (1941), 89; Papworth also painted water-colours of this type, exhibiting the *Hall of Hela, the regions of Eternal Punishment* (untraced) in R.A. 1807; W. J. Papworth, *J. B. Papworth* (1879), 29.

fluidity of oil painting. The colours are opaque; the darks very black; the lighter parts painted in vivid reds and green; the handling is dry and tight; he could give little differentiation of texture and his treatment of water is always the merest convention: but these faults, or at least some of them, facilitated the translation of his paintings into engravings, many of which he carried out himself. It is through these engravings that Martin's work can best be appreciated today. Many of his paintings, despite their fame and size, have disappeared; some have blackened and decayed so as to be mere shadows; with renewed interest in him, several have recently come to light again and been successfully cleaned, but we still at first hand have only a very partial knowledge of the great pieces which caused so much sensation when they were first exhibited. The work which first won him celebrity was his *Joshua*:[1] this was hung in the Royal Academy of 1816, but 'hidden', he complained, in the ante-room. It contains all the repertory which was to become typical of Martin's work: the rocky hills, the huge architecture, the lowering clouds, the sense of scale portentously rendered by the contrast with tiny figures. Scale Martin undoubtedly achieved. Proportion was his dominating interest. Of *The Deluge*,[2] which he regarded as one of his chief pictures, he wrote: 'The highest mountain in the Picture will be found to be 15,000 Ft., the next in height 10,000 Ft. and the middle-ground perpendicular rock 4,000 feet.' *The Bard* (Pl. 40 *b*), exhibited the year after *Joshua*, shows the same recipe: the hills rise beyond the immense castle; perched on a great black crag the small, gesticulating figure of the bard utters his curse on Edward's army winding through the defile far below; half-way up the hillside a baggage train, hardly visible, serves as another point of proportion. 'Grandeur and originality', 'the sublime', are the recurrent terms used of Martin: in the exhibition of the British Institution in 1821, his *Belshazzar's Feast*[3] had to be railed off from the crowds thronging to see it. He became Historical Landscape Painter to Prince Leopold and Princess Charlotte; later the Prince

[1] Freemasons' Hall, Aldwych, London: see T. Balston in *Burl. Mag.* xcvi (1954), 350.   [2] Known only in engravings.

[3] Coll. P. S. Martin, Esq.: several variants are known.

Consort commissioned a painting from him (*The Eve of the Deluge*); he was awarded the gold medal at the Brussels exhibition, and his former patron, Leopold, now king of the Belgians, made him a knight of the order of Leopold; Joseph Bonaparte, ex-king of Spain, invited him to dinner and gave him a pair of candlesticks that had belonged to Napoleon. He was praised, courted, and fashionable, and when his London popularity waned his pictures of *The Last Judgement*[1] toured round England with much admiration and were still touring some eighteen years after his death in 1854.

For a time the chief rival to Martin was the painter Francis Danby. He was an Irishman, who when twenty came to London in 1813, did the Welsh tour, so obligatory on aspiring artists, and duly painted a romantic sunset sketch of Conway castle (Pl. 11 *b*). After Wales Danby settled in Bristol and in 1820 exhibited in the Academy his *Upas Tree*,[2] the poisonous tree in a dark moonlit glen surrounded by mouldering bones. Then in the Academy of 1825 came *The Delivery of Israel out of Egypt* (Pl. 41). This with its crowded and minute figures, its sweep of rocky hills, its pillar of fire rending the clouds, was a direct challenge to Martin; and contemporary gossip said that the Academicians wanted a rival to Martin, who now always exhibited at the British Institution. Whatever was the truth of this, Danby's painting in 1826, *The Opening of the Sixth Seal*, a great bombastic display of lightning and heaving rocks, now blackened into dull insignificance, was even more of the Martin type. It was bought by Beckford and it is now in the National Gallery in Dublin.

These apocalyptic visions are, however, only an episode in Danby's art. He comes in much of his work nearer to the pastoral school, where mourning nymphs pose in golden landscapes or weep in bosky shades. Made an A.R.A. in 1826, he came up for election as R.A. in 1829 and was defeated by Constable by one vote. Constable had had long to wait: already *The Haywain*, exhibited in Paris in 1826, had made him an international figure, but the 'imagination' of Danby had a greater contemporary appeal

[1] Two are in the coll. of Mrs. Robert Frank, the third in the Tate.
[2] In the Sheepshanks Coll. in the V. and A., in a sad state of deterioration.

than Constable's inspired power of observation; they had for some years been recognized as opposites:

> The awful pause, till wrath awake,
> And God arise the world to shake.
> Thése, these are themes, that may proclaim,
> So DANBY finds, an artist's fame.
> Learn this, ye painters of dead stumps,
> Old barges, and canals, and pumps . . . [1]

It was, however, no controversy between imagination and nature that was to interrupt Danby's career. Some time between 1829 and 1832 he left England and settled in Geneva: the reason in Victorian writers such as the Redgraves was only hinted at; 'domestic difficulties', 'moral obliquity'. Researches in the Geneva records have now pieced together the story; Danby was living there with his mistress, Helen Evans, and ten children, three hers, seven by his wife. As the children were with him, it is likely that his wife had deserted him, possibly owing to unfaithfulness; after Danby's death in 1861, she married the painter Paul Falconer Poole, and as they were both elderly, though Poole was about sixteen years younger than Danby, it is reasonable to think there had been some previous romance. Danby had befriended Poole, and the latter disappeared from London, going to Southampton, about the same time as Danby went to Geneva. 'I know', Redgrave wrote much later, 'they must have looked on each other with bitter feelings.'[2]

Whatever the exact story, there was enough to prejudice Danby's chances of academic rank: he returned, it is true, to England and attempted in *The Deluge* (1840)[3] to resume Martin's manner: but it was the sunset landscapes or seascapes, with their flushed clouds, which occupied his later years, 'solemn and beautiful works'

---

[1] Quoted, from *Rhymes Latin and English* (1826), by John Eagles, by G. Grigson in *The Harp of Aeolus* (1947), 69; see also H. W. Haüsermann, 'Francis Danby at Geneva', *Burl. Mag.* xci (1949), 227. Danby seems to have been unconnected with the Danbys of Turner's ménage, but the Danby scandal must have made Turner all the more secretive about a private life that fell short of Academy standards.

[2] F. M. Redgrave, *Richard Redgrave* (1891), 251.

[3] Coll. Miss G. Herbert, Abergavenny: study in the Tate.

as they seemed to Ford Madox Brown looking back on them in 1888.[1] Curiously enough the concluding piece of nineteenth-century imaginative landscape was the work of Poole, *The Vision of Ezekiel*, painted in the 1870's, a strange and powerful echo of the awe of the mountains that had haunted the earlier years of the century (Pl. 38 *a*).

Apart from the purveyors of the awe-inspiring, there existed a school of landscape painters that looked to Gainsborough and the Dutch masters, Ruisdael and Hobbema, as the great exemplars. In Norwich John Crome had established an important local school, but in his lifetime and for some long period after it his paintings were little known, despite thirteen works exhibited at the Royal Academy between 1806 and 1818, except in his native Norwich. In his *Boulevard des Italiens* (Pl. 24 *a*), the product of his one visit to the Continent in 1814, with its lively figures, its booth in the corner with piled-up paintings in their gilt frames, its line of sway-ing trees between the houses, he showed that a populated street scene was as firmly and imaginatively within his range as his native lonely spaces; but it was to them that he always returned and he remained faithful to the open skies and the dark massed heath of East Anglia. Space, *plein air*, was his subject. His *Poringland Oak* is the climax of a long tradition of foliage painting, handed down to him from Gainsborough and the Dutch masters; its spatial relation to the sky beyond is something of his own. The long ridge of *Mousehold Heath* has little sense of the texture of the earth's carpet or of the planes of its composition; to our eyes, taught by Constable, the Impressionists, Cézanne, it is a somewhat drab, formless work, but it deals with immensity and there is poetic alchemy in it; it stands with Hardy's 'Egdon' as the final distillation of English waste land.

Of the younger men working with him James Stark (1794–1859) is the most distinct personality, whose Norfolk scenes are painted with great competence, and are on the whole singularly well pre-served, clear and fresh in their colouring; but he was essentially

---

[1] *Mag. of Art*, xi (1888), 124. 'His latest years/Divulged those immaterial ecstacies', wrote E. H. W. Meyerstein in a poem, 'At Danby's Grave', *Oxford Mag.* (1952), 288, that is a significant indication of the revived interest in his paintings.

a pupil and his work lacks any genuine individual impulse. George Vincent (1796–*c.* 1836) is a much more interesting artist, and also a much more uneven one, for he fell on troubled days and some of his later painting is weak and slipshod. There is, however, a body of painting of the Norwich school, much of it as yet insecurely attributed, which contains some anonymous paintings of considerable merit and the sum of which is greater than that of the known followers of Crome.[1]

In the metropolis itself, Callcott in the later twenties and thirties was held by many to 'surpass all others in his branch'.[2] Lines of carriages waited at his door for the visitors to his studio when his pictures were shown there on the eve of the Academy. In 1827 he had married Maria Graham, a widow, already well known as a literary figure.[3] Charles Eastlake, the future President of the Royal Academy, was a friend and had, in 1820, drawn the illustrations, with considerable charm, for her *Three Months Passed in the Mountains East of Rome*, a study of the romantic subject of brigandage. Always interested in pictures, she now took to writing on art, particularly after their honeymoon tour through Germany and Italy—Botticelli she noted was very like Stothard. But her lasting fame came through a quite different type of work, her *Little Arthur's History of England* (1835). Within a few years of her second marriage she became a bed-ridden invalid, but her room became one of the great meeting places for artistic society in London. Richard Redgrave wrote a famous account of it: 'the long summer evenings . . . the little bed on which the lady sat . . . propped up with pillows covered with rich draperies . . . the old furniture of the quaint, picturesque, irregular room'.[4] Like the Eastlakes later, it was as a couple that the Callcotts played so great a part in the art life of their day, and when she died in 1842 he survived her for only three years. In 1837, the year of her accession, Queen Victoria

---

[1] W. F. Dickes, *The Norwich School of Painting* (1905).

[2] Whitley, ii. 235. See obituary notice, *Art Union* (1845), 15.

[3] See R. B. Gotch, *Maria, Lady Callcott* (1937).

[4] *A Century of British Painters*, ed. Ruthven Todd (1947), 375; she once surprised her visitors by the remark, 'I should rather be called a bitch than a female', an almost Regency comment on the new Victorian cult of the ladylike; A. T. Story, *Life of John Linnell* (1892), i. 272.

conferred knighthood on him, a tribute to his character, social standing, and pleasant, carefully modulated art.

John Constable, born in 1776, was three years senior to Callcott, but, whereas the latter became an Associate of the Academy in 1806, a full member in 1810, Constable had to wait for his Associateship till 1819, his R.A. till 1829. Too much can be made of the lack of appreciation of Constable in his own time. The critic of the *Morning Chronicle* waged a long and destructive war against him;[1] he saw academic honours pass him by in favour of much lesser men; but other journals were, if not more discerning (for the *Morning Chronicle* knew what it attacked), more sympathetic; Paris extended him a recognition rarely given to English painters. *The Cornfield*, 'more than usually studied' as the painter said of it,[2] a somewhat timid painting on which recent criticisms of his work had left their trace, was presented to and readily received by the National Gallery within a few months of his death; and though it was not till the close of the century that his repute was firmly established, there was a considerable traffic in forgeries of his work in the 1850's. Today he is to many the greatest and best loved of English painters, and sometimes is acclaimed as the father of Impressionism, perhaps too readily, for the highlights on his shadows, the splitting of colours into contrasted points, the tendency to work towards a higher key, taught something to Delacroix, may have influenced Rousseau and Troyon, but never led the artist himself near to the prismatic analysis of the Impressionists: 'the power of Chiaro Oscuro', as he constantly says in his letters, was one of his main preoccupations and this modelling by light and shade, of which to him Rembrandt's *Mill* was the great example,[3] is far from the reflecting surfaces of Monet and Pissarro.

[1] Whitley, ii. 194.

[2] R. B. Beckett, *John Constable and the Fishers* (1952), 235. C. R. Leslie's *Life of John Constable* (1st ed. 1843; revised 1845; ed. revised and enlarged by A. Shirley 1937; ed. by Jonathan Mayne 1951; references are to Shirley's ed.) is the basic authority. See also C. J. Holmes, *Constable and his Influence on Landscape Painting* (1902); Lord Windsor, *John Constable, R.A.* (1903); P. Leslie, *Letters from John Constable to C. R. Leslie* (1932); S. J. Key, *Constable* (1948).

[3] Third Lecture: Leslie, op. cit. 315; on all this question see Douglas Cooper, *The Courtauld Collection* (1954), 44.

He has often been compared with Wordsworth.[1] They had met in 1807 and at Sir George Beaumont's house there was always much talk of the poet and reading from his poems. Constable himself quotes them constantly. They shared the belief that the simple and commonplace were often 'more consonant to nature, that is, to eternal nature and the great moving spirit of things'.[2] Constable's aim was to understand a landscape by constant study and by reproducing it in all its changing aspects. He is one of the most dedicated of painters. It was his naturalism that was at the time romantic and revolutionary. 'Our own Glover', wrote Henry Matthews in *The Diary of an Invalid* (1820), 'had, perhaps, made the greatest possible exertions to surmount the difficulty, and give with fidelity the real colours of nature; but I believe the beauty of his pictures is in an inverse ratio to their fidelity; and that nature must be stripped of her green livery, and dressed in the browns of the painters, or confined to her own autumnal tints in order to be transferred to canvas.' 'This is too bad', wrote John Constable to his friend Archdeacon John Fisher, 'and one would throw the book out of the window, but that its grossness is its own cure.'[3] It was the same argument that he had constantly with Sir George Beaumont, who remained faithful to his 'brown tree' and all the range of colours that it stood for.[4] Constable had first met Sir George when the latter came to visit his mother, whose house, Dunmow, was at Dedham. In Owen's great portrait of her, the tower of Dedham church, that was to be almost the symbol of the new world of landscape, can be seen through the window (Pl. 8). It was here in his native Essex, the county that, as he so often said, made him a painter, that this strapping young fellow of nineteen, the 'handsome miller', saw Sir George's Claude, the small *Hagar* with which he always travelled.[5] From then on he sought to combine the principles of design on which the great masters had

---

[1] See Sir Kenneth Clark, *Landscape into Art* (1949).

[2] Wordsworth writing to Christopher North, June 1802: *Wordsworth Poetry and Prose*, ed. W. M. Merchant (1955), 843. 'That unsophisticate species of painting which, affecting not the *beau ideal* of art, endeavours to depict nature, though studied upon scientific principles, in her genuine simplicity.' *Library of Fine Art*, i (1831), 177.

[3] R. B. Beckett, op. cit. 68.   [4] Leslie, op. cit. 155; cf. *P.P.* xv (1850), 16.

[5] Now in the National Gallery.

built up their pictures with a new closeness of observation of the component parts. One of his earliest paintings, from the year 1802 when he had made his way to London and was a pupil of the Academy School, the vertical view of Dedham Vale (V. and A.) is closely linked with the scheme of the *Hagar*, and at the end of his life he elaborated it into the much larger version now in the Scottish National Gallery. Larger and much higher in key; for between these two paintings Constable has traversed a wide gamut of colour. In his major pictures it is the clear fresh foliage of early summer that sets the colouring: only in one, *The Cenotaph* (1836), did he show 'autumnal tints' and that was possibly due to the memorial nature of the painting, showing as it did Reynolds's monument in the grounds of Coleorton and expressly intended as a commemoration both of Reynolds and of Sir George Beaumont, so that their names could appear 'once more in the catalogue, for the last time at the old place'.[1] The sketches in fact often lack the vernal greens of the finished pictures; they are personal transcripts of the artist's communing with nature, and something of his own sadness often goes into them. 'My mind has been so much depressed, that I have scarcely been able to do any one thing. . . . I am now, however, busy on a large landscape; I find it of use to myself, though little noticed by others. Still the trees and the clouds seem to ask me to do something like them.'[2] It was through the sketches that he reached, with infinite pains, the serenity of the finished picture. There was constant experiment and alteration and, for all his protests against the misleading nature of art, the final design is disciplined by the traditions of the Academy. It is perhaps characteristic that the painting which gave him most trouble, *Waterloo Bridge*, a theme explored in many versions and meditated over for some fifteen years,[3] is that in which the design is least conventional. It is a study in recession, the various distances being clearly marked along a diagonal from Whitehall steps in the left foreground to the dome of St. Paul's in the right background, and the problem is to balance the strongly marked house frontage on the left with the

[1] Leslie, op. cit. 341; 1836 was the last R.A. exhibition in Somerset House.
[2] Ibid. 312.
[3] Denys Sutton, 'Constable's Whitehall', *The Connoisseur*, cxxxvi (1956), 249.

distant though emphatic dome and chimneys on the right. Constable only reached his Academy version (1822: Pl. 47) by using a balustrade with an urn at either end as a centralizing feature in the foreground. It is also perhaps characteristic of this interest in picture making that when he lectured his favourite subject was an analysis of Titian's *Peter Martyr*, a painting which he only knew in an engraving: he could explore the conception, could 'sift that picture to the bottom',[1] but its 'breadth and tone' he had to accept at second hand.

The framework was a traditional one; it was on the details that Constable poured out his deep concentration. The Dutch artists whom he admired were 'a stay-at-home people' and to him that was the cause of their originality.[2] He himself never left England and his subjects are mainly concentrated in a few localities, his native Suffolk, Osmington, Dorset, and Salisbury (where he stayed with Archdeacon Fisher), Brighton, where he was taken by his wife's health, and Hampstead Heath, all localities he knew well and had studied repeatedly and at leisure:[3] the subjects of his works form a history of his affections. In a painting such as *The Hay Wain* (R.A. 1821) there is a lifetime's experience of the changing facets of this familiar scene, so that every ripple, every submerged piece of colouring, every point of clinging moisture or glinting stone were so firmly in mind that for his own content he could scrape them in with his palette-knife, almost modelling the paint, giving to the full-scale sketch an amazing sense of transitory phenomena, constantly shifting, so that the sketch seems alive, a chord of more than one vibration, compared to the steadied rendering of the Academy work. *The Hay Wain* measures $51\frac{1}{4}$ in. by 73 in. It takes its place in the series of 6 ft. canvases, which Constable regarded as the final test of his art. It was only two years ago that he had painted the first of them, which John Fisher purchased for 100 guineas, the climax of their friendship, this deep, permanent relationship which Constable seemed especially capable of inspiring amongst younger men, the archdeacon, John Dunthorne, both of

[1] Leslie, op. cit. 347, 379. He set the picture with models in the life class.
[2] Ibid. 399.
[3] Sir Kenneth Clark, *The Hay Wain* (Gallery Books No. 5, n.d.).

whom he lost in the same sad year, 1832 ('I am unfortunate in my friendships'), George Constable of Arundel, C. R. Leslie. With his usual asceticism about names, which at times makes identification of his pictures so difficult, Constable exhibited it as *A Scene on the River Stour*, but it almost at once came to be known as *The White Horse* (Pl. 44 *b*). 'We will call it if you please', wrote John Fisher, '*Life and the Pale Horse*.' It is a lovely, peaceful English summer afternoon, and it set, perhaps for the first time, a tradition for the rendering of English landscape, the sentiment of which is now a little staled by tasteless repetition, a staleness that the overcareful, slightly dry rendering cannot entirely overcome; for compared with *The Hay Wain*, *The White Horse* lacks a uniform atmospheric sense; the foliage is thinly drawn and too finely registered.

Between *The Hay Wain* and its successors, *The Leaping Horse* (V. and A.), *The Chain Pier, Brighton*, the various views of Salisbury cathedral from the meadows, came a further development. Constable had been studying very closely the nature of clouds, aided by the important work of Luke Howard, *The Climate of London*, which appeared between 1818 and 1820, containing his classification of types of clouds.[1] In 1821–2 'skying' as he called it was Constable's main preoccupation, and to these years belong the group of cloudscapes in which he mastered the accurate presentation of the weather. The place of truth in art is too endless a discussion to be given space here, but there can be no doubt that the findings of science have often been a great stimulus to painting, and that its authority has brought a deepened conviction and more complete achievement. The skies of Constable's later period, from which it has been said the coming weather can easily be foretold, fulfil the search for the movement, the transience of nature, which was always the theme of his sketches. On Brighton beach the squall is just breaking: umbrellas are up, the sudden gust ruffles the waves and blows forward the women's skirts, while on the cliff beyond the sun still shines. Compare this splendid work with Turner's version of the same theme (Pl. 45). Constable shows the squall approaching, the waves stirred by the wind, the clothes of the people on the beach blown about them; it is a moment of

[1] See K. Badt, *John Constable's Clouds* (1950).

transition; Turner paints the light spreading over the water, a study in reflections, concentratedly luminous, light rather than weather. Constable's precision precludes him from the imaginings of Turner. When Turner rouses a storm, some ill-starred bark is dashed to pieces in it. When Constable thought of shipwreck, he gives a stormy sky over the emptiness of Osmington shore.[1]

Like Turner, Constable sought for his work the wider popularity of engraving, but the story of *The Various subjects of Landscape, characteristic of English scenery* was a very different one from that of the *Liber Studiorum*.[2] Where Turner had in his namesake an engraver of established repute, Constable employed a young man, David Lucas,[3] who had only just completed his apprenticeship. Under Constable's close direction, Lucas produced some plates of extraordinary vigour and freshness, real translations of Constable's genius into another medium, but financially there was loss, and Constable's alternate bursts of enthusiasm and lapses into weariness were ill calculated to forward a successful enterprise. 'In some of these Subjects', said the Prospectus, 'an attempt has been made to arrest the more abrupt and transient appearance of the Chiar'-oscuro of Nature', and in fact in the mezzotints the strong contrasts of light and shade which underlie all Constable's designs emerge too forcibly, unmitigated by the shimmer of his painted surface, and hints of conventional romantic melodrama perturb the renderings of 'the transient appearances'. Where Turner himself mastered the new medium, Constable only directed it, a little fussily, though with generous impulses of appreciation: 'Your quiet way—is I well know the *best* and *only* way.'[4]

In 1828 Maria Constable, the wife to whom he was so deeply devoted, died of the consumption that had long been weakening her. The full-scale sketch of *Hadleigh Castle* is the expression of his grief for her. Nowhere else in paint has English romanticism made

---

[1] In the Louvre: study in the Tate. Constable had in mind the wreck of the *Abergavenny* (1805), when Capt. John Wordsworth, the poet's brother and Mrs. John Fisher's cousin, perished: Leslie, op. cit. 306.

[2] A. Shirley, *The Published Mezzotints of David Lucas after John Constable* (1930).

[3] Lucas was born in 1802, the son of a Northamptonshire grazier; his best work was done for Constable, but he never gained much employment elsewhere and he died in Fulham Workhouse in 1881.   [4] Shirley, op. cit. 233, 141.

such music out of a melancholy near despair. The critics, however, complained of this 'accursed bespattering with blanc d'argent'.[1] There can be little doubt that Constable found these attacks very wounding and in the last years of his life, bereaved and worried, he became at times morose, and his tongue, which always had a sharpened edge to it as is not uncommon in men who have a sense of lonely rectitude, was often cutting. As the Redgraves wrote of him,[2] 'Leslie has painted him *couleur de rose*, and transfused his own kindly and simple spirit into the biography. The landscape painter, though of a manly nature, was eminently sarcastic, and was very clever at saying the bitterest things in a witty manner.' The man himself, sincere, restless in intellect though unswerving in his main ideas, not over clear in thought but steady in progress, profoundly conservative by nature and politics however strange and new were some of the elements of his art, generous to the unfortunate, emerges clearly in his letters: with more casual acquaintances and with the world at large he was not altogether happy in his contacts, and this perhaps explains his slow recognition at the Academy; but that is now a small matter, for he is with the immortals. He died in the night of 30/31 March 1837, from a sudden seizure, the exact nature of which was not clearly diagnosed. He was in his sixty-first year.

Meanwhile his reputation was growing elsewhere. *The Hay Wain* had returned unsold from the Academy of 1821, but there had been inquiries about its purchase from a Parisian dealer, with the curiously un-Parisian name of John Arrowsmith. After negotiations which showed all Constable's distrust of the foreigner, *The Hay Wain*, *The Lock on the Stour*, and a small *Yarmouth Jetty* were sold for £250 with a view to being exhibited in the Salon of 1824. The critics were not impressed: their doyen, Delécluze, thought that negligence had its pedantry as much as excessive care.[3] But the

---

[1] Whitley, ii. 165: the finished painting (R.A. 1829) is untraced: see C. Holmes in *Burl. Mag.* lxviii (1936), 107 and 294.   [2] *Century of British Painters* (ed. 1947), 372.
[3] Leslie, op. cit. 176; Beckett, op. cit. 163; H. Isherwood Kay, 'The Hay Wain', *Burl. Mag.* lxii (1933), 285. There is considerable uncertainty as to the versions exhibited in Paris, and their present location. *The Lock* may be that in the Huntington Coll., California, the *Yarmouth Jetty* that in the Glenconner Coll. *A View of Hampstead* was shown in the Salon, probably the painting now in the Louvre.

artists themselves were enthusiastic. William Brockedon, painter of the Alpine passes, wrote to Constable: 'The French have been forcibly struck by (your pictures), and they have created a division in the School of the landscape painters of France . . . the next exhibition in Paris will teem with your imitators. . . . I saw one draw another to your pictures with this expression, "Look at these landscapes by an Englishman,—the ground appears to be covered with dew".'[1] By the end of 1825 there were at least twenty-five Constables in Paris, and the Louvre had been negotiating, unsuccessfully, with Arrowsmith for the purchase of *The Hay Wain*. Delacroix, many years later, spoke of the impact Constable's work had upon him, and there is a well-known tale how on seeing *The Hay Wain* on its arrival at the Salon he hurriedly repainted his own *Massacres de Scio*, emotionally so remote from Suffolk subjects; but Delacroix, warned by Géricault of the interest of English art, had already in 1823 seen a sketch by Constable, 'admirable chose et incroyable', in the studio of the landscape painter, Régnier,[2] and there had been time for this new influence to be absorbed more gradually and less dramatically.

Meanwhile at the age of forty-four Turner in 1819 paid his first visit to Venice. There he concentrated on drawing a large series of pencil sketches: St. Mark's, the Dogana, the Salute, San Giorgio, the Rialto, all are carefully noted, with scrupulous accuracy but with here and there that almost shorthand power of selection which is always there to remind us of the rapid, intense application behind Turner's vision. On his return some of these drawings were turned into water-colours, of considerable merit, but conventional in their registration of the thing seen. Venice, which was to be so deeply his final inspiration, had at first nothing of the transforming impact of the Alps: or perhaps the impact was there, but required a longer maturing.

From Venice he went on to Rome. Here again we have sketchbooks full of wonderfully exact drawings and a few water-colours,

---

[1] Leslie, op. cit. 176.

[2] R. Escholier, *Delacroix*, i (1926), 123; M. Florisoone, 'Constable and the Massacres de Scio', *Journ. W.C.I.* (1957), 180. Almost at the same time as Delacroix, Thomas Barker of Bath was painting the same massacre in fresco on the wall of Doric House in Bath: see *Art Union Journ.* iii (1841), 69.

beautifully evocative, but with none of his later fury of imagination: these themes too required a period of gestation. The first large oil of Rome (6 ft. by 11 ft.)—*Rome from the Vatican: Raffaelle accompanied by La Fornarina, preparing his pictures for the decoration of the Loggia*—is as cumbersome as its title, a singularly artificial attempt to combine scenic and narrative content. It is too pondered a work, and the tribute to Raphael, couched in the form almost of a cheap novelette, obtrudes on the landscape. There is no new vision here: it is the golden Turner of the Carthage paintings, a little daunted by the splendours he had seen. It was not till two years later, in *The Bay of Baiae,* that the glow of the south adds meaning to his oils.

Despite Italy, he was in the twenties drawing on his experience of other painters, Rembrandt and Watteau, with a little of his contemporary, Stothard mixed into it: 'he would', wrote Constable to Archdeacon Fisher in 1825, 'be Lord over all'.[1] Much of his time also was taken up by sketching tours for engraved work, in particular for the *Rivers of England* and the *Rivers of France*. In these sketches Turner was taking great liberties in recording the site: different viewpoints were combined in one scene; castle and church towers became points of emphasis rather than architectural records; colours were contrasted in strong patches of blue and red; the matter was subordinated to his own intellectualization of the thing seen in terms of diffused light and colour. This process at work in the unrestrained sphere of imaginary subjects can be seen in a painting exhibited in 1832, *Nebuchadnezzar and the Burning Fiery Furnace* (Pl. 43). His friend, George Jones, had selected this theme for himself; Turner, for whom the furnace had obvious attractions, thought that he would paint it too and the friends agreed on exactly similar shape and size. George Jones's painting is a careful, academic work, the figures precise and rather dry, the colouring with some rich passages but entirely conventional. In Turner's painting it is quite impossible to tell what is happening—the mysterious figure of the brazen image looms up in the background; the figures of Shadrach, Meshach, and Abednego, the three children, are barely visible in a brilliant flame-coloured glow

[1] Beckett, op. cit. 208.

which spreads in widening circles over the picture space, reaching a climax in the thick, brilliant painting of the princess of Babylon's parasol and dress, where light falling on rich materials is contrasted with the haze from the furnace itself.[1]

The Fiery Furnace is a fantasy on a given theme. At this same period, Turner was also steadily deepening his observation of natural phenomena. In his two paintings of *Mortlake Terrace* (exhibited 1826 and 1827), now respectively in the Frick Collection and the National Gallery at Washington, the long shadows of the trees are luminous and full of colour, the qualities of evening and morning sunshine wonderfully distinguished and the diagonal of the parapet is a demonstration of a softened, light-diffused outline. They are his most peaceful and amongst his most instructive works.[2] A few years later, in 1829 and 1830, he was painting at Petworth the fields by the lake with deer browsing or stags fighting, silhouettes against the rising or setting sun; or a ship smoothly passing through the Chichester canal,[3] paintings where every shape and colour are conditioned and varied by the angles at which light falls on them and are yet absorbed as a whole into the sunshine, not mere reflectors of it. And in the house itself, he filled a sketchbook with notes of the rooms, the gallery with Flaxman's *St. Michael*, the stairway, the colour of a falling curtain, the guests at ease after dinner, mere rapid, blot-like notes, where everything is alive and everything exists in terms of colour. Then, probably on his last visit before Lord Egremont's death in 1837, he painted in oils his *Interior at Petworth*, unfinished perhaps but surely complete for him, where all linear definition is submerged in his sensuous delight in the rich colouring of stuffs and decoration. 'The idea that the world is made up of solid objects with lines round them ceased to trouble him.'[4]

In 1833 Turner exhibited his first oil painting of Venice, *The*

[1] Jones told Ruskin that when Turner's version got the better place, Turner 'did all in his power to get the pictures changed'. *Diaries of John Ruskin*, ed. Joan Evans (1956), 248.

[2] See C. J. Holmes, 'Three paintings by Turner', *Burl. Mag.* xiv (1908), 17.

[3] *The Fighting Stags* and *Chichester Canal* are both at Petworth.

[4] Sir Kenneth Clark, 'Turner at Petworth', *The Ambassador* (1949, No. 8), 84; see also *C.L.* lviii (1925), 966.

Bridge of Sighs, Ducal Palace and Custom House, Venice: Canaletti [sic] painting. It was a small panel, 20 in. by 22 in.: the reference to Canaletto, however ridiculous the small figure painting a picture already fixed in a heavy gilt frame, shows that Turner had examined and appreciated the work of his predecessor, even if he had rejected his methods; topographical exactitude is disregarded, and the Dogana is swung round to provide a viewpoint which in fact does not exist; and the mellow, even sunlight that fills Canaletto's Venice is replaced in Turner by a shimmering hazy light, broken reflections from the water, broken light on the carved architectural façades. In the centre of this small panel, Turner's vision of Venice begins to come alive. He returned, probably in 1835, to the city itself. Now he was on familiar terms and there were no more delays. He exhibited in 1836 a view of St. Mark's Square, with the campanile and St. Mark's itself. It appears in photographs to be a grand, exciting work and it roused the young Ruskin to his first acclamation of Turner: other criticism centred on the strangeness of the picture, on the fact that from two figures in the foreground it was called *Juliet and her nurse*, and on the fantastic colours and the night sky lit up with bursting fireworks.[1] It is, however, the sketches and oil paintings that followed his third visit in 1840 that have permanently linked Turner's name with that of Venice. In *The Sun of Venice going to Sea*, the city, so carefully noted in the first sketchbooks, has been reduced to gradations of light, set in the flecked blue of the sky and the flecked green of the water; the boats themselves are vague, brown shadows; only in the billowing sail, vividly caught by the sun, is there actuality; in *San Benedetto looking towards Fusine* there is not even that; all the forms blend, disappear, re-emerge into the atmosphere. It is effortless painting; his hand is completely rendering his concept of air and water.

It is now a procession of great masterpieces. The classical subjects had reached the climax of their golden swagger in *Ulysses deriding Polyphemus* (1829), only to dissolve in their turn into the brilliant haze of *Mercury and Argus* (Pl. 42 *b*), or the lurid, storm-shot

---

[1] Coll. Mrs. G. Macculloch Miller, New York; reproduced *Catalogue of Pictures Collected by Yale Alumni*, Yale (1956), pl. 45: 35 in. by 47 in. Juliet has, of course, no business in Venice.

vapours of *Hero and Leander* (1837). He had, too, been proceeding with his shipwreck themes. In 1831 *The Lifeboat and Manly Apparatus going off to a vessel making signals of Distress* (V. and A.); in 1834 *The Wreckers—coast of Northumberland, with a steam boat assisting a ship off shore* (Pittsburg). A steamboat: two years earlier, in *Fingal's Cave*, the smoke from a steamship's funnel blends with the spray— it was a new effect in Turner's repertory.[1]

Two pictures mark the climax of his sea horrors. *The Fire at Sea*, which he never completed or exhibited, is the greatest cascade of flame that he painted, blazing out against a turbulent sea. It is a splendid and fearful subject, and the child's corpse floating in the foreground is only one item of the ferocity with which he imagined it. *The Fire* probably dates from the middle thirties. *Typhon Coming on: Slavers throwing overboard the Dead and Dying*, exhibited in 1840, is as terrible a subject as could be desired.

I believe [wrote Ruskin] if I were reduced to rest Turner's immortality upon any single work, I should choose this. . . . Purple and blue, the lurid shadows of the hollow breakers are cast upon the mist of night, which gathers cold and low, advancing like the shadow of death upon the guilty ship as it labours amidst the lightning of the sea, its thin masts written upon the sky in lines of blood, girded with condemnation in that fearful hue which signs the sky with horror, and mixes its flaming flood with the sunlight, and, cast far along the desolate heave of the sepulchral waves, incarnadines the multitudinous sea.[2]

In this flaming, lurid turmoil, of which no reproduction can give any impression, Turner has hardly specified the horror of his theme. The detail is submerged in the general attack on the eyes. Terrible shapes loom out as bodingly as in any of Picasso's later

---

[1] G. Grigson, 'Fingal's Cave', *Arch. Rev.* civ (1948), 51. The cave was discovered in 1772, and had an immediate romantic appeal; the painting, the first Turner to go to America, was formerly in the New York Public Library and is now in an English private collection.

[2] *Works*, iii. 572. Turner must have read of the *Zong*, the slave ship whose large cargo of slaves in an epidemic were thrown overboard rather than let die of disease for which no insurance money would have been paid (1783); see T. Clarkson, *History of the Abolition of the Slave Trade*, 2nd ed. (1839), 80; but the 'mad seas' and 'the direful sharks' come from Thomson's account of the slave ship in the canto of 'Summer' in the *Seasons*; see Ann Livermore in *The Connoisseur Year Book* (1957), 80.

paintings, and the half-submerged corpse of the negress, the broken chain clanking ironically around the projecting leg, while some strange monster swims towards its prey, is the last nightmare of the deep (Pl. 39 *b*).

With the coming of steam, marine painting lost one of its most splendidly decorative features, the rigging of the sailing ships. Turner found some compensation in the blasts of smoke belching up to create new patterns with the mist and cloud. He had never rivalled in his rigging the accuracy of the marine painters of the previous century, and accuracy of detail, as opposed to grasp of essentials, had never been his strong point. Few artists absorbed so readily and so carelessly and concentrated so wholeheartedly on the main purpose, and there is, as constantly pointed out, little accuracy either in ship or lighting, in the famous elegiac painting (R.A. 1839) with which he celebrated the passing of the old order, the *Téméraire*, a veteran battleship of Trafalgar, tugged to her last berth to be broken up, her rigging all stripped and pale, and the impudent tug belching in front of her. 'Of all pictures', wrote Ruskin, 'of subjects not visibly involving human pain, this is, I believe, the most pathetic that was ever painted.'[1]

Three years later a heavier cloud of smoke, a great mourning trail, blows across one of Turner's canvases. David Wilkie, travelling from Alexandria by one of the new East Indian steamers, the *Oriental*, died at sea near Malta. *Peace—burial at Sea*, in its strange octagonal setting as though a memorial plaque, contrasts the ragged cloud of smoke melting into the atmosphere with the hard outline of the auxiliary sails. Again there is no realism; but there is also no doubt as to the placid shimmer of the sea and the contrast with the sky. Turner was now in the full development of the last phase of his painting. Steadily he had been pursuing the problem of outlines seen in varying lights and of the dissolution of shape into atmosphere. In 1837 his *Snow storm, avalanche and inundation in the Val d'Aosta* (Art Institute of Chicago) shows the mountains and storm merging into one. In his last sea-storm pieces the same process is at work. In the Academy of 1842 he exhibited his *Snowstorm* with the sub-title *Steamboat off a harbour's mouth making*

[1] *Works*, xiii. 170.

signals in shallow water and going by the lead. The Author was in this storm on the night the Ariel left Harwich. Not only was he in it, but, at the age of sixty-seven, tied to a beam on the deck so that he could observe the whole course of the storm. The critics parodied the *Fallacies of Hope*:

> O Art, how vast thy mighty wonders are
> To those who roam upon the extraordinary deep!
> Maelstrom, thy hand is here.

'Soapsuds and white wash', Ruskin heard him muttering, 'I wonder what they think the sea is like.'[1]

Two years later, in 1844, he exhibited *Rain, Steam and Speed*. It is a salute to the new railway age. The train roars along the track, and a hare, the old natural type of velocity, vainly tries to outdistance it. The steam fuses with the mist, the forms dissolve in it as in some kind of Götterdämmerung, the end of an epoch. Turner's career too was drawing to an end. He had seven more years to live and there are flashes of genius in some of the work done in them. His imagination was as tense as ever, but hand and eye were faltering, and his technique became more and more careless. He hardly sought to please the public, and they were not pleased. More and more pictures were left unsold to be rolled up, at times to moulder in the gallery of his house in Queen Anne Street or patch a wall to expel the winter's flaw.

The attacks of the critics on Turner's later paintings had roused a champion, a young man, who in 1836 was only seventeen when he wrote a defence, which Turner discouraged him from publishing. John Ruskin, after this first contact, went to Oxford, and it was as by 'A graduate of Oxford' that *Modern Painters, Volume I* appeared in 1843. It was the beginning of a vast structure that was to have a lasting effect on all thought about the visual arts. Turner, the most unvocal of artists, had found a prophet whose prose in its romantic splendour matched the level of the master's painting. In richness, resource, and profusion they are alike. In a generation of new patrons, the generation of the Reform Bill, who were easily pleased with the accepted conventions of naturalistic imitation,

[1] Finberg, op. cit. 390; P. G. Hamerton, *Life of J. M. W. Turner* (1895), 345.

Ruskin in this first volume reaffirmed the classical tradition that the arts are the vehicle of thought. 'Painting, or art generally, as such, with all its technicalities, difficulties, and particular ends, is nothing but a noble and expressive language, invaluable as the vehicle of thought, but by itself nothing. He who has learned what is commonly considered the whole art of painting, that is, the art of representing any natural object faithfully, has as yet only learned the language by which his thoughts are to be expressed. He has done just as much towards being that which we ought to respect as a great painter, as a man who has learnt how to express himself grammatically and melodiously has towards being a great poet.'[1] But whereas in the eighteenth century, thought was shown in interpretation of subject, to Ruskin it was shown in the analysis and study of nature. The first approach, the direct contact of a sketch, might well have more 'thought' in it, than the carefully finished picture. 'If one atom of thought has vanished, all colour, all finish, all execution, all ornament, are too dearly bought.'[2] To an age much drawn to all forms of technical accomplishment, these were salutary words. Yet while he probed into botany and geology, he could write that 'Constable perceives in a landscape that the grass is wet, the meadows flat, and the boughs shady; that is to say, about as much as, I suppose, might in general be apprehended, between them, by an intelligent faun and a skylark.'[3] Bemused by the violent, insatiable imagination of Turner, he could find no logical sequence of argument to explain him, and the majestic words flowed on full of insight and inconsistency.

The data on which he worked, the comparisons on which he drew, were the paintings of his time, and names now little thought of are prominently embedded in his writings. One example must serve. In his praise of marine painters Ruskin couples Turner with a younger artist, Clarkson Stanfield.[4] Born in 1793, Stanfield served at sea till an injury to his foot forced him to take up another profession. He became a scene painter at Drury Lane, where he made a great name for himself. Scenery was then at its most elaborate and included dioramas, where a slowly unrolling back-cloth revealed a whole series of pictures—one of Stanfield's in-

[1] *Works*, iii. 87. [2] Ibid. i. 91. [3] Ibid. v. 172. [4] See ibid. iii. 226, 254, 535.

cluded the progress of a ship from the building yards to its wreck. His paintings, many of them large in size, retain much of the bold simplification and hard, clear silhouettes of the stage, but he had great knowledge of the sea and of cloud formations. In *The Abandoned* (Pl. 66 *a*), to judge from reproductions, he produced one of the most desolate and powerful of English wreck pieces. His *Last of the Crew* (Sheffield) is another study in this grim obsession with sea dangers. His waves are closely studied and Ruskin wrote that 'One work of Stanfield alone presents us with as much concentrated knowledge of sea and sky, as, diluted, would have lasted one of the old masters his life.' But while the forms, the surface shimmer, the contrasting colours of deep or shallow water are exactly rendered, Stanfield was lacking in any great power of handling paint. The fusion of sea and sky, cloud, rain, and wave in Turner were beyond his scope. 'We should like him', Ruskin continued, 'to be less clever and more affecting—less wonderful and more terrible.' It is a strange comment on the deeply felt drama of his wrecks, but in much of Stanfield's work, such as the large series of Italian landscapes formerly at Bowood,[1] it is the scene painter rather than the observer of nature that is to the fore. Finely planned, they are yet flat and conventional, coloured according to recipe, and the peasant figures are stock properties with none of that liveliness which since Wilkie had been an expected attribute of English art.

There was, while Constable was dying, Turner painting at his most abstract, and Ruskin writing, a growing vogue for landscapes where an acceptable 'view' was the main subject, and fields, meadows, and hills, 'lakes and brooks and streams, crossed by picturesque bridges or forded by quaint carts',[2] were in the studio reduced to a common standard of arrangement and atmosphere. Constable's vacant place was filled at the Academy by the election of Frederick Richard Lee, who, patronized by William Wells[3] of

[1] Christie's, 16.5.1952, lots 138–42; see Dr. Waagen, *Treasures of Art in Great Britain*, iii (1854), 166.

[2] Redgrave, *Century of British Painters* (1947), 388; writing of Thomas Creswick, who in the mid century was the chief purveyor of 'good taste' in landscape.

[3] 'My pictures', Constable wrote of him, 'do not come into his rules or whims of the art, and he said I had "lost my way".' Leslie, op. cit. 218.

Redleaf, had gradually been making a name for himself as a landscape painter. 'Pretty enough', Constable had thought him, and Lee, who began his career as an ensign in the 56th Foot and for all his long life was a keen shot and yachtsman, is the perfect figure of the unintellectual, superficial artist that England has frequently produced, painting competently and repetitively, selling his pictures and not bothering much about more abstruse qualities. His green fields and limpid streams readily pleased and dominated a period in English landscape when emotion and observation were alike at a discount. The great art of Turner and Constable, as though it had overstrained the understanding of their contemporaries, leads to these trivial decencies. When T. S. Cooper, the animal painter, whose sheep have an unforgettable woolliness, joined forces with Lee, their triumph was complete.[1]

[1] M. H. Grant, *Old English Landscape Painters*, ii (n.d.), 349: 'Mr. Lee bids fair to become the Hobbema of his time and country' (Q.R. lxii, 1838, 161).

V

STATUARY

THE pediments and porticoes of the Regency classical style demanded the co-operation of sculptors, and the stucco façades had their parallels in various compositions by which statuary could be provided both more cheaply and more durably than in stone. Of these coade stone was the most celebrated, a product whose supply and marketing was organized by Mrs. Eleanor Coade from her manufactory in Lambeth.[1] She claimed that her stone 'had a property of resisting the frost and consequently of retaining that sharpness in which it excels every kind of stone sculpture'. Mrs. Coade herself died in 1796, but the firm continued in active production, first under her daughter, another Eleanor Coade, then under William Croggan and his son till 1836. Most of the sculptors of the day experimented at one time or other with this material, and much of their work has justified Mrs. Coade's claim. The statues on Sir John Soane's houses at Pitzhanger (Pl. 35 *b*) and Lincoln's Inn Fields or the great tympanum of the death of Nelson, designed by Benjamin West, on the west colonnade of Greenwich Hospital are singularly unweathered. Two of the artists particularly associated with these ornamental pieces were John Rossi and J. G. Bubb, who for a time (*c.* 1818), despite earlier quarrels, worked in partnership, using a kind of terracotta instead of the Coade patent. Bubb's pediments and friezes can still be seen in London and Bristol, particularly the great pediment of Cumberland Terrace and the much finer relief and statues on the Bristol Commercial Rooms. His main venture into monumental sculpture was not a happy one; when in 1806 he won the commission for Pitt's memorial in the Guildhall, it was generally held that the cheapness of his tender was the first consideration. It is an unsightly mass of figures that solidly survived the bombing of the hall. The Common Council of the City were not fortunate in their

[1] G. B. Hamilton in *Arch. Rev.* cxvi (1945), 295.

patronage: James Smith's Nelson memorial (1810) is only little better than that of Bubb. These ineptitudes in stone, groups too large for the genius of their creators, were not now to be tolerated, for there were available sculptors of far different range and distinction, and the decorator, the worker in synthetic stone, had to take second place to the disciples of Canova and the hard, shining stone of Carrara.

Few artists have enjoyed such general European acceptance as that accorded to Antonio Canova.[1] A cosmopolitan aristocracy, that was soon to lose its arbitrament of taste to newer patrons, acclaimed him with a fine disregard of wars, nationality, and politics. His studio in Rome was the central inspiration of neo-classic sculpture, where Thorwaldsen the Dane and Flaxman the Englishman learnt the true doctrines and became his chief disciples. Flaxman returned home in 1794, and England was quick to learn the new Roman idiom. A great age of statuary, so it seemed, was beginning and the triumphs over Napoleon provided worthy objects of lasting commemoration. Improvements in 'pointing' instruments had much increased the accuracy with which plaster models could be exactly copied, even in hard Italian marble, though for the chiselling English artists were much dependent on Italian workmen. The decision in 1795 to relieve the overcrowding in Westminster Abbey by initiating a series of memorials in St. Paul's to 'Heroes who had recently lost their lives in the service of their country' came opportunely. A grant for sepulchral monuments had been voted in 1789 and now a committee was set up, 'the Committee of Taste' it was soon nicknamed, to select subjects and artists. At once there was much gossip about it: 'Rossi to be employed . . . Flaxman is to have one . . . only Englishmen are to be employed . . . Banks on account of his political principles will not.' This last was a wrong guess. In 1798 Banks was writing that he had been summoned by the committee to discuss three monu-

---

[1] F. J. B. Watson, 'Canova and the English', *Arch. Rev.* cxxii (1957), 403. *The Works of Antonio Canova engraved in outline by Henry Moses* appeared in England in 3 vols. in 1822–4, and any comparison with contemporary English sculpture shows clearly the profound influence of these designs. Henry Moses (1782?–1870) was the leading purveyor of outline drawings of works of art.

K

ments for 'Naval Heroes, who have been killed in attempting to
kill Others'.[1] It provided two of his last commissions. Born in
1735, he was undoubtedly the doyen of British monumental
sculptors at the turn of the century. He could handle eighteenth-
century elegance in groups such as his *Shakespeare between Painting
and Poetry* (1789) for the doorway of Boydell's Gallery,[2] but his
two groups in St. Paul's are thoroughly neo-classical in conception.
Both are of naval captains. Captain Burgess (1802) is a whiskered
but nude figure, his nakedness masked only by some scanty
drapery falling from the shoulder (Pl. 48 a). Allan Cunningham
states that the drapery was at first even scantier and only lengthened
after clerical protest. A winged victory presents him with a sword,
and on the pediment are mourning seamen and a triumph of
shields and despondent prisoners. Here the rhythm of the design
and the careful, emotional restraint are not without moving
qualities, but there is something irresistibly comic about the interview between the heroic captain and his muse. Captain George
Westcott, slightly more clad in a Greek chiton, sinks into the arms
of another impersonated victory. 'No artist has contrived with
such small means to give so much offence . . . artists were long in
learning to tell in a simple way that a man died for his country.'[3]

   To the naval captains succeeded the Peninsular warriors.[4] John
Bacon commemorated General Craufurd and General Mackinnon
who fell at Ciudad Rodrigo, and in his group of the *Burial of Sir
John Moore* (Pl. 48 b) created one of the most dramatic and tensely
felt renderings of these heroic death-scenes. His pupil, Charles
Manning,[5] rises to a moment of excellence in his Hardinge monument. Sebastian Gahagan, Nolleken's poorly paid assistant, produced his most important work in memory of Sir Thomas

   [1] Farrington *Diary*, unpublished passages printed C. F. Bell, *Annals of Thomas Banks*
(1938), 115, 118: for Banks see also Allan Cunningham, *Lives of the most eminent
British Painters, Sculptors and Architects* (1830), iii. 82.
   [2] Now in the Public Gardens at Stratford-upon-Avon.
   [3] *Q.R.* xxxiv (1826), 126.
   [4] For a brief and unfavourable summary of what she calls the Peninsular School see
K. A. Esdaile, *English Monumental Sculpture since the Renaissance* (1927), 73.
   [5] The Mannings were a family of sculptors: Samuel Manning's monument to
Charles Grant (1824) in St. George's, Bloomsbury, has considerable merit.

Picton, killed at Waterloo, a highly classical group with a fine mourning Eros and Canova's influence clearly apparent: Sir Richard Westmacott represented Sir Ralph Abercrombie falling from his horse into the arms of a massive Highlander, while sphinxes on either side indicate the Egyptian setting of his death. Humphrey Hopper's 'lamentable mass of marble'[1] to General Hay, and Josephus John Kendrick's groups where Hercules and Minerva shake hands before a medallion of Sir William Myers or a sprawling Britannia weeps for General Ross—these betray the inability of lesser men to struggle with so stern a discipline.

One monument, though doubtfully successful, requires some more detailed comment. Sir William Ponsonby had been killed at Waterloo when his horse stumbled, and his memorial is a large equestrian piece (Pl. 49 a). It was commissioned from William Theed, who had recently completed his *Hercules capturing the Thracian Horses* on the pediment of the Royal Mews, and no doubt another equally successful horse was hoped for: but Theed died in 1817, before the group was completed, and it was carried through by a younger sculptor, Edward Hodges Baily. It was the opening of a most prosperous career; it was also in the type of charger and in the treatment of the drapery a tribute to a new source of influence, the Elgin marbles. In 1801 Thomas Bruce, seventh earl of Elgin and at that time British ambassador at the Porte, obtained a firman for drawing, measuring and taking casts at the 'Temple of the Idols', as the Turks called the Parthenon: the permit extended also to the taking away of pieces of stone with inscriptions or figures.[2] The scheme had been suggested by Thomas Harrison, the architect, when he was working for Elgin at Broomhall, and J. M. W. Turner was invited to accompany the expedition to sketch the antiquities. Turner, though then only twenty-four, asked for too high a remuneration, and eventually an Italian, Giovanni Battista Lusieri, was engaged, a man whose zeal was largely responsible for the course of events. Drawing and modelling

[1] Gunnis, *Dictionary*: this and Kendrick's two groups are in Westminster abbey.
[2] The most authoritative account is A. H. Smith, 'Lord Elgin and his Collection', *Journ. of Hellenic Studies*, xxxvi (1916), 163–372. See also A. Michaelis, *Ancient Marbles in Great Britain* (1882).

was the original aim, but as Elgin saw the constant quarrying on the Acropolis and the wanton destruction of the sculptures, he determined to save them by taking them to England. The ship on which many of them were loaded sank off Cerigo and it was not till three years later that they were salvaged at great cost. Elgin himself was detained in France on his return journey and a curious painting in the Elgin collection shows his three small children, with their Greek nurses, holding up miniatures of their father and mother, the prisoners of Bonaparte. In 1806 he was released and the marbles, which had been lying in cases in London, were at last exhibited. At once there was an outcry, led by Byron, against the pillager of Athens. Richard Payne Knight, more interested in bronzes than marbles, dismissed the Elgin sculptures as largely Roman of the time of Hadrian, and when in 1816 a select committee[1] was appointed to consider the purchase of the collection for the British Museum his evidence was hostile. In the interval before the Commission, England had played a leading part in the decision that the artistic booty of Europe collected by Napoleon in Paris should be returned to its original owners.[2] This had raised sharply the question of rights in works of art, and the committee was anxious to establish that the marbles had been properly acquired, which, if the Turkish knowledge of and acquiescence in their removal was the test, they certainly had been. Canova, the great Canova, the master exponent of neo-classicism, came to London and praised the marbles highly, stressing their importance for the future of English sculpture and never questioning English rights in them. Benjamin Robert Haydon joined in the battle with all his usual unbalanced vehemence, and his lively attack was translated into French and Italian and quoted by Goethe.[3] The marbles were purchased for £35,000, less than half the sum which Lord Elgin estimated that he had spent on them. Eight years later,

---

[1] The Select Committee's Report (*P.P. 1816*, iii. 49) is also printed in *The Elgin Marbles*, publ. for J. Taylor (1816): in the introduction Elgin is praised for 'rescuing these precious remains of ancient art from the destroying hand of time, and from the more destroying hand of an uncivilised people'.

[2] D. M. Quynn, 'Art Confiscations of the Napoleonic Wars', *American Historical Rev.* l (1945), 437.

[3] B. R. Haydon, *Lectures on Painting and Design*, ii (1846), lecture xiii.

on the death of Payne Knight, his collection of bronzes and coins and his great series of Claude drawings were left to the British Museum: the two rivals met at length on common ground. The impact of the marbles was at once considerable. Models of them were in great demand, and John Henning first carved them in intaglio and then went on to carve them as a frieze on the Athenaeum and the Hyde Park Arch. Many a Regency interior showed friezes of horsemen, either in relief or as wallpaper;[1] and on other monuments than that of Sir William Ponsonby the victims of Waterloo fall from horses whose ancestors pranced on the Parthenon.[2]

Of the St. Paul's memorials the most important was naturally that to Nelson. It was a commission for which there were many competitors, and in 1808 it was awarded to John Flaxman. It is an elaborate design: Nelson stands, leaning on an anchor, surrounded by personifications of the sea; his face is cut boldly, with deep simplified furrows, generalized rather than individual, the hero not the man; below, in contrast to the sombre aloofness of the central figure, Britannia points out the admiral to two young boys, a rather unnecessary underlining of the exemplary purpose of such pieces of statuary, but a subject, the instruction of youth, to which Flaxman always brought an engaging freshness.

It was only in 1797, at the age of forty-two, that Flaxman had been elected A.R.A., and his rising prestige was marked by the commission for the monument to Lord Mansfield in Westminster Abbey, completed in 1801. This massive erection, the first free standing, or as the term then was 'insulated', monument to be set up in the Abbey, can hardly be judged today for it has been moved from its original position in the north transept and is enclosed in the transept aisle, up against the northern wall; but as a group it can never have been other than clumsy. The head of the great Chief Justice, based on Reynolds's portrait of him, has Flaxman's generalized dignity, but the seated posture is ill fitted for the angle

[1] See 'Select Committee on Arts and Manufactures', *P.P. 1835*, v. 436, 451, and *1836*, ix. 65.

[2] Cf. the younger Bacon's monument to Sir Henry Walton Ellis in Worcester cathedral.

of sight from ground level, and the figures of Wisdom and Justice, though they have a fine linear rhythm of their own, are clamped too closely to the main block: they remain 'the thoughtful occupants of a monument',[1] stereotyped and uninventive; only in the figure of the condemned youth at the back of the monument (Pl. 49 b) does Flaxman's purity of line show to its full advantage, the one point also where some intensity of feeling penetrates the classical calm.

Flaxman's 'insulated' figures are comparatively few. Largest of all would have been his 230 feet high figure of Britannia, which he suggested erecting on the hill-side at Greenwich as a memorial to the Battle of the Nile:[2] but this, probably fortunately, was never carried out. Sir Joshua Reynolds in St. Paul's; Sir John Moore cast in bronze in George Square, Glasgow; the 'colossal marble statue' of the rajah of Tanjore still standing in his palace, where Bishop Heber had seen it in 1826;[3] Robert Burns in Edinburgh, all show a certain stiffness, a lack of internal rhythm, which comes perhaps from the absence of those 'protruding or flying folds', which Flaxman so much deprecated in Bernini, then regarded as the nadir of sculptural taste.[4] His happiest statue is perhaps that to Sir Matthew White Ridley (d. 1813) in Newcastle cathedral, but this, though fully in the round, is placed against a carved background with emblems of triumph to which Flaxman has given considerable linear value, and the full acceptance of the classical toga for Sir Matthew's garment has removed the need of any hampering compromise.

'For a bust', said the much-quoted Fuseli, 'give me Nollekens. Had you required a group of figures, I should have recommended

---

[1] Q.R. xxxvi. 128.

[2] *A Letter to the Committee for raising the Naval Pillar*, London, 1799 (reprinted *Library of Fine Arts*, ii (1831), 45). Cunningham says of him (iii. 326): 'He had a serious leaning to allegory, and dealt largely in British Lions, Victorys and Britannias.'

[3] R. Heber, *Narrative of a Journey through India*, new ed., 2 vols. (1873), ii. 266. There is also in the mission church a relief by Flaxman showing the rajah saying farewell to the missionary Schwartz, on the latter's death-bed. See E. Croft Murray, 'An Account Book of John Flaxman, R.A.', *Walpole Soc.* xxviii (1940), 79.

[4] 'It would have been better for sculpture had Bernini never lived.' R. Westmacott, *Handbook of Sculpture* (1864), 313.

Flaxman.'[1] In a relief or in some close-knit group of figures Flaxman's powers could have a fuller scope than he ever found in the upright standing figure. Lady Fitzharris (1815) (Pl. 50 b) sits reading to her children, united with them in an intricate pattern that maintains itself from whatever angle the work is seen. Here also is that fusion of the sculptural and the homely in which Flaxman excelled.

Sentiment [he said in one of his Academy lectures] is the life and soul of fine art. . . . By this quality a firm alliance is formed with the affections in all works of art. With an earnest watchfulness for their preservation, we are made to perceive the most sublime and terrific subjects, following the course of sentiment through the current and mazes of intelligence and passion to the most delicate and tender ties and sympathies of affection;—the benign exertions of spiritual natures; the tremendous fall of rebel angels or Titans; the immovable fortitude or contending energy of patriotism; the sincerity of friendship, and the irresistible harmony of connubial, maternal, fraternal and filial love.[2]

This is an unusually vivid passage in a series of discourses mainly devoted to an analysis of ancient, medieval and renaissance art, but it is not one that is very lucid as exposition. 'When Mr. Flaxman reasons', Hazlitt said of the lectures, 'he reasons ill':[3] it serves, however, to show how the emotions were classified. The pathos which to us today seems over-sweet and mawkish was then the balancing opposed extreme to Fuseli's nightmares, Turner's heaving shipwrecks, or John Martin's apocalyptic landscapes. To Flaxman the idealization of human everyday affections was more congenial than the transmutation of the terrible into the sublime. Figures reading seem to have had a special appeal for him. Sir William Jones on his monument in University College, Oxford, writes in his book while he discusses his digest of laws with Hindu sages, a work of 1801 that contains some of the finest modelling in any of Flaxman's statuary; at Winchester cathedral Dr. Warton (1801) instructs his boys, book in hand, and at Harrow parish church the founder, John Lyon, is in a similar pose (1815). Monu-

---

[1] Cunningham, *Lives*, iii (1830), 182; see also W. G. Constable, *John Flaxman* (1927).   [2] *Lectures on Sculpture*, 2nd ed. (1838), 163.
[3] *Centenary Edition of Collected Works*, xvi (1933), 338.

ments such as these, while they occasionally show neo-classic motifs and are sometimes based on classic poses, had a freshness and originality which go some way to explain the immense admiration in which Flaxman was held by contemporaries and by the mid-nineteenth century.

It is all the stranger that one of the most enduring of his claims to renown rests on his drawings for the *Iliad* and *Odyssey*. These were commissioned by Mrs. Hare-Naylor, a gifted and eccentric Englishwoman, who, through the connivance of Georgiana, duchess of Devonshire, had eloped to Rome with a canon of Winchester. The patronage behind these chaste and simple line drawings had therefore its Regency elements of fantasy. They were published, engraved by Tommaso Piroli in Rome in 1793, in England in 1795 (with some of the plates re-engraved by Blake replacing some by Piroli that had been destroyed), in Germany in 1804, another English edition in 1805, and further European editions followed. Meanwhile, presumably via Mrs. Hare-Naylor and Georgiana, the latter's mother, the Dowager Countess Spencer, ordered thirty-one illustrations from Aeschylus (engraved by Piroli, London, 1795), and Thomas Hope ordered 109 illustrations from Dante (engraved by Piroli, Rome 1802, London 1807).[1]

All these quickly enjoyed great popularity and the Homeric drawings still have a place in the visual imagination. Later generations knew them as illustrations to A. J. Church's *Tales from the Iliad and Odyssey*, and learned instinctively to see with Flaxman's eyes Penelope at the loom, Ulysses drawing the bow upon the suitors, Athene descending from the skies, or Ajax defying the Trojans. Ever since his drawings for Wedgwood Flaxman had been much interested by Greek vase painting; these drawings are an attempt to re-create the linear rhythms of this art, and the poses, the strongly marked profiles, the economy of means are all taken from them. The gentle, pious mind of Flaxman was, however, singularly unsuited to the often lecherous humours of the vase paintings. He uses their methods in the furtherance of idealized art, but his goddesses, Venus and Thetis, his Andromaches, Hecubas, and Penelopes cannot escape a slight tinge of contemporary feeling.

[1] For bibliography of the various editions see Constable, op. cit. 98.

The coyness of Helen, the youthful, almost childish desire of Paris would hardly have burned the topless towers of Ilium. The travel-stained Ulysses is a wonderfully boyish figure as laid by Phoenician sailors on his own coast. The battle-scenes are on the whole more successful: stylized as a ballet, they have an exciting rhythm which makes up for their lack of ferocity. Dante was a harder matter, for here, not knowing Botticelli's drawings which might well have appealed deeply to him, he had to seek within himself, and both understanding and emotions are superficial. Dante and Virgil are dull, lay figures, and one only has to compare Flaxman's Francesca and Paolo with that of Blake (Pl. 27) to see how thin was the former's poetic passion.

To appreciate Flaxman as draughtsman, it is necessary to look at the drawings themselves. As with his sculpture, carved by other hands from half-scale models,[1] so his drawings are mainly known at second hand. Piroli was a competent engraver, but he understood Flaxman's intentions perhaps too well. The clarity and firmness of the line becomes even more emphatic and facial expressions, to which Flaxman in his own drawings could give a flicker of intensity, in the engravings are often reduced to insipidity. Blake's engravings of Flaxman's drawings for Hesiod have a more sensitive touch. Published in 1816–17, they have escaped from the limiting example of the vases and are the happiest achievement of Flaxman's linear sense (Pl. 36 a). He was designing now with a new fluency, already apparent in the very beautiful relief on the silver gilt vase, with Paul Storr's mark and the date 1812, which Queen Charlotte gave to the Prince Regent (Pl. 36 b). This work was commissioned by the great silversmiths, Rundell and Bridge, and it was for them also that the Achilles shield,[2] 9 feet in circumference, was executed. This latter Flaxman always regarded as one of his most important works. It was a truly classical subject, that had been a pleasant matter of aesthetic speculation since Pope's essay on it in his translation of the *Iliad* accompanied by Barlow's engraved version,

[1] There is a notable collection of these models in University College, London.

[2] Completed 1818: silver casts were made for the king, the duke of York, the duke of Northumberland, and the earl of Lonsdale.

which in its turn was based on N. Vleughel's design in Boivin's *Le Bouclier d'Achille*, published in Paris in 1715.

In the long friendship with Blake the Hesiod designs are perhaps the most significant point. Much as they had in common, there is little contact in their art. From his 'dear sculptor of eternity' Blake may have learned a tauter linear rhythm than he himself readily controlled, but Flaxman, despite his admiration for both Blake's poems and drawings, was himself far removed from the prophetic turmoils of his friend. Flaxman's influence must be sought elsewhere. His designs soon became well known on the Continent, and in days when line drawings were a current form of reproduction, they rapidly became the great pattern book of neo-classicism. Ingres kept on his table a drawing by Flaxman of the chained Prometheus, placed him in the foreground of his *Apotheosis of Homer*, and copied his Zeus and, more surprisingly, his Francesca and Paolo reading the fatal book. Regnault, Prud'hon, Guérin, all show traces of these much-studied drawings, and in England they underlie much of the vivid colour and lusciousness of Etty and the mythological scenes of James Ward. The classics to a society much permeated by new elements were a sure and approved touchstone, and Flaxman, with an unerring sense, interpreted them in the current visual conventions: but to him they were not mere narratives. In Homer he sought out scenes where a moral could be found or easily allegorized; and if that was lacking, these figures were still the schoolmasters of style, the true classic sense of form, didactic in shape even if not in meaning. It is this earnest elegance that has given Flaxman's art its lasting quality. He could be naïve, but he was never trivial.

Younger than Flaxman by twenty years, but arriving as a student in Rome while his senior was still working there, Richard Westmacott, whose father, another Richard, was a sculptor of some standing, early achieved considerable repute and in particular succeeded his father as a fashionable supplier of carved chimney pieces, a branch of the art much in demand and one in which the merits of each piece were carefully assessed by rival house owners. Westmacott's greatest triumph in this line was a dragon chimney piece for the Pavilion at Brighton, but by then he had established himself in every form of sculpture and begun the long line of memorials which are a widely characteristic feature of English churches. The greatest of these was his monument (1810) to Charles James Fox in Westminster Abbey. There is a large grandiloquence about the group, and the kneeling negro, symbol of Fox's efforts for the abolition of slavery, is a nobly executed conception (Pl. 53 b). Much praised by Canova, it must always hold a high place in any anthology of English sculpture. Westmacott, unfortunately, often falls below this notable achievement. Some of his reliefs have a certain emotional intensity, seen at its best in the Yorke memorial at Wimpole, and his angels or nymphs can have a suave decorative grace; in his touching memorial in Westminster Abbey to Mrs. Warren (*The Distressed Mother*: 1816) he imitates worn homespun on the marble with a realism that belongs to a later phase; but his skill could not inform so large an output as he undertook. He was knighted in 1837 and died in 1856, leaving a son who carried on his work on similar lines but with the lessening of vitality that comes from too strong a parental influence. With Sir Richard's two brothers, the Westmacotts form a dynasty which dominated the sculptural activities of the first half of the century, but even the combined family prestige and the considerable fortune and social status of its leading representative could not equal the renown and prosperity of their great rival, Francis Leggatt Chantrey.

Born in 1781, the son of a Yorkshire farmer,[1] Chantrey began his career as a grocer's apprentice in Sheffield, left that for apprenticeship to a local woodcarver, and made his way to London in 1802. Soon he attracted the attention of Samuel Rogers and received generous encouragement from Nollekens, still the accepted practitioner in portrait busts. Shrewd at money making and according to his pupil and biographer, J. T. Smith,[2] at keeping it, Nollekens was much employed and could give to a head a combination of

---

[1] There are lives of Chantrey by George Jones (1849), John Holland (1851), A. J. Raymond (1904), and H. Armitage (1915); as with many self-made artists he was uncertain of his age: when giving evidence in the case of *Carew* v. *Burrell* (*Report from shorthand notes* (1840), 59) he said he was '54 or 56' when he was in fact 59.

[2] *Nollekens and his Times* (1828): this malicious and readable book has several times been reprinted: ed. G. W. Stonier (1945).

individuality with classical reserve that greatly pleased his distinguished patrons. Compared with his busts, those of Chantrey
are more genial and natural; he could suggest the yielding roundness of flesh without straining the limits of his medium, and his
famous head of Sir Walter Scott (Pl. 61 *a*) seemed to Lockhart the
best likeness of that much-portrayed author.[1] Only William Behnes
among his contemporaries could equal him, and Behnes, ill regu-
lated and unfortunate in his life, is very uneven in his art. His
mourning figure of Beriah Botfield (1825: Norton, Northants.),
very recognizably the same young man as gazes confidently out
of Phillips's portrait (Pl. 9), is a most sympathetic rendering of
romantic melancholy.

In 1812 an opportunity for large-scale work came to Chantrey
through a commission from Thomas Johnes, the great Welsh
collector and scholar, whose only daughter had died as a young
girl. The monument dominated the small church at Hafod, built
in 1803 at Johnes's expense from designs by Wyatt, 'a neat edifice
with rather a modern look' George Borrow called it.[2] The small
church, till its destruction by fire in 1932, was dominated by a
great marble group that showed Marianne Johnes lying on a couch,
mourned by her parents, with her palette, brushes, and lyre beside
her, and a book half slipping from her hand. Twenty years earlier
Banks had shown Penelope Boothby lying asleep on her tomb at
Ashbourne, a small English girl with no classical allusions. It was
the beginning of a new readiness to be directly affecting. Stothard
in his paintings played on similar sensibilities, and it was probably he who provided Chantrey with the design for the Johnes
memorial and with some suggestions for *The Sleeping Children*,
the work that finally established his repute. Mrs. Robinson,
daughter of a dean of Lichfield, had tragically lost her two young
daughters, and commissioned a monument to them for the cathedral. Chantrey's model was exhibited at the Academy of 1817, and

[1] Its popularity led to many replicas, few of which had any direct work from
Chantrey on them, and to a large-scale piracy of plaster casts.

[2] Hafod House was built in 1786, and rebuilt after a fire in 1807, by Thomas
Baldwin for Thomas Johnes in an elaborate Gothic style: Turner painted one of his
most romantic water-colours of it (Pl. 12 *b*). See E. Inglis-Jones, *Peacocks in Paradise*
(1950). The ruins of the house were demolished in 1958.

aroused something of the enthusiasm that attended the early showings of Wilkie. All England mourned with Mrs. Robinson and the tomb long seemed 'a production for delicacy, pathos and tender feeling unparalleled in the whole range of modern sculpture'.[1] Today the pathos seems a little mawkish, with the curls, the chubby cheeks, the fading snowdrops (Pl. 54 a): there is a discordance between the subject and the style; Chantrey's clean lines and firm carving, essentially suited for marble, make too definite a statement out of these maternal sorrows. The large Pike Watts monument at Ilam (Staffordshire), showing the dying father blessing his wife and children, is a sounder example of his skill and the sentiment is kept within reasonable bounds, though the style falters, for the Grecian couch on which the sick man reclines is supported on a plinth with Gothic mouldings, an improper mingling, not infrequent in England, that Canova would never have tolerated. Less linear than Flaxman, Chantrey had a far greater sense of volume, which he could convey by very economical effects of modelling, effects that could easily be transferred by intermediaries to the marble block. He was also tactfully skilful in his suggestion both of classic drapery and modern costume. Canning in Westminster Yard wears unmistakably a toga but with stockings beneath it: William Pitt in Hanover Square is cloaked rather than togad: and the high relief of the seated figure of John Phelips at Wells uses quite frankly a voluminous dressing gown. Bishops in their lawn sleeves and flowing robes provided an actual compromise between old convention and existing fact and Bishop Heber at St. Paul's or Bishop Ryder at Lichfield (Pl. 50 a) show 'how very eligible such costume may become under the hand of a master'.[2] One of his most ingenious pieces shows a compromise of another kind, and his lovely group of Mrs. Jordan posing as Charity with two of the FitzClarence children (Pl. 61 b), commissioned by the royal lover after his accession, is one of the latest and not least typical of Regency

[1] J. Croston, *Chantrey's Peak Scenery* (1886), 12; see also 'Memoir of Chantrey', in *European Mag.*, lxxxi (1822), 6.

[2] *European Mag.* lxxxv (1824), 457, refering to another of his statues, that of Dr. Jackson at Christ Church, Oxford.

inventions. In his large output there is naturally much inequality.[1] The sensitivity of the carving varies with the assistant employed and the amount of working up given by the master,[2] but at his best his art is of a high order. In the reclining figure of Mrs. Boulter at Great Tew a gentle rhythm runs through the whole pose, the transition of head, neck and torso has rarely been more successfully rendered, and the face in its expression has surpassed sentiment and reached serenity (Frontispiece). Eminently sensible and successful, he left a considerable fortune, and the Chantrey Bequest has, if not without controversy, served to keep at least his name remembered.

The full inheritance of the classic tradition came to a boy, born in 1790 close to Conway, that shrine of romanticism, John Gibson. Thanks to the support and patronage of the Liverpool Maecenas, William Roscoe, he received some training in sculpture. Roscoe's interests lay in the Italian Renaissance; the author of lives of Lorenzo de Medici and Leo X, like Lorenzo a banker by profession, he sought to emulate their patronage and make Liverpool a Florence of the north. Raphael was to him the climax of achievement in the visual arts and he taught to the young boy, who modelled for his fireplace one of the grisailles from the Stanza della Segnatura, a respect for simplicity of statement and for ideal beauty. 'The works of the ancients', he told him, 'will teach you how to select the scattered beauties displayed in Nature. The Greek statue is Nature in the abstract, therefore when we contemplate those sublime works we feel elevated.'[3] It was a lesson that John Gibson never forgot. When in 1817 he came to London, Flaxman gave him much encouragement and urged him to go to Rome. 'Mr. Chantrey', however, 'did not think that there was

---

[1] Chantrey's models were bequeathed to the University of Oxford, and have recently been rearranged in the Ashmolean Museum, though the passage of time has taken a toll of considerable damage to them.

[2] For an account of Chantrey's methods of work see J. Holland, *Memorials of Chantrey* (1851), 294. Allan Cunningham and Henry Weekes were among his assistants.

[3] Lady Eastlake, *Life of John Gibson* (1870), 34; see George Chandler, *William Roscoe* (1953); J. R. Hale, *England and the Italian Renaissance* (1954), chap. iv. Archer Shee's portrait of Roscoe in his library, with Fox's bust on the table beside him, is a telling record of this phase of northern culture (Pl. 7 b).

any necessity for a sculptor to go there, he thought that in London might be found every requisite for his improvement.'[1] But to Rome he went and in September 1817, with £150 collected by his friends in Liverpool, he set out on his journey. There his drawings at once arrested Canova's attention, and the world-famous sculptor took him into his studio and treated him as one of his favourite pupils.

At Rome Gibson remained, with a few brief visits to England, until his death there in January 1866. In his naïve autobiography we have a vivid picture of the life of the English artist community; of the visits of wealthy English patrons such as the duke of Devonshire and Sir George Beaumont; of the rule of taste under Canova and Thorwaldsen, with whom Gibson, true to their tradition as opposed to the rising anti-classicism of Lorenzo Bartolini, came to rank as a third genius; of the Rome of the siege of 1848, shells bursting in the studio, Garibaldi 'beautiful, lawless and brave'. We have, too, a picture of the man himself, single-minded, unambitious and ungrasping, devoted to his art, very loyal to his friends, his brother 'Mr. Ben', Mrs. Robinson, Mrs. Huskisson, Mrs. Sandbach, the Eastlakes, charming the Queen and the Prince Consort with his unaffected manners. His statues have a clean, simple line, trivial sometimes in subject, shepherd boys and girls with butterflies, but without the contemporary sentiment of Chantrey's children, without, too, the poignancy that the latter sometimes reached. Gradually these statues and reliefs came back to some of the great houses of England. In Liverpool his statue of Huskisson, clad in a toga with one arm bare, roused some controversy when erected in his mausoleum built by Foster in St. James's cemetery, and was perhaps a strange tribute to this earliest victim of the railway age, but his widow stood firm and the statue was not only accepted but another version ordered for the Custom House.[2] In Foster's Ionic funerary chapel (Pl. 51 b), above the cemetery gorge, there are more of Gibson's monuments, William

[1] See autobiography quoted by T. Matthews, *The Biography of John Gibson* (1911), 40; Chantrey was a thorough Briton and later deeply suspicious of the Prince Consort's leanings towards German art.

[2] Now moved to Prince's Boulevard: there is a third version in Pimlico Gardens, London, originally designed for the London Royal Exchange.

Hammerton, Emily Robinson, William Earle, his wrinkled hand wearily marking the passage in his book (Pl. 51 *a*): nowhere can the rhythms and idealization of English neo-classicism be more surely experienced. 'In you', wrote Lord Lytton in his dedicatory epistle to *Zanoni* (1846), 'we behold the three great and long undetected principles of Grecian Art, simplicity, calm and concentration.' Strangely enough, to this severity Gibson sometimes in his later work added colour, rightly believing this to have been the Greek practice. When exhibited with two others of his tinted statues at the Exhibition of 1862, his 'tinted Venus' provided dinner-table talk for all fashionable London.

By his will Gibson left his models and unsold works to the Royal Academy, thereby explicitly following the examples of Canova and Thorwaldsen. Today some are shown on the stairs to the Diploma Gallery, and little noticed. There is dullness and sometimes insipidity in their formal elegance, but they are beautifully modelled, and in the marble beautifully carved; for, unlike most English sculptors, Gibson had constantly his chisel in his hand, and he had to a rare degree a sense of the smooth planes, the broad but subtle modulations to which Italian marble lends itself. The surface of his bodies is never dull, whatever vacancy of mind seems to possess them. Something of his lost repute will some time be restored to him and then the pages of Lady Eastlake's book, itself so mannered in its treatment, will once more be turned, and the young man from Conway, who went to the Continent speaking only English and Welsh and 'the latter was of no use to me in Paris', the devout Christian solving with little awareness of the difficulties the old problems of Christianity and pagan legend, the upright, much loved man will once more be found one of the most appealing characters in the annals of English art.

Working with Gibson in Rome was Richard Wyatt, whose fine classical line and sureness of taste find their happiest example in the Legh memorial at Winwick (Pl. 52 *b*). Taste was less assured in the case of his cousin, Matthew Cotes, son of James Wyatt the architect. His large monument to Princess Charlotte, in St. George's chapel, Windsor, is one of the most surprising of Regency pieces. The death of this princess in childbirth, after a year of married life with the man of her own determined choice, had moved the country as few events before or since; robust in appearance, humorous and courageous in character, the princess had filled a sentimental need that few of her relatives had been able to satisfy:

> in the dust
> The fair haired daughter of the isles is laid
> The love of millions. How we did entrust
> Futurity to her.[1]

The suicide of her doctor, Sir Richard Croft, seemed to confirm the rumours that the case had been sadly mishandled and deepened the tragedy. Arthur William Devis, famous for his painting of *The Death of Nelson*,[2] painted for the church at Esher *The Apotheosis of Princess Charlotte* in which the princess is carried up to heaven by angels, one of whom carries her still-born child. The theme is based on baroque versions of the Assumption, and it is at first sight a strange and somewhat dubious treatment, even in a moment of such charged emotion. But there had been some precedents. The Rev. Matthew Peters had round the turn of the century popularized pictures of pious families soaring upward at the last day and of angels carrying children to paradise. They were sentimental exuberances and the churchmanship of the eighteenth century had been a little starved of such nourishment. West had painted the apotheosis of Nelson, George Carter that of David Garrick. Flaxman in 1784, at Gloucester, had shown Mrs. Sarah Morley and her child, both drowned at sea, borne heavenward by angels. That, however, had been in low relief. The monument designed by Matthew Cotes Wyatt, set up by George IV in 1824 and subscribed for by 1s. contributions, is in very full relief. Against carved stone drapery the princess soars upward, carved in the round and fastened by iron bars to the back wall. On either side, also carved in the round, are substantial angels: below, covered by a sheet, is the dead body, the fingers of one hand protruding, with macabre effect, from beneath the covering, mourned by two veiled figures. The princess is lightly clad, the draperies moulded to her figure: reticence is at a discount: a dramatic *tour de force* is aimed at, and

---

[1] Byron, *Childe Harold*, Canto iv, 169.   [2] Maritime Museum, Greenwich.

the orange glass originally set in the west window of the chapel cast a heavenly glow upon it. An age used to the cartoons of Gillray, the horrors of Fuseli, the awe-inspiring catastrophes depicted by John Martin, could take this full-blooded performance. To us it seems overstated and in doubtful taste: but it is the expression of an epoch and an endeavour rare in English art (Pl. 55). Four years later Wyatt repeated the floating figure and stained glass lighting even more dramatically for a memorial to the duchess of Rutland in the small Romanesque mausoleum at Belvoir Castle. He had already made a striking statue of the duchess for the saloon at Belvoir, where his brother, Benjamin Dean Wyatt, something of a specialist in French designs, collaborated with him in producing one of the grandest of Regency decorations. The gold frieze of peacocks, the Manners's crest, is linked with Matthew's ceiling paintings of the triumph of Juno over Io, and two magnificent birds watch her engaged in the macabre occupation of removing the eyes from the decapitated head of Argus. The whole story of the rebuilding of Belvoir and the patronage of the Duchess Elizabeth is redolent of the fancies of the time.[1]

These were but some of the most celebrated names. There were in this wonderfully abundant period many others. If royal patronage and official commissions are to be accepted as evidence, Peter Turnerelli, Sculptor-in-Ordinary to the Royal Family, was one of the outstanding sculptors of the Regency. His work included the Jubilee bust of George III (1810), busts of eminent generals for Carlton House, and the 'nuptial busts' of Princess Charlotte and Prince Leopold. John Edward Carew was given the rare opportunity of ideal works for Lord Egremont at Petworth, which he carried out with a softer modelling than true neo-classicism allowed (Pl. 81 a). Ill-founded hopes on his part led to a celebrated lawsuit with Lord Egremont's successors, a telling document of the relations between patron and artist.[2] Thomas Campbell, an Edinburgh man who studied in Rome, executed the statue of Paulina Borghese that is at Chatsworth, and is seen to considerable advan-

---

[1] Christopher Hussey in *C.L.* cxx (1956), 1456, 1500.

[2] *Report of the Trial of the Cause Carew against Burrell, Bt. and another* taken in shorthand by Mr. Cooke (1840): both Westmacott and Chantrey gave evidence.

tage in the statue of Lord Hopetoun standing with his horse in the courtyard of the Royal Bank of Scotland, Edinburgh. Another Scot, William Scoular, had considerable repute for classical and fancy subjects and made for Queen Adelaide, then duchess of Clarence, a touching small figure of her dead child that recalls the pathos of Chantrey's *Sleeping Children*.[1] Peter Hollins in his recumbent statues of Lady Bradford (1842, Weston, Staffs.), with its relief of floating angels whose draperies have an almost *art nouveau* curve, and Mrs. Thompson (1838, Malvern priory) equals the finest of Chantrey's female figures, with an added softness of modelling and flow of line that is his own. His seated figure of Dr. Warneford (1840) in the Warneford Hospital, Oxford, shows another side of his considerable gifts. Robert William Sievier, an encyclopaedic genius who abandoned sculpture for the manufacture of elastic fabrics and experiments with telegraphy, modelled with great precision and delicacy and gave strikingly life-like appearance to his figures, such as that of Lord Harcourt in St. George's chapel, Windsor (1832). In this approach to realism the lead was taken by Samuel Joseph, whose statue of Wilberforce (Pl. 53 a), set up in 1838 in Westminster Abbey, marks a break with traditions of idealism. No one could be less classical than this seated figure, his legs crossed, his expression humorous and lively, his hand playing with his cravat, the book just closed. New men were coming to the fore, restless under the strict discipline which had curbed Flaxman, Chantrey, and Westmacott in their sentimentalism; but with the loosening of restriction the great era was in fact over.

Not, however, before its achievement was far flung. In St. Paul's church, Halifax, New Brunswick, the body of R. J. Uniacke (d. 1834) lies on his bier, signed 'John Gibson Romae'; Flaxman sent out to Barbados a relief for the tomb of John Braithwaite, and used, reasonably enough, the same design three years later for a memorial in Ledbury; India has many monuments, such as Chantrey's great relief of Bishop Heber in St. George's, Madras;[2]

[1] At Windsor: reproduced M. Hopkirk, *Queen Adelaide* (1946).
[2] Reproduced as frontispiece to vol. ii of Mrs. Heber's *Life of Reginald Heber* (1830).

Chantrey's George Washington is in the Boston State House; Baily's Governor Bourke still looks out over the bay of Sydney; instance after instance could be given: sculpture was imperial as well as classical.

VI

THE AGE OF WILKIE

THE opening years of the century were full of plans for the encouragement of the arts, often with a side glance at their possible influence on manufactures. Benjamin West brought forward in 1802 proposals to form a 'National Association for the Encouragement of Works of Dignity and Importance in Art', and in 1805 Archer Shee's *Rhymes on Art*, which enjoyed a considerable vogue, urged the claims of the arts on national consideration. One result of these exhortations was the opening in 1806 of the British Institution in Boydell's Shakespeare Gallery in Pall Mall. It aimed at showing and selling modern works, awarding premiums, and also holding exhibitions of old masters, largely drawn from private collections, for artists to copy. The control of the Institution was in the hands of a committee of subscribers, of whom none was a professional artist and amongst whom Lord Strafford, Sir George Beaumont, and Richard Payne Knight were prominent. Valentine Green, the engraver, was Keeper, and his design for the 1811 catalogue, 'an ass in the Greek pallium teaching', was a manifesto of the Institution's support of national and contemporary art against the more traditional approach of the Royal Academy.

The press naturally enough proceeded to play off one body against the other; *The Times*, for instance, backed the Institution and did not begin giving notices to the Academy till 1824; but others soon found the Institution equally open to criticism for partiality and exclusiveness. The formation in 1823 of the Society of British Artists[1] was the scheme of a dissident group, using James Elmes's *Annals of the Fine Arts* as their main organ and supported by Haydon, Martin, and other well-known opponents of the Academy. It had a chequered career in its rooms in Suffolk Street, for the standards achieved were never wholly convincing: 'We

---

[1] For the Society of British Artists see Whitley, ii *passim* and *European Mag.* lxxxiv (1823), 150; for criticism of the Academy, *Annals of the Fine Arts*, iii (1818), Preface.

hope', wrote the critic of the *European Magazine* in 1825, 'the foolish thing will be given up'; but in 1841 it was still sufficiently vigorous to obtain a royal charter.

The Royal Academy itself was still housed in Somerset House, as rebuilt by Sir William Chambers in 1780. The entrance hall, furnished with large casts of classical subjects and leading to the famous elliptical staircase, with which Rowlandson had made such play (Pl. 21 *a*), can be seen delineated as it was in 1810 in Ackermann's *Repository of Arts, No. 17*.[1] There were frequent complaints of its ill-kept arrangements. Visitors mounted 'the extremely inconvenient, wretchedly dark, filthy dirty and eminently disagreeable staircase of the Royal Academy, slipping over scattered orange peels, covering their gloves with dust, if accidentally touching any part of the balusters or walls, during the horrid ascent, the abominations of which are scarcely compensated by the entertaining absurdity of beholding Hercules with his apples in a brass wire bird cage, at the bottom of it'.[2] But despite such disadvantages, the annual exhibitions remained the great centre of British art, and were on the whole genuinely representative of its trends and most skilled practice. An Academy exhibition gives a cross-section of English painting and sculpture, and the year 1813 may serve as well as another for the purpose of a brief survey.

It was a year which to a writer in the first volume of the *New Monthly Magazine*[3] seemed to promise a fresh era in the arts, largely through the government's patronage of the great architectural schemes for Marylebone Park; but English painting too, he thought, held now an established place in European art. No. 1 in the exhibition was George Dawe's *A child rescued by its mother from an eagle's nest* (Pl. 56). It was a subject already treated by Blake for Hayley's *Ballads*, but there the story has the more fantastic ending of child and mother carried to earth on the eagle's wings and belongs

[1] S. C. Hutchinson, *The Homes of the Royal Academy* (1956). W. Sandby, *The History of the Royal Academy of Arts*, 2 vols. (1862), is the basic account: see also J. E. Hodgson and F. A. Eaton, *The Royal Academy and its Members* (1905); *The Royal Academy from Reynolds to Millais*, ed. C. Holme (Studio Special Number, 1904); W. R. M. Lamb, *The Royal Academy* (1951).

[2] (T. E. Hook), *Love and Pride* (1833), i. 41.

[3] i (1814), 66.

to a visionary, more ethereal world (Pl. 20 a). In Dawe's version it is the terror and melodrama that is emphasized; the vast beat of the eagle's wings and the giddy precariousness of the matronly figure belong to the excitements of the new age. 'Tamely conceived and indifferently executed' was the view of the critic in *Bell's Weekly Messenger*,[1] but if it is tame, then the demand for agonies was acute indeed. Lawrence was represented by a group of eight portraits, of which that of Sir Thomas Graham (United Service Club), martially posed before a battle-scene, was the most ambitious, that of James Watt (coll. Miss Boulton, Tew Manor) the most interesting subject. The veteran Northcote exhibited, besides several portraits, a scene of lion hunting, one of the subjects coming into vogue with the romantics, and a biblical scene of *Joseph and his brethren* (engraving in Witt Library). Another biblical scene, *Moses and Aaron before Pharaoh, King of Egypt* (Grittleton House), was by the President, Benjamin West. Stothard contributed a group of Shakespeare's characters (V. and A.), but it was hung above the work of a younger artist, and as Stothard himself admits, his picture only obtained a glance from the crowd when they could not get close enough to admire the delicate precision of David Wilkie's *Blind Man's Buff* (Buckingham Palace). Of the younger artists, Wilkie now held the most assured place, and in 1813 was a member of the hanging committee, his colleagues being James Ward of whose nine exhibits seven were of horses and one of dogs, and Richard Westmacott. Turner showed his two strangely different paintings, *The Deluge* and *Frosty Morning*. Constable showed his *Landscape: boys fishing*,[2] one of his earliest achievements in the maturity of his style, and *Landscape: morning*. Of the younger men, William Mulready showed two paintings, *Boys playing at cricket* and *Punch*, both in the vein that Wilkie was so rapidly popularizing;[3] William Collins won much praise with his pathetic *Disposal of a favourite lamb* (Pl. 64 a). The Bristol painter, Edward Bird, had a series of paintings showing the career of a poacher.

---

[1] 1813, 150. For Dawe see *Library of Fine Arts*, i (1831), 9. These Academy sensationalisms are now replaced by the cinema and the illustrated press.

[2] Reproduced C. R. Leslie, *Memoir of Constable*, ed. A. Shirley (1937), pl. 48, coll. Hartree family. The *Landscape: morning* is untraced.

[3] For these two paintings see J. Dafforne, *Pictures by W. Mulready*, 11.

Three years earlier a critic had classed him with Wilkie as having 'fully established the superiority of English artists over those of the Flemish School, in that great requisite of painting, the union of morality with the accurate and lively representation of domestic scenes'.[1] The poacher ended up duly penitent and presumably fulfilled these requirements.

Of the portrait painters, other than Lawrence, William Owen had a fine, straightforward portrait of Dr. William Howley (N.P.G.), who that same year became bishop of London and was to become in 1828 the last of the prince archbishops of Canterbury. Owen's paintings are always distinguished by the careful renderings of the costume, and in this the surplice, so often a dull patch in ecclesiastical portraits, is treated with a real sense of texture. Phillips had a large painting of the Prince Regent on horseback, in which the action of His Royal Highness seemed to the *Morning Chronicle*[2] 'singular and commanding'. Beechey's portrait of the Right Honourable Spencer Perceval had a particular and tragic interest, for in the previous May the Prime Minister had been assassinated in the lobby of the House of Commons: another of his portraits, that of Sir Francis Bourgeois, was also of a man recently deceased, for in January 1811 the founder of the Dulwich Gallery had died as a result of a riding accident.[3]

In subject painting the rising generation was represented by Etty, whose *Whisper of Love* and *Indian Warrior* sound like his normal style, though his third exhibit, *The Fireside*, suggests something more in the Wilkie vein.[4] Fuseli did not exhibit, but R. T. Bone's *Nymph and Cupid* was probably, to judge from his drawings, a derivative piece reflecting the Fuseli manner: H. P. Bone's *Goblin Cave* was a scene from *The Lady of the Lake*. The young American artist, C. R. Leslie, attracted some attention by his *Murder* (coll.

[1] *Bell's Weekly Messenger* (1810), 157 and (1811), 149. One of the series, *The Game-keeper's Return* (panel 18 in. by 23 in.), was in Christie's 10 June 1955, lot 27: another, *The Poacher in Prison*, is in the Guildhall Gallery.

[2] Notice of the Academy, 3 and 4 May: untraced.

[3] For these two portraits see W. Roberts, *Sir William Beechey* (1907), 124.

[4] *The Fireside* was popularized as a subject of Cowper's poem: Fuseli has a bizarre rendering of it (Ganz Coll., Oberhofen). The Ettys, the Bones, and the Hilton are all untraced.

J. R. Boone, Esq., Towson, Maryland), a grotesque piece, to judge from a photograph, which suggests that the artist was well advised to turn to lighter subjects. William Hilton, now in his twenty-seventh year, was admired for his *Mary anointing the feet of Jesus*, which was purchased by the British Institution. His was a careful, pondered achievement, a reaction against the violence of the mannerist school, and it is sad that much of it, such as his master-piece, *Edith finding the Body of Harold*,[1] should be such sorry wrecks of corrugated asphaltum. He died in 1839, disappointed by lack of patronage, broken by the death of his wife, Peter de Wint's sister.

In landscape, apart from Constable and Turner, there were two paintings by Sir George Beaumont, several Welsh castles, a *Ship in distress off Scarborough* by T. C. Hofland (which won him a premium of £100 from the British Institution and established his reputation), and a *Poetical effect at Melrose described in the Lay of the Last Minstrel* by Joseph Gandy, items which show romanticism gaining ground.[2] In a vast landscape, the distance marked by clumps of trees and emphasized by the minute scale of the figures, *Adam's first sight of Eve*[3] was represented by John Martin, soon to be one of the most admired portents of the age.

Any connoisseur, either English or continental, looking back at this Academy from any point in the next thirty years would probably have selected as the most important picture Wilkie's *Blind Man's Buff* (Pl. 58 a). A new bias had been given to English art by this young, lanky Scot from the Fifeshire manse of Cults.[4]

[1] It now languishes in the cellars of the Tate Gallery, and is little likely to be restored to presentable condition. For its condition see J. C. Horsley, *Recollections of a Royal Academician* (1903), 228.

[2] The Hofland and Gandy are untraced: the former was bought by the marquis of Stafford; Redgrave, *Century of British Painters* (ed. 1947), 454.

[3] It was found in 1945 by Mr. Evelyn Waugh in an hotel in Ardrossan: it is now in the Glasgow Art Gallery. See T. Balston, *John Martin* (1947), 36.

[4] The manse at Cults in Fifeshire, built in 1797 for Wilkie's father, the small walled garden with its sundial, the tiny sessions house, the church with its raised pulpit dominating the congregation, remain unchanged since Wilkie knew them as a boy and are as he drew them, but on the church wall are the reliefs of his parents, made by Chantrey, and of Wilkie himself by Samuel Joseph, whose statue of him is now in the Tate Gallery.

It is difficult today to realize the immense prestige he secured among his contemporaries. When John Martin, in 1853, twelve years after Wilkie's death, painted his vast canvas of the *Last Judgement*, he placed Wilkie with Michelangelo, Leonardo da Vinci, Raphael, Titian, Rubens, and Dürer in his group of painters.[1] Anecdotal painting, scenes of everyday life with a moral, pathetic, or comical twist to them, had never since Hogarth lost their popular appeal in England. Wheatley and Walton had invested them with an eighteenth-century elegance which owed something to the example of Greuze, but it was not till the coming of Wilkie that the homely scene was presented with all the technical attributes of pose and colour that hitherto had been the preserve of high historical art.[2] Wilkie persuaded his father to send him when fourteen to the Trustees Academy in Edinburgh: there he stayed for four years, learning what the northern capital could teach him, gazing in the print sellers and auction rooms at the etchings and engravings of Rembrandt and Ostade, the latter a name that recurs persistently in all his letters and writings. When he came to London in 1805, his first painting exhibited in the Royal Academy, in 1806, was *The Village Politicians* (earl of Mansfield). It is a small picture, 2 ft. 6 in. by 3 ft. 4 in., showing a group of countrymen seated round a table in the inn discussing an article in the *Gazetteer*. It was hung 'on the chimney', that is above the fireplace in the main room, a much favoured place. The crowd round it was so great that when Haydon, having read the favourable notice of it in the news, hurried to see it, 'there was no getting in sideways or edge-ways'. Wilkie, pale as death, kept saying, 'Dear, dear, it's jest wonderful.'[3] It is difficult today to imagine the interest that this simple-seeming work aroused. The celebrated connoisseur, John Julius Angerstein, whose collection was shortly to provide the basis for the National Gallery, pointed it out at the Academy dinner as 'the star of the collection':[4] Northcote disliked it, but

[1] The identifications come from Martin's key to the painting. See above, p. 107.

[2] The main authority for Wilkie is Allan Cunningham, *The Life of David Wilkie*, 3 vols. (1843). See also Lord Ronald Sutherland Gower, *Sir David Wilkie* (1902), and W. Bayne, *Sir David Wilkie* (1903).

[3] *Autobiography of B. R. Haydon*, ed. Tom Taylor (new ed., 2 vols., 1926), i. 36.

[4] Cunningham, *Life*, i. 115.

saw in it the beginning of 'the Pauper Style': 'Young man', said Fuseli, 'that is a dangerous work.' The tradition, as Angerstein rightly saw, was that of Teniers and Hogarth. The former artist had deeply impressed the young Scotsman, when he first saw paintings by him in London: 'pictures by Teniers, for clear touching certainly go to the height of human perfection in art: they make all other pictures look misty beside them'.[1] This 'clear touching' remained for long Wilkie's main preoccupation; he worked over and over his small figures, scraping out and re-forming them, studying each touch of the brush and filling his interiors with luminous shadows. His subjects were drawn from the village life with which he was best familiar, and were studies in character rather than moral tales painted with a message. His originality in fact lay in his refusal to go outside his most intimate range of experience and the scrupulous care with which he worked. He came at a moment when the small Dutch masters, much sought after by the Prince Regent,[2] were coming into favour, and he produced with convincing sincerity an English equivalent which pleased by the homeliness of its subject and yet employed the manners of accepted academic tradition.

Amongst the various distinguished patrons whom Wilkie's art now attracted, Sir George Beaumont was almost inevitably one. He found for the young artist a token of encouragement of singular appropriateness, Hogarth's mahlstick, and he commissioned from him *The Blind Fiddler*, exhibited at the Academy in 1807 and given with Sir George's collection to the National Gallery in 1826. This carefully designed picture, with its exact details of still life, its sentiment, its genuine sense of the bond of the music between listeners and performer, has always been one of his most popular works; but it lacks the Watteau-like pointedness of pose and gesture that he could give to his smaller figures in more crowded, lively scenes such as the *Village Festival*, painted for Angerstein in 1811, *Blind Man's Buff* (1812)[3] and *The Penny Wedding* (1819)

[1] Ibid. 79.
[2] *The Athenaeum* (1829), 753, refers to 'a fatal predilection for specimens of Dutch excellence in the first patron in the realm'.
[3] *Bell's Weekly Messenger*, 9 May 1813. 'This excellent artist is declining into a

for the Prince Regent, or, on a somewhat larger scale, his *Chelsea Pensioners Reading the Gazette of the Battle of Waterloo* (Apsley House) for the duke of Wellington in 1822. These commissions testify to the position that the young artist had rapidly secured. In 1817 he was staying at Abbotsford painting a somewhat clumsy group of the Scott family, posed as cottagers (Edinburgh); in 1820 he completed *Reading the Will* for the king of Bavaria, who gave it a place of honour among his Dutch masters.[1] Everyone painted Wilkie (Pl. 60), this sandy-haired, dishevelled, long-limbed man, with his drawled east coast 'Really' that all his London friends imitated, earnest and persistent to the point of being boring, but with a charm of sincerity that made his gaucheries endearing. Phillips makes him a romantic character, in a sweeping black cloak, very handsome and certainly a little untrue, though, as always with Phillips, one suspects that he has given us an insight that more prosaic renderings miss. Jackson shows him, in a drawing of 1807, alert, the mouth half open, eager to speak. Beechey painted him, in 1808, with his palette in his hand and a sketch of *The Blind Fiddler* behind him, more round-faced and cherubic. Owen gave him a firmer, blunter look.[2] Wilkie in his own two self-portraits gives the keen youth, but recently arrived in London (S.N.P.G.), and then, some ten years later, the more rounded, thoughtful face, still under the same tousled crop of hair. Andrew Geddes painted him, very pleased with his dressing gown and leaning against a handsome tapestry chair that his mother had sent him (S.N.P.G.).[3]

With Raeburn in Edinburgh, Wilkie in London, Walter Scott an international figure, and Abbotsford a constant centre of

prettyism, similar to Watteau. He should shake off this feebleness.' For Wilkie's interest in the Dulwich Watteaus see Mrs. [A. T.] Thomson, *Recollections of Literary Characters* (1854), ii. 168.

[1] Now in the Neue Pinakothek, Munich.

[2] Robinson & Fisher Sale, 3 March 1927: photograph, Witt Library.

[3] Cunningham, op. cit. 359: the same chair figures in Wilkie's *Letter of Introduction* (Edinburgh) and several of his other paintings. A set of similar chairs is in the possession of the earl of Crawford and Balcarres and comes from Crawford Priory, the great house at Cults, where in 1811 Lady Mary Crawford was busy with a new Gothic house: 'one end', wrote Wilkie to his brother, 'is a castle, the other a Gothic chapel' (Cunningham, op. cit. 336). It seems possible that some chairs may have been given to the manse at the time of the alterations.

pilgrimage, the cultural association of Scotland and England had rarely been closer or more balanced. This association was now, in 1822, to receive its great apotheosis, the visit of George IV to Edinburgh, the first visit since the Union of the Kingdoms. The New Town was awaiting him. Charlotte Square had been completed to Robert Adam's designs in 1800, and Playfair and Gillespie Graham were laying out squares and crescents in a severely Grecian style, now and then tempered by experiments in Gothic. As the day approached, excitement grew. Wilkie travelled north with William Collins and Andrew Geddes: the clans gathered in their tartans, with bagpipes playing. Wilkie had secured a position at Holyrood: Collins was down at Leith harbour, when 'who should start up upon the occasion to see the same occurrence, but J. M. W. Turner, Esq., R.A.P.P!!! who is now with us we cannot tell how'.[1] He had in fact come up by boat and filled two sketchbooks on the journey there and back. There are two unfinished oils in the Tate Gallery of the Lord Provost's banquet in the Parliament House and of the king at the High Church of St. Giles. 'The painters', writes Wilkie Collins in his memoir of his father,[2] 'soon became involved in all the choicest dissipations of the Northern Metropolis, at that period when court gaiety and conviviality outmanœuvred Scotch prudence. . . . Wilkie forgot his discretion in a "new sky-blue coat", and caroused with the rest, when the mirthful dinner closed, in gastronomic triumph, the bustling day' and, led by Sir Walter Scott, the whole company danced round the table. This particular dinner was to celebrate the knighthood conferred on Raeburn on the last day of the king's visit.[3]

Wilkie painted two pictures commemorating this occasion, a large, life-size portrait of the king, wearing the kilt, an imposing, muscular figure, defying the monarch's own reputed statement 'I cannot help smiling at myself', and the *Entry of George IV into*

[1] Letter from Wilkie to his sister (Cunningham, *Life*, ii. 85): P.P. stands for Professor of Perspective. [2] i. 200.

[3] For this banquet a Chamberlain Worcester dinner service was borrowed from an Edinburgh resident. Part of it still exists and is the property of Mrs. W. E. Bassett of Melbourne. Each piece has a painted view of a Gothic building, and the service is an admirable example of the new romantic taste. It has the pattern-number 176, which dates it *c.* 1800 (Pl. 37 *a*).

Holyrood House. The latter, of which he also did a finished sketch, is for Wilkie at this time a large painting, 49 in. by 76 in.,[1] and it was one that gave him infinite trouble. He had gone to Edinburgh full of plans for his painting of John Knox preaching: this was his instinctive preoccupation, to which the royal painting was an interruption, and it was not in fact completed till many years afterwards, when Wilkie had returned from his long travels abroad. It was finally submitted for royal inspection in 1830 only a few months before the king's death. By then the fatal use of asphaltum was impairing the lasting qualities of his work, and indeed his portrait of the king, 'the most glazed and deepest-toned picture I have ever tried', is sadly corrugated, and the *Entry* is cracked in the darker passages; but its sense of movement and excitement, the immense variety of poses and of inner rhythms within these poses make it one of Wilkie's masterpieces and one of the most genuinely baroque of English paintings. It is a pondered design, and in his drawings we can follow his mind at work, how a stalwart Highlander in a sketch of ladies arriving in their carriages becomes the Duke of Argyll and two pages are also lifted from the same rapid note of an actual occasion (Pl. 59). For the finished painting is not actual at all: the king himself strikes a magnificent pose, a piece of courtly glorification. It is 'the Regency' at its height, with its climax in the debauched, florid, but withal royally charming and never quite unlikeable central figure.

A career that had seemed so steadily successful suffered in 1824 a series of reverses; these took the form of family misfortunes leading to a nervous breakdown in the artist's health. Wilkie had never been robust: tall and thin, shy in manner except when warmed by friendship, there had always been an element of frailty in him, and his strength, which he had often overtaxed in the prolonged care he gave to the production of a picture, now gave way. He became listless and incapable of work; the doctors were divided as to cause and cure; finally in the summer of 1825 he

---

[1] See S. Sitwell and F. Bamford, *Edinburgh* (1948), 220, where there is a detailed account of the ceremonies. Both paintings are in Holyrood: the smaller and better preserved version of the *Entry* is in the Scottish National Portrait Gallery (Pl. 59 *b*).

decided to go abroad and try the effect of changed surroundings. Aided by a generous gift from Sir George Beaumont, he began a foreign tour which was to last for three years.

Wilkie's success had naturally attracted followers. William Collins, his disciple and close friend, was the son of an Irishman who had settled in England as a journalist and picture dealer. Against such a background it is not surprising that the young William took to painting.[1] The success in 1813 of his picture *The Disposal of a favourite Lamb* has already been mentioned. The title sufficiently indicates its pathetic and anecdotal subject, which enormously pleased the public, and an engraving from it rapidly passed into fifteen thousand impressions, though compared with Wilkie's delicacy of pose the children are wooden and their gestures clumsy. In 1814 Collins was elected an Associate and six years later became an R.A.; in these intervening years he had found a new subject for his brush, seascapes, in which the figures of children on the beach played a subordinate part, and which he treated with a clear and luminous realization of the sky. His stretches of sand on a still day have, both in oil and water-colour, an opalescent quality which was his peculiar but limited gift. His woods and hedgerows, the background to his urchins swinging on gates or his villagers proceeding to church, could at times degenerate into dull formulas. Constable, who knew him well, could never forgive him his early success and some patronizing remarks attributed to him: 'Collins', he wrote to Archdeacon Fisher in 1825, 'has a coast scene with fish as usual, and a landscape like a large cow-turd.'[2] Collins himself was probably unaware of this resentment and wrote feelingly to Leslie of 'our lamented friend' when Leslie was compiling the *Life*.[3] With Wilkie his friendship was continuous and in periods of absence they exchanged long letters, where it is clear that each talked with deep confidence to the other. Collins's elder son, born in 1824, had Wilkie as his second name and the painter as his godfather; his celebrity as

---

[1] For Collins see W. Wilkie Collins, *Memoirs of the Life of William Collins*, 2 vols. (1848).

[2] R. B. Beckett, *Constable and the Fishers* (1952), 214.

[3] Leslie, *Life of Constable* (ed. 1937), 366.

Wilkie Collins the novelist was to give fresh fame to this old friendship.

Of all the exponents of this new style, William Mulready, next to Wilkie, was perhaps the most talented. Born in County Clare in 1786, the son of a leather-breeches maker, he was brought by his family to London some five years later.[1] His early career shows the varied money-making concerns to which a young artist might address himself, illustrating books for William Godwin, who was eking out his insufficient means by publishing tales for children; working on the great panoramas, Seringapatam, Acre, Agincourt, exhibited by R. K. Porter between 1800 and 1803; painting water-colour studies of ruined abbeys and country scenes under the influence of John Varley, whose sister he married; and experimenting with historical pieces. In the British Institution of 1808 he exhibited a painting, *The Rattle*, which is the first of his genre figure pieces. Undoubtedly it owed much to the success of Wilkie in the exhibition of 1806. The two artists were acquainted and Wilkie in 1814 painted Mulready as the lover in *Duncan Gray* (V. and A.), but they were never intimate. Robust, something of a pugilist, coping with an unhappy marriage and four children, Mulready's was a very different temperament: his artist friends were John Varley, William Hunt, and John Linnell; his chief patron Sir John Swinburne, a quite different group from that which surrounded Wilkie. He had a wonderful eye for the ungainly movements of small boys, and in his later years he found unusual harmonies of violet, green, and brown which give a particular poetic quality to the simple incidents he depicts.

While anecdote triumphed, historical painting languished. Nothing could be more contrary to the career of Wilkie than that of Benjamin Robert Haydon. Born in the same year as Hilton, he was to find the same lack of consistent patronage and his frustration and intransigence were to make much stir in England and bring no good to himself or his favourite causes. Coming

[1] F. G. Stephens, *Memorials of William Mulready* (1867, revised ed. 1890); J. Dafforne, *Pictures of William Mulready* (n.d.). His best-known paintings are carved in outline round the tomb on which he lies in effigy, under a wonderfully incorrect gothic canopy in Kensal Green. *The Rattle* is untraced.

to London from Exeter, he received a commission from Lord Mulgrave for a painting, the *Death of Dentatus* (marquess of Normanby), a large work on a six-foot canvas, which he characteristically painted and repainted, particularly after he had seen the Elgin marbles in their unworthy resting place in the pent house at the back of Lord Elgin's house in Park Lane. These became his models, which he constantly drew and on which he based his whole theory of proportion and anatomical knowledge. Of this study the final version of *Dentatus* was the first result: it is possible to recognize in the pose of the figure on the ground the torso of the *Theseus*; but Dentatus himself, muscular and violent, is an almost comic creation, suggesting that Fuseli and Martin were wise to abandon realism in their visionary scenes. *Dentatus* was accepted by the Academy but hung in what Haydon considered the poor light of the octagon room; in fact it was a position that had been occupied by several of Sir Joshua's pictures. His reaction against this supposed slight is characteristic of him; he never forgot his grievances, filling the pages of the twenty-seven volumes of his journal with self-pity and bombastic but curiously vivid rumblings of his damaged pride. He lives today by these pages, published by Tom Taylor in 1853, a document in near madness, but with some true pathos in the corruption of something that was also near greatness.[1] His paintings have darkened and the ground has come through: asphaltum he avoided and criticized Wilkie for his devotion to it, but his own technique has led to changes almost equally disastrous. He was not without his moments of success: three of his paintings, *The Judgement of Solomon* (1814), *Christ's Entry into Jerusalem* (1820), and *The Raising of Lazarus* (1823) were much praised and drew large crowds when they were exhibited: the first is now lost, the second is in St. Mary's Seminary, Norwood, Ohio, the third in the possession of the Tate Gallery, on loan to the Gallery in Plymouth. Meanwhile he put everything to his own disadvantage: alienating patrons such as Sir George

[1] Memoir by James Elmes in *Annals of Fine Arts*, v (1820), 335; E. George, *The Life and Death of Benjamin Robert Haydon* (1948). The *Autobiography and Memoirs* were selected from Haydon's journals by Tom Taylor in 1853: new ed. (A. P. D. Penrose) 2 vols. (1926), with detailed index. There is a one-volume edition by H. Elwin (1950) with a useful selection of plates.

Beaumont by accepting commissions and then not carrying them out; attacking prominent authorities such as Payne Knight in pamphlets; approaching the Academy, as he did in 1826 and 1827, and then storming at them because they failed immediately to elect him: he was three times imprisoned for debt, and five of his children died.

In 1820 the English public had the opportunity of seeing historical painting of a more contemporary kind. Géricault's *Raft of the Medusa* had been exhibited in the Salon of 1819 and had at once become a subject of controversy. The Director of the Musées Royaux purchased it, but did not propose to hang it, and Géricault, inspired by the recent success of Le Thière's *Judgment of Brutus* in England,[1] retrieved his vast canvas from the gallery cellars and brought it to England. Here was a work on the popular shipwreck theme of a melodramatic force that no English painter could equal. The public responded; Géricault seems to have made money out of his venture and later showed *The Raft* in Dublin also. But we have few comments on it from English artists: its fiercely propagandist, controversial spirit appears to have passed unnoticed and it probably seemed only an example of that large-scale historical painting, in which it was generally agreed the continent had the supremacy. Géricault himself was more observant.[2] He was warm in praise of the English school as shown in the Academy exhibition, and impatient with the familiar French attitude of dispraising all art but their own. 'How useful to our painters would it be', he writes, 'to see the touching expressions of Wilky.' Of the painting itself (*The Chelsea Pensioners*),

I will speak only of one figure which seemed to me the most perfect, whose pose and expressions draw tears, however much one holds them back. It is a soldier's wife who, thinking only of her husband, searches with harassed, restless eyes the list of the dead. . . . There is no crape or mourning: rather the wine flows on every table and the sky is un-furrowed by any fatally presaging lightnings. But it reaches a final pathos like nature herself. I am not afraid that you will tax me with

[1] Exhibited 1817: Whitley, i. 271.
[2] Géricault, *Raconté par lui même et par ses amis*, ed. Pierre Cailler (Geneva, 1947), 103; see Lee Johnson, 'The "Raft of the Medusa" in Great Britain', *Burl. Mag.* xcvi (1954), 249.

anglomania. You know as well as I what we have that is good and
what we lack.

'Like nature herself.' These anecdotes, these touching expressions,
these wonderfully telling gestures have for us the flavour of a
period piece and the unfashionable fault of too much story-telling.
In the break-up of the great classical tradition, they played their
part, the search for natural conduct, along with Constable's clouds
and with Ward and Landseer's animal paintings, of which in
the same letter Géricault wrote that 'the masters have produced
nothing better in this genre'.

In early May of 1825 another French visitor arrived in London,
Eugène Delacroix. The impact of Constable upon him has already
been mentioned, but it was not only Constable that drew him to
England. There had been other English exhibitors in the Salon of
1824, R. P. Bonington (five pictures), Copley and Thales Fielding,
James Roberts, J. D. Harding, and William Wyld. Thales Fielding
had helped him on the background of *The Massacre of Scio*, that
background where English influence has often been detected, and
Delacroix in return worked on Fielding's Salon painting, *Macbeth
and the Witches*, which Stendhal noticed with appreciation in his
review of the Salon in the *Journal de Paris*. Delacroix in England
was at first hostile and unhappy,[1] shocked by the absence 'of
all that we call architecture', miserable at the lack of sun, at
the constant *jour d'éclipse*; but soon his interests were aroused: the
displays in the shops, the design of the rowing boat in which the
Fieldings took him down the Thames to Richmond, the theatres,
above all Shakespeare. English painting he found admirable when
on a small scale: the history paintings encouraged by the British
Institution seemed to him merely maladroit reminiscences of the
old masters. Many years later (1858), looking back on these
experiences, he wrote of the happy memories of his visit and
recalled the work of Wilkie, Etty, Lawrence, and the Fieldings.
Constable and Turner were veritable reformers from whom the
French had learned much.[2] For a moment the two movements, the
English and the French, draw together, but only to separate, only

[1] A. Joubin, *Correspondance générale de Eugène Delacroix* (1936-9), i. 135.
[2] Ibid. iv. 57.

for the great achievements of Delacroix, remote from English art
of the thirties and forties, to create romanticism in European terms.
Bonington, whose historical paintings both in oil and water-colour
have something of the vibrating power of Delacroix, though
lighter in feeling, might, had he lived, have bridged something of
this gap. George Hayter, a thoroughly eclectic artist, at times
seems to ape French manners, but his *Circassian Women sold to
Brigands* (Pl. 62 *b*) is a timid attempt at oriental abandon.[1]

The year of Delacroix's visit, 1825, had seen the Academy
dominated, at least spatially, by a canvas by William Etty, one of
the names singled out by Delacroix. The painter was then thirty-
eight years old, had served as a pupil of Lawrence, and had some
success in the Academy of 1820 with his *Coral Finders* (coll. B.
Welsh, Esq.), a Regency classical piece, lush, decorative and gay;
it was a surprising product for this devout, serious-minded York-
shireman, but two years earlier the equally serious Hilton had
shown his *Rape of Europa* (Petworth), an equally voluptuous piece,
and one where the influence of Boucher is very apparent, though
he was an artist rarely, if ever, mentioned by his English followers.
Since then Etty, though he was a lonely traveller, suspicious of
foreign ways, had spent seven months in Venice. '*Venezia, cara
Venezia* . . . the birthplace and cradle of colour and idol of my
professional life . . . I felt *at home most in Venice*.'[2] *The Combat*,
however, his exhibit of 1825, measuring 10 ft. 4 in. by 13 ft. 3 in.,
recalls the grand manner of Bologna or Rome rather than Venice.
A group of three figures, linked in a design of large sweeping
movements, it is one of the most striking triumphs of English
High Art (Pl. 62 *a*). Neglect has taken toll of it; the colours have
darkened; the contrasting flecks of black and white with which
Etty intensified the glow of his flesh painting have become out of
tone; but with judicious cleaning it might still in some large
gallery fill a telling place. Much admired on its exhibition, it

[1] J. B. Gold in *C.L.* cxxiii (1958), 689.
[2] 'Autobiography', *Art Journ.* xi (1849), 38. See also for Etty the *Life* by A. Gilchrist
(1855); W. C. Monkhouse, *Pictures by Etty* (n.d.); W. Gaunt and F. Gordon Roe,
Etty and the Nude (Leigh-on-Sea, 1954); Dennis Farr, *William Etty* (1958), an exhaustive
treatment of his work.

alarmed by its size and only found a purchaser, in a moment of enthusiasm which he later regretted, in John Martin.

As a result of *The Combat*, Etty received a commission from Lord Darnley for a painting of *The Judgement of Paris*[1]. This has echoes of Rubens and of Marcantonio's engraving, but these are fused into a richly textured design of Etty's own imagining. He was now painting at the full height of his powers, and was determined to follow *The Combat* with works of similar heroic scale. Between 1825 and 1830 he completed a trilogy of great canvases of *Judith*, and, an even larger one, *Benaiah slaying two lionlike Men of Moab*. These great machines frightened English patrons: but in 1831 *The Combat*, *Benaiah*, and the three *Judiths* were purchased by the Royal Scottish Academy and were later transferred to the Scottish National Gallery, where in my youth they hung impressively on the second line of the largest room. Now the cellars have them, and it is long since *Benaiah* has been unrolled.

Etty in 1828 had become a full Academician. There was increasing criticism of his paintings on the grounds of indecency: 'entirely too luscious', said *The Times*, 'for the public eye'.[2] In 1835 the *Observer* claimed that 'the Lord Mayor himself deserves at once to be sent to the treadmill for imprisoning a little Italian boy for hawking about the streets a naked Cupid, if such lascivious scenes are allowed to be exhibited at the Royal Academy with impunity'. The Academy remained unmoved, but the criticisms are understandable. Etty throughout all his life continued to attend the life class at the Royal Academy, and has left innumerable studies of the nudes that he made there; the young guardsmen, who provided the male models, in heroic attitudes or tied up as though for martyrdom; the female models in a wide variety of poses, many of which served for figures in his finished works. In these studies his painting is often found at its best, and all his intensity went into them; but when it comes to his ideal subjects the figures remain models, and the women with their style of hair, their bodies obviously used to corsets, retain a disturbing sense of the

[1] Now at Port Sunlight.
[2] See Whitley, ii. 145 and 299.

contemporary.[1] A shy, pious bachelor, Etty found in his painting
a sensuous outlet. No English artist has so systematically attempted
to set down his reaction to the nude. He never wholly succeeded,
and it may be that his shortcomings helped to turn English art
from the representation of the unclothed human form, whose
functions and construction we understand with our closest inti-
macies and whose idealization touches our most sensitive responses:
but in his glowing colour, occasionally in his handling of paint, he
caught reflections of the Venetians and of Rubens that have escaped
most other English artists.

With Etty's large canvases, historical painting in the grand
manner may be said to reach its climax. Hilton till his death in 1839
was to continue his correct and academic art; Haydon's unhappy
career had still some twenty years to run, but on his release from
the King's Bench prison—a second imprisonment for debt—he
turned to more popular subjects, *The Mock Election*, purchased
by George IV, *Chairing the Member* (Pl. 63 *b*), and *Punch or May
Day*. These are Hogarthian subjects, intricate designs and vividly
coloured patterns, full of anecdotal detail. 'How fine, how very
fine that is', Wilkie said, standing in front of *Punch*,[2] and in the
three soldiers facing the mob in *Chairing the Member*, correct but
slightly anxious, Haydon achieved something nearer the heroic
than the contortions of Dentatus. His genre paintings have survived
more successfully than his immenser conceptions.

Another artist singled out by Géricault was Edwin Landseer.[3]
When only sixteen years old, at the exhibition of the Society of
Painters in Oil and Water-colour in 1818, he had shown *Fighting
dogs getting wind*. It was purchased by Sir George Beaumont and
was the subject of a long criticism in *The Examiner*.[4] 'The gasping,
and cavernous, and redly-stained mouths, the flaming eyes, the
Prostrate Dog, and his antagonist standing exultingly over him,

[1] 'Town models distorted by the modiste's art.' Holman Hunt, *Preraphaelites*, i. 49,
and in *Contemporary Rev.* xlix (1886), 475.

[2] E. George, *Haydon* (1948), 165, 193.

[3] F. G. Stephens, *Memoirs of Sir Edwin Landseer* (3rd ed. 1880); W. Cosmo Monkhouse, *Works of Sir Edwin Landseer* (n.d.); A. Graves, *Catalogue of the Works of Sir Edwin
Landseer, R.A.* (n.d.); J. A. Manson, *Sir Edwin Landseer. R.A.* (1902).

[4] 1818, 269: quoted Stephens, loc. cit. 43: untraced.

the inveterate rage that superior strength inflames but cannot sub-
due, with the broad and bright relief of the objects, give a wonder-
producing vitality to the canvas.' This is high praise for a young
boy's work, 'My little dog-boy', as Fuseli called him in the
Academy classes.[1] Géricault's reference is to the Royal Academy of
1821 and there Landseer's picture was *Rat Catchers*,[2] four dogs,
excitedly sniffing a rat hole in a barn, a very lively, vigorous piece
of painting, where the rough hair of the terriers is broadly rendered.
Three years later, again at the British Institution, he exhibited a
painting which firmly established his fame: here anecdote, fashionable anecdote, is superimposed on an animal scene, and the fatal
recipe of Landseer's success was first drawn up. A monkey has
seized a cat and is using its paw to move hot chestnuts off a stove,
despite the pathetic protests of the victim's kittens; the howling cat
is horribly realistic, and the subject might almost be thought a
caricature of a romantic horror piece: but, painted like a small
Dutch masterpiece, it has a skill and intensity of its own which
excludes any satirical element; in sentiment it is a peculiarly un-
pleasing work.[3] It enjoyed, however, great popularity: Landseer's
own estimate of its market value, given at the height of his fame,
was £3,000 as opposed to the £100 for which he originally sold
it. The die was now cast: the pathetic, sentimental and grotesque,
the parade of beasts as classic worthies had begun; dogs postured
as Diogenes and Alexander[4] or as Dignity and Impudence, and a
reputation was established which was to gain in engravings a world-
wide popularity. There were still possibilities of other things. In
Chevy Chase, exhibited at the Royal Academy in 1826,[5] where he
had been elected an Associate as soon as he reached the statutory
age of twenty-four, he painted a scene of animal fury, the hounds
leaping on the stag, the prancing horses, which, if it owes a some-

[1] Leslie, *Memoir*, i. 39.

[2] Coll. Nicholas Argenti, Esq.

[3] Engraved C. G. Lewis.

[4] R.A. 1848, with a long paragraph giving the story: now in the Tate Gallery. In
1825 a painting of a duck flapping its wings beside a dead drake was entitled *Hector and
Andromache*, though this was later changed to *The Widow* (eng. J. Burnet). *Dignity and
Impudence* perished in the Tate flood of 1928.

[5] Birmingham Art Gallery: variant in Graves Gallery, Sheffield.

what inadequately absorbed debt to Snyders, is still a remarkable document of English romanticism (Pl. 25 a).

Meanwhile Wilkie was on the continent. His letters home,[1] many of them to William Collins, give a remarkably vivid picture of the conditions of travel and also a reflective commentary on the pictures that he saw. In Italy Correggio meant most to him: in Munich he found his own *Reading the Will*: at Dresden the *Sistine Madonna* seemed to him 'dry and wretched from neglect' though 'the heads are truly divine', and once again it was Correggio that fascinated him and he analyses in detail the use of colour in the *Notte*. The Dresden Collection was comparatively unknown in England; even Sir Thomas Lawrence had never seen it, and Wilkie thought that Howard alone of present Academicians had visited it. The final stage of Wilkie's foreign tour, after he had returned from Germany to Rome, took him to even more unfamiliar territory. He reached Madrid in October 1827. The impact of Velazquez upon him was considerable. 'I can almost fancy myself', he writes, 'among English pictures. Sir Joshua, Romney and Raeburn, whether from imitation or instinct, seem powerfully imbued with his style, and some of our own time, even to our landscape painters, seem to possess the same affinity.'

Throughout the later stages of his journey, Wilkie had been regaining health, and in Spain he could once more apply himself to painting and returned with seven subjects, three Spanish and four Italian, which he exhibited in the Academy of 1829. The Spanish pictures were all purchased by the King, and one of them, *The Maid of Saragossa*, particularly pleased the public. They mark a change not only in matter but in method. The scale of the figures is now much larger in proportion to the pictorial space and there is a far firmer organization of the main design; the sweeping gesture of the Saragossan maid, urging on the defenders of her city, belongs worthily to the grand manner and the painting itself is looser and aims at greater breadth. Something is lost. The acutely observed attitudes and gestures of his peasant scenes are never recaptured; when he turns, as in the Irish scenes of the second half of the thirties, the *Peep o'day Boy* (1836) (Pl. 58 b) painted for the great

[1] Allan Cunningham, *Life* (1843), ii. 170–7, 215, 245, 288, 326.

collector Vernon, and the *Irish Whiskey Still* (1840) bought by the king of Holland,[1] to cottage subjects, he retains the larger arrangement, the more confident sense of space, that he had learned abroad. He was, too, attempting canvases of a much greater size. His eighth picture in the Academy of 1829 was a portrait of the earl of Kellie, begun in 1824 for the Hall of his own country town, Cupar, but only now completed. It is 95 in. by 68 in. and is in fact too large for the painter's ability: the life-size seated figure is well conceived, the head vital and forceful, but a vague curtain inadequately fills the upper space. *William IV* and *Queen Adelaide*, presented by the latter to the University of Oxford in 1838, are 104 in. high; one of his most successful subject pieces, *The Empress Josephine and the Fortune Teller* (1834) (Edinburgh), measures 83 in. by 62 in., and in the work which occupied so much of his time during the thirties, *Sir David Baird finding the body of Tippoo Saib* (138 in. by 107 in.) (Pl. 57), he attempted not unsuccessfully a great baroque composition.[2] These new departures did not escape considerable criticism. 'Though Wilkie found many to admire these new productions of his genius, still the prevailing opinion was that he had quitted a path in which he had no rival, for one wherein he had not a few superiors.'[3] It was even put about that when Wilkie left for the Holy Land in 1840, it was as a disappointed man, whose royal patronage was leaving him and whose popularity was on the wane. For this view there seems to be no serious evidence. Wilkie in 1829 had been welcomed back to a position of unusual authority in English art; he had been thought of as President of the Royal Academy on Lawrence's death and it was perhaps undue marks of royal favour that prejudiced his case; he was knighted in 1836; he was consulted by everyone and filled a distinguished place in London society. His own statement as to his intentions in visiting the Holy Land may be accepted without further enlargement. He talked to Collins on the eve of his departure 'with all his early enthusiasm on the advantage he

[1] Now in the National Gallery of Scotland.
[2] Baird had died in 1829: Wilkie's figure is based on Raeburn's portrait, engraved as frontispiece to *Life of Sir David Baird* (1832). The drama of Baird's victory at Seringapatam (1799), where he had previously endured four years' captivity, long fascinated England.   [3] S. C. Hall, *Vernon Gallery*, iii, pl. 15.

might derive from painting upon Holy Land, on the very ground on which the event he was to embody had actually occurred'. In long letters written from Jerusalem to Sir Robert Peel he discusses the traditional Italian interpretation of the milieu of sacred history, the conventions of Raphael and Leonardo, the 'nearer verisimilitude' of the Venetians through their intercourse with the Levant. 'A Martin Luther in painting is as much called for as in theology, to sweep away the abuses by which our divine pursuit is encumbered', a last glint of the earnestness of the son of the Fifeshire manse.[1]

These were plans and expectations that were not to be fulfilled. The sketches which Wilkie made in Palestine were never to be worked up.[2] He left after five weeks, his travels having been much limited by the plague and quarantine regulations, and sailed for Alexandria, where he painted his brilliant small portrait of Mohammed Ali: at Malta symptoms which had already been disturbing turned much worse and he died at sea one day after leaving the island (1 June 1841). The news was received in England as that of a national calamity: 'his works', wrote his brother Academicians in their formal letter of condolence to his brother and sister, 'are known and admired wherever the arts are appreciated and he has achieved a celebrity unsurpassed in modern times': but it was in a painting that the emotions of his sudden loss found their true expression, in the beam of light falling across the dark silhouette of the ship in Turner's *Peace—Burial at Sea*.

The more ambitious range of subjects tackled by Wilkie in his last phase, regretted as it was by many critics, reflected a swing in popular taste. The passing of the Reform Bill meant even more as a symbol than as a political fact, and there was a new confidence in middle-class assertions of their likes and dislikes. The genre scenes that owed so much to Wilkie's early paintings continued to give pleasure and William Collins, Mulready, Thomas Webster

[1] Cunningham, *Life*, ii. 416.

[2] A volume of lithographs from them drawn by Joseph Nash, *Sir David Wilkie's Sketches in Turkey, Syria and Egypt*, was published in 1843: from the sketches on which Wilkie noted 'Study for the Nativity' and 'Study for the "Ecce Homo", Jerusalem', it is clear that he had kept his main purpose in view and that the completed paintings might well have opened a new phase of his art.

(Pl. 96 *a*), and others continued to provide them.[1] In 1836 the humours of everyday life received in another medium the rich commendation of *The Pickwick Papers*. But in the poems of Mrs. Hemans or the early novels of Lytton there was a mixture of sentiment and costume romance which found eager acceptance, and which seemed, misleadingly, well suited to the visual arts. The neo-classical repertory was exhausted. Charles Eastlake, working in Rome, drew on it for his *The Spartan Isadas* (1827: Chatsworth), but soon turned aside to more appealing scenes of Italian peasants, whose blind mothers, snake-bitten children, or pilgrim ecstasies lent them some particular, if occasionally morbid, interest, and in his more historical pieces such as *The Champion* (Pl. 65 *b*) looked for inspiration to Venice rather than ancient Rome, painting as it seemed to Haydon 'with Titianesque simplicity',[2] though it is rather Palma's moonfaced ladies that seem the closest point of contact. Others, in the desperate search for a subject, ransacked literature, the Waverley novels, *The Vicar of Wakefield*, *The Spectator*, Cervantes, Molière, La Motte Fouqué. Shakespeare as ever was a fascinating challenge, but now it was Autolycus, Petruchio, and Malvolio that attracted rather than the great tragic figures. Painting had long depended on recognizable symbols and the associations of traditional poses for much of its communicative power. For religious and classical themes, or even for portraiture, there was a wealth of allusion, familiar and therefore sufficiently unobtrusive not to diminish the primary impact of the design. The stories told by English painters in the eighteen-thirties had no such accepted and enriching iconography. Their points had to be made explicit; it was narration rather than the use of a known convention to crystallize a visual experience. Of these story-tellers, C. R. Leslie, dear to us as Constable's biographer, was one of the most expert. Born in London, of American parents, he was taken home to Philadelphia while a child and brought up there. America still claims him as one of her painters, but, sent by friends to study

---

[1] 'We have enough, and far more than enough, of the familiar in the humours of the dog-kennel . . . and the waggeries of mischievous schoolboys' (*Fraser's Mag.* iii, 1831, 680).

[2] Lady Eastlake, *Memoir* preceding her husband's *Contributions to the Literature of the Fine Arts*, 2nd ser. (1870), 104.

in England and helped by his fellow countrymen, West and Washington Allston, he became the representative artist of a minor phase of English art.[1] He was much patronized by Lord Egremont, of whom he has left a very sympathetic account, and often stayed at Petworth. Leslie admired Hogarth, but for his narrative power rather than his brush work, and in his own painted anecdotes not only smoothed the surface but polished the manners. His *Princes in the Tower* (Pl. 65 a) shows how he could turn a tale of horror to prettiness. Perhaps youthful America has some part in this inadequate emotional approach, for it was shared by Leslie's fellow countryman, Gilbert Newton, who died insane in 1835 and whose palette and brushes are carved on the tomb raised to him by his friends in the cemetery of Wimbledon parish church.

Daniel Maclise was a very different character. Born in 1811,[2] he was only a young man in the twenties when Leslie was at the height of his popularity. His ready gift for portrait sketches in pencil found him employment with *Fraser's Magazine*, when in 1830[3] there began a series of caricatures of eminent literary figures, mainly by 'Alfred Croquis', which was Maclise's pseudonym. This is one of the great English collections of caricatures rivalling those of Spy in *Vanity Fair* and wonderfully vivid in their economy of statement. Samuel Rogers, Thomas Moore, Walter Scott, John Galt, James Morier, William Wordsworth, William Roscoe (Fig. 5), Thomas Carlyle, Michael Faraday, S. T. Coleridge, Harriet Martineau, Lord John Russell, the list could go on with almost equal interest for all its eighty-four plates.[4] This literary, journalist

[1] See *Art. Journ.* N.S. ii (1856), 73, 105; *Autobiographical Recollections of the Life of C. R. Leslie*, ed. Tom Taylor (1860). Bellenden Ker, one of the founders in 1848 of the Arundel Society, described the British School in 1841 as 'Mr. Eastlake, Mr. Turner, Mr. Landseer, Mr. Maclise, Mr. Leslie, Mr. Etty, Mr. Briggs and several young artists coming forward, Mr. Herbert, Mr. Cope etc.' *P.P. 1841*, vi. 405. Henry Briggs's (1791–1844) historical and Shakespearian pieces form a link between the Boydell tradition and the Leslie–Maclise group. For Herbert and Cope see below, pp. 216, 282.

[2] For a controversy about the date of Maclise's birth see Redgrave, *Dictionary*. The chief source of information is W. J. O'Driscoll, *A Memoir of Daniel Maclise* (1871).

[3] The *Magazine* was begun in that year by Dr. William Maginn, like Maclise by origin from Cork, who 'in consequence of some differences with *Blackwood*, had quitted the modern Athens'.

[4] See W. Bates, *The Maclise Portrait Gallery*, new ed. (1898). Many of the drawings are in the Forster Collection in the Victoria and Albert Museum.

world was one in which Maclise remained at home. John Forster and Charles Dickens were his closest friends and it was with them, rather than with fellow artists, that much of his time was spent.

FIG. 5. *Daniel Maclise: William Roscoe*

The tall, good-looking, powerful Irishman was always conscientious about Academy and other duties, but in a period when most artists congregated together, he was detached and of another world. It is not then surprising that literary themes attracted him. In 1829 his painting, *Olivia and Malvolio*, was exhibited in the

Royal Academy.[1] Its clear colours, great dramatic sense, and graceful flow of line had an individuality which made it at once notable. The thirties saw a continual series of similar works and similar success: in 1836 he was elected A.R.A., when only twenty-four, and in 1840 a full member. His literary pictures reached their climax in *The Play Scene from Hamlet* (R.A. 1842). As narrative painting this reaches a high level: the figures are grouped with powerful dramatic effect and are strongly characterized; largely seen in shadow, the modelling still remains rounded and firm. The design, as in many of Maclise's works, is based on that popular Victorian formula, the vignette, a central oval space, clearly lit, while the surrounding groups and details merge into an outer border and gradually become deeper in tone towards the edges of the canvas. His paintings are wonderfully preserved. The modelling is at times over hard, reminiscent of contemporary continental work such as that of Steinle or Ary Scheffer, and the colouring, if striking and appropriate, is, as the Pre-Raphaelites strongly felt, 'untrue in light and shade'. Yet, they admitted, 'idiom and inspiration are both essentially his own'; they were 'real works . . . of extraordinary invention'.[2] It was not, however, till state patronage opened new opportunities that he was to reach his highest achievement.

Meanwhile private patronage was dominated by two men, representing a very different class from that of the Regency aristocrats, Robert Vernon and John Sheepshanks. Vernon[3] was a self-made man, who had acquired a fortune through supplying horses to the army during the Napoleonic war. His collection represented his own taste, and the works were generally commissioned directly from the artist. Etty with eleven paintings, including the well-known *Youth at the Prow*, was the most largely represented painter, but there were landscapes by Wilson, Turner, Constable, Callcott, Creswick, Clarkson Stanfield, F. R. Lee, and T. S. Cooper, a

---

[1] The version in the Tate Gallery is *c.* 1840, painted for Robert Vernon: see O'Driscoll, p. 40.

[2] See Ford Madox Brown in *Mag. of Art*, xi (1888), 123.

[3] See Vernon Heath, *Recollections* (1892), and S. C. Hall, *The Vernon Gallery*, 3 vols. (1854).

considerable group of Stothards, Landseer's *The Hunted Stag* (Pl. 25 b), *War*, and *Peace*, three of his most dramatic compositions,[1] Wilkie's splendidly designed *Peep o'day Boy*, the masterpiece of his later period, and important works by James Ward, Gilbert Newton, Henry Briggs, G. Jones, F. Goodall, Thomas Uwins, E. M. Ward, C. R. Leslie, Charles Eastlake, Daniel Maclise, and others. Vernon's portrait, a handsome, distinguished looking man, with his King Charles spaniel in his lap, was painted by H. W. Pickersgill, and a marble bust by Behnes was presented to the National Gallery, from subscribers headed by the queen: more significant than either of these was perhaps the photograph taken of him by his nephew, which required an exposure of eight minutes.[2] He died in 1850 and is buried in the chapel at Ardington, which he added to the village church, placing in it a large statue by Baily of *Prayer*, a kneeling female figure. His collection, three years before his death, was presented to the nation and is now in the Tate Gallery, though many items from it, fallen out of first rank favour, are generally on loan.

John Sheepshanks came of an industrial Yorkshire family, and had a wealthy background and greater education: but his selection of paintings is very similar to that of Vernon's. His collection,[3] which he was anxious should be used for educational purposes, was given in 1857 to the new South Kensington Museum, and, though he generously stated that he had no wish that it should be kept apart, it can still be seen there, intact if not completely exhibited, a representative display of early Victorian achievement. Turner's *Vessel in Distress off Yarmouth* (1831) was perhaps the most notable work, William Collins's *Rustic Civility* the most widely popular.

[1] *The Hunted Stag* with its dark water and darker hills, and the bright red tongues of the dogs is a real romantic 'horror' piece: *War* and *Peace* were destroyed in the flood at the Tate in 1928.   [2] Vernon Heath, *Recollections*, 50.

[3] Richard Redgrave, *The Sheepshanks Gallery* (twenty pictures reproduced in permanent tint by the autotype process) (1870). The autotypes are remarkably fine.

VII

THE BATTLE OF THE STYLES

INTERESTED circles at the opening of the century debated the battle of the styles as one between Roman and Greek. The first volume of *The Antiquities of Athens* by James Stuart (d. 1788) and Nicholas Revett (d. 1804) had appeared in 1762, but its immediate impact had been small. The great Romanist Sir William Chambers, could when lecturing in the sixties scornfully refer to the pomp with which 'the Grecian antiquities have lately been ushered into the World and what Encomiums have been lavished upon things that in Reality deserve little or no Notice'.[1] In 1791, however, he was a little less confident: 'latterly the *Gusto Greco* has again ventured to peep forth, and once more threatens an invasion'.[2] The invasion was, however, a leisurely one, and it was not till 1816 that Stuart's unpublished papers were collected by Josiah Taylor into a fourth volume of *The Antiquities of Athens*. By then 'the opposite and vicious style of Robert Adam'[3] was securely displaced, but the 'chastness and purity' of the Grecian advocates had still to contend with the ready eclecticism of Regency taste and the uninhibited designs of John Nash. In establishing a new bulwark of correctness, 'white and modern, the handwriting of our race, in this practical nineteenth century, on its square plain masonry and Doric shafts',[4] two names stand out, William Wilkins, the most scholarly of the Grecians, and Sir Robert Smirke, perhaps the dullest.

Wilkins was the protégé of Thomas Hope, and it was through his advocacy that, as a young man of twenty-six, he obtained in

[1] Quoted L. Lawrence, 'Stuart and Revett', *Journ. of Warburg Institute*, ii (1938), 136. For the Greek revival in England see M. L. Clarke, *Greek Studies in England 1700–1830* (Cambridge, 1945).

[2] *Elements of Civil Architecture*, i (ed. 1825), 135; see N. Pevsner and S. Lang, 'Apollo or Baboon', *Arch. Rev.* civ (1948), 271. For general topics in this chapter see works quoted p. 66, n. 1.   [3] Joseph Gwilt, *Encyclopaedia of Architecture* (1842).

[4] Lord Lytton, *A Strange Story*, ii. 36, written as late as 1862.

1806 the commission for Downing College, Cambridge, to be carried out in the purest Grecian style. Wyatt had already prepared designs and their rejection in favour of this unknown practitioner, but recently returned from four years travel in Greece, marked a turning-point.[1] With its low, flat skyline, broken only by a pediment, raised on Ionic columns closely modelled on those of the Erechtheum, Downing was a novelty in collegiate architecture (Pl. 35 *a*). The judges showed a little apprehension that 'the unpleasant communication between the kitchen and the Hall by a winding subterraneous passage of 140 feet . . . will prove very inconvenient', but these were subordinate matters to the purity of style. In the following year the East India College commissioned Wilkins to design a building at Haileybury,[2] thereby bringing the new Grecian style into school as well as college architecture. In these academic spheres, University College, Gower Street, was Wilkins's most important undertaking. As it stands today, it is his work only in the central block and flanking walls. The high podium with steps going up within it to the great open line of columns is a very notable invention. At the National Gallery, the commission for which was awarded to Wilkins in 1832, with some gossip about how he got it, there were endless compromises to be made. The flight of steps leading up to the portico had to be radically altered, which Wilkins, always good at steps, did with great ingenuity, in order not to obscure the view of St. Martin's spire from Pall Mall. The Corinthian columns from Carlton House had to be re-employed in the portico. Contemporary discussion of the design was vigorous, and it has on the whole found few supporters. The dome must always have been insignificant, 'Mr. Wilkins' toadstool' the *Spectator* called it; dwarfed by the Nelson column it has become squat and unconvincing. Meanwhile in 1809 he had re-

---

[1] Gavin Walkley in *Journ. R.I.B.A.* xlv (1938), 970 and 1014, and more fully in typescript Medal Essay in R.I.B.A. library. See also A. Beresford Pite, 'The Work of William Wilkins', *Journ. R.I.B.A.* 3rd ser. xl (1932-3), 121; R. Willis and J. W. Clark, *Architectural History of Cambridge*, ii. 753.

[2] F. W. Bourdillon in *C.L.* xl (1916), 486. Wilkins's fine west front is crushed by the high dome of the chapel built in 1878, an effect that does much to vindicate Wilkins's scaling of his dome in the National Gallery. See also W. J. W. Blunt, *The Haileybury Buildings* (1936).

built Grange Park, Hampshire, with a liberal use of Roman cement, as a temple with a hexastyle Doric portico, the most uncompromisingly Grecian dwelling in England, whose owner, Henry Drummond, was determined to rival Dance's nearby portal at Stratton, built for the Barings.[1] At York, Wilkins built a Greek museum for the Philosophical Society (1827–8), so that the abbey ruins became a Gothic feature in the gardens of a classical mansion.[2] St. George's Hospital at Hyde Park Corner (1828–9) is, despite later enlargements, one of his most characteristic buildings, where his subdued good manners and his scholarly mouldings, too refined for English weather and English light, can still be conveniently studied.

Wilkins died in 1839 and, by his own wish, was buried in the chapel of Corpus Christi College, Cambridge, in the New Court that he had designed in 1823,[3] 'the work' as his sepulchral inscription states 'which found most favour in his own eyes'.[4] This court is in the Gothic style, but it is a veneer of Gothic on a classically regular framework. The screen of King's College, almost opposite, shows Wilkins's Gothic manner in a more accentuated, individual mood, which recalls Hawksmoor at All Souls rather than the middle ages. Classical scholarship was a recognized accomplishment; the romantic movement had still some way to progress before medieval studies could be placed on any equal footing with them; but Wilkins, the protégé of the neo-Greeks in 1806, asked to be buried in Gothic and by 1823 could write to the Master of Trinity that he considered Gothic architecture to be his forte.[5]

---

[1] Grange Park in fact was sold to the Barings: both S. P. and C. R. Cockerell (1823–5 and 1852) made additions to it: meanwhile Henry Drummond had become an Irvingite, building the large Catholic Apostolic Gothic church at Albury in 1843 (designed by W. H. Brooks) and employing Pugin to remodel the Manor House, already reconstructed by Soane in 1800.

[2] Walkley, *Thesis*, 103; see also *The Harcourt Papers*, ed. E. W. Harcourt, xiii (n.d.), 180.

[3] 'The change from a state of war to that of peace had occasioned an influx of students to the Universities, so that there was a demand for increased accommodation within the walls of the Colleges': the Master, Dr. Lamb, quoted in R. Willis and J. W. Clark, *The Architectural History of Cambridge*, i. 302.

[4] Moved from the chapel and now on the library staircase.

[5] Walkley, *Thesis*, 65.

While Wilkins was at work on the National Gallery, Robert Smirke[1] was carrying out his scheme for the British Museum, which had outgrown its accommodation in Montagu House, the seventeenth-century essay in the French manner which stood on the Bloomsbury site now occupied by Smirke's Grecian building. The eastern wing, containing the long gallery for the library of George III presented by George IV, was the first to be built, in 1823–6, and was followed by the west and north wings, making a quadrangle behind Montagu House. Then the house itself was demolished and the present portico with its colonnade of giant Ionic columns and Sir Richard Westmacott's carved tympanum was finally completed in 1847. During this long interval Schinkel had been building the Altes Museum in Berlin, using the same giant order, the same screen of columns. The two buildings sprang from a similar impulse and possibly there was some interchange of ideas between them.[2] Certainly there is a greater sense of projection and depth, a greater boldness of attack than Smirke achieved in his other great public work, the General Post Office (1824–9), whose long façade, low podium, and shallow portico must have composed a somewhat tepid ensemble.[3]

Smirke retired from practice with the completion of the museum, though he did not die till 1867, then eighty-seven years old. His father, the painter of scenes of comedy and sentiment, a strong republican whose election to the Keepership of the Royal Academy had been quashed by royal intervention, did not die till his ninety-fourth year in 1845: his art had been essentially English in the tradition of Hogarth; in the Boydell Gallery, to which he made many contributions, he had stood against the grand manner of Reynolds's preaching. He must have wondered at the immense success of his son in this stern, classical idiom. Now, when so many of his larger designs have been demolished or bombarded, Smirke's Ionic portico to the Royal College of Physicians stands at the corner

[1] Sir E. Smirke in *Journ. R.I.B.A.*

[2] N. Pevsner, 'British Museum', *Arch. Rev.* cxiii (1953), 179; L. Ettlinger, *Arch. Rev.* xcvii (1945), 131.

[3] 'The Passing of the G.P.O.', *Architects and Builders Journ.* xxxvi (1912), 220; though not demolished till 1913, the Post Office had been completely altered by the addition of an attic storey in 1874.

of Trafalgar Square, a joint testimony with Wilkins's Gallery to the merits and limitations of this phase of English architecture.

There were in it other able practitioners. Decimus Burton, born in 1800, had before he was thirty built the Athenaeum Club, one of the most satisfying of Grecian buildings, though now its effect must be imagined with the later attic storey removed, and the whole neighbourhood reduced in height.[1] The Athenaeum frieze is one of Burton's pleasantest ornaments, and the same cavalcade rides on his Ionic colonnade to the gateway of Hyde Park, and was intended to figure also on his much larger, more Roman archway, originally aligned with the centre of the screen, and still today dominating the approach to Buckingham Palace (Pl. 34 a).[2] The lodges of the Park with their small Doric porticoes remain a most telling feature of this part of London, and in the Strand the fine surviving bow of Charing Cross Hospital is another reminder of Burton's skill. He left his distinctive mark on the metropolis, before he turned to town layout at Tunbridge Wells and Brighton,[3] and at the small Lancashire port of Fleetwood, for a time a link on the new rail and sea route to Scotland, where the lighthouse with its balustrades and corbelled balcony is one of his pleasantest fancies.[4]

Eight years older than Decimus Burton, Philip Hardwick has left almost as strong a classical imprint on the London scene; but his buildings are more various and scattered. At Telford's great scheme for St. Katharine's Docks, the Doric colonnade and attached Doric columns are probably due to Hardwick's influence. Even more striking was his use of Doric in his arch and screen completed in 1837 for the station of the London and Birmingham Railway at Euston. At the outset of the railway age passengers were invited to leave through this severely classical gateway, a salute from the old world to the new. Now much dwarfed by

[1] For Burton see R. P. Jones in *Arch. Rev.* xvii (1905), 109, 155, and P. A. Clarke, *James and Decimus Burton*, unpublished thesis (1949), library of R.I.B.A.

[2] See Burton's water-colour sketch of the two arches now in the R.I.B.A., reproduced in Richardson, *Monumental Classic Architecture* (1914), 63. For the later history of the arch see D. Stroud in *Arch. Rev.* cvi (1949), 397, and below, p. 303.

[3] See above, p. 183.

[4] P. Fletewood-Hesketh, *Murray's Lancashire Architectural Guide* (1955), 90.

neighbouring buildings, cramped in and shorn of its ironwork railings and outer lodges, Hardwick's arch retains today an ineffaceable dignity.

The excesses of the French Revolution, the growth of new centres of population, ill-housed, turbulent, untaught, the vigour of Dissent, the influx of Irish labour, cheap and papist, all gave to the Church in the early nineteenth century a new position as a bulwark of society. At the same time much opinion, some educated, some not, resented the large incomes of the episcopacy, the ill-kept cathedrals, the pluralities and absentee rectors. It was against this background that at the close of the war there came an urgent demand for the building of many new churches. John Bowdler, whose brother Thomas was to give a new word to the English language, formed a committee to petition for the erection of churches out of public funds in the populous parts of England. In 1818 the Church Building Society was founded under royal patronage to enrol subscribers for a similar purpose and in the same year Parliament voted £1,000,000 for new churches. In 1818 the Act was passed, a board of commissioners was set up and proceeded to survey the problem. They laid down that the buildings should be solid and durable; that the character of an ecclesiastical edifice for divine worship according to the rites of the United Kingdom of England and Ireland was to be preserved, both externally and internally; that there should be a general competition for plans, with a view to calling forth professional talent, and that the largest amount of grant for any single church should be £20,000. On the first survey it was decided to build eighty-five churches, providing sittings for about 144,190 persons, of which 'about one-third will be in free seats, to be appropriated to the use of the poor'.[1]

By the second report of 1822[2] ten churches had been built. Of these seven were Gothic, two Doric, one Ionic. Of the thirty other churches in course of construction, seventeen, among them St. Luke's, Chelsea, were in the Gothic style. On the whole, however, London for some little time preferred Grecian styles, the provinces Gothic.[3]

[1] *P.P. 1821*, x. 1 ff.   [2] *P.P. 1822*, xi. 1 ff.   [3] *P.P. 1827*, vii. 1 ff.

In London [said a writer in the *Quarterly Review*][1] we have but few specimens of Gothic amongst the new churches. The Commissioners have now determined to adopt nothing but pure Grecian architecture. We greatly regret this resolution, inasmuch as it will tend to give a character of the dullest monotony to the new buildings. The design for the new Gothic church at Chelsea was passed before they had adopted this resolution. This fine building will be distinguished by the peculiarity of possessing a groined vaulting of stone, the first which has been executed since the revival of Gothic architecture.

The architect of St. Luke's, Chelsea, thus singled out for praise, was James Savage, hitherto mainly known as a builder of bridges and throughout his career much interested in constructional problems; this bias no doubt led him to undertake the stone vault, supported by external flying buttresses, which aroused in contemporaries so much admiration for his boldness and talent, though the *Gentleman's Magazine*, in a laudatory notice,[2] had to admit that the style of the vaulting was two centuries older than that of the building. Externally little changed, St. Luke's is a Perpendicular building, faced in Bath stone over brick; its tall tower and its too slender crockets have a Regency elegance (Pl. 68 *b*); the interior is strikingly lofty, with a very high ground arcade supporting a gallery half-way up the pillars, a small triforium opening and large clerestory windows; the aisles are lit by windows above the gallery level, and the gallery divides the aisles into two stages, the lower of which is almost permanently in shadow. This in itself creates a completely un-Gothic form of light and shade, and St. Luke's lacks any of the normal Gothic volumes; despite its elaborate elevation the side walls seem thin and flat, with no articulation, and the very meagre tracery of the windows completes this effect. It is impossible to avoid a feeling of doubt as to the stability of this high, narrow hall, though in fact it has resisted blasts its builder never thought of: as an engineer Savage is admirable.

In all, the churches built were 214 and in the same period much enlargement and adaptation was being carried out by the Church Building Society or private patrons, alterations which generally took the form either of increase of seating accommodation or the

[1] xxvii (1822), 323.   [2] xcvi (1826), 201.

addition of a tower and spire. St. Mary, Bathwick (1814–20) in
Bath by John Pinch, aided by the Commissioners, is a good
example of the predominantly fifteenth-century style which was
generally copied. Inside the pews faced a large three-decker pulpit
at the west end and had their backs to the sanctuary.[1] Francis
Goodwin, an inveterate entrant for all the competitions of the time
and a prolific publisher of pattern books in every style and for
every purpose,[2] architect of the exceedingly Ionic Manchester
Town Hall,[3] used Gothic for his churches, a thin, eclectic Gothic
that can be seen at Holy Trinity, Bordesley, Birmingham (1823).
Very different was the firmer accuracy of Thomas Rickman, the
architectural historian: many of his churches have been altered,
and one of his largest, the nave added to the fourteenth-century
tower at Christ Church, Coventry, has been bombed, but several of
his Commissioners' churches still survive and are always respectable, and where expense was less rigidly enforced, as at Hampton
Lucy (Warwicks.), he showed that imaginative control of his
medium which he revealed at the fullest in his handling of the
New Court at St. John's, Cambridge.[4] Charles Barry's St. Peter's,
Brighton (1824–8) (Pl. 68 a), closes finely the vista up the Steyne,
and its buttressed tower and high ogival entrance arch, all still very
white and gleaming in Portland stone, is one of the most successful
of ecclesiastical scenic effects and a worthy forerunner of its architect's later triumphs. William Tite's Scottish Presbyterian church
in Regent Square, Holborn (1824–7), built to accommodate the
crowds flocking to hear Edward Irving, where the young Pugin
was taken to worship by his mother, is perhaps as characteristic an
example as any of this period of Gothic. It was modelled on the
west façade of York Minster, but not very sensitively.[5] Edward

[1] W. Ison, The Georgian Buildings of Bath (1948), 81.

[2] Domestic Architecture. . . . A Series of Designs in the Grecian, Italian and Old English
Styles (1833–4); reissued 1835 as Rural Architecture. The output of such publications
was very large indeed, and a full list would be a lengthy document: for a compendious
example, with a remarkable bibliography of books consulted, see J. C. Loudon,
Encyclopaedia of Cottage, Farm and Villa Architecture and Furniture (1833: new ed. 1846).

[3] Demolished 1912: see C. Stewart, The Stones of Manchester (1956), 18: the entrance
colonnade was re-erected at Heaton Park.

[4] See M. Whiffen in Arch. Rev. xcvii (1945), 160.

[5] The interior was bombed, but the façade still stands.

Garbett's church at Theale (1820–2) was an early and brilliant experiment in the style of Salisbury.[1]

Greek temples do not, at first sight, lend themselves over easily to the requirements of the Anglican liturgy,[2] but eighteenth-century services centred on the pulpit and the reading-desk, and the tendency in church design was to bring these as near the altar as possible, or rather to do away with deep chancels and to bring the altar close to the pulpit and desk. The chancels were unsuitable for mattins and sermon, and, if relegated to occasional communions, they tended to be ill-kept or even used for storing the various utensils required for cleaning the church. A flat or shallow-ended church was economical of space, brought everything in view of as many of the congregation as possible in their double tiers of ground and gallery sittings, facilitated the conduct of the service, and, a new point of some significance, was much more easily heated. The font was sometimes moved up to the east end to join pulpit and altar. If some of the congregation organized themselves for singing, or if on special occasions professional singers were hired, they generally used the west end gallery. For all these purposes the rectangular Grecian designs were more easily adaptable than the Gothic. The only problem was that a Grecian design had to have a portico, and high stone columns with heavy pediments were expensive items. Of the Commissioners' churches in the Grecian style, St. James's, Bermondsey (1827–9), with its tower in diminishing quadrilateral sections is one of the most distinguished[3] and it is characteristic of the period that its architect was the same James Savage who had already built the pioneer Gothic St. Luke's, Chelsea. More lavish in its accumulation of detail, the parish church of St. Pancras, built by William Inwood and his son Henry in 1819–22, copies closely the motifs of the Erechtheum, even to utilizing the portico of the caryatids, carved in synthetic stone by John Rossi, for its twin vestries. Above, its tower repeats in each of two stages the columned octagon of the Tower of the Winds,

[1] See Q.R. xxvii (1822), 309, and *Journ. W.C.I.* xviii (1955), 173.

[2] See G. W. O. Addleshaw and F. Etchells, *The Architectural Setting of Anglican Worship* (1948).

[3] See an appreciation of it by H. S. Goodhart-Rendel in *English Architecture since the Regency* (1953), 50.

which with the choragic monument of Lysicrates had to do constant service as Greek substitutes for a steeple. At St. Matthew's, Brixton (1822), C. F. Porden, in one of the severest London churches, boldly moved his tower to the east end, breaking away from the dominant example of Gibbs's St. Martin-in-the-Fields, which had proved a difficult model in many other cases. Somewhat repetitively, Smirke's heavy Doric or peristylar Ionic porticoes still exist, or partially survive, at the churches of St. James's, Hackney, St. Anne's, Wandsworth, and St. Mary's, Wyndham Place. At St. Marylebone New Church (1813–17) Thomas Hardwick placed caryatids on the tower and Ionic columns as supports for the gallery, but on the portico, as a second thought after its commencement, the Corinthian order was used (Pl. 31 *a*).

For magnificence, as Nash well knew, the Corinthian order could not long be neglected. George Basevi used it in stucco for his houses in Belgrave Square, which, with its tributary streets and crescents, was laid out from 1825 onwards by the great builder, Thomas Cubitt, with an imaginative sense of space relationships which fortunately can still be appreciated today. Basevi, a pupil of Soane, represents an eclectic rather than a purist tradition. In 1836 he won the competition for a design for the FitzWilliam Museum at Cambridge and that building, with its projecting columned portico and elaborate Corinthian order, is his most individual achievement,[1] though one that he was not fated to complete, for, while working at it in 1845, he was called over to Ely cathedral for consultation on the state of the western tower and, when inspecting it, fell from it to his death. Cockerell, who completed so often the work of other men, designed an interior entrance, which must have answered Basevi's outside approach, but which in its turn was much modified by the lesser genius of the younger Barry.

Charles Robert Cockerell, who succeeded Basevi at the Fitz-William Museum, is in imaginative power and sense of general effect the most impressive English architectural genius of the century. He can give unquestioning satisfaction, where Soane can

---

[1] See his own drawing of the front elevation reproduced in R. J. Willis and J. W. Clark, *The Architectural History of the University of Cambridge* (1886), iii. 210.

only interest by his ingenuity and invention. Like Soane, he must today be largely judged by photographs of buildings no longer extant or greatly altered and by sketches of unexecuted projects. Hanover Chapel in Regent Street, his admired solution for a classical church, was demolished in 1896,[1] his Westminster Insurance Office in the Strand in 1908; his Sun Insurance Office in Threadneedle Street still retains his segment-headed windows and banded rustication but has been much rebuilt in its upper storeys. Born in 1788, son of the Samuel Cockerell who had designed Sezincote, he spent his twenty-first year in the office of Robert Smirke, at that time busied with the rebuilding of Covent Garden Theatre. Then he departed for an adventurous journey through war-infested waters to Constantinople, and spent the next five years in Turkey and Greece and two more in Italy, not returning to England till 1817. They were years in which he had obtained great fame, but as an archaeologist not an architect. At Aegina he had seen emerging from the earth the head of a warrior, 'perfect in every feature', the forerunner of the sixteen figures which eventually the German members of the party obtained for Munich.[2] At Bassae, crawling into a fox's hole, Cockerell uncovered a relief, which led to the discovery of the Phigaleian Marbles, now in the British Museum. When he left Athens, his friend the Turkish commandant of the Acropolis rolled one of the remaining slabs of the Parthenon frieze down the rocks so that Cockerell could smuggle it away.

He found London occupied with the Regent Park schemes of John Nash, and one of his earliest works was the Hanover chapel, orthodox Grecian in style, an Ionic portico with a pediment and two square towers on either side. Almost at the same time, however, he made one of his few essays in Gothic at St. David's College, Lampeter, where his flattened arches, thin buttresses and pepperpot towers have a meagre appearance, most unlike his customary feeling for projection. In 1839 Cockerell won the competition for

[1] P. Waterhouse, 'Hanover Chapel', *Journ. R.I.B.A.*, 3rd ser. iv (1897), 111.

[2] R. P. Cockerell in *Arch. Rev.* xii (1902), 43–47 and 129–46. See also S. Smirke in *R.I.B.A. Trans.* (1863–4), 17; J. M. Brydon in *Journ. R.I.B.A.* vii (1899–1900), 347; E. Prestwich in *Journ. R.I.B.A.* xviii (1911), 669. The *Journ. R.I.B.A.* articles contain important photographs of Cockerell's buildings before their destruction or alteration.

the Ashmolean Museum and Taylor Institution in Oxford, which
happily survives little altered and always admirable. A centre
block of galleries, with an Ionic portico, unites two higher wings,
round which the cornice continues. On the street front an Ionic
screen supports four heroic statues, carved by Cockerell's favourite
assistant, William Grinsell Nicholl. The third storey is crowned
by an elaborate cornice. The round hooded arches breaking through
the cornice and the parallel cornices of the top and first storey are
characteristic features of his style (Pl. 67 b). Examples of his use of
them are to be seen at the banks in Liverpool, Manchester, and
Bristol which he built for the Bank of England to whom he
became architect in 1833. His work is always recognizable and
individual. 'The man is a great artist, though I don't believe in the
style he works in', Pugin said of him, a tribute worth the having.[1]
His church of Holy Trinity, Hotwells, Clifton (1829–33) (Pl. 31 b),[2]
with its great arch and pediment whose lower line is broken by a
dove descending in a glory of rays, is one of his most remarkable
inventions and in feeling is far more baroque than classical. Where
Soane had evolved his own mouldings and decorative details,
Cockerell borrowed from his wide classical knowledge, putting to
contemporary use some of the motifs of his own discoveries.[3] He
was a great synthesist, whose works always have unity whatever
their components, and his sense of style prepared the way for a
mid-Victorian architecture more integrated, even though more
elaborate, than the Regency and early Victorian compilations.
In the decorations of St. George's Hall, Liverpool (1851–4),
Cockerell's cast iron balconies supported by caryatids, plaster wall
decorations, Corinthian columns and great chandeliers were to
have all too many successors, for his elegant splendour handled by
others easily degenerated into civic bombast. In particular the
spandrel figures of the Great Hall, their wings spread like the
Lincoln angels, their loose drapery flowing in new curves, were to
have many art nouveau progeny (Pl. 73 c). At Liverpool, however,

[1] Journ. R.I.B.A. 3rd ser. vii (1900), 351.
[2] The interior was destroyed by bombing, 1940–1.
[3] As for instance the frieze of the Phigaleian Marbles round the stair-well of the
Ashmolean Museum.

splendour is genuinely achieved (Pl. 74 a), and achieved in a building of the most impressive magnitude.

In 1838, the city of Liverpool, in honour of the coronation, laid the foundation stone of a new concert hall and the following year advertised a competition for designs. Out of seventy-five entries, the award was given to that of Harvey Lonsdale Elmes, a young man of twenty-five, working with his father, James Elmes, well known for his editing of *Metropolitan Improvements* and *London in the Nineteenth Century*. Before work began on the concert hall a second competition was advertised for designs for new Assize Courts and this again was won by Elmes, who submitted plans for a strictly symmetrical building with a long portico in the Doric order. The Grecian tradition was strong in Liverpool. John Foster, son of the city architect of the same name, had returned in 1814 from travels in Greece and Asia Minor, in which Cockerell had been his companion, and he had shared in the réclame of the excavations at Aegina and Bassae. Foster's Custom House (1828–39)[1] was intended in its large scale to signify the prosperity of Liverpool, but its Ionic formula and its carefully unemphatic dome hardly told under the blackening and encrusting of its surfaces: bombed in 1940, its demolition had already been under discussion. In its uncompromising accuracy and simplicity it was, with Thomas Harrison's rebuilding (1793–1820) of Chester castle as a worthy rival, one of the most notable monuments of the Greek revival in England, and the north could claim as great a purity of taste as London and the south.

Neither of Elmes's prize-winning designs was however used, for it was decided to combine the two buildings into one block and he prepared new drawings for a great central hall with court rooms on either side. Meanwhile he visited Munich and Berlin and the vast proportions and spatial unity of his new designs were certainly influenced by Schinkel's work, while the vault, executed in hollow brick, may have been inspired by some recently published proposals for the restoration of the Baths of Caracalla.[2] Externally a

[1] L. B. Budden, 'The Liverpool Custom House and its Architect', *The Architects and Builders Journ.* xxxvi (1912), 164. For Foster's cemetery chapel see above, p. 143.
[2] By G. A. Blouet, 1828.

great pillared portico dominated the eastern façade, while a similar shorter portico on the south side received the greater emphasis of a double row of columns, though in practice it never became the

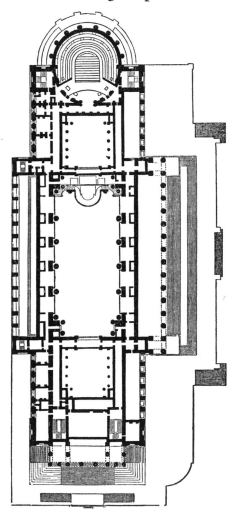

Fig. 6. *Plan of St. George's Hall, Liverpool*

main entrance. The western side had a series of engaged pilasters but its effect depended mainly on the patterning of its window spaces. The northern end is a semicircular apsidal termination (Fig. 6). There is a continuous strongly marked cornice, above which rises the attic of the central hall. Carried out in cream coloured sandstone, the building has now blackened and its contrasts have been lessened, but it is still extraordinarily happy in its proportions. The order is Corinthian, not the Doric of Elmes's Assize Court plan. The Town Hall begun in Birmingham in 1832 and still in construction at the time of the Liverpool commission[1] was a careful version of a Corinthian temple raised on a podium and was a scheme with which Elmes must have been familiar. St. George's, however, belongs to a freer classicism than that of Wilkins and Smirke, or of the Birmingham architects, Hansom and Welch. The rich capitals of the fluted columns are Roman in type, though the mouldings above them have a Greek refinement. Inside, red granite columns, superior Elmes thought to 'any scagliola, however gorgeous', the great encaustic floor, now generally covered, the elaborate bronze grilles and the coffered ceiling form one of the most magnificent of English interiors, but the details were to be mainly Cockerell's work, for Elmes's health had been steadily declining. In 1847 he was in an advanced state of consumption; too late he was hurried away to Jamaica for a milder winter and died there at the end of November. He was only thirty-three. One of England's greatest buildings was to have no successors.[2]

In England St. George's Hall seems a little belated, for already in 1838 Gothic had won great triumphs and a new, fanatical note had been sounded in the propaganda for it. Hitherto it had been used for churches, for a certain number of baronial dwellings, where an instinct for castellation had been only temporarily submerged under Palladianism, for some follies and picturesque features and for some pieces of Regency pastiche, but not on the whole for serious civic buildings, the heart of the matter in the England of the Reform Bill. 'For civil purposes . . . the town hall, exchange or senate house, the Greek, Roman or Italian styles are universally admitted to be applicable.' So Francis Goodwin had written in 1833.[3] A year later, on 16 October 1834, London

---

[1] See *Architectural Mag.* ii (1836), 16.

[2] See R. P. Jones, 'The Life and Work of Harvey Lonsdale Elmes', *Arch. Rev.* xv (1904), 231: G. Henn, *St. George's Hall, Liverpool* (Liverpool, 1949).

[3] *Domestic Architecture*, No. 5.

crowded to the river to see the Old Palace of Westminster blazing to its destruction. It was a cataclysm such as Martin, Danby, and Turner had dreamed of, and Turner was there and later made various versions of the theme. Haydon, also in the crowd, thought of the new scope for state patronage and for 'painting the House of Lords'. The following year the Commission, after considering the claims of Smirke and Pennethorne as official architects of the Office of Woods and Works,[1] announced that the Houses of Parliament were to be rebuilt in either the Gothic or Elizabethan style and announced a competition for the purpose.[2] Only six months were allotted for the competitors to prepare and submit their designs, but so unique and important was the opportunity that ninety-seven architects entered. The first prize was awarded to Charles Barry, the second to J. C. Buckler, one of the more noted protagonists of the Gothic style, the third to David Hamilton of Glasgow, and the fourth to E. Kempthorne. When the announcement of the awards had been made, the storm broke. In March of 1836 there was an exhibition of the unsuccessful designs, and this was followed by a meeting of the competitors, among whom a party secured the support of Joseph Hume in Parliament for an attack on the Commissioners and their conduct of the competition. A brisk interchange of pamphlets denounced the Gothic style as ecclesiastical and obscurantist or the Grecian as pagan and un-English. The Commissioners found it difficult to state in what the 'superior beauty and grandeur' of Barry's design lay: unity of

[1] In 1815 Smirke, Soane, and Nash had been attached as 'official architects' to the Board of Works: in 1832 the Board was reformed as the Office of Woods and Works, and James Pennethorne was commissioned to prepare plans for improvements in the Metropolis: in 1851 this scheme reverted to the Board of Works, from which 'metropolitan improvements' were transferred in 1856 to the Metropolitan Board of Works (see L. Brett, 'The Crown Builds', *Arch. Rev.* cxiii (1953), 7).

[2] The exact procedure was as follows: a committee of both Houses (*P.P. 1835*, xviii. 1) drew up instructions and specifications: the selection of the architect was entrusted to four Commissioners (*P.P. 1836*, xxxvi. 487) and their report was in turn submitted to a Select Committee, appointed in Feb. 1836 (*P.P. 1836*, xxi. 43). The basic accounts of the building are in A. Barry, *Life and Works of Sir Charles Barry* (1867), and C. Eastlake, *A History of the Gothic Revival* (1872). See also K. Clark, *The Gothic Revival* (2nd ed. 1950), H. R. Hitchcock, *Early Victorian Architecture* (2 vols. 1954), and M. Hastings, *Parliament House* (1950).

design and its general proportions were as far as they were prepared to go on this 'point of feeling and taste': nor were they much
clearer about the exact scope of the term Elizabethan.[1] The press
and the pamphleteers largely employed moral words such as
'manly', 'dignified', and 'chaste', equally applicable or inapplicable
to either side. The problems of the controversialists are easily
understood. Barry's design had its greatest merit in its picturesque
use of the site, the long river front leading away from the bridge
to the corner mass of the Victoria tower, with the balancing clock
tower at the east end as a more slender, less emphatic accent; on
the northern side Westminster Hall was masked by Soane's Law
Courts, Gothicized against his will[2] and finally demolished in
1883: Barry always wished to replace them by a row of offices
continuing his general wall treatment, with a large towered
entrance to New Palace Yard, thereby removing the 'disjointed,
and incongruous character of the present building on the land side',[3]
which incidentally shows his basic classical bias, though there
would still have been a recession of the western half and the gateway set at an angle across the eastern corner would have been a
picturesque feature. It is probably fortunate that this was not
carried out and that Westminster Hall was to be allowed to
dominate the northern vista, a dominance that Barry was anxious
to avoid. Within, the unequal and often non-rectangular courts,
the vaulted corridors and staircases retained something of the
sense of growth of the old assemblage of buildings, but Barry's
medievalism was visual not constructional. His ornament is applied
to regular façades, with long rows of evenly spaced windows, little
projection and strongly marked string courses which firmly
emphasize the horizontal line. 'Late medieval and Tudor', he called
it, and the elevation as engraved for the committee of acceptance[4]
had already dispensed with some of the Gothic detail of the drawing;

[1] *P.P. 1836*, xxi. 49, 53. The *Edinburgh Review* (lxv, 1837, 175) commented on 'the
absurdity of building, in the nineteenth century, according to the taste of the twelfth
or sixteenth' in reviewing W. R. Hamilton's pamphlets on the New Houses of
Parliament.

[2] See his *Proceedings Respecting the New Law Courts at Westminster* (1828).

[3] *Life and Works*, 289.

[4] *P.P. 1836,* xxi: the original drawings are in the library of the R.I.B.A.

there was, Barry said, to be no panelling of the exterior walls as in Henry VII's chapel. Expense was no doubt one reason: Joseph Hume was belabouring the cost of Gothic detail, and Barry had reduced his estimate to £707,104 for six years' work, a surprisingly low figure and one that proved very illusory in view of the twenty years building campaign, eventually costing about £2,000,000. The original estimate, however, remained the basis of Barry's personal fees, despite constant protests from the architect himself and eventually from the Royal Institute of British Architects, founded in 1834 under the presidency of Thomas Philip, earl de Grey, with Barry, Papworth, and P. F. Robinson as vice-presidents and T. L. Donaldson as secretary.[1] Donaldson, in his long life of ninety years, twenty-three of which were to be spent as Professor of Architecture at University College, London, did more than anyone for the R.I.B.A., more than most for architecture in general. In the parliamentary controversies, his balanced view and moderating influence were firmly on Barry's side.

Charles Barry, born in 1795, was in 1836 an established architect, who had spent some time travelling in Italy, Greece, Syria, and Egypt,[2] had built several Gothic churches and since 1833 had been employed by King Edward VI's School, Birmingham, on new buildings in the Perpendicular style. His best-known work, however, the Travellers' Club in Pall Mall (1829–31), was in the Italian manner, and the success of its design, the prominent site and the influential nature of its membership gave new prestige to this third dominant style, which, though not absent from Regency country houses, was only emerging from the disfavour into which the most accepted Anglo-Italian version, the Palladian, had fallen. The heavy cornice, rusticated quoins and strongly marked edicular treatment of the windows give to the Travellers' Club[3] a variety of surface light and shade which many Grecian buildings lacked, and the Italian palaces which it recalled, many of them built in their day by

[1] See J. A. Gotch, *The Growth and Work of the Royal Institute of British Architects* (1934).

[2] M. Whiffen, 'Journeys of Charles Barry', *Arch. Rev.* cv (1949), 211.

[3] W. H. Leeds, *The Travellers' Club House . . . Accompanied by an Essay on the Present State of Architectural Study and the Revival of the Italian Style* (1839). 'It was reserved for Mr. Barry to introduce the cornicione here', ibid. 23.

merchant princes and bankers, seemed appropriate to the great clubs of the reform period and a generation which had seen a William Roscoe modelling himself on Lorenzo de' Medici. The Reform Club, for which Barry won a competition in 1837, is, unlike the Travellers, a free-standing building, and the space allowed of a large central hall. It was also from the beginning a three-storeyed elevation, unlike the original two storeys of its forerunner. Its evenly spaced windows are less interesting than the grouped windows of the Travellers' southern façade, but it firmly stamped the Italian pattern on London clubland, and ten years later Sydney Smirke attempted to rival it with his Venetian design for the Carlton Club next door, whose splendour now, since its destruction in the second war, is only a memory. Meanwhile Barry was converting an earlier house at Trentham into a great colonnaded palazzo for the duke of Sutherland, set in a formal garden designed by William Nesfield, Barry's frequent collaborator:[1] but from such schemes, original in many of their details, Barry was now diverted by the ever-increasing demands of the new Palace of Westminster.

Work on the foundations and the river wall began in 1837, but the first stone of the new buildings was not laid till April 1840. There was much clearance of ruined buildings to be done, estimates to be drawn up and decisions to be taken as to the stone to be used. The Bolsover quarries were those favoured, but the supply from them was insufficient and Anson stone was also employed. From the beginning it was realized that the London atmosphere, at this time steadily worsening, constituted a major risk to a pinnacled building, rich in stone carving, forming, as a Member of Parliament was later to complain,[2] 'the most magnificent aviary for swallows and sparrows the world ever saw'. Problems of repair were becoming apparent even before the building was completed. In 1847 the House of Lords was occupied, the House of Commons in 1852: Big Ben, another theme of much controversy, was installed in 1859: the Victoria Tower was completed in 1867, seven years after Barry's death. He had been knighted in 1852 when the Queen for the first time entered by the royal stairway at the foot

[1] *I.L.N.* xi (1847), 248; *C.L.* iii. 272, 304: Trentham is now largely demolished.
[2] *Hansard*, cxi (1850), 330: today pigeons and starlings are the menace.

of the Tower. It had been a long and often acrimonious business; a
tiresome dispute about methods of ventilation filled the forties; the
Commissioners for the decoration of the New Palace pursued their
elaborate schemes without adequate consultation with the architect. 'Sua mortifera est victoria', Peel had said when defending
Barry against Hume's petition, and to the prolonged conduct
of an affair so publicly bandied and scrutinized posterity has
added doubts as to Barry's part and good faith in the actual
design.

In the work at King Edward's School, Birmingham, Barry had
been employing the young Augustus Welby Pugin, son of Nash's
draughtsman, to design much of the Gothic detail. Pugin was in
his early twenties and had already had a varied career, designing
Gothic furniture for Wyatville at Windsor, stage sets at Covent
Garden, and a Gothic house for himself, St. Marie's Grange, at
Salisbury. He had visited and drawn many of the cathedrals,
churches, and colleges of England and formed an intense dislike
of Wyatt 'the destroyer' and his restorations. He had sailed his own
ship as far as the Firth of Forth, where he was wrecked, and he had
very recently joined the Roman Church. Barry, working at great
pressure, employed him on the drawings for the Westminster
competition, and Pugin also assisted, in the same task, the Edinburgh architect, Gillespie Graham, who had befriended him at the
time of his shipwreck. A discerning critic in the *Morning Post*
commented on the fact that these two sets of drawings were by
the same hand and showed 'the genuine spirit of Gothic architecture'. The elevations for Barry's entry bear this out and are closely
related to Pugin's admitted sketches. Pugin, however, never
claimed to have designed the building. 'The plan', he said, 'was
Barry's own.' This was unquestionably the case. Pugin could at
no stage of his career have organized this great group of buildings,
and, had he attempted to do so, his mixture of genius and pedantry
would have produced some quite other result. There was also a
long break, between 1836 and 1845, in his connexion with Barry.
His son, however, felt strongly that his father's share had never
been fully recognized. Some letters lent to Barry after Pugin's
death and dealing with their collaboration curiously went astray:

there were public debate and recrimination in which both sides overstated their case.[1]

The decorations remain, and in the collection of Pugin's drawings for them, now in the Victoria and Albert Museum, the exuberance of his skill can be seen in its initial stages. His name had not occurred amongst the competitors in the Exhibition of Decorative Work for the New Palace of Westminster held in 1844, but his influence had been felt there, in the designs of Messrs. Hardman of Birmingham for ironwork and in the encaustic tiles of Messrs. Minton of Stoke-on-Trent, though these latter owed also much to the genius of Owen Jones, whose great work on the Alhambra appeared between 1842 and 1845 and whose mosaic designs in the 1844 Exhibition were used for some of the Westminster floors. From 1845 Pugin's genius permeates the whole, the tremendous gilt framework for the throne, the great armorial displays, the restless, brilliant use of colour, and the individuality and certainty of the motifs. There is an insistency about everything Pugin touched: not always pleasing, he is always noticeable and memorable. Outside, the rising Victoria Tower took on a new richness of pattern work. At some period, not clearly certain but probably before Pugin's re-employment, Barry's decision to leave the walls unpanelled was reversed, and the exterior texture assumed a richness that matched the almost gaudy splendour within.

A lesser, more balanced, equally industrious figure played his part, the stonemason and carver, John Thomas, who, like Pugin, had worked for Barry on King Edward's School, and who continuously was in charge of the stonework for the New Palace. Thomas's carvings are a frequent feature of the London scene: on the pediment of Philip Hardwick's Great Western Hotel at Paddington, in the waiting hall at Euston, the frieze round the United Service Club, the life-size wooden figures of judges for Lincoln's Inn Hall; elsewhere Birmingham, Manchester, Bristol, Edinburgh, Glasgow, Windsor, and Balmoral have, or had, examples of his prodigious output. Much of this is in a style that

---

[1] See, in addition to the authorities already quoted, R. Dell, 'Who was the Architect of the Houses of Parliament?', *Burl. Mag.* viii (1906), 404. There is an important and more contemporary summing up of the case in *The Ecclesiologist*, xxix (1868), 44, 105.

can best be described as debased classical, but at Westminster he found himself and created a team of workmen who set the standard for later Gothic revival figure-sculpture. His full, easy-flowing drapery is handled with considerable skill, and both in pose and expression he was inventive while at the same time adequately traditional. Figures from Pugin's designs are seldom satisfactory: the forms are thin, the poses stilted, and he had constant difficulty in adjusting them to the available space in his niches. Thomas in the rows of kings and queens on the doorways of the central hall at Westminster admirably solves such problems, and his larger figures on the Victoria Tower have genuine monumental feeling.

These three men, Barry, Pugin, and Thomas, in their varying degrees created this familiar and famous building, which, with all its shortcomings, its ephemeral fashions, its inconveniences, has the symbol-making greatness: the silhouette that Barry invented became part of British history. Greater architects have given more disciplined and ennobling pleasures; few have found as widespread a response. In the Thames fogs or twilight, wet with English rain, begrimed with London dirt, in full sunlight and moving shadows, it fits its place, climate, and functions, defying architectural purists in its apotheosis of the picturesque.

Gothic, however inexact, now reigned in high places, but the commissions that poured in on Barry were mainly for Jacobean or Italianate buildings. For the earl of Carnarvon he rebuilt Highclere in what he called the Anglo-Italian style; in fact its affinities are more with Jacobean building, from which it takes its strapwork balustrade and obelisk finials. Its use of towers and its strongly marked string courses recall Westminster, and it was in 1837, while enthusiasm for the New Palace had not been blunted by interference and frustration, that Barry designed it. It was, according to his son, one of his favourite works. Compared, however, with Harlaxton Hall,[1] begun by Anthony Salvin three years before Highclere and not completed till the mid-forties, Barry's Jacobean is as personal as his Gothic. Whereas Highclere is a rectangle round a central hall, Harlaxton is built on the traditional E shape

[1] A. Oswald in *C.L.* lxxxii (1937), 374.

plan,[1] and its oriel windows, its skyline of high chimneys, gables, and cupola-topped turrets are completely different in conception from the flat walls, regularly spaced windows, and masking balustrade of Highclere. Seen from the entrance gate, beyond the dip and rise of its mile-long drive, Harlaxton is as dramatic in its impact as any building in England, and the approach through an elaborate gatehouse up to the curved forecourt is a continuous intensification of the first impression. The front elevation is composed of Jacobean motifs used with great vigour and certainty. The Ancaster stone has retained its clean cut edges, and the strapwork, rustication, and prominent string courses are unsoftened by weathering (Pl. 72 *b*). There is a brutal quality about Salvin's decoration which reaches its climax in the heavy, projecting voussoirs, huge scrolls, and carved overhanging trophies of the entrance hall. Then, perhaps to accord with the patron's collection, William Burn took over the interior,[2] and the great staircase rises from an Italian door with twisted columns, almost certainly imported, through plaster draperies and cherubs to a painted sky, where a figure of Time leans over unrolling a plan of the building. Much employed in Scottish baronial buildings, William Burn, here and at Montagu House (1859–62), belatedly realized baroque profusion in English settings. Victorian architects were indeed various and enterprising in their undertakings. Salvin was to rival the impressiveness of Harlaxton in his Edwardian castle at Peckforton (1846–50): in the Jacobean manner, Paxton and Stokes produced for the Rothschilds at Mentmore (1852–4) a building that stylistically is half-way between Highclere and Harlaxton and as lavish as either.[3]

In Barry's later works he returned to his earlier models. Bridgewater House (1847–57) was built for Lord Francis Egerton, one of the accepted arbiters of taste, who had served on numerous commissions; it has many of the features of the Reform Club, but is much more profuse in its decoration, and the curved pediments of the first-storey windows have elaborate carvings by John Thomas

---

[1] Compare the plan of a Tudor house as given in T. F. Hunt's *Exemplars of Tudor Architecture* (1830), pl. xi.　　[2] C. Hussey in *C.L.* cxxi (1957), 704, 764.

[3] See for these and other examples H.-L. Hitchcock, op. cit., chap. viii, 'Manorial and Castellated Country Houses'; for Paxton see below, p. 257.

(Pl. 72 *a*). Dorchester House was the admitted rival to Bridgewater House. Its architect was Lewis Vulliamy, son of a famous clock-maker of Swiss extraction. He was known as a builder of Gothic churches, but at All Saints, Ennismore Gardens, had experimented with Italian Romanesque, collaborating with 'Alhambra' Jones on the interior decorations.[1] At Dorchester House, where he was employed by Robert Holford, the shipping magnate and art collector, he used the Italian style, but without the consistency of Barry. Now only a memory, it lacked as seen from the Park the coherence of Barry's designs; the corner pavilions rising above a heavy cornice were insufficiently linked with the main building, and this villa silhouette fitted uneasily into a street frontage. Dor-chester House was, however, fortunate in its interiors. Whereas Barry had had to see his great hall at Bridgewater House garishly decorated by the German, Götzenberger, Vulliamy was followed by Alfred Stevens, who created there what must have been one of the finest interiors in England, derivative from Michelangelo in much of the figure carving, but derivative with the acute perceptions of independent genius.

With these two great mansions the Italian style was established, and continued to be used throughout the country for another fifty years. Philip Hardwick's hall at Euston Station (1847),[2] which has some claim to be the grandest room in London, was based on Peruzzi's great chamber in the Palazzo Massimi. When Queen Victoria found a secluded spot at Osborne where 'we can walk anywhere without being followed or mobbed', the Prince Consort with the help of Thomas Cubitt, the London contractor, designed in 1845 a house with Italian campaniles, a two-storeyed loggia, terraced gardens and laurel shrubberies,[3] these last ensuring the popularity of one of the unhappiest features of nineteenth-century gardening. In the new streets of London, in Marylebone and Kensington, and in the residential areas of provincial towns Italianate towers rose above the roof-line of new terraces, as in R. W. Jearrad's Lypiatt Terrace at Cheltenham (Pl. 32 *a*). In 1839

[1] The church underwent considerable alteration in 1892.
[2] Mainly carried out by his son, Philip Charles Hardwick.
[3] *Osborne House*: Ministry of Works Guide (1915).

Edward Walters built for Richard Cobden in Manchester a warehouse, where motifs from Italian palazzi were adapted to new commercial purposes, and fourteen years later the same architect borrowed details from Verona for his Free Trade Hall. 'For us', wrote Caroline Norton in *The Child of the Islands* (1845), 'the streets, broad-built and populous, For them unhealthy corners, garrets dim.' These 'black palaces' must have been in sinister contrast to the terrible slums around them.[1]

While Italian was established by royal patronage, and the Gothic style gained steadily on the Grecian for churches and public buildings, French influences were apparent on the new hotels, one of the characteristic features of the age. Philip Hardwick and his son were responsible for the Great Western Hotel at Paddington. The selected style was, according to the *Illustrated London News*,[2] 'French of Louis XIV or later'. In fact, despite the central balcony on caryatids carved by John Thomas,[3] its high mansard, stone dormers, curved roof, and cupolas suggest, even if they precede, Napoleon III's rebuilding of the Louvre, a work which was to be much noted in England. Many hotels followed the example of the Great Western, and French motifs became increasingly common.[4] In the railway stations too the mingling of styles was at work.[5] James Pritchett's Ionic portico at Huddersfield (1847) is in the line of succession from Euston. Daniel Mocatta used at Brighton (1841) the Italian style and two years later Lewis Cubitt built a great Italian tower, with rusticated quoins, to surmount the station entry at Dover. Tite borrowed Barry's club-house style for Southampton, but in his Windsor Station, with its royal entrance, Gothic seemed inevitable. Bristol Temple Meads was the most ambitious venture into Tudor. In country areas the veranda sheltering the platform gave opportunities for some pleasant use of cast iron ornament, and the tracing of patterns from station to station can still beguile a journey.

Here and there some of the Regency repertory of styles made

[1] C. Stewart, *The Stones of Manchester* (1956), chap. ii.   [2] xxi (1852), 538.
[3] These were removed *c.* 1935, when the entrance doorway was much modified.
[4] See H. R. Hitchcock, *Victorian Architecture*, i, chap. vii; *I.L.N.* xxi (1852), 538.
[5] Christian Barman, *An Introduction to Railway Architecture* (1950).

sporadic reappearances. The Egyptian was particularly favoured in the new cemeteries which were replacing the repugnantly un-hygienic London graveyards: in Kensal Green (opened in 1833) the mausoleum of Andrew Ducraux (1837), the lessee of the Royal Amphitheatre, 'erected by genius for the reception of its own remains', is basically Egyptian with a riot of symbolic urns, angels, winged horses and beehives: and at Highgate (1838) Egyptian pilasters were much used by Stephen Geary in his dramatic gate-ways and catacombs (Pl. 32 d).[1] One of its last manifestations was in Brunel's[2] pylons for the Clifton suspension bridge, where the effect was to have been completed by metal hieroglyphs set into the stonework; but the long and complex history of the bridge's erection (1837–63) led to the modification of the original scheme and the hieroglyphs were never inserted. The Moorish style had behind it the authority of 'Alhambra' Jones, and was used in the work of Brunel and Matthew Digby Wyatt at Paddington Station, where Brunel had stipulated that the designs should be suited to the materials employed, a sound mid-Victorian view, but where, wonderfully inventive as the patterns are, Saracenic is the word that most easily comes to mind.

The classical style died the hardest. When in 1838 another fire, this time destroying the Royal Exchange, led to another competi-tion and more controversies, the Gresham Trustees stipulated that the design should be in the 'Grecian, Roman or Italian style'.[3] William Grellier was awarded the first prize, but after more than usually dubious proceedings the commission was assigned to William Tite, whose main western façade, despite some muddled eclecticism in other parts of the building, is a firmly classical porch with eight giant Corinthian columns and a triangular pediment. Cockerell also was a competitor. His design exists in an elaborate water-colour sketch and would have been one of his most striking

[1] J. A. Picton, 'On Cemeteries', *Architectural Mag.* ii (1837), 426. Messrs. Poulton and Woodman's cemetery chapels (1837–9) in 'the Decorated Gothic style' at Basing-stoke are good examples of a class of building much in demand at the time of the Revival: *Building News*, v (1859), 358. R. P. Ross Williamson, 'Victorian Necropolis', *Arch. Rev.* xcii. 87.

[2] See L. T. C. Rolt, *Isambard Kingdom Brunel* (1957).

[3] K. Esdaile, 'Battles Royal: No. 1', *Architect and Building News*, cxxv (1931), 47.

buildings: the advanced statue-bearing columns round which the entablature returns and the large arches behind them have a full-blooded dramatic impact, beside which his Taylorian façade at Oxford seems timidly experimental (Pl. 67). It might well have been the fulfilment of his genius, giving deeper meaning to all his other works.

Sir Charles Barry died in 1860. He was at the time engaged on the town hall at Halifax, which was completed by his son, E. M. Barry, after his death. The hall is lit with two rows of windows, of equal height and broken entablatures on free-standing columns; the upper entablatures are marked by ornamental finials on the low balustrade; it is one of the richest of Barry's Italian schemes; but at one corner of the building rises a large tower and spire, the latter with three ornamental galleries, thoroughly un-Italianate in appearance. This is Victorian architecture at its most lavishly monumental (Pl. 75 b). Five years earlier Cuthbert Brodrick had been building the town hall at Leeds and infusing the classic patterns of St. George's Hall with some of Barry's exuberance.[1] James Pennethorne's building for London University in Burlington Gardens (1866–70) has Italian towers, rusticated ground storey and applied columns, which support a skyline of statues round whose capitals the cornice breaks with a Soanian effect. John Gibson, Barry's pupil, in his National Provincial Bank in Bishopsgate (1865), profusely covered with carved reliefs, entered by its great rounded archway, topped by a row of marble figures, created in that stronghold of nineteenth-century architecture the typical example of Victorian profusion unrestrained.

[1] D. Harbron in *Arch. Rev.* lxxix (1936), 33.

VIII

STATE PATRONAGE

WHILE contemporary painting attracted a growing amount of attention in the periodicals, the old masters, the objects of so many artists' continental pilgrimages, were given a new availability. In 1824 the House of Commons voted £60,000 for the purchase of the Angerstein collection. John Julius Angerstein, a Russian by origin and one of the creators of the modern 'Lloyds', a friend of Lawrence and West, had built up a princely fortune and spent much of it on paintings. The collection was not numerous, thirty-eight paintings in all, but included Sebastiano del Piombo's *Raising of Lazarus* (No. 1 in the Gallery catalogue and still one of its largest pictures), Rubens's *Rape of the Sabines*, five splendid Claudes, Titian's *Venus and Adonis*, Hogarth's *Mariage à la mode*, and Wilkie's *Village Festival* (the only work by a living artist). Several pieces went under distinguished names which they do not now retain. There was considerable negotiation with the executors, in which the two principal dealers of the day, William Seguier and Samuel Woodburn, were much consulted: there was also the problem of housing, which was solved temporarily by the purchase of the remainder of the lease of Angerstein's house, No. 100 Pall Mall. It was quite unsuited to the purpose, even when a new top light was added to the drawing room, and it soon became hopelessly inadequate as more pictures were acquired by gift and purchase: Correggio's *Madonna of the Basket* in 1825; Titian's *Bacchus and Ariadne* in 1826, not without criticism of its condition and subject. 'The figure of Bacchus', said a writer in the *New Monthly Magazine*,[1] 'borders on the ridiculous.' Almost as great a picture came in the same year by gift, Rubens's *Château de Steen*, the most important painting in Sir George Beaumont's collection. Sir George had been largely responsible for a National Gallery being founded and had early expressed his

[1] xviii (1826), pt. 3, 461.

intention of presenting his collection to it. It was one already well known to practising artists, many of whom had enjoyed Sir George's hospitality at Coleorton Hall, the house George Dance built for him in 1804–8 in a highly individual Gothic style (Pl. 29 *a*). 'We ... breakfasted', wrote Haydon of his visit, 'with the Rubens' landscape, and did nothing, morning, noon or night, but think of painting, talk of painting, dream of painting and wake to paint again.'[1] The third great foundation collection was that bequeathed in 1831 by the Rev. William Holwell Carr, with Tintoretto's *St. George*, Rembrandt's *Woman Bathing*, and Luini's *Christ Teaching*, then generally considered to be a genuine Leonardo. The control of the Gallery was almost entirely in the hands of the Keeper. A committee of first six, then eight gentlemen was nominated by the Treasury with somewhat vaguely defined powers and met but seldom, in fact not at all in the first three and a half years of the Gallery's history. Problems that were to prove lasting ones early appeared: press campaigns against purchases, criticisms of the hanging, Sunday opening, discussions about glazing and debates as to cleaning.

The rooms at 100 Pall Mall were soon sadly inadequate. A highly finished water-colour of this date by Frederick Mackenzie gives us some idea of how they were arranged: one wall is dominated by the Sebastiano, which stretched from the ceiling to the elaborate cornice; but for the most part the pictures hung in triple tiers; the rooms were filled with the chairs and easels of the copyists. The issue was eventually forced by the threatened collapse of No. 100 owing to the excavations for the foundations of the Reform Club next door, and the Gallery had to be moved down the Mall to No. 105. This was only a temporary resting place, and after much debate the foundation stone of Wilkins's new Gallery was laid in February 1834, on a site near Charing Cross created by the removal of the King's Mews and a number of other crowded buildings.

The Gallery opened in its new quarters in April 1838. A year earlier the east wing had been occupied by the Royal Academy,

[1] *Autobiography* (ed. 1926), i. 96; see catalogue, *Sir George Beaumont and his Circle*, Leicester Museum and Art Galleries (1953).

who had held their first exhibition there in 1837. From the start the two bodies were uneasy neighbours, all the more so because their union coincided with an organized attack upon the Academy's privileges. In 1835 a select committee of the House of Commons had been appointed primarily to investigate the best means of extending the principles of design among the manufacturing population: on this it reported briefly at the end of the year, recommending the resumption of its sittings to discuss the state of the higher branches of art and the best mode of advancing them.[1] This, however, was assigned to a new committee, under the chairmanship of William Ewart, the well-known Liberal member for Liverpool. The earlier committee had included patrons such as Lord Francis Egerton and Sir Robert Peel: the new one contained no titles and represented the reformers of 1832 and the 'avowed indifference' of Lord Melbourne. It had been influenced by the attacks on the Academy made in Parliament by Joseph Hume, an agitation in which Ewart had taken part. The evidence given before the committee is a remarkable document.[2] Haydon stormed at the Academy, lectured on the history of art, and rehearsed his own particular grievances, all in a series of positive assertions: he was followed by John Martin who was little less voluble: it was undoubtedly the President of the Academy, Archer Shee, who came well out of the case.[3] The committee pressed him with questions and failed to understand the most simple answers, but he kept his temper and argued that it was only as a body with some privileges that the Academy could hope to stimulate artistic ambitions. On the questions of the joint tenancy of the new building he was emphatic that the Academy had only agreed to move from Somerset House, which it held in royal gift, on the understanding that it would have the same conditions of tenure at Trafalgar Square. The case for the Academy as a school of art, as a benevolent society for artists, not necessarily academicians, in distress, and as providing recognition and encouragement

---

[1] *P.P. 1835*, v. 373–518.

[2] *P.P. 1836*, ix. 1–409.

[3] M. A. Shee, *Life of Sir Martin Archer Shee* (1860), ii. 85. The *Life* contains a full account of the dispute of the thirties.

for leading practitioners was, somewhat doubtfully, accepted as proven.

Another concern of the Select Committee was 'the want of instruction in design amongst our industrious population'. In his evidence C. R. Cockerell stated his belief that

the attempt to supersede the work of the mind and hand by mechanical process for the sake of economy, will always have the effect of degrading and ultimately ruining art. . . . Some years ago His Grace the Duke of Northumberland had the liberality to lay out a large sum in his house at Charing-cross on manufactures, wholly English and of unusual magnificence. I followed the execution of these in various manufactures, and found them always at a loss for design and models well understood, and confessing, according to their own words, the deficiency of the master hand.[1]

This was the general burden of all the evidence given by various representatives of English trades. Paisley shawls that had long enjoyed an international popularity were being displaced by French patterns: firms such as Coade & Sealey, Rundell & Bridge, or Wedgwood used to employ artists of eminence, Bacon, Rossi, Flaxman, Stothard, Theed, and Baily; now they employed lesser men in order to meet the demand for cheap articles.

The want of instruction [the committee summed up] experienced by our workmen in the Arts is strongly adverted to by many witnesses. . . . Mr. Martin (the celebrated painter) complains of the want of correct design in the china trade; Mr. Papworth (an eminent architect) of its absence in the interior decorative architecture of our houses, and in furniture. Hence the adoption of the designs of the era of Louis XV (commonly dignified with the name of Louis XIV), a style inferior in taste and execution. To a similar want of enlightened information in art, Mr. Cockerell attributes the prevailing fashion for Elizabethan Architecture, a style which (whatever may be the occasional excellencies of its execution) is undoubtedly of spurious origin.[2]

Regret was expressed at the absence of art history in the teaching of

---

[1] *P.P. 1836*, ix. 118. Northumberland House was demolished in 1874: the central feature of the redecoration scheme under the third duke was probably the great staircase designed by Thomas Cundy: see *Survey of London*, xviii (1947), pl. 7.

[2] *P.P. 1836*, ix. 3.

the universities, but one of the witnesses, Mr. James Morrison, doubted whether Oxford or Cambridge could ever be suitable places for the study of the fine arts. Here and there a more cheerful, self-reliant note was struck. J. Jobson Smith of Messrs. Stewart, Smith & Co., Sheffield, boasted that their grates, fenders, and stove fronts were considered by Chantrey the finest that he had seen; at Worcester the china trade was increasing; a very beautiful service was being made for the pasha of Egypt; the operatives had been attending Mr. Constable's lectures at the Literary and Scientific Institution 'with great profit to themselves'; but there was general agreement that design suffered from the lack of any adequate patent protection, which was limited to models of human figures or animals or 'any subject being matter of invention in sculpture'. Schools of design and museums where works of art could be seen were sadly lacking compared to the provision of them in France; libraries were inadequate. Despite repeated questioning by the committee, no one in England seemed to be making much use of the fuller knowledge about classical interior decoration provided by Pompeii.

The main outcome of the Select Committee of 1836 was the registration of patents for decorative design[1] and the creation of the Government School of Design, housed in the rooms at Somerset House vacated by the Academy. There were many problems to be settled. Should the new School teach how to draw? Should it encourage designers or train men in crafts? The Council of the School, on which there were two painters, Eastlake and Callcott, a sculptor, Chantrey, and an architect, Cockerell, found themselves at a loss and commissioned William Dyce to examine the state schools in France, Prussia, and Bavaria. On his return, though he urged that we 'must cease to look upon the mere establishment of schools of design as an infallible nostrum', he was appointed the Director in 1840.[2] This young Scotsman, thirty-four years old, was a singularly gifted man, who had studied art in Rome, where he had made close contacts with the Nazarenes; and

---

[1] *An Act to secure to Proprietors of Design for Articles of Manufacture the Copyright of such Designs for a limited Time*, 2 Vict. xvii.

[2] For Dyce see article by J. Dafforne in *Art Journ.* vi (1860), 293.

then, disappointed by the unreceptivity of his native Aberdeen to 'early Christian art', had turned to natural science and won a prize for an essay on electro-magnetism: he had next become a successful, if on the whole conventional, portrait painter and a member of the Scottish Academy, at the time still seeking its royal charter, which it received in 1838. He was to prove himself an able organizer and a strong character who held to his own views and intentions, and when, in 1843, a clash came between his opinions and those of the Council, he resigned the directorship. The School tended to fall between two stools, industrial design or fine art; the Council wanted artists as opposed to ornamentists, whereas Dyce advocated a more practical approach.[1]

In 1841 the government took a further step in the organization of art. Sir Robert Peel appointed a select committee to consider 'the promotion of the fine arts of this Country in connexion with the rebuilding of the Houses of Parliament'.[2] After hearing various witnesses, of whom Archer Shee was once more notably to the point, William Dyce the best informed as to fresco painting, and Charles Eastlake the most learned, the committee recommended the appointment of a royal commission, reassuringly stating that 'independently of the beneficial and elevating influence of the fine arts upon a people, every pecuniary outlay, either for the purpose of forming or extending collections of Works of Art in this country, has been directly instrumental in creating new objects of industry and of enjoyment, and therefore in adding, at the same time, to the wealth of the country'.

At Peel's invitation the Prince Consort agreed to act as president of the commission. He had been married barely two years and little was as yet known of him: Peel, so it was said,[3] wanted 'some neutral ground in public matters on which a royal individual . . . could safely tread'. The royal patrons 'were not yet much dis-

---

[1] See 'Report by the Provisional Council of the School of Design', *P.P. 1841*, xiii. 533; Dyce, *The National Gallery, its formation and management considered in a letter addressed by permission to Prince Albert* (1853).

[2] T. S. R. Boase, 'The Decoration of the New Palace of Westminster', *Journ. W.C.I.* xvii (1954), 319, where full references are given to the various parliamentary reports and to contemporary criticisms.

[3] *Q.R.* cxi (1862), 175 (obituary notice of the Prince Consort by Lady Eastlake).

tinguished for their encouragement of high art'.[1] Callcott had been knighted; George Hayter (knighted in 1842) had been appointed the Queen's portrait and history painter, and entrusted with the painting of the coronation and the official portrait of the Queen in coronation robes, an ably managed, grandiloquent piece. Hayter's matrimonial affairs (he had made an early and unfortunate marriage and was now living with a lady who was not his wife) were not considered suitable for the moral standard required by the Academy and he was never a member of that body: these difficulties, however, did not debar him from royal favour and in fact seem to have intrigued the Queen in her early, light-hearted days.[2] The royal painter in water-colour, Alfred Chalon, was, however, an Academician of some standing, and his water-colour of the Queen, the head from which was used for many colonial stamps, was to be the key-piece for the young Victoria's iconography.[3] All in all, royal patronage was not regarded as important or distinguished. There was too some fear that the Prince might lean too heavily towards the German school, and there had been suggestions at the Select Committee that a German artist should be invited to undertake the work. The school of Munich under Peter von Cornelius, who visited London in 1841, enjoyed a prestige which today it is hard to appreciate. His vast designs are cold, correct, and lifeless, but they were in fresco, a method almost untried in England, but one, it was generally agreed, that must be used at Westminster. It had long been felt that it was a national discredit that this highest form of art was lacking.[4] The Select Committee had arisen out of a motion in Parliament for a grant for experiments in fresco painting. Dyce and Eastlake were strongly of opinion that it should be attempted; and the latter was appointed secretary to the Commission, the first step in a career which was to lead to the presidency of the Royal Academy and the directorship of the National Gallery.

The Commissioners now announced a competition for cartoon

[1] *Athenaeum* (1843), 675.
[2] Information from Mr. John Woodward, who is working on Hayter's papers.
[3] R. Lowe, 'The Chalon Portrait', *Journ. of Royal Soc. of Art*, ciii (1955), 342.
[4] T. Uwins, *Autobiography*, ii. 268.

drawings 'executed in chalk or charcoal, not less than ten nor more than fifteen feet in their longest dimension; the figures to be not less than the size of life, illustrating subjects from British History or from the works of Spenser, Shakespeare or Milton'. The opening of the exhibition of the cartoons, 140 in all, in Westminster Hall in the summer of 1843, inaugurated by a visit of the Queen, caused the widest interest. 'It was a surprising scene, new to English art, and in its immense quantity and high excellence astonishing everyone. . . . Instead of our being without historic art, in London, it was found to be plentiful and admirable.' So wrote William Bell Scott,[1] a little sarcastically for he notes that, of the prize-winners, Selous had hitherto been 'an assistant painter of panoramas' and Townsend 'a surgeon now become artist'. The winners were in fact comparatively unknown men: the £300 premiums were assigned to Edward Armitage for his *Caesar's Invasion of Britain*, G. F. Watts for *Caractacus led in triumph through the streets of Rome* (Pl. 78 a), and C. W. Cope for *The First Trial by Jury*. £200 prizes were awarded to J. C. Horsley, J. Z. Bell, and H. J. Townsend, £100 to W. E. Frost, E. T. Parris, H. C. Selous, John Bridges, and Joseph Severn. Some of the more senior artists, however, were included in an additional award of ten £100 prizes, paid out of the money taken in the first fortnight of the exhibition. The spectacle of Westminster Hall crowded with these giant productions is preserved for us in a woodcut in the *Illustrated London News*.[2] Screens were erected along the side walls up to the springing of the roof, with a long central screen down the middle of the hall, and on these the cartoons were fixed in two serried rows, practically touching one another: between the arches a third row of cartoons partially blocked the windows and must have considerably obscured the light. In the first two weeks, at an admission price of 1s. a head, there was an average attendance of 1,800 a day: then the exhibition was opened free and was crowded throughout, 'with most respectably dressed people' *The Times* noted with some relief.[3]

[1] *Autobiographical Notes* (1892), i. 169.   [2] iii, 1843, 17.

[3] For an account of the crowds at the exhibition see *Memoir of Sir Charles Eastlake* in the second series of his *Contributions to the Literature of the Fine Arts*, 173, and Mrs. S. C. Hall in *Art-Union Journal*, v (1843), 219. B. Simmons wrote a poem, 'Westminster Hall on a free admission day', in *Blackwood's Edinburgh Magazine*, lvi (1844), 652.

Amongst the prize-winners, none was as yet even an Associate of the Royal Academy. The entries had been made anonymously and it might well seem that the result was something of a setback to the official body. More established artists had not been prepared to risk their reputation and to spend time on work for which there was no certain remuneration. As the names leaked out, it became clear that the competitors mainly belonged to the younger generation. With the exception of Henry Howard, the secretary of the Academy, Haydon was probably the most senior artist represented and he received no award. The entry in his diary for 1 July begins: 'A day of great misery. I said to my dear love, "I am not included".'[1] Already he had been much distracted by the death of Wilkie, an artist whom, in the pages of his *Journal*, he constantly abuses for sycophancy and treachery, but obviously with an uneasy feeling that Wilkie's success, which he admitted to be deserved, was based on qualities of character which he himself sadly lacked. Yet he struggled on, and in 1846 opened on Easter Monday an exhibition in a room at the Egyptian Hall of two new large-scale paintings, *Aristides* (who of course stood for Haydon himself, and in fact had the sub-title 'The Injustice of Democracy') and *Nero* (Pl. 63 *a*). The advertisement recalled Haydon's forty-two years devoted to 'simplifying the principles of art for the instruction of the People' and the 'utter neglect' he had received.[2] The exhibition was a complete failure, unpleasantly emphasized by the crowds flocking to another room in the same building where Barnum was exhibiting a dwarf, General Tom Thumb. He was once more in desperate financial straits. Peel, whom he had so often provoked and criticized, answered an appeal with a gift of £50. But the gift was not even used: on the morning of 22 June, 1846, having tried to shoot himself, he cut his throat with a razor. He lives in the vehemence of his journals: his paintings, save for the genre scenes, are little prized and little like to be so, and many have drifted into

[1] *Autobiography* (1926), ii. 752.
[2] Both these paintings are now in Melbourne, brought there by Haydon's friend Twentyman, who received them in part payment of debts owing to him on Haydon's death and who settled in Australia. They are now in the collection of Sir H. Gengoult Smith, but the *Aristides*, much damaged, is stored in the Exhibition Building.

oblivion. Short-sighted, technically inadequate, he could not in his chosen medium speak 'definitively of those mighty things', yet, as the obituary notice in the *Art-Union Journal* put it, 'Whatever were his mistakes, Mr. Haydon was a great movement in Art.'[1]

Amongst other unsuccessful exhibitors were the two Scott brothers, David and William. The former, whose Byronic gloom is well depicted in Scott Lauder's portrait (S.N.P.G.) of him, is the most profoundly imaginative British painter of the second quarter of the century. An Edinburgh man by birth and training, he had studied in Rome and in Paris, and held Michelangelo and Caravaggio as the two greatest painters. His *Philoctetes* (1839),[2] painted with great breadth and atmosphere, and his *Traitor's Gate* (1841), a strange, deeply shadowed invention, are among the most arresting history pieces of the romantic movement, and in his drawings for *The Ancient Mariner* and *The Pilgrim's Progress* he is one of the few successors to Blake, whose designs for Blair's *Grave*, known in childhood, had made a lasting impression on him. His Westminster cartoons, *Wallace and the battle of Stirling* and *Drake on the Quarter-deck, witnessing the Fire-ships destroying the Spanish Armada*, were, his brother wrote, 'slight' and 'wilfully un-elaborated', 'their execution was dangerous, even fatal to come before a jury with Sir Charles Eastlake at its head'.[3] William Scott's own fresco, *The Britons surprising the Roman Wall*, received some favourable comment, and his most striking success as a painter was to be in mural decoration, in the eight large canvases for Wallington House.[4]

Of the Westminster cartoons few now remain. Drawn on paper, 'in chalk or charcoal', they have mostly perished. The prize-winning exhibits were sent on a provincial tour, and then probably

---

[1] vii (1846), 216.

[2] See *Burl. Mag.* xci (1949), 153. For Scott see W. B. Scott, *Memoir of David Scott* (1850); A. L. Simpson, *Life of David Scott*, as preface to illustrated edition of *The Ancient Mariner* (1885); J. M. Gray, *David Scott and his Works* (Edinburgh, 1884). The *Philoctetes* and *Traitor's Gate* are in the National Gallery of Scotland; thirty-two of the original drawings for *The Pilgrim's Progress* are in the Sunderland Free Library; neither they nor the *Mariner* drawings were accepted for publication till after Scott's death.

[3] *Autobiographical Notes* (1892), i. 169.

[4] *c.* 1855–60: R. Ironside in *Arch. Rev.* xcii (1942), 147.

cut up: that at least happened to Watts's *Caractacus*, three fragments
of which, along with a sketch of the whole design, are in the
Victoria and Albert Museum. Many, however, of the cartoons,
including all the prize-winners and the supplementary list of ten
awards made out of the profits of the exhibition, were published
in lithograph.

Meanwhile the Commissioners were proceeding with exhaustive
thoroughness rather than with the dilatoriness that the public
sometimes attributed to them. Every care was taken to secure the
most up-to-date information about fresco technique: long and
learned discussions were held as to suitable subjects, and there were
further exhibitions of sculpture, applied arts, specimens of fresco,
more cartoons and large-scale oils. It was somewhat hard on the
artists: these endeavours absorbed all their time and yet brought
little reward, for even a prize hardly reimbursed them. Encouragement was given by the Prince himself. A small pavilion or summer
house in the grounds of Buckingham Palace was selected and it
was decided that the central octagonal room should be decorated
with arabesques and lunettes illustrating *Comus*, the lunettes being
entrusted to Clarkson Stanfield, Uwins, Leslie, Sir William Ross,
Landseer, Dyce, Maclise, and Eastlake. The artists ran almost
comically true to form: Stanfield has a piece of stage-scenery
landscape; Leslie a conversation piece with some pretty accessories;
Landseer a rout of animal-headed monsters ('the crowd presenting
every phase of bestial Expression');[1] Eastlake an abstracted virtue
surrounded by Raphaelesque cherubs; Dyce a Nazarene simplicity
of statement in the scene where the Brothers restore the Lady to her
parents. Sir William Ross (1794–1860, knighted 1842, R.A. 1843)
was best known as the most fashionable miniature painter of the
day, but he had begun work as a history painter and his cartoon of
The Angel Raffaelle discoursing with Adam had won a £100 premium
in 1843.[2] Dyce had only been called in when Etty had failed to
give satisfaction with a lunette originally allotted to him. He could

[1] *The Art-Union Journ.* (1845), 259, and *Art Journ.* (1865), 6. Landseer's oil study
(56 in. by 44 in.) for his fresco is now in the Tate Gallery. See L. Grüner, *The Decorations
of the Garden Pavilion in the Grounds of Buckingham Palace* (1846).
[2] *Art Journ.* (1860), 72.

not manage the unfamiliar medium, and his royal patrons were probably right in the words attributed to them: 'Poor man, he doesn't know what we want.'[1]

The Prince meanwhile was forming that collection of Italian primitives and Flemish fifteenth-century painters which marks a turning-point in taste in England. He was buying also contemporary English paintings, but the greatest name, Turner, is missing from his list. Dyce was probably his favourite, and, though he had not exhibited in the cartoons exhibition, he was invited to contribute a design for one of the spaces in the House of Lords, to represent the *Baptism of Ethelbert*. He had, however, in the Academy of 1844 shown a painting, *Joash and the Arrow of Deliverance* (Pl. 84 *a*), which stood out from all the other exhibits. Its bold simplification, flat planes and high seriousness belong to the Nazarene and Munich schools which he so much admired, but it has a strength of design and modelling that few of the Germans could equal. It was a masterpiece in a style new to England, relying on expressive form not on anecdotal detail. In the previous year, the Academy picture which caused the most sensation was P. F. Poole's *Solomon Eagle* (Pl. 66 *b*): this is broadly painted as opposed to Dyce's firm outlines, and though light in tone it has many and more conventional gradations of light and shade; above all it is full of dispersed anecdotal interest; the facile contrast of the masked and elegant revellers with the stark prophet; the barred houses; the bearers of the dead; here the existing tradition was powerfully expressing itself, but it pales beside Dyce's statement. Prince Albert purchased the latter's *Madonna and Child*, a reminiscence of quattrocento art, which still hangs at Osborne where the Prince commissioned Dyce to paint on the staircase a fresco of Neptune giving the Empire of the Sea to Britannia.

The remaining five panels in the House of Lords were eventually assigned two each to Maclise and Cope, and one to Horsley: the Lords and Commons corridors were each to have eight scenes drawn from the seventeenth century, and these were entrusted to

---

[1] Gilchrist, *Life of William Etty* (1855), ii, 150–69. The Garden Pavilion was taken down in 1928. The paintings had been much ruined by damp: see J. Steegman, *Consort of Taste* (1950), 205.

Cope and E. M. Ward: the Queen's robing room, with Arthurian subjects, went to Dyce: the upper waiting hall had a series of smaller frescoes from English poetry by Cope, Horsley, Herbert, Armitage, Watts and Tenniel: of further schemes, Maclise undertook two large frescoes, *The Meeting of Wellington and Blücher* and *The Death of Nelson*, in the Royal Gallery, and J. R. Herbert's paintings of *Moses and the Tables of the Law* and of the *Judgment of Daniel* in the peers' robing-room. These had in 1863 been completed or partially worked and at that date further contracts were cancelled, and the Commission, which by then had outlived its enthusiasm and its President, wound up its affairs. The death of Prince Albert in 1861 was the real end of the undertaking. His had been the directing mind and without his determined support the enterprise would probably have ended much sooner, under parliamentary attacks for expense, press ridicule of the delays and some of the results, jealousies and feuds of artists, and the intractability of the medium in English damp and London dirt.

The achievement was disproportionate to the effort involved. A new generation of artists had essayed the grand manner, but few with success and few persisted in it. Dyce in fresco never achieved the nobility of some of his oil painting, the *Ethelbert* is little more than a Raphaelesque pastiche and his Arthurian allegories cannot adequately fill the wall space at their disposal (Pl. 78 *b*); he was happier at Osborne than anywhere in the Palace of Westminster. G. F. Watts was twenty-six when he received the premium for his cartoon; he had many of the gifts of a decorative painter, and the great fresco in Lincoln's Inn Hall, painted after he had spent four years in Italy on the proceeds of his award, shows that here was in the making a genuine designer on the larger scale. Begun in 1853 it was completed in 1859, single-handed in true fresco on a wet ground, a vast undertaking, for the fresco at its lowest level is 45 feet long and 40 feet at its middle height. The design owes much to the *School of Athens* and must always suffer from the comparison, but its marked rhythms are its own and both in sense and form it shows much intellectual grasp.[1] It was during his Italian sojourn, at the Holland's Villa Careggi, that he painted the large canvas

[1] W. H. Draper, 'The Watts Fresco in Lincoln's Inn', *Burl. Mag.* ix (1906), 8.

(3 ft. 35 in. by 8 ft. 96 in.), now in the Tate, of a *Story from Boccaccio*, which shows a far richer colour sense than survives in the faded and twice-cleaned fresco: it is a very splendid decorative piece such as few English artists have rivalled. But this immense early promise was not to last, perhaps through lack of encouragement. His later allegories of love and death and hope were to win wide popularity, but their somewhat vague symbolism is clad in a misty, iridescent light which, sometimes arresting, cannot please for long. Something was lacking. Protected by admiring and wealthy ladies from too abrupt contacts with the outside world, he remained a constant worker, turning in old age to sculpture, producing always some notable portraits, but in the imaginary field which was his main concern capable only of relaxed visions.

The others, with the one exception of Maclise, are lesser men, and the frescoes of the poets in the upper waiting hall perished early and are now but blackened, damp-corrupted wrecks, generally covered from sight. John Tenniel's flaccid *St. Cecilia* (Dryden), which was painted thinly with very fluid washes, has proved more resistant than the others; but Tenniel was to make his name with cartoons of another kind, in the pages of *Punch* where the term was first used in parody of the Westminster exhibits, and with book illustration where as the creator of Alice and her companions he was to endow the English mind with one of its most lasting set of images.

Edward Armitage was a pupil of Delaroche and had worked with him on the famous hemicycle in the École des Beaux-Arts, which was regarded as one of the great examples of fresco painting. He represents the French school, as opposed to the more dominating German influence with which the tension really lay. In the competition for large oil paintings, his *Battle of Meamee* had received a prize and was purchased by the Queen. It commemorated a recent British victory when, in February 1843, Sir Charles Napier with a small force had defeated the armies of the ameers of Scinde. It is a muddled, undistinguished work, a conventional nineteenth-century battle-piece which was to have many followers.

C. W. Cope's seventeenth-century scenes in the Lords corridor, painted on plaster laid on slate panels detached from the wall and many of them executed in waterglass, a process which Prince Albert strongly advocated, are the best preserved of all the frescoes. Cope's straightforward narrative gifts and naturalistic style were much to the liking of the Prince, and he purchased one of his largest oil paintings, *The Death of Wolsey*, for Osborne. E. M. Ward is a more interesting painter, whose historical anecdotes have a genuine liveliness and dramatic invention; his frescoes have worn less well and are in patches badly discoloured, but in them he at times breaks away from the insipidity of expression that was all too clearly apparent in most of the attempts to ape the grand manner. English painters in the thirties had as their ideal of feminine beauty an oval face, with a high forehead, small mouth and large, vacant eyes. In Leslie's paintings, the early works of Maclise, Eastlake's Italian peasants, the pathetic governesses and seamstresses of Redgrave, Etty's luscious ladies and the pages of the *Keepsake* annuals, the type recurs, and no doubt corresponds to the views of the 'reformed' upper middle class male about ladylike docility. It, however, lent itself but little to high allegory or the great historic gesture.

It was, therefore, perhaps fortunate that Maclise's two great frescoes in the Royal Gallery were, with the exception of two or three women tending the wounded on board the *Victory*, male subjects. They are long, narrow paintings, scenes of carnage, rising in the *Wellington and Blücher* to the triangular apex made by the meeting of the two generals, falling in the case of the *Nelson* to the V-shaped group around the stricken leader. Within the general scheme lesser designs build up to the main feature, and when the colours had their original brilliance, the reds of the uniforms must have told boldly in the *Wellington*, whereas it is the blue-grey smoke clouds that hold together the *Nelson*.[1] There is a rich inventiveness of gesture, pose, and expression, and if there is carnage there is also compassion, in the man binding up the wounded guardsman's leg, in the group raising the body of 'young gallant Howard',[2] in the woman bathing the bleeding sailor's head and in the dazed, desperate look of the young powder monkey. English

[1] The oil version of the *Nelson* is at Liverpool in excellent preservation.
[2] Byron in *Childe Harold*, Canto III, xxix.

art in the high, romantic vein has seldom reached such narrative power and found such force and range to set it out (Pl. 79).

The Commissioners had also concerned themselves with sculpture and works of decorative art. Here as has already been mentioned they soon ran into conflict with Sir Charles Barry, who regarded these matters as the province of the architect. The Commissioners, however, held firm; the sculpture was exhibited in Westminster Hall along with more cartoons and examples of fresco painting, and there was general comment on how much better it looked there than in the cramped space of the Academy. The three sculptors singled out for special commendation by the Commissioners were W. Calder Marshall, John Bell, and John Henry Foley. The pieces that drew most popular attention were the two large groups by J. G. Lough, containing three colossal horses between them; they were, as the *Athenaeum* put it, 'remarkable for size, beauty and eccentricity';[1] 'executed in a manner which almost dumbs panegyric' wrote the *Literary Gazette*.[2] They were not, however, commended by the Commission, who may have thought them somewhat too melodramatic for their purpose. Lough was in fact one of the most interesting and individual sculptors of the period. Unfortunately he had much of Haydon's temperament: Cecilia Ridley could write of him in 1843: 'He no doubt thinks more highly of himself than he ought, and sets a higher value on *genius* than it has, and he has not firmness of mind and principle to struggle against the trials that weigh down upon him.'[3] His great *Milo and the Lion* (1827), later cast in bronze for Sir Matthew Ridley and now at Blagdon, is an alarming but striking piece of out-door ornament. His statue of James Losh in classical dress, carried out in Rome in 1836 and now on the stairway of the Newcastle Literary and Philosophical Society, has the long neck and vaguely mannerist treatment which characterize much of Lough's work, and which recur in his monument to Bishop Middleton in St. Paul's cathedral (1832), where the first Protestant bishop of India stands with outstretched arms, his lawn sleeves ingeniously

---

[1] *Athenaeum* (1844), 628.   [2] *Literary Gazette* (1844), 209.
[3] *Life and Letters of Cecilia Ridley,* ed. by Lady Ridley (1958), 145: I am most grateful to Lady Ridley for information about Lough from family papers at Blagdon.

carved, blessing an Indian man and woman (Pl. 5 b), and in the moving effigy of his daughter in Kensal Green cemetery. The Commissioners, however, gave no premiums for sculpture, and contented themselves with announcing in 1847 that the three selected artists had each been assigned a marble statue for St. Stephen's Hall, Hampden to Foley, Falkland to Bell, and Clarendon to Calder Marshall. Further commissions were given later to MacDowell and Baily. John Bell, whose bronze *Eagle Slayer*[1] of the 1844 Exhibition was distributed as bronze statuettes by the Art Union and was to be an admired piece in the Great Exhibition of 1851, was a man in the early thirties, whose chief commissions were still to come; William Calder Marshall, born in 1813, was two years his junior. They were to be in the second half of the century two of the main providers of memorial statues. John Henry Foley (1818–74) was a more original and romantic artist.[2] Trained in the Royal Academy School, his *Death of Abel* had been favourably noticed in 1839, but his *Youth at the Stream*[3] in the 1844 Exhibition was his first considerable work, one that already shows the clean, bold lines and grace of pose which always distinguish his work. Patrick MacDowell (1799–1870), born in Belfast, had long maintained himself by hack-work for the figure-shops, till his statue of *A Girl Reading* attracted the attention of Lord Francis Egerton, whose commission for it in marble led to the patronage of other collectors. E. H. Baily (1788–1867), an R.A. since 1820, was a much more established sculptor, who had been frequently employed on government undertakings such as the Marble Arch or the National Gallery. Flaxman's favourite pupil, he sometimes comes near his master's rhythms in work such as the floating muses on the Denys monument at Easton Neston; but at times he is ponderous, and the vast group of the *Three Graces* at Grittleton House has bulk rather than beauty; he was betwixt and between the classical idiom and the realism of the mid-century; Lord Pomfret (1830), also at Easton Neston, sits in a toga by a Greek

---

[1] Now, stripped of his bow, in the garden of the Bethnal Green Museum.

[2] W. C. Monkhouse, *The Works of John Henry Foley, R.A.*, London (n.d.); see S. C. Hall in *Art Journ.* (1874), 305; and G. F. Teniswood, ibid. (1875), 22.

[3] Hunt, *Book of Art*, 138.

vase; Thomas Fleming (1852) in Manchester cathedral stands erect in knee breeches. Since November 1843, when his statue of Nelson was raised to its lofty station[1] in Trafalgar Square, he had provided England with one of its best-known silhouettes.

Two statues require particular mention. In 1854 John Gibson was commissioned to carve a statue of the Queen between the figures of Justice and Clemency for the Palace of Westminster. Solemn on her massive throne, the young Queen sits between two huge allegorical figures, uneasily set before a Gothic arch. Unwieldy as it is, this group is one of the greatest pieces of English neo-classical sculpture, uncompromising in its impassivity, carved in boldly simplified planes by the hand of a master.[2] To Barry, however, it was out of scale, another insult to his building. When his turn came, after his death in 1860, J. H. Foley's statue of him on the stair-landing between the upper and lower waiting rooms shows him seated, a little wearied, as he must often have sat in the prolonged last stages of the great work.

Charles Eastlake had remained secretary of the Commission throughout all its long course of business. He had worked with Prince Albert on terms of mutual respect and friendship, and his deep knowledge and calm tact had done much to ease the many controversies. He had, however, been accumulating other tasks, sadly at the expense of his own somewhat frigid but competent art. In 1843 he had succeeded William Seguier, on the latter's death, as Keeper of the National Gallery, a post of many distractions. The question of the permanence of fresco painting, so eagerly canvassed throughout the sessions of the Commission, had roused an interest in wider problems of cleaning and preservation. This now rebounded on the National Gallery. Seguier had protected the pictures, then unglazed, with a mixture of mastic in turpentine and boiled linseed oil, known as 'Gallery varnish', and susceptible to rapid darkening in the polluted London atmosphere.[3] Eastlake proceeded to remove some of this heavy covering and in 1846 five

[1] See woodcut in *I.L.N.* iii (1843), 332.
[2] *I.L.N.* xxxi (1857), 206: the two supporting figures have recently (1957) been taken away, leaving only that of the Queen.
[3] *An Exhibition of Cleaned Pictures*: The National Gallery (1947).

pictures were cleaned. The outcry was immediate and 'Verax' (J. Morris Moore, a dealer) wrote in *The Times* (29 Oct. 1846)[1] that *Peace and War* had been 'completely flayed' and 'the fine rich glazings have been completely scoured off'. The Velazquez *Boar Hunt* was reduced 'from its pure and solemn tone' to 'a chalky film'. The *Boar Hunt* had in fact been largely repainted in the 1830's by George Lance, a pupil of Haydon and an exhibitor at the Academy.[2] In face of the protests and in view of his other commitments, Eastlake resigned in 1847 and was succeeded by Thomas Uwins, who boldly proclaimed his adherence to the policy of cleaning. The Trustees, however, hesitated. Sir Robert Peel, who had been studying the writings of Buchanan on glazes, was genuinely disturbed about the whole problem.[3] In 1852, however, Peel being dead, the Trustees decided to proceed with cleaning. At once the outcry arose again: it was vehemently declared that, in particular, Claude's *Isaac and Rebecca* and Canaletto's *View of Venice* were completely ruined. As the Commissioners put it, 'fervent love of the art seems to have kindled some personal animosity.'[4]

The Report of the Select Committee of 1853 and the evidence heard before it is a portentous volume running to 965 folio pages, and few galleries can ever have had their problems discussed at such exhaustive length. The Committee, while confessing that it was difficult to reach any clear conclusion about the results of the cleaning, made one recommendation which was at once acted upon, namely that there should be a salaried Director appointed by the Treasury, and that every recommendation for the purchase of a picture should originate with him. They also recommended that the Gallery should be moved to Kensington Gore, where land was now held by the Commissioners for the Exhibition of 1851, but this more formidable proposition was left in abeyance and was to prove the basic idea not of a new National Gallery but of the Victoria and Albert Museum.

[1] Verax, *The Abuses of the National Gallery* (1847); the author of *Modern Painters* wrote a moderate, well-informed letter about the cleaning, and Verax had much fun at the expense of his style and his partiality for Mr. Turner.

[2] *P.P. 1852–3*, xxxv. 396. For Lance see *Art Journ.* iii (1857), 305.

[3] *P.P. 1850*, xv. 29.   [4] *P.P. 1852–3*, xxxv. 11.

Eastlake was appointed to the post of Director. It was a splendid vindication of him from all the attacks in the forties. In 1850 he had been elected President of the Royal Academy and knighted. More important, he had married in 1849 Elizabeth Rigby, whose articles in the *Quarterly Review* had long been a factor in the formation of English taste. She brought to the marriage a learning and intelligence which could match his own, and a taste that perhaps was surer and which certainly played its part in the great purchases, the results of annual travels abroad, of Eastlake's directorship. In a remarkable phrase, the Committee of 1853 had stated that 'what Chaucer and Spenser are to Shakespeare and Milton, Giotto and Masaccio are to the great masters of the Florentine School.'[1] Ottley, the Prince Consort, Eastlake himself had all worked towards this changing viewpoint, and perhaps the landmark in his acquisitions was the great Uccello *Rout of San Romano*. Sir Robert Peel, Eastlake said, 'rather opposed the purchase of works by the early Italian masters: his expression always was "I think we should not collect curiosities" ':[2] but the primitives were rapidly ceasing to seem curious.

[1] *P.P. 1852-3*, xxxv. 16. Lord Lindsay's *History of Christian Art* (1847) had given much space to the 'vast genius' of Giotto: see J. Steegman in *Journ. W.C.I.* x (1947), 123.

[2] *P.P. 1852-3*, xxxv. 471. There is an admirable account of the Eastlakes in J. Steegman, *Consort of Taste* (1950); see also F. W. Rae in *The Fine Arts*, N.S. i (1866), 52.

IX

RESTORATION AND REVIVAL

'THE humid and corrosive quality of the atmosphere', wrote the *Monthly Review* in 1800, 'is continually obliterating the specimens of antient art with which our pious forefathers embellished the country. Some have perished; others are seen "nodding to their fall"; and even where no gross acts of folly or omission can be charged on clergymen or their parishioners, the tooth of time has committed cruel depredations.'[1] The growth of antiquarian interest in the past was accompanied by a new sense of responsibility for the upkeep and restoration of ancient monuments,[2] a responsibility often misplaced in its activities. The eighteenth century had already seen some important enterprises, though many of them were rather purgings of worn 'barbaric' ornament, old tombs, old screens, old pulpits and stalls, than genuine efforts of conservation. James Essex (d. 1784)[3] was a genuine antiquarian, and one whose views about open vistas, throughout the whole length of the church, were to underlie some of the bitterest of nineteenth-century controversies. Three years after Essex's death James Wyatt began restorations at Westminster abbey and also at Lichfield. These soon unleashed a prolonged attack on him in the pages of *The Gentleman's Magazine*, conducted by John Carter, 'antiquity's most resolute friend', whose drawings of Gothic detail and buildings were the handbook of Bishop Milner and the new purists. Durham was the main centre of their battle,

---

[1] xxxii. 421.

[2] For a general survey of this subject see M. Briggs, *Goths and Vandals* (1952), chaps. vi–x. Nineteenth-century books on the cathedrals generally contain some details as to recent restorations, but in most cases an exact account of nineteenth-century repairs and alterations has yet to be written: a notable exception is A. F. L. Clarke and H. M. Colvin, 'Rebuilding and Repair of Berkshire Churches during the seventeenth, eighteenth and early nineteenth centuries', *Berks. Archaeol. Journ.* liii (1953), 65, liv (1954–5), 58, and lv (1956–7), 73.

[3] D. R. Stewart in *Arch. Rev.* cviii (1950), 317.

and it was largely owing to Carter's 'most furious clamour'[1] that 'the Restorer' was prevented from removing the Galilee to provide a carriage approach and taking down the Neville screen to secure a vista. From the outside of the cathedral, where the stone was crumbling, Wyatt scraped about 4 inches of masonry, much of it work that needed doing, but less drastically. The old chapter house was destroyed, though, as was probably often the truth, the rough and ready methods, which took no care of tombs and carving,[2] were due to the chapter architect, Morpeth, not to Wyatt himself, who was seldom on the spot and whose fee of five guineas a day plus expenses discouraged the chapters from too frequent recourse to his advice. Salisbury lost its bell tower and two chantry chapels; Lichfield and Hereford were other sufferers. Wyatt was ever ready, and his clients willing enough to agree. 'I like', he wrote to the President of Magdalen, 'the idea which has been suggested of taking down the old quadrangle very much; it is in a very bad state and very inconvenient.'[3] This eager vandalism was largely due to a desire to tidy up the buildings and make them serviceable; and his patrons, believing that they represented an age of aesthetic enlightenment, were anxious to improve rather than preserve: Wyatt's use of plaster work or 'Roman cement' encouraged replacement of Gothic detail on a large scale. Others joined in the business. At St. David's cathedral, John Nash in 1791–3 rebuilt the upper half of the west front in a manner that was completely remodelled by Gilbert Scott some ninety years later.[4] At Canterbury it was Lanfranc's north-west tower, the surviving evidence of his work, which was pulled down in 1832, and a new tower built by George Austin matching Chichele's one on the south-west. York Minster had a more dramatic disaster. In 1829 the choir was gutted by a fire, set alight by Jonathan Martin, the lunatic brother of John Martin the painter. It was restored, on the whole very sensibly, by Robert Smirke, and an attempt to move the screen, a subject on which views passionately

[1] R. W. Billings, *Cathedral Church at Durham* (1843), 13–15.
[2] *O.H.E.A.* iii. 223.
[3] T. S. R. Boase, 'An Oxford College and the Gothic Revival', *Journ. W.C.I.* xviii (1955), 149.   [4] I. Wynn Jones in *Arch. Rev.* cxii (1952), 263.

varied, was defeated by the combined efforts of Archdeacon Markham and William Etty.

At Rochester a new name appeared in 1825: Lewis Nockalls Cottingham was till his death in 1847 to be the leading Gothic restorer, filling the gap between Wyatt and Gilbert Scott. His drawings of King Henry VII's chapel and of Westminster Hall and his full-scale *Working Drawings for Gothic Ornament* testify to his knowledge and exercised a deep influence on the growth of Gothic accuracy. At Rochester and later at Hereford Cottingham could be drastic enough, but he did much to further Gothic carving, and in the later stages of his career, at Bury St. Edmunds and possibly at Kilpeck, he was inventing medieval detail with such fluency that it is hard to tell the true from the false. Wyatt's ornament is easily recognizable: Scott's workshop had standardized types, competently cut, that can hardly be mistaken: but in the intervening period, while a new race of revivalist stone-carvers was being trained, it is often difficult to assess the genuineness of our medieval heritage. Blore at Peterborough and Ripon, Salvin, most disastrously, at Norwich were other practitioners in these activities. The prelude to the revival was this prolonged probing into the original structures.

The early Gothic debates had been concerned with antiquarian and stylistic differences, and the odium involved had been mainly academic.[1] Now a note of a quite different fervour was to be sounded, and the Christian style was to be based on the two foundation stones of the Catholic Church and of functionalism. To be true to the first it must provide for its ritual by practising the second. In 1829 a young English convert, a layman, Ambrose Phillipps, was watching the celebrations in St. Peter's for the passing of the Catholic Emancipation Act in England—'Santa Emancipazione' the peasants called it, thinking a new saint had been added to the calendar.[2] The removal of Catholic disabilities was a measure

[1] For the phases of the Gothic Revival see *Arch. Rev.*, 'Gothic Number', xcvii (1945), 148: an attack on Gothic in *Annals of Fine Arts*, ii (1818), 172, argues that the purposes of Gothic were no longer understood, and that it merely conveyed a sensuous feeling of awe, exactly the attitude Pugin sought to dispel. H.-R. Hitchcock, *Early Victorian Architecture in Britain*, 2 vols. (1954), and B. F. L. Clarke, *Church Builders of the Nineteenth Century* (1938), are essential guides to the whole subject.

[2] E. S. Purcell, *Life and Letters of Ambrose Phillipps de Lisle*, i. 161.

where the political implications, the liberal conscience about freedom, the agitation in Ireland, had bulked larger than the actual
position of the Roman Catholic Church in England, for the old
Catholic gentry, with their private chapels and chaplains as the
main centres of ecclesiastical influence, were not altogether anxious
for change, and the existing restrictions had been less and less
strictly enforced. With the French Revolution the English colleges
on the Continent fled to England and English priests were once
more trained in this country. Even some religious communities
found refuge, like the Benedictine nuns whom Milner established
at Winchester. Small, inconspicuous Catholic chapels were being
built in the first quarter of the nineteenth century (St. Aloysius,
Phoenix Street, Somers Town, is a still unchanged example); now
with emancipation larger schemes were considered. In 1834 in
Birmingham Bishop Walsh presided as Vicar Apostolic over a
meeting where it was resolved that 'a commodious and splendid
Catholic church, bearing testimony to the increased and increasing
liberality of our Protestant fellow-countrymen and in some degree
worthy of Catholic worship be erected in the town of Birmingham'. The chief mover in this scheme was John Hardman, a
wealthy Catholic citizen, whose son, John Hardman junior, was
founding an important firm, still in existence, which was to become under Pugin's influence the chief providers of ecclesiastical
ironwork and the leaders in the revival of stained glass. The
Hardmans were extremely devout Catholics, and for the daughter,
Sister Juliana, Pugin built a convent that was to influence later
architects by its simple Gothic forms used straightforwardly for
constructional purposes.

Other forces were tending to make Birmingham a leading
Catholic centre. Following the earlier and much more modest
Catholic Relief Act of 1791, one of whose clauses licensed Catholic
seminaries in England, a Catholic college had been founded outside
Birmingham at Oscott. Here in 1833 the designs for a group of
collegiate buildings were entrusted to Joseph Potter of Lichfield.[1]
The Oscott designs were on the traditional lines of Regency Gothic,
with regular 'Tudor' windows and a castellated tower with a

[1] For Potter's work at Plas Newydd see C. Hussey in *C.L.* cxviii (1955), 1198, 1252.

double oriel window above the gateway. To aid the project the patronage of the sixteenth earl of Shrewsbury, the leading Catholic peer in the Midlands, was sought and gained. The 'good Earl John' had succeeded his uncle in 1827. He succeeded also to his uncle's vast scheme for Alton Towers, where a great garden had been laid out and a new mansion begun in the Gothic style.[1] In 1832, it is said, when in London looking for designs for Gothic furniture and fittings, the earl saw some drawings by Augustus Welby Pugin, then a young man of twenty-one. This may mark the beginning of the connexion between the peer and the architect, but if so it took some years for their relationship to become a close one, and it was not till August 1836 that Pugin paid his first visit to Alton Towers.[2] The younger Pugin had been born in 1812. From his father, Nash's draughtsman, he received a sound education in the drawing of Gothic buildings and details, from his mother a strong distaste for her form of rigid Presbyterianism, a reaction which led him after her death in 1833 to join within two years the Roman Church. With his conversion a new purposefulness was added. 'I can assure you', he wrote to his friend Osmond, a Salisbury stonemason, in January 1835, 'that, after a most close and impartial investigation, I feel perfectly convinced the Roman Catholic Church is the only true one, and the only one in which the grand and sublime style of church architecture can ever be restored.'[3] Years afterwards in 1848, on the occasion of his third marriage, he wrote to another friend, J. R. Bloxam, 'I take this early opportunity of letting you know that I have got an admirable wife who is devoted to the true style.'[4] It was the true, Christian Catholic style that dominated his life, and when he was not building in it, he was propagating its principles by his writings.

In 1836 appeared *Contrasts: or, a Parallel between the noble Edifices*

[1] D. Gwynn, *Lord Shrewsbury, Pugin and the Gothic Revival* (1946).

[2] Phoebe Stanton, 'Some Comments on the Life and Work of Augustus Welby Northmore Pugin', *Journ. R.I.B.A.* 3rd ser. lx (1952), 47. See also B. Ferrey, *Recollections of A. N. W. Pugin* (1861); P. Waterhouse, 'Life and Work of Welby Pugin', *Arch. Rev.*, vols. iii and iv (1897–8); and M. Trappes-Lomax, *Pugin* (1932). Dr. Stanton's thesis (Univ. of London, 1950) is the definitive work on Pugin but it has not been published in full. [3] Ferrey, op. cit. 88.

[4] Manuscript letters of Pugin to Bloxam: Magdalen College, Oxford.

of the Middle Ages, and Corresponding Buildings of the present Day; shewing the Decline of Taste. Pugin could write as well as draw: there is a Miltonic delight in Latinate words, an excited power of invective and a nice taste in satire. Much of his case was being argued at the same time in France by Montalembert, and between the first edition of *Contrasts* and the second in 1842, Pugin expanded and strengthened his case by study of the French author.

· A Catholic church [he writes] not only requires pillars, arches, windows, screens, and niches, but it *requires them to be disposed according to a certain traditional form*; it demands a chancel set aside for sacrifice, and screened off from the people; it requires a stone altar, a sacrarium, sedilia for the officiating priests, and an elevated rood loft from whence the Holy Gospel may be chaunted to the assembled faithful; . . . and unless a building destined for a church possesses all these requisites, however correctly its details may be copied from ancient authorities, it is a mere modern conventicle, and cannot by any means be accounted a revival of Catholic art.[1]

The words roll on, echoing the rhythms of the Athanasian Creed. But it was not only words: *Contrasts* depended largely on its drawings. Side by side the new and the old were shown: Inwood's St. Pancras chapel (now St. Mary's, Somers Town) opposed to Bishop Skirlaw's rich Decorated church at Swine, Yorkshire: King's College, the Strand, against Christ Church, Oxford: the Catholic town (an added plate in the second edition), full of Puginesque churches, and the New Town, with a large jail in the foreground, factory chimneys everywhere, the church tower re-built and chimneys appearing through the roof, a Grecian par-sonage—and of course the figures in the middle ages are gay, courteous, and compassionate, in the present brutal and de-graded.

In 1834–5 Pugin was in Birmingham, working for Barry on King Edward's School and also busy with Barry and Gillespie Graham's drawings for the Westminster competition. In 1837 he obtained a new patron, Charles Scarisbrick, an eccentric Lancashire Catholic recluse, at his house at Scarisbrick, where as usual Pugin had to add to and adapt another architect's design, and where his

[1] *Contrasts* (2nd ed.), 58.

own scheme was never completed and cannot be studied here except to note that the original clock-tower, fantastically heightened by Pugin's son, Edward, is almost certainly the model followed for 'Big Ben'.[1] At Alton Towers a local architect, Fradgley, had already been employed, and the main building had been carried out to his design, to say nothing of a Swiss cottage for a blind Welsh harper and a Gothic temple—how Pugin would have rejected such a term—in the garden. Pugin added the chapel, some rooms, a conservatory and the entrance lodges. This joint composition is not altogether successful. The castles of the Revival are often insensitive in texture, too smooth and competent, as at Smirke's Eastnor (Pl. 15 a); but they seldom fail to produce striking silhouettes, and Eastnor, surrounded by its walled terraces, seen across its lake, is as genuinely romantic a design as could be desired. Alton Towers, now gutted and roofless, is a jumble of towers that form no coherent group, either with themselves or their setting, a much less coherent ensemble than was achieved at Scarisbrick. There was an element of sham in this modern castellation, which Pugin himself often attacked, and which accorded ill with his principles. The gardens, rich in varied trees, are axially unrelated to the castle, and Pugin's work, distinguished at close view, confuses the general aspect. As always, it was the interior decoration, now dismantled, that best suited his genius (Pl. 73 b).

The mansion itself was only a small part of the work undertaken for or through the earl. At Oscott in 1837, following the réclame of *Contrasts*, Pugin was appointed Professor of Ecclesiastical Art and Antiquities. Very shortly he seems to have superseded Potter as architect in charge, took the chapel and its fittings in hand, knocked out Potter's east end to build an apsidal sanctuary and designed a Gothic reredos. When in 1838 the chapel was dedicated, 'Pugin', so a young visiting priest, William Bernard Ullathorne, who ten years later was to be Vicar Apostolic of the Central District, describes him, 'Pugin, with his eyes flashing through his tears, was in raptures, declaring it the first great day for England since the Reformation.'[2] The chapel, rich in colour and ornament,

---

[1] M. Girouard in *C.L.* cxxiii (1958), 506 and 580.
[2] *Autobiography of Archbishop Ullathorne* (1891–2), i. 135.

is indeed one of the masterpieces of the Revival, but it was not merely an architectural triumph.

At Alton Pugin had met another friend of Lord Shrewsbury's, Ambrose Phillipps. He was a young man, only a few years older than Pugin, like him a convert to Roman Catholicism, who had on his Leicestershire estate of Grace Dieu, where there were the ruins of an Augustinian priory, established, largely on borrowed money, a community of Trappist monks. Phillipps was as enthusiastic for plainsong as Pugin was for the Catholic style. Meagre and often tawdry as were the Catholic chapels, they had endeavoured to make some amends by an elaboration of music, in contradistinction to the raucous English choirs singing away, quite unorganized, in the parish church gallery (Pl. 96 *a*). Professionals, both men and women, performed some of the livelier eighteenth-century church music, Haydn in particular, and their performances were billed at the church door. This to Pugin and Phillipps was anathema. Between them they evolved a vision of the *ecclesia anglicana*, based on the Sarum use, clothed in the ample vestments they found depicted on brasses, accompanied by Gregorian chant and situated in buildings of the best pointed style. Pugin began his career in the theatre, designing sets for an operatic production of *Kenilworth*, and there is always something of the theatre, of the production as a whole, in his approach to his buildings. His churches were always the setting for ceremonial. 'It was on that occasion', wrote Ullathorne of the Oscott dedication, 'that the old French style of vestment and surplice was changed for those of ampler form.' It was in fact the opening move in a vestiarian controversy as bitter as that which was soon to divide the Church of England. These innovations were naturally enough not always acceptable to the older Catholic clergy, particularly to Bishop Baines, Vicar Apostolic of the Western District.

The clergy [wrote Pugin to Phillipps with many underlinings] will put down religion . . . the very men who do not hesitate to violate rubrics every day to suit their convenience or their pockets, now swelling with indignation and horror at the idea of an ample surplice or chasuble such as almost every saint in the Calendar wore. Administer baptism out of an old physick phial; reserve the Blessed Sacrament in a *dirty cupboard*; . . . burn gas on the altar; have everything as *mean*, as *pitiful*, as *shabby* as you please; hire Protestant performers to sing . . . do all this and you will be right. But if you venture to speak of ancient glory and ecclesiastical dignity, oh, you are a man of extravagant opinions . . . and *ecclesiastical censure* awaits you.[1]

True enough, it did. In 1839 a letter was sent from the Office of Propaganda in Rome to Bishop Walsh, the Vicar Apostolic of the Central District and a strong supporter of Pugin and Phillipps, expressing disapproval of the new vestments and ceremonials and referring to Pugin as 'an architect recently converted from heresy'. It was a serious blow; from now on Pugin was battling within his own church, becoming in his pronouncements ever more hysterical, but never wavering in his convictions, fighting what was to be a losing battle against the Italianate influences in English Roman Catholicism, and eventually leaving most of the outcome of his struggles not to Rome but to the more moderate section of Anglo-Catholicism, who looked for decent ceremonial but had no intention of following Newman and others in their migration. Lord Shrewsbury, however, despite these turmoils, which he viewed with a certain aristocratic detachment, continued his support. At Alton in 1841 Pugin was building a school and almshouses for him, with a chapel, warden's lodging, cloister and schoolmaster's house, solidly constructed in stone, with joists and beams in English oak. The chapel, with an ornate screen, painted ceiling and figured tiles, shows Pugin the decorator: the simplicity of the other buildings shows Pugin the constructor, for once allowed the quality of material which he was usually denied.

Pugin's career as a church builder had begun with two small chapels for Phillipps, works where cheapness was a main consideration, and Pugin was always prepared to build cheaply as long as there was no pretence about it. Between many of his drawings, rapidly sketched out when a building was first mooted, and the actual building itself, there is often a wide economic gap. The design he produced in 1838 for the Roman Catholic church of St. George at Southwark was for an immensely lofty church, with a central tower and transepts in the Decorated style. Not altogether

---

[1] Purcell, *Life and Letters of Ambrose Phillipps*, ii. 223.

surprisingly Southwark turned it down at once. In the end they accepted a design for a church without clerestory and with aisles almost equal in height to the nave, producing a three-gabled west front, the whole built in yellow London brick. It was to be crowned with a western tower and spire, but this never advanced beyond the preliminary stages. The three high-pitched roofs stood out well above a heavily built-up neighbourhood and with the tower might have provided a striking silhouette; but today St. George's, rebuilt from a blitzed ruin, has little of Pugin's work in it.

Meanwhile Pugin had been engaged on another large church, where plans went more smoothly. Wiseman had on his return from Italy been deeply struck by the cramped conditions of English Catholicism and he became one of the great supporters of the new Birmingham 'cathedral'. In 1839, backed by Bishop Walsh, Lord Shrewsbury, and John Hardman and with Pugin as architect, old St. Chad's was demolished and a new building begun on its site. St. Chad's is 156 feet in length, 58 feet broad and 75 feet high. The site was not an easy one as the ground slopes away to the east, and Pugin had to build up the lady chapel and apse and sacristies from a lower level to meet his high transept. The effect is actually very successful. For a church one day likely to be a cathedral, Pugin held that two west towers were appropriate. These with their spires rising from a gabled roof are curiously Germanic and must owe something to Pugin's continental journeys.[1] The junction between the central gable and the towers is clumsy and the sculpture is inadequate to the size of the façade. Inside there is no clerestory; the high columns are too thin and slight, as so often in Pugin's work, and the tie beams of the roof are awkwardly fixed. The windows are filled with stained glass, much of it by the Hardman family, and the window of the north transept, the window of the Immaculate Conception, was presented in memory of John Hardman junior in 1867; he is shown in a panel of it, robed as cantor, a tribute to the work he did for plainsong as master of St. Chad's choir. His father, who died in 1844, had presented the high altar and the rood screen, the latter one of Pugin's most

[1] Or possibly to Whewell's *German Architecture* (1835).

characteristic and elaborate works and one which Catholics would rather have been without (Pl. 69).[1] On 19 June 1841 the cathedral was consecrated: the High Mass that followed was musically exclusively Gregorian.[2]

It was, however, Pugin's smaller churches that were perhaps more important. At St. Wilfrid's, Hulme, then on the outskirts of Manchester, he built a church to seat 800, which with the priest's house included was only to cost £5,000. Even so, it has aisles, a small clerestory, a tower, and a small pyramidal spire. There is a marked break between the nave and chancel and the tower is set at the south-west corner. This was now to become Pugin's regular practice and to be followed by innumerable imitators. It is only possible here to refer to two other churches. St. Giles' at Cheadle in Staffordshire, completed in 1846, was built for Lord Shrewsbury, and here for once no expense was spared. The pinnacled spire, 200 feet high, soars up from the valley above the orange-brown sandstone church (Pl. 70 a). The lead-covered roof is steeply pitched. ('Nothing', he writes of it, 'like high roofs covered with lead' and characteristically follows the remark, 'I am happy to say the furious curate has left and all is going on quietly again.') Inside there is colour everywhere, an elaborate screen, much brass work by Hardman, and a richness of decorative effect that few English churches can equal. Great gilt leopards, for which it would be hard to find a precedent, fill the panels of the western door (Pl. 73 a). Even at Cheadle, there had been difficulties. Lord Shrewsbury had suddenly decided that he would like a gallery at the west end. 'A gallery', Pugin wrote to him, 'at Cheadle, perfect Cheadle, my consolation in all my afflictions! When it is erected I shall almost turn Jonathan Martin and set fire to the building.' 'Five Protestant archdeacons,' he adds, 'are pulling down galleries of every kind. All the works of the Camden and Oxford Societies denounce them.'[3]

His own church, which he himself financed, St. Augustine's,

[1] 'Dr. Wiseman has at last shewn his real sentiments by attempting to abolish the great Rood-Screen'; Pugin to Ambrose Phillipps, Purcell, *Life and Letters*, ii. 213.
[2] *A History of St. Chad's Cathedral, Birmingham*, by the cathedral clergy: Birmingham, 1904.   [3] *Journ. R.I.B.A.* lx (1953), 47.

Ramsgate, at the point where he thought St. Augustine had landed, is curiously unlike the Midland churches.[1] The interior walls are faced with cream coloured Caen stone, unplastered and therefore without painted decoration. Working with the best materials, Pugin seems only anxious to display them. A spire was originally intended and the large central pillars to support it are too massive for the nave, and the sense of space seems defective. From outside the group formed by the church and his own house, both with surfaces of black flints, has some fine detail, but lacks the central emphasis that the spire might have given. Inside a chantry chapel, below one of Hardman's windows, is Pugin's tomb with a recumbent effigy and his children as mourners.

For the rest the best summary of his church building is the view that Pugin drew for his *Apology for the Revival of Christian Architecture in England*, published in 1843: here beside St. George's, St. Chad's, St. Giles', Cheadle, St. Marie's, Derby, can be seen the cathedral at Killarney and the parish church of St. Michael at Gorey in Wexford (Lord Shrewsbury was earl of Wexford). Pugin's Irish churches were a considerable part of his architectural achievement. In 1843 he wrote from Wexford, 'There will be 2 cathedral churches, 3 parochial ones, 3 conventual and 1 collegiate all carried out with fonts, altars, vestments, surplices, stained windows . . . really there is wonderful faith and devotion in this county after all.' As usual, these enthusiastic designs were not entirely carried out, but several were completed and with all this in hand he was, he writes in a letter of about the same date, sending out 'models of churches, tombstones, fonts, altars . . . tiles, glass, etc. to Hobart Town to start the good style in the Antipodes'.[2]

Between 1837 and 1841 Pugin stayed much at Oscott, where he had a room assigned to him. He was busy designing furniture and fittings and instructing John Hardman's craftsmen in making them; but Oscott was a platform as well as a workshop. His lectures there were published in 1841 as *The True Principles of Pointed or Christian Architecture*. 'The two great rules of design are these: first that there

---

[1] J. Summerson, 'Pugin at Ramsgate', *Arch. Rev.* ciii (1948), 163.
[2] One of his most unchanged and also accessible churches is that of St. Thomas of Canterbury, Fulham (1848): see *I.L.N.* xxxi (1857), 130.

should be no features about a building which are not necessary for convenience, construction or propriety; second, that all ornament should consist of enrichment of the essential construction of the building . . .'; further 'the construction should vary with the material employed and the designs should be adapted to the material in which they are executed.'[1] These were views which, lit by *The Seven Lamps of Architecture*, were to become accepted principles, not to be seriously challenged till Geoffrey Scott overthrew them, as it were overnight, in his *Architecture of Humanism* (1914). Pugin elaborates his theses with the methods of *Contrasts*, showing the right way and the wrong; locks, papering, windows, fireplaces, chimneys, all the details in which he always rejoiced are brought under review. Two years later his *Apology for the Revival of Christian Architecture* takes up the battle, more violently, with more specific examples of what was in Pugin's favourite phrase 'not at all the thing'. It was dedicated to Lord Shrewsbury with an engraved initial letter in which Pugin presents his book to the earl, both of them in medieval costume (Fig. 7). 'It is easy enough to tell us to *Revive*', wrote a reviewer in *Fraser's Magazine*,[2] 'but . . . the great drama of history does not admit of encores . . . . Unfortunate for us as it may be, we of this present nineteenth century cannot by any possibility put ourselves into the exact position of foregone times; which being the case, the best thing that we can do is to console ourselves philosophically with the reflection that we have at least escaped the misfortune of being born in the twentieth.'

In 1840 Pugin made a new friend, John Rouse Bloxam, of Magdalen College, Oxford, who had been Newman's curate at Littlemore and was to remain devoted to him, but never followed him to Rome. Bloxam was a scholarly antiquarian and liturgist, and a man of much personal charm; he was also cautious and discreet. Newman, Ward, and the leaders at Oxford were not archaeologically minded: Newman in fact after his conversion and

---

[1] For Pugin's principles and constructional as opposed to archaeological use of Gothic see Phoebe B. Stanton, 'Principles of Design versus Revivalism', *Journ. of Soc. of Architectural Historians*, xiii. 3 (Univ. of Virginia, 1954), 20.

[2] xxviii (1843), 600.

the Oratorians with whom he was so closely associated were to
become the main supporters of the Italian style. Pugin in the forties
built a house for Ward, but he found him 'a sash window man'
and, far worse, averse to chancel screens. 'Mr. Pugin', wrote

FIG. 7. *A. W. Pugin: Initial*

Newman in 1848, 'is a genius . . . but he is intolerant, and if I might
use a strong word, a bigot. He sees nothing good in any school of
Christian art except that of which he himself is so great an ornament.'[1] The group of buildings round the Oratory gradually grew,
Italian and Renaissance in design, till the great church was designed
by Herbert Gribble in 1878. It marks the great defeat of Pugin's
teaching within his own communion.

For Bloxam's rooms in Magdalen, however, he designed a
corona of lights, a triptych, a prie-dieu, all carried out by John
Hardman, and eventually for Magdalen a Gothic gateway replacing a much finer one by Nicholas Stone. Ward involved him
in a far larger Oxford scheme, the rebuilding of the chapel and
Broad Street front of Balliol. Pugin prepared detailed plans and
elevations and for Ward himself a book of small drawings of the

[1] Purcell, op. cit. ii. 205.

proposed work, bound in red velvet with metal clasps.[1] 'You have no idea', he wrote to Bloxam, 'how I have worked at these drawings. I have never exerted myself so before, for I quite delight in this opportunity of setting forth real collegiate architecture on the old principles.'[2] Then suddenly the scheme was dropped, apparently because various benefactors objected to a Catholic architect. He had much difficulty in getting the college to pay for the drawings: he had spent much time over it. The whole business rankled, as we can see in his letters to Bloxam: Ward himself went over to Rome and became as Italianate as any.

It was in Cambridge rather than in Oxford that the true style found support. In 1839 a group of enthusiasts there founded the Camden Society to 'promote the study of Ecclesiastical Architecture and the restoration of mutilated architectural remains'. They issued pamphlets, and in their journal, *The Ecclesiologist*,[3] published regular lists of churches that were approved or condemned. In much they agreed with Pugin, though they were apt, much to his indignation, to refer to him as 'a schismatic': they did not insist on screens, they became involved in a great elaboration of church symbolism, and they came down firmly in favour of the Gothic of the later fourteenth century. Romanesque they thought might be suitable for New Zealand.[4] The architect whom eventually they selected for their model church, All Saints, Margaret Street, was William Butterfield.

Elsewhere things were stirring. If Birmingham was the centre of the Roman revival, Leeds was a key position for Anglo-Catholicism. It became so through the vicariate of W. F. Hook at the parish church from 1837 to 1859. The old church was a cruciform medieval building, in which there was a large chancel beyond the crossing, so that the altar was almost invisible from the nave and matins were in fact read west of the crossing; the choir and organ were in a gallery over the western arch of the crossing.

[1] The drawings are in the possession of Balliol College.

[2] Manuscript letters, Magdalen College.

[3] The term was an unfamiliar one: the *British Critic* referred in 1837 (xxi. 220) to 'Ecclesialogy [*sic*] a science which may treat of the proper construction of the Church'.

[4] They were probably unaware of the beautiful small Romanesque churches that James Blackburn, transported for forgery, was building in Tasmania.

Leeds presented all the problems of a town of rapid growth: in 1801 the population was 53,162, in 1831 it was 123,393. Church provision was inadequate, and the parish church of St. Peter shared in this general inadequacy[1] and also proved to be structurally unsound and in urgent need of repair. Hook was never a member of the Tractarian group, though he deeply admired much for which they stood and though some of the Leeds evangelicals closely identified him with it. 'Tract XC', he wrote to Newman,[2] is' a little bit of a scrape, but it does us good to get into scrapes sometimes.' His connexions were rather with Dr. John Jebb whose two works, *The Cathedral Service of the Church of England*, based on lectures given at Leeds, and his *Choral Service of the United Church of England and Ireland*, were published in the early forties. Jebb was a great propagandist of the surpliced choir, which was rapidly to become a marked feature of Anglican worship in parish churches as well as in the cathedrals, where it had always existed, though when we hear of Goss and the St. Paul's choir attempting the *Hallelujah Chorus* on a day on which only one bass and one tenor had turned up, we may doubt how well the tradition was being maintained. Even in cathedrals, Jebb advocated the removal of screens, or at least the substitution of light, open ones, such as that which Gilbert Scott substituted for Cosin's heavy, magnificent barrier at Durham. Jebb's desire to link the congregation through the choir with the sanctuary was much more practical in a parish church than in the long medieval cathedrals, and the parish church of Leeds was the first to set out the new liturgical arrangements.[3]

The architect was R. D. Chantrell, a Leeds man, who since 1820 had been designing churches and other buildings. These churches were without chancels—in most cases these were added later—and were typical Gothic of the twenties. St. Peter's is fifteenth century rather than fourteenth, but stylistically it has considerable ambigui-

---

[1] W. R. W. Stephens, *Life and Letters of William Farquhar Hook* (1878), i. 381. 'It is impossible to perform the service of the sanctuary with that order and decency with which we ought to perform them.'

[2] Ibid. ii. 67.

[3] See G. W. O. Addleshaw and F. Etchells, *The Architectural Setting of Anglican Worship* (1948), chap. vii.

ties: the style, says its historian, James Rusby,[1] was 'a transition from the Decorated to the Perpendicular, which enabled the architect to introduce a considerable variety of forms': its fine, panelled tower is placed unusually over the north transept, which was the main entrance from the street, and gives a misleading external emphasis, quite different from that of Pugin's side towers, which are never allowed to obstruct the main axial scheme. Internally, seating was one of the main requirements and the church was provided with galleries set back beyond the main pillars, on iron pillars, and ornamented with elaborate tabernacle work. A broad chancel was provided for the choir and the altar was raised above it by a flight of steps (Pl. 70 b): the altar itself with an enlarged copy of Correggio's *Agony in the Garden* and a crimson velvet covering given by Queen Adelaide hardly answered to new ecclesiological requirements, of which Hook would only partially have approved. Chantrell's views were clear enough and he later termed the *Ecclesiologist* 'a mischievous tissue of imbecility and fanaticism'.[2]

In 1845 Pugin renewed his contact with Barry and from then on the decoration of the Houses of Parliament was his main task, though not sufficient for his restless energy. It was now that he published two of his most important works, *The Glossary of Ecclesiastical Ornament and Costume* (1844), with magnificent coloured plates that were to have considerable influence on the polychromatic phase of the revival, and *Floriated Ornament* (1849), again in colour and showing Pugin's genius at its best. It was these decorative activities that brought him the direction of the medieval court for the Great Exhibition of 1851, an uncongenial task in many ways. He disliked the Crystal Palace, and many exhibits throughout the Exhibition were Gothic fantasies such as those he had denounced in the *True Principles*. The strain of it all was telling: he had never been able to relax; ceaseless work, ceaseless controversy, three marriages and a broken engagement had burned him out. In 1852 his mind gave way and happily the end was not long delayed. He died on 14 September 1852.

[1] J. Rusby, ed. by J. G. Simpson, *St. Peter's at Leeds* (1896); and R. W. Moore, *A History of the Parish Church of Leeds* (1877).
[2] Quoted B. F. L. Clarke, *Church Builders* (1938), 100.

In 1844 a competition was announced, on an international basis, for a new Lutheran church, the Nikolaikirche, in Hamburg. The following year the prize was awarded to George Gilbert Scott.[1] It was continental recognition of the status of the English revival, and it established the position of the architect, even if the Camdenians marked him down for this dallying with Lutheranism. The first landmark had been reached in the most prosperous and characteristic architectural career of the nineteenth century. Industrious, capable of organizing a large office, confident in his own judgement but anxious that the patron should be pleased, accurate in his estimates, quick to absorb new ideas but sensitive to what the public liked, he had many of the qualities requisite for success. 'That an architect', Goodhart-Rendel has written of him, 'who, during a working career of forty years, built or interfered with nearly five hundred churches, thirty-nine cathedrals and minsters, twenty-five universities and colleges, and many other buildings beside, was a remarkable man it would be foolish to deny.'[2] He had begun his career in partnership with Moffat building new poor houses, these successors to the new jails that had exercised Nash and his contemporaries; occasionally a jail itself, notably the red brick castle at Reading. In 1844 he was thirty-three, one year older than Pugin, and he had recently completed a large church, St. Giles's, Camberwell, costing £14,500 and holding a congregation of 1,500. It is built of Kentish rubble trimmed with Caen stone, a combination that stands up well to London climate and tells through its coating of dirt. It has a deep chancel, but originally had galleries, a typical Scott compromise: the capitals, early Decorated foliage, are carved with the certainty and competence which Scott, at the expense of sensitivity, was always to secure. Its tower and spire are well seen from the open green on the southern side and still deserve much of the praise given by contemporaries.[3]

[1] Sir Gilbert Scott, *Personal and Professional Recollections* (1879).

[2] *English Architecture since the Regency* (1953), 95.

[3] No attempt can be made here to survey Scott's vast output: he himself considered All Souls', Halifax, one of the best of his churches (Pl. 77 a). J. B. Philip superintended the carving and may well have played a considerable part in the final development of Scott's ornament; see *A Description of All Souls' Church, Haley Hill, Halifax* (Halifax, 1859). The Episcopalian cathedral of St. Mary in Edinburgh begun in 1874 was his

The forties were years that saw much church building, largely new churches for the growth of London south of the river, urged on by Bishop Blomfield of London with what Sydney Smith called 'his ungovernable passion for business', or for the rapidly developing industrial towns: expanding trade and population provided a challenge that Tractarian zeal was very ready to meet. Henry Clutton, J. M. Derick, Ambrose Poynter, Benjamin Ferrey, Pugin's muddled biographer and pupil, Edmund Sharpe, author of *Architectural Parallels*, Thomas Cundy, I. H. Stevens, were some of the architects who were designing them. The most accepted style, with all the drive of the *Ecclesiologist* behind it, was the 'Middle Pointed', but here and there experiments were made as in J. W. Wild's brick version of Italian Romanesque in Christ Church, Streatham (1840–2), or T. H. Wyatt and D. Brandon's lavish and more accurate 'Lombardic' church at Wilton, erected by the Herberts, a rare piece of aristocratic church building. At Leamington the vicar, John Craig, began in 1843 a vast and prolonged rebuilding of the parish church, acting as his own architect and borrowing from various continental styles to produce one of the largest and most individual of Victorian churches. On the whole, however, it was the influence, allied if not completely at one, of Pugin and the Camdenians which predominated; and of new south London churches, the Roman Catholic 'Our Lady of Victories', Clapham (1849–51), by Pugin's pupil, William Wilkinson Wardell, is as distinguished as any. Wardell in 1857 emigrated to Australia and his greatest works are in the Southern Hemisphere; St. Patrick's Roman Catholic cathedral, Melbourne, begun by him in 1860, with its fine vaulting and masonry, its wide transepts, apsidal chevet, its organized spaciousness, beyond Pugin's compass, and its silhouette of towers is perhaps the greatest triumph of the English Gothic revival.[1]

In 1849 Gilbert Scott was appointed, in succession to Blore, Surveyor of the Fabric of Westminster Abbey. It was a post that bestowed recognition as the leader of Gothic practice in the Anglican tradition, not Puginist or Camdenian, but that of the *via*

last great undertaking, the largest church to be erected in Britain since Wren's St. Paul's.   [1] For Wardell see obituary notice, *Tablet*, Nov. 1899.

media. It marked also his arrival as chief restorer of the day. Few men have been so fully recognized as arbiter of archaeological taste; Buckler might attack him at Lincoln, where Scott had volunteered his criticism unasked; Edmund Beckett, afterwards Lord Grimthorpe, might quarrel with him at St. Albans, but cathedral chapters felt secure in his authority. Technically Scott could be audacious and brilliant, underbuilding the western façade of Ripon and practically rebuilding the lower tower of Salisbury underneath the load of its later storeys and the spire. His taste was more questionable. He removed much of Wyatt's, Blore's, and Nash's earlier restorations, replacing them with his own crisp stone masonry and carving. Where Wyatt had left a vista, Scott complied with the new ritualism and restored chancel screens, slender, open work metal erections, carried out by Skidmore of Coventry, 'somewhat aberrantly' as Scott constantly complained.[1] 'A portentous Georgian pulpit' or 'a plastered ceiling' had much to fear from him.[2] Before his death in 1878 all his theories were to be called in question by William Morris and the Society for the Protection of Ancient Buildings, founded in 1877, but the grand rows of the seventies and eighties in which Lord Grimthorpe was to be the central and surprisingly vituperative figure, the conflagrations in which archaeological, liturgical, and architectural passions blazed most luridly, lie outside the period of this volume.[3]

The same year, 1849, that saw Scott appointed at Westminster, saw two other events of considerable architectural significance, the appearance in May of Ruskin's *Seven Lamps of Architecture* and the signing of a contract by Beresford-Hope, on behalf of the Ecclesiological Society, with William Butterfield for the building of a church which, along with that of St. Mary Magdalene being erected contemporaneously by R. C. Carpenter in Munster Square, should be ecclesiologically a model of 'the right thing'. The two favoured architects were each given an opportunity to display their prowess. For Carpenter it was the close and climax of his brief career, and he died in 1855. He had since 1846 been working in

---

[1] *Recollections*, 288. For Scott's screen at Winchester see *C.L.* xxv (1909), 747.
[2] Dean Burgon in Preface to *Recollections*, xvi.
[3] See P. Ferriday, *Lord Grimthorpe* (1957).

Brighton, building for Father Arthur Wagner, one of the most redoubtable exponents of Tractarianism, the church of St. Paul's, whose tower with its long lancet windows can be so well seen descending West Street (Pl. 71 *a*), and whose interior alarmed Brighton by its stalled chancel and rood screen.[1] St. Mary Magdalene,[2] liturgically correct enough, is with its high aisles, its three gabled west front, its thin columns and polychromatic painting (now much faded) a typically Puginesque church, and Pugin, as also at St. Paul's, Brighton, provided the design for Hardman's east window. The tower that Carpenter designed was never carried out and it would have given a much-needed emphasis to a somewhat characterless and depressing block. There is, however, nothing jaded about Butterfield's work at All Saints, Margaret Street, which, though commissioned in 1849, was not consecrated till ten years later.[3] On an awkward site, dictated by the persistence of the congregation of the previous church, he built a tower topped by a wooden spire such as had not been seen before in England, and which has North Germany as its nearest relative, though there is no evidence that Butterfield had visited Germany (Pl. 71 *c*). He was, however, building a brick church, and therefore might well have looked to the great brick churches of the North European plain. And it was frankly brick. The age of stucco was now over and all had to be true in ecclesiastical building. All Saints was an expensive church, costing approximately £70,000, almost as much as the Nikolaikirche, and this was largely due to the very varied and rare stones that were used for its polychromy. Outside there are bands, diapers, and zigzags of darker materials, breaking the flat surfaces; within, though in the dark interior they hardly tell, patterns of brilliantly contrasted colours are composed with glazed tiles, various marbles and even red mastic (Pl. 71 *b*). The frescoes,

[1] See H. S. Goodhart-Rendel, 'The Churches of Brighton and Hove', *Arch. Rev.* xliv (1918), 27; H. Hamilton Maugham, *Wagner of Brighton* (Dublin, 1949).

[2] T. E. Sedgwick, *Description and History of the Church of St. Mary Magdalene, Munster Square* (1902).

[3] For Butterfield see 'Memoir' in *Journ. R.I.B.A.* vii (1900), 241; John Summerson in *Arch. Rev.* xcvii (1945), 166, reprinted in *Heavenly Mansions* (1949): and a most discerning account in Hitchcock, *Early Victorian Architecture*, chap. xviii: H. Redfern in *Architect and Building News*, clxxviii (1944), 21.

Dyce's saints in the east end, were painted on heavily gilt back-grounds: the windows, mainly by the French designer, Gérente, are unusually harsh and garish. These violent contrasts were as bold and striking as those, the *Ecclesiologist* noted, of paintings by Millais or Holman Hunt; as bold also as the silhouette of the tower rising from its cramped courtyard and the awkward adjustment of the gabled porch to the wall of the choir school. Everything built by Butterfield has this same arresting quality, vigorous and un-couth. Ecclesiologically he might be correct enough; architecturally he was a rebel, who was using Gothic for his own ends, not in a desire to reproduce effects from the past. The slim, pencil-like tower of Balliol chapel rising above the mixed grey and blue tiles of its roof: the blare of the mosaic walls inside Keble chapel as opposed to its great, looming mass outside—for the patterning in the brick, dulled from its first brilliance, seems now to emphasize rather than break the mass:[1] his gabled eastern tower at Stoke Newington, now standing above blitzed ruins: his octagonal eastern tower at Rugby with its projecting gargoyles, grimly assertive above the most unlovable of school chapels; all these are individual works, new not revived architecture, often ugly, always memorable and always Victorian, of their own time and no other.

We do not know whether Butterfield read *The Seven Lamps of Architecture*. There are curious similarities between the church and the book. The zones, 'cloudings and flamings' or spots, resolving themselves into chequers and zigzags, stars or other shapes are all here,[2] and here too something of the bold, sketchy work that Ruskin advocated. There is, however, no clear contact between them. Ruskin only once mentions Butterfield by name,[3] with commendation among a group of original and independent archi-tects, but there is a sneering reference in a note added to *The Seven Lamps* in 1880 to 'the stupidest traceries that can be cut cheapest, as in the cloisters of the missionary school at Canterbury',[4] that is in Butterfield's rebuilding of St. Augustine's. It was rather some

[1] 'Mr. Butterfield has taken the strong step of playing confidently into the hand of time'; M. R. Ricardo in *Journ. R.I.B.A.* iii (1896), 369.

[2] The Lamp of Beauty, *Works*, viii. 180.

[3] I am relying on the Index to the *Works*: the reference is in a paper delivered in 1865. [4] *Works*, viii. 128.

common trend to which they both were susceptible, in their differing responses. *The Seven Lamps of Architecture* made an immediate stir in educated circles, and a second edition appeared in 1855, but *The Stones of Venice*, of which the first volume was published in 1851, was slow in selling. These long and far from easy volumes exerted only a gradual influence. There was, however, in their abundance nourishment for many ideas that others were seeking after. The debate about architecture had been conducted within a limited stylistic framework, to which Pugin had added liturgical fanaticism. Ruskin provided it with a moral and social content thoroughly in keeping with all that was most earnest in the thought of the time. *The Seven Lamps* appeared in 1848, the year of revolution, and the author was full of forebodings: 'It is no time for the idleness of metaphysics, or the entertainment of the arts. The blasphemies of the earth are sounding louder, and its miseries heaped heavier every day. . . . I have paused, not once or twice, as I wrote . . . as the thought has crossed me, how soon all Architecture may be vain, except that which is not made with hands': and he concludes, bizarre and sinister as Blake or Fuseli, with the words 'The sun was risen upon the earth when Lot entered into Zoar'.[1] His great periods, 'often intoxicated with inspiration not to be expressed',[2] stretch from earth to heaven, and his condemnation of false materials, of 'members which . . . profess to have a duty and have none', sounded like some new revelation: 'that building will generally be the noblest, which to an intelligent eye discovers the great secrets of its structure': yet it could only achieve full nobility if it was based on joy in the work; 'so long as men work as men, putting their hearts into what they do . . . there will be that in the handling which is above all price'.[3]

G. E. Street was ten years younger than Butterfield.[4] In 1850, when he was twenty-six, an article by him in the *Ecclesiologist*, 'On the proper Characteristics of a town church', crystallized many of the theories and impulses that were crowding in. Kent ragstone,

---

[1] Op. cit. 25, 265–6.

[2] See Professor Kerr, 'Ruskin and Emotional Architecture', *Journ. R.I.B.A.* vii (1900), 181.　　　　　　　　　　　　　　[3] Op. cit. 61, 214.

[4] A. E. Street, *Memoir of G. E. Street* (1888).

which Scott's St. Giles's, Camberwell, had made the approved material, was now condemned as too rustic to be appropriate in a town area. If plain hewn ashlar could not be used, then brick was the next best: for light there must be a large clerestory, and if necessary the high pitch, which both Pugin and the ecclesiologists had thought essential, could be flattened out: foreign examples he considered could be studied with profit. Street had been trained in Gilbert Scott's office. In 1855 he had entered for the competition for a cathedral at Lille, and won the second premium.[1] The first went to William Burges, three years his junior, whose design was an immensely scholarly study in the Gothic of Northern France. Burges was a great designer of furniture, fittings, and plate; his figured mosaic floor in Worcester College chapel was, he thought, 'the finest executed in this way since the Romans left the island';[2] and the house he eventually built for himself at 9 Melbury Road, Kensington (1875–80), was designed and furnished with a Pre-Raphaelite accuracy of detail. St. Finbar's cathedral, Cork (1863), is his greatest building and is a wonderfully rich and successful rehandling of a past style, but compared to Street's church of St. Philip and St. James, Oxford, completed, except for the spire, a year earlier, Cork cathedral is mere academic good taste. St. Philip and St. James is a remarkably plastic conception:[3] the tower, rising square from the transepts, with a broached octagonal spire with four canopied windows, does not soar, but emphasizes the sense of mass: the apse, the short transepts, the small bell tower, the shallow porch all firmly build up into a single block from which no elaboration of carving is allowed to detract: some bands of darker stone and inlaid decorations of the window arches give some slight polychromatic effect, but also stress the horizontal as opposed to the vertical lines. Inside there is a low arcade of four wide bays, surmounted by a clerestory of deeply splayed but severely unornamented windows; the eastern arch of the arcade

---

[1] For the competition see A. E. Street, op. cit. 24–31. 'The architecture of France met its Agincourt at Lille.' French patriotism could not stomach this and 'a certain well known priest, aided by a local architect . . . concocted a new design in which many elements, much watered, both of Mr. Burges's and of my father's design, were recognisable.' [2] *Ecclesiologist*, xxvi (1865), 336.

[3] H. W. Taunt, *North Oxford and its Mother Church* (n.d.).

breaks into the wall of the chancel arch without completing its curve, a device that Butterfield used at All Saints, thereby leaving as clear as possible the view of the altar and achieving a functional abruptness of statement. The pillars of the arcade are of polished Aberdeen granite and the capitals are elaborately cut and strongly emphatic; one of them, subscribed for by the choir, has angels with musical instruments; apart from the capitals and the colour contrast of the pillars decoration is concentrated in the apse. In no other of his many churches is there such a complete revelation of a strongly marked personality. 'He felt—none more strongly—how paramount the beauty of usefulness is.'[1]

Compared to the preciseness of Pugin and the tact of Scott, there is a robust provocativeness about Butterfield and Street: but they in their turn were not unprovoked. The fifties and sixties saw attacks on Tractarianism, which in the forties had been mainly matter of university politics, spreading to wider and more blatant fields. The restoration of the Roman hierarchy had given a new and sinister connotation to anything that savoured of Romanizing. At Hawksmoor's church of St. George's-in-the-East, the services in 1859 were interrupted by a howling mob, the fittings destroyed, the clergy assaulted, while a reinforced posse of police remained comparatively inactive. It was the culmination of a growing and almost licensed ribaldry, which vented itself first by scribbled insults on the church walls and then by open violence. Later, legal action was to be instituted against the clergy concerned. Butterfield and Street were both committed to the cause,[2] the former spending his reserved, bachelor life in association with High Church clergy, the latter a sidesman at All Saints, Margaret Street, and a frequent singer in church choirs. Their architecture has the vigour and aggressiveness of defiant martyrdom.

Something of their freedom in handling the Gothic idiom can be found in the work of other architects: Samuel Teulon in

[1] *Memoir*, 60. Anglicanism shared in the expansiveness of the time, and Street designed the English churches at Genoa and Rome: his Crimean Memorial Chapel at Constantinople is very characteristic of his forceful style (*Building News*, xv (1868), 571).

[2] 'Among Anglican architects, Carpenter and Butterfield were the apostles of the high church school—I, of the multitude.' Gilbert Scott, *Recollections*, 42.

particular seldom fails to be interesting and is often distinguished: Henry Woodyer, one of Butterfield's few pupils, can show, as at St. Paul's, Wokingham, a restrained and pleasant use of some of his master's methods, coupled with an inventive fancy in tracery that is entirely his own. On the whole, however, a more traditional use predominated.[1] John Raphael Brandon's Catholic Apostolic church in Gordon Square (1853) seemed to Eastlake 'one of the grandest and most effective modern churches which have marked the Revival', at a time when 'the completely original designs which were produced did but little credit to the Gothic cause or to their respective authors'.[2] Brandon's exactness of detail was based on long research published in 1847 in his *Analysis of Gothic Architecture*. It was a tradition that still had life in it and was to inspire the work of J. L. Pearson, G. F. Bodley, and others in the last quarter of the century. The style was being used also for civic buildings. E. W. Godwin's Town Hall at Northampton (1864) owes something to *The Stones of Venice* and is a remarkable accumulation of details, some of them fine enough, though it is hardly co-ordinated as a whole. 'In this style', Ruskin wrote in the second edition of *The Seven Lamps* (1855), for in the first his dislike of Pugin still coloured his attitude towards the Revival, 'let us build the church, the palace and the cottage; but chiefly let us use it for civil and domestic buildings.' For the palace there was a representative in Balmoral, built by the Aberdeen architect, William Smith, in 1853–5, under constant interference from Prince Albert, though the Scottish baronial style might not satisfy Ruskinian requirements. Now in the ever-growing towns terraces were displaying pointed doorways between pillars and carved capitals, and the gables and mullions of Gothic were vying with the Italian cornices and towers in villas throughout the country;[3] or the motifs were combined in mixtures which seemed significant of the virile independence of the age, even though here and there a high-pitched Mansard roof suggests that this British energy has some Parisian impulse behind it. Highbury or St. John's Wood responded readily: even in south and east

---

[1] See H.-R. Hitchcock, 'High Victorian Gothic', *Victorian Studies*, i (1957), 47.
[2] *History of the Gothic Revival* (1872): the author was a nephew of Sir Charles's.
[3] See J. Summerson, 'The London Suburban Villa', *Arch. Rev.* civ (1948), 63.

London the drab rows of Georgian terraces, recognizably Georgian even though ornament was minimal, began to feel the Gothic urge. When in 1862-4, the Baroness Burdett-Coutts built some model blocks of flats and a market at Columbia Square in Bethnal Green, designed by H. A. Darbishire, the style was elaborately Gothic and the towered, gabled market with its heraldic beasts, now boarded up in disrepair and soon no doubt to disappear, is one of the great curiosities of the period (Pl. 33 a).[1]

Many of the trends of the time met in one building, the Science Museum in Oxford. As a result of a competition, in which there had been thirty-two designs submitted, the work was entrusted to Benjamin Woodward, a young Irishman who had recently designed a library for Trinity College, Dublin, on Ruskinian lines. Oxford needless to say had been vocal on the question of styles, apart from the more vehement question of establishing science, and Woodward's Veronese Gothic was only carried through Congregation by a majority of two votes. Dr. Acland, however, the prime mover of the whole scheme and a friend of Ruskin since Christ Church days, seemed satisfied, even though the laboratory was a copy of the octagonal kitchen at Glastonbury: Ruskin assured him that 'the power and essence of Gothic . . . lay in its adaptability to all need'.[2] Where, if not on a building devoted to natural science, should there be scope for genuinely naturalistic foliage and beasts, fresh inventions copied from actual plants and animals, carved, he was delighted to find, by Woodward's Irish stonemasons who took a real interest in their job and in the true tradition caricatured any university officials who tried to interfere with them. It was to be a combined temple of art and nature in which all of whom Ruskin approved were to co-operate. Rossetti sensibly declined, though he soon turned his interest to Woodward's other Oxford building, the Union Debating Hall; but Woolner designed a porch, which was unfortunately never erected, and he and young Alexander Munro made a series of statues of great scientists[3] to stand against pillars in the central hall, whose glass roof was surprisingly

[1] M. Girouard in *C.L.* cxxiii (1958), 812.
[2] See H. W. Acland, *The Oxford Museum* (3rd ed., 1893), 45.
[3] Queen Victoria presented the first four of them.

supported by ironwork foliage. These last, inevitably by Skidmore of Coventry, were perhaps hardly Ruskinian, despite the accuracy of the fronds (Fig. 8); but the long frontage, with its windows

FIG. 8. *Ironwork spandrel of roof, Oxford Museum*

rising straight from the string course, its polychromy and decorative roundels, its high-pitched dormered roof certainly owed much to the Ruskinian canon. Funds failed in 1859,[1] and it was left incompletely decorated. It has never been greatly admired, but it has a staying quality which holds its own amongst the vast growth

[1] Acland (op. cit. 16) sadly contrasts the 'rigorously restrained expenditure' with the contrary treatment of Cockerell's Taylorian Institution.

of more modern laboratories around it. Here with but a road between it and Keble the most powerful phase of Victorianism finds concentrated expression.

In 1857 Gilbert Scott gave his own version of Victorian Gothic housing[1] in the block built in the Broad Sanctuary at Westminster. On such a site Gothic was tactfully appropriate, and the open *parvis* before the Abbey was no normal street frontage. The building came at a critical moment in Scott's career. In the previous year, 1856, a competition had been held for a new Foreign Office and a new War Office or a block combining the two. They were won by two little known architects, Coe and Garling, and Scott's design for a Gothic Foreign Office was placed third, a design of high-pitched roofs and gables, somewhat disconcertingly broken by staircase turrets, half-way, in their diagonal slope, between Blois and Pisa.[2] Palmerston, however, decided to disregard the awards and to assign the building to Pennethorne as architect to the Board of Works. Scott found himself, in his own words, 'at liberty to stir'. Palmerston for a brief period was replaced by Derby and Disraeli, and Scott was given the commission. Then Palmerston in 1859 returned to power, and would have none of Scott's design. 'This battle', as Palmerston called it, in rather old-fashioned terminology, 'of the Gothic and Palladian styles'[3] was a long-drawn-out contest, and in the end the Foreign Office and the India Office, which in the course of the dispute had been substituted for the War Office, were built by Scott in the Italian style. It was generally felt, particularly by the Goths, that he ought rather to have resigned his commission. Had he done so the all important view across St. James's Park, the vista towards the Horse Guards Parade so ingeniously planned by Nash,[4] might have fared much worse. Scott's deep set window arches break the heaviness of this large massive building, and his square Italian towers and steps up to Downing Street are used with some feeling for the picturesque. The statuary is well placed and the white Portland stone of the

[1] His *Remarks on Secular and Domestic Architecture* appeared the same year.
[2] Reproduced Goodhart-Rendel, *English Architecture since the Regency*, 116. See Mrs. Esdaile, 'Battles Royal', *Architect and Building News*, cxxvi (1931), 125.
[3] *Hansard* (164), 535.
[4] S. Lang, 'St. James's Park', *Arch. Rev.* cx (1951), 293.

plinth and string courses varies the surface. Scott himself, however, felt extreme shame and sorrow and in 1860, when he won the competition, and he won more competitions than he lost, for the St. Pancras Railway Station, he solaced his wounded integrity by a Gothic design of splendid intricacy, which should be in every way ill-suited for its purpose, but which has weathered well and now holds an assured place in London's architecture (Pl. 76 a). Palmerston's victory indeed hardly checked the cult of municipal Gothic. In Manchester when a new Town Hall was begun in 1869, it was uncompromisingly Gothic, though some foreign elements, some influence from Butterfield and Street, were superimposed on its middle-pointed framework (Pl. 74 b).[1] Its architect was Alfred Waterhouse, who had recently been working at Balliol College and whose hard, highly individual style and clear planning were to be a powerful ingredient in late Victorian building.

The climax of Street's career is marked by the last of the celebrated competitions, whose contentious stories have occurred so frequently in this volume. In 1866 six architects, Scott, Street, T. H. Wyatt, Edward Barry, P. C. Hardwick, and Alfred Waterhouse,[2] were asked to contribute designs for new Law Courts. Wyatt and Hardwick declined: then there were complaints in Parliament that the field had been too limited: further competitors entered: the judges recommended that Street's elevation should be accepted and Barry's interior arrangements: Scott protested at this as a breach of the terms: there were arguments for almost a year and eventually the building was assigned to Street, Barry being accepted as architect for a new National Gallery, which was never built.[3] There were endless debates, about the site, about the style, about the interior arrangements; at the climax of the building operations they were held up by a six months' strike. The result

---

[1] W. E. A. Axon, *An Architectural and General Description of the Town Hall, Manchester* (Manchester, 1878); F. B. Oakley, 'Manchester', *Journ. R.I.B.A.* vii (1900), 453.

[2] The dynastic element is strong: Thomas Henry Wyatt, for long David Brandon's partner, was the brother of Matthew Digby Wyatt and their grandfather was a first cousin of James Wyatt. Edward Barry was the son of a greater father, P. C. Hardwick the son and grandson of architects. Scott was to be the founder of a new dynasty.

[3] There is a full account in A. E. Street, *Memoir*, chap. viii.

is, perhaps not surprisingly, disappointing and provides the final proof that nineteenth-century Gothic adaptations make unsatisfactory street façades; but there are many ingenuities of planning and in the unity and refinement of the detail something comes through of Street's enthusiasm and sensitivity. The Great Hall (Pl. 76 *b*) achieves the nobility at which it aims. He died, worn out by the worries of this great undertaking and before its completion, on 18 December 1881. Four days earlier had died an architect who had, as the obituary notice in the *Builder* phrased it, 'held a distinguished place among English architects in his own day', Decimus Burton, and the same writer noted how these two deaths stressed 'the extraordinary rapidity with which the pendulum of architectural taste in this country has swung from one extreme to another'.[1]

[1] *The Builder*, xli (1881), 780. Anthony Salvin and William Burges were also among 'death's trophies of this year 1881': see *Proceedings of R.I.B.A.* (1881–2), 97.

X

THE GREAT EXHIBITION

IN the parliamentary discussions about art and commerce national prestige and profit had been intermingling themes. Less explicitly, it was clear that if art could be shown to return sound trading dividends, then the Puritan conscience could be at rest from doubts as to its frivolity. Long before Parliament, however, an independent body, the Society of Arts, had been interesting itself in this sane and serious approach.[1] Founded in 1754 'for the Encouragement of the Arts, Manufactures and Commerce of the Country', it had been prominently active in the second half of the eighteenth century, but had lately fallen on less energetic days, until in 1843 Prince Albert agreed to accept the presidency of the Society. This was followed by the grant of a Royal Charter in 1847. Some small exhibitions were organized and premiums offered for designs of a tea service and some beer mugs, which were won by an exhibit by Felix Summerly carried out by Herbert Minton. Felix Summerly was the pseudonym of a member of the Society, Henry Cole, a civil servant aged thirty-eight, whose restless industry had already found outlets editing railway charts with antiquarian notes; producing books for children, illustrated by Mulready, Horsley, Redgrave, Linnell, and others; publishing the first Christmas card (designed by Maclise); and securing the establishment of a docks at Grimsby.[2] Inspired by the success of his tea service, he started a series of 'Art Manufactures' (an early use of the term) and also began with Redgrave the *Journal of Design and Manufactures*, which ran for only three years[3] but was not without its importance at the time. Thanks largely to Cole's energy in approaching manufacturers, the Society's exhibitions of 1847 and

[1] O. Hudson and K. W. Luckhurst, *The Royal Society of Arts* (1954).

[2] Sir Henry Cole, *Fifty Years of Public Work* (2 vols. 1884).

[3] 1849 to 1852—6 vols.: its inserted patterns of fabrics are of first importance for the study of early Victorian textiles.

1848 attracted far wider attention than previously, and in the latter year there were seventy thousand visitors. The following year Cole and Matthew Digby Wyatt, a member of the Wyatt dynasty, went to Paris to report on the Quinquennial Exhibition of French Industry. In France there had been some talk of holding an international exhibition, but the idea, though strongly sponsored, had been turned down by the Chamber. Cole, an ardent Free Trader, eagerly and persistently adopted it. He came back full of a new enthusiasm, having won over Herbert Minton, who had also been in Paris, to his views. Francis Fuller, another member of the Society who had visited Paris, in a chance train conversation between Southampton and London with Thomas Cubitt, on his way back from Osborne, outlined the possibility of holding a world exhibition in London under the patronage of the Prince Consort. Cubitt took the first opportunity of repeating the conversation to his royal patron. At the annual prize-giving at the Royal Society of Arts its secretary, Scott Russell, openly referred to their President's desire for a comprehensive exhibition in 1851. The four protagonists, Cole, Fuller, Cubitt, Scott Russell, were shortly summoned to meet the Prince and the scheme for an exhibition was finally launched.[1]

The intervening period before its opening on 1 May 1851 was to see many intrigues, anxieties, setbacks and strokes of luck. Peel was sympathetic but the government was cautious, and it was not till January 1850 that a Royal Commission was issued to deal with all the problems involved. The story has often been told, and here can only be glanced at: how *The Times* came out in support and then veered against; how the residents of Kensington protested against the violation of Hyde Park, the felling of its trees (with Colonel Sibthorp, M.P., as leading dendrophile), the hordes of vagabonds who would undoubtedly frequent it; how Sir Robert Peel on 29 June 1850, riding in the Park after a meeting of the

---

[1] There is a large literature on the Exhibition: of recent works see C. Hobhouse, *1851 and the Crystal Palace* (revised ed. 1950); C. H. Gibbs-Smith, *The Great Exhibition* (1950); Yvonne ffrench, *The Great Exhibition* (1951); K. W. Luckhurst, *The Great Exhibition of 1851* (Royal Soc. of Arts: 1951); C. R. Fay, *Palace of Industry, 1851* (1951); Asa Briggs, *Victorian People* (1954).

Commissioners, was thrown from his horse and died four days later; how the Commissioners' plan for the building, with a great sheet-iron dome designed by Brunel, was greeted with derision; how Mr. Joseph Paxton came to the rescue with a rival design; and how *Punch* christened it the Crystal Palace. Throughout these debates and vexations it was largely the steady and thoughtful persistence of the Prince Consort that maintained the project.[1] He of all the protagonists grasped most fully the wide implications of the Exhibition, and could voice, with authority and pondered eloquence, the hopes that surrounded it. These today seem to us strangely, ironically miscalculated, and the confident optimism outlined in the Prince's Mansion House speech of March 1850 is now a museum specimen of human fallibility. Free trade, division of labour, increase in means of communication, the stimulus of competition and capital were all, he argued, leading men to a new sense of unity and to a fuller discovery of 'the laws by which the Almighty governs his creation'.[2] Without the prophetic element the fervours of 1851 would be incompletely understood, but in fact it was the climax of a mood rather than the beginning of a millenium.

The part that the arts, whether fine or otherwise, were to play in it was never very clearly defined. Three practising artists were Commissioners, Richard Westmacott, Charles Barry, and Charles Eastlake. The last seemed to *The Times* 'rather unfortunately selected as a representative of pictorial art' and, even if he had not already practically abandoned painting for writing and administration, his correct, academic studies of Italian peasantry or scenes of chivalry (Pl. 65 *b*) had little contact with the machine age. 'Art', the Prince had said in his speech, 'teaches us the immutable laws of beauty and symmetry, and gives to our productions forms in accordance with them.' No one can have attached any very clear meaning to this statement, but it reflects the current belief that the rules of absolute beauty might be discovered by diligent quest, as were being discovered the 'laws of power, motion and transformation'.

[1] See Theodore Martin, *The Life of the Prince Consort*: 5 vols. (1875–80), vol. ii.
[2] *The Principal Speeches and Addresses of the Prince Consort* (1862), 111.

In this *mystique* of the marriage of art and industry one master-piece, however, could be affirmatively quoted, the Crystal Palace itself. Technically it had many features never before so publicly used. Its designer, Joseph Paxton, was one of the remarkable figures of the time. Born in 1803, a farmer's son, he had become in 1826 head gardener at Chatsworth.[1] William George Spencer Cavendish, sixth duke of Devonshire, had recently added horti-cultural to his many aesthetic interests. Faced by his master's demand for exotic plants, Paxton had turned his great inventive capacity to the perfecting of conservatories, using cast-iron columns, large panes of sheet-glass and his own type of sash-bar, the basic framework of his constructions. The Great Conservatory at Chatsworth, completed in 1840 and demolished in 1920, covered an acre in extent: much admired by Queen Victoria, who drove through it in a carriage on her visit to Chatsworth in 1843, it stimulated the authorities at Kew Gardens to the erection in 1844 of their great Palm House, designed by Decimus Burton, who had some hand in Paxton's Chatsworth plans. Still standing, the Palm House represents today this form of Victorian luxury, which private incomes now are unable to heat or to maintain. It was followed by another Paxton building at Chatsworth, the Lily House, erected in 1850 for the exuberant flowering of Victoria Regia, a lily from British Guiana, a structure of glass built on the most economical of frameworks.[2] By the time he designed it, Paxton, still holding the office of head gardener, was advising the duke on most of his affairs, was a recognized authority on many problems of architecture and engineering, and was designing with his architect son-in-law, George Stokes, a castellated mansion at the Cavendish Irish seat of Lismore. On a visit to London in June 1850 he found everyone in a state of despondency about the Commission's design for the Exhibition building. A mutual friend took him to see Cole; Lord Granville, the Vice-President of the Commission, was a nephew of the duke of Devonshire; the

---

[1] V. R. Markham, *Paxton and the Bachelor Duke* (1935).

[2] Nathaniel Ward's *Growth of Plants in Close-Glazed Cases* (1833) had given great impetus to the construction of greenhouses. Paxton knew Rouhault's Serres in the Jardin des Plantes at Paris built in 1833: see P. Norton Shand in *Arch. Rev.* lxxxi (1939), 65.

Prince Consort summoned Paxton to an interview and examined the plans, which he had produced in a week's intense work. The Prince was converted, but the Building Committee, not unnaturally, hesitated. Glass, restricted in use by an excise duty only recently removed, was unknown as a building commodity; they could hardly believe that it would even be forthcoming in sufficient supply. Paxton forced the issue. He gave a drawing of his design to the *Illustrated London News*, who had recently published that of the Commissioners. The new drawing appeared on 6 July and at once won approval. At the last moment the Building Committee gave way. There were only some nine months before the Exhibition was due to open. Thanks to the standardization of its units, the building was completed in time for the exhibits to be unpacked and arranged, though the confusion of the last days seemed to be beyond any human control.[1] Three tiers of shining, flat-roofed terraces, with a central transept whose curved roof rose above them, it covered in all eighteen acres of ground space; its galleries provided an additional five acres. It included two of the great elms which had been so stoutly defended; it withstood a severe gale when half completed; it was ingeniously ventilated to prevent condensation. Londoners took this magical, machine-made building to their hearts long before the May Day opening arrived. It was the first birthday of Victoria's youngest son, afterwards the duke of Connaught. Winterhalter painted the duke of Wellington presenting his good wishes to the royal parents, and beyond them in the background, sparkling in the sun, is the Crystal Palace, the symbol of hope and peace and prosperity.

If the Palace was the most celebrated ferrovitreous construction

---

[1] The account by M. Digby Wyatt of 'The Construction of the Building' prefaces the official *Descriptive and Illustrated Catalogue of the Great Exhibition, 1851* (for which Tenniel designed the cover). See also C. Downes, *The Buildings erected in Hyde Park for the Great Exhibition* (1852); Tallis (J. & Co.), *The Crystal Palace described and illustrated by beautiful engravings, chiefly from Daguerreotypes* (3 vols., 1856); Dickinson Brothers, *Comprehensive Pictures of the Great Exhibition from the originals painted . . . for Prince Albert* (2 vols., 1854). The *I.L.N.* (vols. xvii–xxi, 1850–2) describes the various stages of building and demolition. W. J. B. Saunders, *The Palace of Industry* (1852), is a short popular account of the building methods. For a recent assessment see P. M. Shand, 'The Crystal Palace as Structure and Precedent', *Arch. Rev.* lxxxi (1937), 65.

of its time it had, in addition to the conservatories, several pre-decessors and rivals. The railway stations,[1] with their great covered platforms, provided in the forties a meeting place for architecture and engineering: the great glazed curves of Newcastle Central, begun in 1846, the elaborate ironwork of Paddington, and the vast arched roof of King's Cross are extant examples of the triumphs of the new techniques. J. B. Bunning's[2] Coal Exchange (1846-9), the most original of the City's commercial buildings, has a glass dome, 60 feet in diameter, raised on thirty-two iron ribs: the stanchions supporting the triple tier of circular galleries from which the offices open and the galleries themselves are all of cast iron, elaborately ornamented, while the walls have painted arabesques of arbaceous ferns and such like motifs, framing small scenes of coal mines and typical miners. When freshly painted, this remarkable building must have been the gayest manifestation of the possibilities of building in iron. Outside, however, the portico is surmounted by the familiar Tower of the Winds, here set between two bronze heraldic beasts (Pl. 75 a). Bunning was a great imaginative decora-tor, much of whose talent was unfortunately spent on ephemeral work for city celebrations: almost his last task was the decorations for the welcome of Alexandra of Denmark to London. His dome precedes the Crystal Palace; that of Sydney Smirke, thought out in conjunction with the Director, Anthony Panizzi, to cover the central court of the British Museum and create a new Reading Room, was begun in 1852 and completed in 1857. While perforce sacrificing much of his father's design, the younger Smirke, always an enterprising architect with a full sense of Victorian display, substituted for the lost courtyard an enclosed space whose propor-tions and scale have been a dignified and not uninspiring shelter to many generations of readers. Had the full scheme of decorations, in which Alfred Stevens was to have played a part,[3] been carried

---

[1] See Hitchcock, *Victorian Architecture*, chap. xv; and C. Barman, *Railway Architec-ture* (1950); C. L. V. Meeks, *The Railroad Station* (Yale University Press, 1956).

[2] See obituary speech by Professor Donaldson, *Sessional Papers of the R.I.B.A.* (1863), v. The opening of the Coal Exchange was the first public appearance of the young Prince of Wales, who accompanied his father.

[3] The model with the scheme of decorative panels is in the possession of the Museum.

out, it would have been one of London's proudest features: as it stands it bears comparison with Henri Labrouste's Salle de Travail des Imprimés in the Bibliothèque Nationale, an almost contemporary undertaking.

These were some of the experimental achievements of Paxton's time, but none had the popular impact of his Palace, and none of their builders had the personal position of the gardener of Chatsworth. Many drawings, prints and some early photographs have preserved for us the appearance of the interior as arranged for the Exhibition. 'The plash of fountains, the luxuriance of tropical foliage, the play of colours from the choicest flowers, carried on into the vistas of the nave by the rich dyes of carpets and stuffs from the costliest looms, were enough to fill eye and mind with a pleasure never to be forgotten.'[1] It is to be noted that the terms used are always 'nave' and 'transept'. This was no great conservatory, but a temple of peace and the arts. The interior decoration was the work of Owen Jones. The underside of every girder was painted red, the columns yellow, picked out with blue.[2] The effect was gay and lively. In arrangement there were no inhibitions against overcrowding: lavishness was the rule: huge carpets hung from the galleries: colossal statues reared themselves above the crowds: there were twenty-four tons of coal in a single block, the largest sheet of plate glass ever made, and a model of the Liverpool Docks, with 1,600 fully rigged ships.[3] We must not, however, linger over the raw materials, the display of machinery, the new gas cookers, the electric telephones, the cameras, the early water-closets, but must come to problems of style, of the application of art to industry. The exhibits, reproduced so freely in catalogues and journals, constitute a great documentation of taste, but one that can hardly be conclusively used. Ornament, now fashionably contrasted with fine art, had become a subject of absorbing interest

[1] Wemyss Reid, *Memoirs and Correspondence of Lyon Playfair*, ii. 363.

[2] 'The steady perseverance of (Mr. Jones) against a violent and clamorous opposition from the self-appointed arbiters of taste, enabled him to carry out his ideas . . . with a success which is now acknowledged by all parties to be complete.' Downes, op. cit. 2.

[3] For contemporary accounts see in particular *The Art Journal's Illustrated Catalogue* and the *I.L.N.* xviii and xix (1851–2).

both as 'embellishing the realities of life'[1] and as sound business. 'The ornamental bread-platter suggested by Bell the Sculptor has positively originated a trade in that article.'[2] There was much discussion as to underlying principles, but fashion is never subordinate to theories and much that pleased would not have been approved. Furniture and household utensils tend in an ordinary family of moderate means to accumulate gradually and to present a haphazard effect. The great houses could have their Egyptian, Grecian, or Gothic rooms: the more bourgeois patronage preferred a medley of the old and new. In the drawings of *Punch*[3] or in book illustrations, the rooms of the time still have, naturally enough, many Regency features, the marble fireplaces with Grecian frets, the Hepplewhite chairs, the Empire writing-tables. Smaller objects were more easily added, the glass-protected shells and imitation flowers, the immensely popular canary in its round-topped cage. The windows had glazing-bars, soon to be replaced by plate glass. The more recent furniture was mainly rosewood, not yet mahogany, and the newer chairs were distinguished by their turned legs, that tendency towards roundness and curves which was the distinguishing feature of the times. In the forties the lighter, gayer colours were replaced by more sombre tints, the rich flock wallpapers matched by deeper coloured carpets, a change that suited perhaps the growing social conscience, awakened by Chartism, cholera, and Lord Shaftesbury's factory acts. Clothes also were becoming more drab, and the régime of black was closing in on male costume.

The immense publicity of the Great Exhibition did much to alter taste, but the portentous pieces of furniture, dinner services, épergnes and fire grates with which contemporary line engravings have made us familiar are in some ways misleading. They were exhibition pieces, designed to make an effect in crowded and competitive display, and, though their ebullience had some influence, they were in no way representative of the normal well-to-do

[1] Dyce in *Journ. of Design*, i (1849), 65; on the whole question see A. Bøe, *From Gothic Revival to Functional Form* (1957), where there is a valuable bibliography.

[2] *Journ. of Design*, i. 1.

[3] See William Gaunt in *Arch. Rev.* cviii (1950), 309; Ralph Dutton, *The Victorian Home* (1954).

home: they were rather, as Redgrave put it,[1] 'something, how-ever outré, that shall obtain . . . the run of the season'. Novelty was at a high premium, particularly in the use of new materials. Papier-mâché chairs and small tables had been in vogue for some years: now gutta-percha sideboards, brass bedsteads, metal tubing chairs, electroplate in various forms, zinc statues, glass fountains, were proof of ever-increasing ingenuity. There was, also, as Redgrave complained, a fine disregard for appropriate use of motifs: 'the funeral urns of the Greeks revived as drinking vessels for the table: the columns of temples turned into candlesticks, and sarcophagi into wine-coolers, while the decorations of ceilings are applied to carpets, and the carved frieze of an Ionic temple to a muslin curtain'. Of such ineptitudes, the Irish bog oak table, whose top was formed by the shield of a crouching naked gladia-tor,[2] was an extreme example (Fig. 9). Amid such eccentricities a unifying style is hard to find. Much of the detail still belonged to the classical period, but it was used now with an unclassical profusion and a frequent interspersion of naturalistic forms. The curve, as Dr. Pevsner has pointed out,[3] is one of the most charac-teristic features of mid-Victorian design, full, generous, bulging curves, echoing and accommodating the crinolines of the lady of the house. In the Medieval Court Pugin's pointed arches might decorate his well-made furnishings,[4] but elsewhere the legs and arms of chairs and couches, the doors and mouldings of cupboards, the cases of pianos, swell out in abandoned curvatures. A papier-mâché easy chair, designed by H. FitzCook and called 'The Day-dreamer', has become an almost classic example of the popular rotundity (Fig. 10). Such pieces were, however, no English speciality. Much continental work shared in these bellying lines, and, despite much English repining about native backwardness, the Exhibition strikingly demonstrated a common European taste.

[1] Supplementary Report on Design: Reports of the Juries: printed for the Royal Commission (1852), 710.

[2] Reproduced Descriptive and Illustrated Catalogue, ii. 827.

[3] High Victorian Design (1951), 49; see also F. G. Roe, Victorian Furniture (1952).

[4] 'Much was to be learnt from the sensible construction of poor Pugin's woodwork': M. Digby Wyatt, 'Form in the Decorative Arts', Lectures on the Results of the Great Exhibition, 2nd ser. (1853), 243.

England, in fact, agitated by its sense of artistic inferiority,[1] was in many instances ahead of her rivals in design as in mechanical invention. Certainly in no other country was there more constant theorizing as to what constituted goodness in ornament.

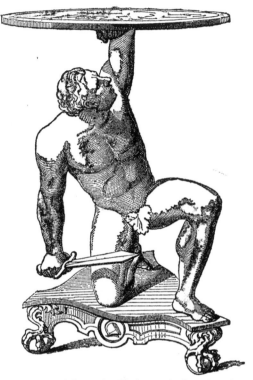

FIG. 9. *Irish bog oak table by J. Fletcher of Cork*

The two prophets of the time were Owen Jones and Matthew Digby Wyatt. Closely associated with the Exhibition, they were respectively entrusted with the subjects of colour and form in the *Lectures on the Results of the Great Exhibition*[2] delivered at the suggestion of Prince Albert; and Owen Jones's *Grammar of Ornament* appeared in 1856. Its splendid coloured plates displayed a most informed selection of ornamental designs of varying ages and countries; its introduction summarized the principles which

[1] It was an old quip that 'the French have *goût*, and we have gout': see *Consideration upon the Expediency of building a Metropolitan Palace* by a Member of Parliament (1825), 21.

[2] 2nd ser. (1853); see N. Pevsner, *Matthew Digby Wyatt* (Cambridge, 1951).

Jones had been for some time advocating. Undoubtedly he had read *The Seven Lamps*,[1] but his views had been already formulated and he and Ruskin shared in a common trend of thought, of which

FIG. 10. *Easy chair of papier mâché* (*The Daydreamer*)

neither individually was the originator, and of which, in short-term influence, Jones, who added practice to persuasion, was the more important exponent. 'Construction', he wrote, 'should be decorated. Decoration should never be purposely constructed':

[1] Reviewed, probably by Wyatt, in *Journ. of Design*, ii (1849–50), 72. For Jones see *Arch. Rev.* lxxxi (1937), 49 and 184.

and for him decoration must always be stylized: 'flowers or other natural objects should not be used as ornaments, but conventional representations founded upon them sufficiently suggestive to convey the intended image to the mind, without destroying the unity

FIG. 11. *Chintz covering designed by Owen Jones*

of the object they are employed to decorate'.[1] Deeply versed as he was in 'the truly enchanted palaces of the Moors',[2] he was a constant advocate of the overall design, and of the growth of lines 'one from the other in gradual undulations'.[3] His own distinguished patterns followed his precepts, and his flat, stylized leaves and geometric formulas (Fig. 11) are completely unlike the

[1] *Grammar of Ornament* (1856), 6.

[2] 'Colour in the Decorative Arts', *Lectures on the Results of the Great Exhibition*, 2nd ser. (1853), 265.

[3] *Journ. of Design*, v (1851), 92. For earlier designs see the series of articles on 'English fabrics printed from wood-blocks between 1790 and 1810' by Peter Floud and Mrs. Barbara Morris, in the *Connoisseur* (1957-8).

realistic profusion (Pl. 82 *a*) that was common to much regency and earlier Victorian furnishings. Other leaders of thought would certainly have been less sweeping. Dyce in his lectures at the School of Design pleaded for flatness in floor and wall designs, but claimed that a wall could simulate openings and that in a panelled scheme, the centres of the panels, flower, fruit, or even landscape and historical subjects, should be realistically treated. These framed designs, whether on wallpapers, carpets, or curtains, belonged to an older tradition, and on the whole were still executed with an experienced sense of suitability. More perturbing were the lush carpet patterns with flowers and ferns in relief which must have been curiously disconcerting to walk on.[1] Possibly it was in china ware that the most ludicrous excesses were perpetrated, and Messrs. Minton's dessert service, presented by the Queen to the emperor of Austria, appears in engravings to have embodied all the most condemned solecisms.

Of the accepted fine arts, painting was limited to one or two examples of works in special processes, such as 'Miller's silica colours'.[2] Sculpture, however, was more largely represented, partially because it was of much assistance to the general appearance: 'the happy and judicious arrangement [of objects of plastic art] in the great structure forms one of its most interesting features',[3] said a contemporary account; the bishops, on the other hand, had written to the Queen protesting that they could not attend the opening ceremony unless some of the nakedness were decently covered.[4] The neo-Grecian school of the first half of the century was represented by John Gibson's *Greek Hunter*, lent by Lord Yarborough, and in Henry Cole's opinion 'the finest piece of sculpture shewn' (Pl. 81 *b*).[5] Two of Gibson's pupils, Thomas and

[1] A selection is illustrated in N. Pevsner, *High Victorian Design*, figs. 72–75. Pugin had earlier attacked floor or wall designs shaded to give relief: cf. A. Bøe, op. cit. 30.

[2] *I.L.N.* xviii (1851), 477; Armitage's *Peace* specially painted for the Exhibition was the largest example.

[3] *Descriptive and Illustrated Cat.* ii. 848: the sculpture section runs from p. 843 to p. 853.   [4] *Journ. of Royal Soc. of Art*, xcix (1951), 547.

[5] 'International Results of the Exhibition of 1851', *Lectures on the Exhibition*, 2nd ser. (1853), 419: the *Hunter* is now in Lincoln Museum: there is a replica in the National Gallery of New South Wales: for reproductions of the sculpture see Tallis, *A Description of Crystal Palace*, i. 38.

Mary Thornycroft, showed a group of *King Alfred and his Mother* which recalls the classical severity of some of Gibson's own work, but their more popular exhibits were equestrian portraits of Queen Victoria and the Prince Consort. J. S. Westmacott showed one of the Magna Carta barons that, cast in zinc, were part of the decorations of the House of Lords. The Prince Consort lent a group of *Theseus and the Amazons* by Joseph Engel, a Hungarian emigrant to England, a rather overpretentious piece, now in the Orangery at Windsor. One of the most dominating pieces must have been that of the two great legal brothers, Eldon and Stowell, designed by M. L. Watson and completed after his death in 1849 by George Nelson. 'Each statue', the *Catalogue* proudly announces, 'is wrought out of a single block of marble, and the whole weighs 20 tons.' Watson, however, deserves better than assessment by weight: vast as are the two statues which now loom over the library that Gilbert Scott designed to hold them in University College, Oxford, they have monumentality as well as bulk.[1] Lough showed a long-necked, mannerist St. Michael triumphing over the devil, and a vast group, previously exhibited in 1844, of a woman and a war horse mourning a dead warrior. Beside some of the foreign exhibits the English sculptures were hard put to it to hold their own: the *Amazon attacked by a Tiger* cast in zinc and bronze by Professor A. Kiss of Berlin, the American Hiram Powers' *Greek Slave* (replica in the Corcoran Gallery, Washington), and R. Monti's *Veiled Vestal* were three of the most popular exhibits, all of them representing a damsel in serious distress, a subject in which Victorian chivalry or sadism or some confusion of the two took a remarkably uninhibited interest. John Bell's chained *Andromeda*, cast in bronze by the Coalbrook Dale Co., was an English exercise on a similar theme. Baron Marochetti, the Piedmontese, who had left France for England in the year of revolutions, showed outside the west entrance his full-size model of the mounted Cœur-de-Lion, which, after much criticism and controversy, was cast in

[1] The commission was originally given to Chantrey but had not been begun at his death. 'There is no man in England', said Allan Cunningham to Lord Eldon, 'who can model like Watson.' For the remarkable story of this monument see Henry Lonsdale, *Life and Works of Musgrave Lewthwaite Watson* (1866), chap. xi. For an appreciation of Watson see W. B. Scott, *British School of Sculpture* (1871), 91.

bronze and placed outside the House of Lords, where it has grown into popular affection: it has a romantic bravura, which the more lingeringly classical English sculptures lacked.[1]

The impact of the sculpture seems to have been considerable, and led to one interesting sequel. At the suggestion of J. B. Bunning, the Corporation of London 'with a view of encouraging the growth of art in this country' voted the sum of £10,000 to be expended in statuary for the Egyptian Hall[2] in the Mansion House. This purpose was gradually effected in the next twenty years. The subjects were vaguely drawn from English literature or history, and Dryden's ode was apparently considered sufficient justification for J. S. Westmacott's[3] *Alexander the Great* (1863). The sculptors employed were mainly those who had come to the fore in the competition for the Houses of Parliament: thus Foley is represented by *Egeria* (1855) and *Caractacus* (1857),[4] the last by general contemporary consent the finest piece, though today this over-muscular, moustachioed figure seems resolutely of its period; W. Calder Marshall by *Griselda* (1855); Patrick MacDowell by *Lea* (1855), a nude in the pose of the Medici *Venus*; E. H. Baily by *The Morning Star* (1854) and, until destroyed by enemy action in 1940, *Genius* (1858); William Theed by *The Bard* (1858) (Pl. 81 c). Theed was the leader in a return to the Renaissance and Michel-angelo, as opposed to the neo-classic tradition, and was entrusted with many memorial statues of the Prince, of which *The Queen and the Prince Consort as Anglo-Saxons* at Windsor is a document in mid-century historical sentiment.[5] Ten years younger than Theed, Joseph Durham still used in his *Hermione* (1858) and *Alastor* (1864) the smooth surfaces and straight falling drapery of neo-classicism. Competent but slightly dull, they lack the charm of his more popular pieces, such as the young cricketer, *Waiting for his Innings*

[1] For a hostile contemporary criticism of Marochetti see F. T. Palgrave, *Essays on Art* (1866), 252.

[2] *Catalogue of Sculpture, Paintings etc. belonging to the Corporation*, i (1867), 43.

[3] A nephew of Sir Richard's, and much employed for architectural sculpture.

[4] See W. Cosmo Monkhouse, *Works of J. M. Foley* (n.d.), 30, and *Art Journ.* vi (1860), 56.

[5] See *Magazine of Art* (Jubilee Number, 1887), 23. Theed's Chetham memorial at Manchester cathedral is one of his finest works.

(Pl. 54 b). The Egyptian Hall is one of the last great English interiors to be decorated with a series of statues in niches, and against their gold backgrounds they make their effect. When, however, they are examined in detail, many of them show that the neo-classic monumental tradition has lost its assurance, and been replaced by timid concessions to historical accuracy in costume and to sentimental expressiveness. J. G. Lough's *Comus* (1856), which rather surprisingly holds, with out-stretched cup, the central position, is an ingenious adaptation of the Belvedere *Apollo*: Henry Weekes,[1] the ablest provider of portrait busts in the mid-century, achieves some dramatic force with his *Sardanapalus*, but these men are lesser descendants of Flaxman, Chantrey, Westmacott, and Gibson, the end of a movement untouched by new impulses of any validity. Perhaps, as it seemed to Cosmo Monkhouse, 'the national unexpressiveness of body . . . made the language of form difficult to teach in England'.[2] In busts and portrait statues a new realism replaced the bold simplifications of neo-classicism; Sir Joseph Boehm, the Austrian who settled in England, in his seated figure of Thomas Carlyle (Pl. 61 d) models the face with an almost painterly quality that recalls Watts's contemporary renderings of the texture of ageing, wrinkled skin.[3] Others, such as Baily in much of his later work, allowed the strict discipline of Flaxman and Canova to degenerate into flaccid limbs and insensitive surfaces.

The Exhibition closed on Saturday, 11 October; four days previously it had had its record attendance of 109,915 visitors. Its success was convincingly established by a surplus balance of £186,437, and the Commissioners for the Exhibition continued and continue as a permanent body for the administration of this fund. Amid general regret the pledge to maintain the open space of the Park was honoured, and the Crystal Palace was dismantled, taken over by a company and re-erected at Sydenham. There it

[1] Biographical Introduction to his *Lectures on Art* (1880). One of Weekes's earliest works had been the figures of the martyrs on Gilbert Scott's Martyrs' Memorial at Oxford. At Christchurch priory he made, for Shelley's son, a great scenic piece of the drowned poet washed ashore.

[2] Op. cit. 5.

[3] There is a terracotta version of the head in the National Portrait Gallery: see David Piper, *The English Face* (1957), 289.

housed varied collections and even more varied performances, till on the night of 30 November 1936 it was destroyed by fire. It was not unmourned: 'To my knowledge', wrote Sigfried Giedion in the *Neue Zürcher Zeitung*, 'the possibilities dormant in the modern civilization we have created have never since been so clearly expressed.' 'I could not tear my eyes', said Le Corbusier, 'from its triumphant harmony.'[1]

While the Palace was being transferred, the Commissioners were purchasing a tract of 87 acres of land in South Kensington, with the intention of creating there a centre for the encouragement of science and art.[2] Towards this end a selection of the exhibits was purchased and for a few years shown in Marlborough House, till in 1857 a building was erected on the new site, under the control of the newly organized Department of Practical Art, of which Henry Cole was secretary and which now replaced the School of Design whose uneasy history has already been discussed.[3] The Crimean War, the disillusioning sequel to the hopes of international goodwill that the Exhibition had fostered, was an unpropitious time for monumental building, and this first museum was a strictly functional hall, with aisles and a gallery, built with corrugated iron sheets and lit by skylights. For display its simplicity must have had, by modern standards, many advantages, but its brutalism, relieved only by a light, cast-iron porch, not unlike the platform covering of a small railway station, shocked contemporary taste. It was never liked, and in 1871 it was taken down and re-assembled inside a brick covering as the Bethnal Green Museum. It had already become insufficient for the various collections that were being concentrated in South Kensington, the Sheepshanks pictures in 1857, followed by the Vernon pictures and Turner bequest, the Queen's loan of the Raphael cartoons in 1865, and in 1869 the National Portrait Gallery, founded by the energetic advocacy of Lord Stanhope in 1856, but as yet only temporarily housed. To meet these growing requirements various galleries

[1] *Arch. Rev.* lxxxi (1937), 1 and 72.
[2] See C. R. Fay, *Palace of Industry*, chap. vii, for the South Kensington schemes: the V. and A. has an important series of drawings showing the buildings at various stages of their development. [3] See above, p. 207.

were being built by the Department's inspector, Captain Francis
Fowke of the Royal Engineers. Fowke was a great user of terracotta, possibly under the influence of Gottfried Semper, a refugee
of 1848, who was patronized by Prince Albert. Semper's first
Dresden Opera House and his monumental version of the Renaissance style certainly influenced the last building with which Fowke
was concerned before his early death in 1865, the Albert Hall
(1867–71), carried out by Major-General Henry Young Darracott
Scott, another Royal Engineers officer, for Paxton's triumph had
temporarily placed the professional architects at a discount. Its glass
and iron dome raised on a brick drum, with a terracotta frieze of
the Triumph of the Arts surrounding it, was in scale and character
something new to London, but the terracotta cult which it popularized is associated with architectural ventures outside the period
of this book.

The Exhibition of 1862,[1] postponed from the year of the decade
on account of the Italian war, opened in the gloom of the Prince
Consort's recent death. It failed, as might perhaps be expected, to
recapture the enthusiasm created by its predecessor,[2] despite exhibits such as the majolica fountain by John Thomas, 36 feet high,
with St. George and the Dragon at the top, running perfumed
water and surrounded by aspidistra-like plants on stone plinths
rising from the edge of the basin, the successor to Osler's 27 foot
crystal fountain in 1851. On the whole, however, the style of the
articles showed a marked decrease in flamboyancy.[3] In the carpets,
wallpapers and hangings it is clear that Owen Jones had not taught
in vain. The Axminster carpets and the new Scottish floor-cloths

[1] *The International Exhibition*: *Illustrated Catalogue of the British Division*, 2 vols.
(1862) with introductory concise history of the Exhibition by John Hollingshead:
T. P. Shaffner and W. Owen, *Illustrated Record of the Exhibition of 1862* (n.d.). See for
the exhibits Cassel's *Illustrated Exhibitor* (1862): for the Exhibition in general, *Journ.
of Royal Soc. of Arts*, x (1862).

[2] See for instance *Spectator*, 3 May 1862, and *What do you think of the Exhibition?*
(extracts from the leading journals, ed. by R. Kemp).

[3] 'As a general rule curves are too freely used in much of our furniture, although
certainly not to the same extent as was done thirty years ago, and the tendency of the
present revival of Gothic and Queen Anne furniture will aid to keep them in check.'
Artistic Homes or How to Furnish with Taste: Sylvia's Home Help Series (n.d. but probably
1881), 11.

from Kirkcaldy were severely stylized in design and the makers of
the kamptulicon, or elastic floor-cloth, proudly boasted that 'most
of the designs are of a purely architectural character'.[1] One Wilton
carpet showed a sad lapse into 'the shaded style', with its musical
instruments drawn in naturalistic relief, but this was a rare instance
(Fig. 12). In furniture the influence of Pugin seemed the main

FIG. 12. *Wilton carpet, Louis XVI style*

heritage from 1851. Straight lines and pointed gables were replacing the swelling curves, and a Gothic bookcase, designed by
R. Norman Shaw (a strange introduction to the dominant architectural personality of the closing years of the century), showed
some of the brusque originality of Butterfield (Pl. 80 *b*). Charles
Eastlake's Gothic designs, in his influential *Hints on Household Taste*
(1868), develop this manner with a coarser, more functional
emphasis on the actual carpentry. To Eastlake's book also was due
the growing cult of the overmantel, 'a set of narrow shelves for
specimens of old china, etc. . . . A little museum may thus be
formed, and remain a source of lasting pleasure to its possessors,
seeing that "a thing of beauty is a joy for ever".' Eastlake needless to say did not envisage the long decadence that was to attend
upon his precepts, though his own mantelpiece shelves are rather

[1] *Illustrated Catalogue* i, sect. iii. 52. See C. Dresser, *Development of Ornamental Art
in the International Exhibition* (1862); and Pevsner in *Arch. Rev.* lxxxi (1937), 183.

forebodingly inscribed with the text that all is vanity.[1] The art of salesmanship and the acquisitive instinct were advancing side by side: a profusion of objects scattered about the room was indicative of taste and also, like the long nails of a mandarin, of ample domestic service. Furniture no longer followed a planned arrangement, but was thickly distributed about the centre of the room: the last quarter of the century was to see in popular household taste the climax of clutter, whatever austerities a Charles Eastlake or a William Morris might advocate.

One departure in 1862 from the pattern of 1851 was a display of British painting, 'the finest and most complete ever brought together'.[2] This was an attempt to repeat the great artistic sensation of the Art Treasures Exhibition at Manchester in 1857, seen by one million fifty-five thousand people and furnished by 'hundreds of cautious collectors'.[3] Manchester owed much to its organizer and cataloguer, George Scharff, the first secretary of the National Portrait Gallery, whose comments on the Exhibition in the *Manchester Guardian* contain a most discriminating account of the growth and change of interest in Italian art in England in the nineteenth century.[4] The pictures were exhibited at Manchester under their owners' attributions, but the excellent light in which they were hung proved a severe test. 'Many a painting that issued forth from the gloomy apartment of a baronial mansion, will go back with a very different character.' In the Exhibition of 1862 the foreign paintings were mainly from the nineteenth century and by living artists: the English gallery was, however, even more ambitious than that at Old Trafford, and its catalogue reads like a summary of nineteenth-century achievement. In both exhibitions a new group of artists attracted considerable attention. 'The life of our Art in this century', wrote Francis Turner Palgrave, 'lies almost entirely in its Schools of Landscape and Incident: both practically inventions of the last sixty years . . . and a more serious style of Incident has lately become common.' This serious style

---

[1] *Hints on Household Taste*, 120.   [2] Cassel's *Exhibitor*, 162.

[3] J. Hollingshead, 'Concise History', *Illustrated Catalogue* (1862), 38.

[4] These articles are reprinted in *A Handbook to the Paintings by Ancient Masters* by G.S. (1857).

was practised by the Pre-Raphaelites, and to Palgrave two names dominate the British gallery: Turner, 'the Shakespeare of another and a hardly less splendid poetical kingdom', and Holman Hunt 'amongst the very small band of high Imaginative Masters who have fully realised their powers'.[1]

[1] *Handbook to the Fine Art Collections in the International Exhibition* (1862), 24, 29, 59.

XI

THE PRE-RAPHAELITES

AS the year of the Great Exhibition drew to a close, on 19 December 1851, Turner died. Toothless, too dependent on stimulants, preserving his privacy and his personal inclinations under an assumed name in a lodging house at Chiswick, 'Old Time', as he himself put it, had 'made sad work' of him. Even Ruskin was estranged and wrote 'closing our intercourse'.[1] His two last entries in the Academy Catalogue (1850), reversions to the tale of Troy that had always had deep meanings for him, were ominously entitled *The Visit to the Tomb* and *The Departure of the Fleet*. In the dirt and dinginess of the Queen Anne Street house, the Academicians assembled for the funeral procession and found the pictures flapping from their frames, covered with fallen plaster. He left behind him an ill-drawn will with many codicils, which led to much litigation;[2] in the end, as he had wished, his paintings and drawings passed to the nation, but nothing came of his intentions to assist ageing and indigent artists. It was a muddled, sordid end to his splendid, imaginative genius. Two years earlier, on 13 November 1849, another painter had died, whose death also marks the passing of an epoch, William Etty. The Society of Arts had that same year arranged a collective exhibition of his works. Edinburgh sent his five great canvases, *The Combat*, *Benaiah*, and the three *Judiths*, but attention was largely concentrated on his new trilogy of *Joan of Arc*, completed in 1847. Ten years earlier he had essayed another huge canvas. *Ulysses and the Sirens* (Manchester: 9 ft. 9 in. by 14 ft. 6 in.), where the drawing falters considerably and the bound Ulysses is a Fuselian contortion of muscles, without any of Fuseli's cunning mystery; to it he gave the alternative title, *The Wages of Sin are Death*. The piety that made him a

---

[1] *Diaries of John Ruskin*, ed. Joan Evans and J. H. Whitehouse, ii (1958), 489.

[2] For the funeral see F. M. Redgrave, *Richard Redgrave* (1891), 81: for the will A. J. Finberg, *J. M. W. Turner* (1939), chap. xxxvii.

congenial friend to Pugin led him in the end to the theme of St. Joan. A little incongruously, the Hon. Mrs. Norton, whose friendship with Lord Melbourne had led to a celebrated divorce case, was the model for Joan. The pictures, though they aroused much comment at the time, have disappeared, and are only known by a rough woodcut of *Joan at the Stake*.[1] Etty's health, however, was failing and probably the trilogy would add little to his reputation. One evening, as he was toiling up the spiral staircase to the Academy drawing schools, he was overtaken by a hurrying young man. Etty signed to him to pass: 'Go, I insist. Your time is more precious than mine.' The young man was William Holman Hunt.[2]

Born in Cheapside, he was the son of a warehouse manager and had been placed in an office by his father, but at the age of sixteen had broken away and settled down to study painting, keeping himself as best he could by any odd job of brush-work that could earn a few shillings. Already he was practising sketching out of doors, protesting that the grass and foliage were green not yellow. Thorough and exact by nature, he refused to take anything on trust, and he found in the gifted boy John Everett Millais, his fellow student in the Academy schools, an enthusiastic response to his views. Revolt was in the air. On 10 April 1848 the two boys, Hunt twenty and Millais nineteen, went to Kennington Common to the great Chartist meeting, which was alarming all London, so that the Queen withdrew to Osborne, members of the aristocracy

[1] D. Farr, *William Etty* (1958), 134.

[2] W. Holman Hunt, *Pre-Raphaelitism and the Pre-Raphaelite Brotherhood*, 2 vols. (1905) i. 93. This remarkable book is the essential account of the Pre-Raphaelite movement, but it states 'the myth' as held by Hunt, and requires some modifications with regard to the part played by Rossetti. There is a large literature on and around the movement. See J. G. Millais, *The Life and Letters of Sir John Everett Millais*, 2 vols. (1899); P. Bate, *The English Pre-Raphaelite Painters, their Associates and Successors* (1901); F. M. Hueffer, *The Pre-Raphaelite Brotherhood* (n.d.); William Gaunt, *The Pre-Raphaelite Tragedy* (1942); R. Ironside and J. Gere, *Pre-Raphaelite Painters* (1948); O. von Schleintz, *William Holman Hunt* (Leipzig, 1907); A. G. Gissing, *William Holman Hunt* (1936); A. L. Baldry, *Sir John Everett Millais* (1899): on Rossetti, see H. C. Marillier, *Dante Gabriel Rossetti* (1899); F. G. Stephens, *Dante Gabriel Rossetti* (1908: reprinted from *Portfolio Monographs*, 1894); O. Doughty, *A Victorian Romantic* (with bibliography: 1949). Helen Rossetti Angeli in *Dante Gabriel Rossetti: His Friends and Enemies* (1949) discusses recent literature, much of it controversial in tone. Letters and diaries have been published in a series of volumes by W. M. Rossetti.

brought up their gamekeepers from the country, and the duke of
Wellington disposed soldiers and guns to control the approaches
to the Houses of Parliament. Hunt and Millais were all for revolution in their own line of business. The greatest names in the past,
the most popular figures of the present were analysed and criticized. Traditional poses, the academic repertory of grouping and
gesture, the 'S' ground plan, theories of light and shade, the
accepted ranges of colour, the triviality of many of the subjects
then popular were the objects of their criticisms. At the Academy
of 1848 Hunt's *The Flight of Madeline and Porphyro during the
drunkenness attending the revelry* (Pl. 85 *a*) is a real attempt to interpret
the scene and find actions appropriate to the story even if the
actions are ungainly; there is also, as in the foreshortening of the
'porter in uneasy sprawl', a determination to shirk no problems
dictated by the theme, however technically difficult they might be.
To Hunt the subject illustrated 'the sacredness of honest responsible
love and the weakness of proud intemperance'; it was that is to
say a serious subject with a message, suitable to the high calling of
art. It is perhaps more important that it was from a poem by Keats.
The Academies of the forties were full of illustrations drawn from
literature, but Hunt did not think that Keats had ever before
provided a subject; he was then little known; his works had not
been reprinted till Moxon's edition of 1846 and Hunt had found
a volume of his poems for 4*d.* on a second-hand stall. Keats and
Tennyson are the voices which stimulated the lyrical excitement
of early Pre-Raphaelite painting, a stimulus eagerly accepted with
no reservations as to the danger of literary content for visual art.

Admiration for Keats and for Hunt's picture brought a new
friend, Dante Gabriel Rossetti. He had been a pupil of Ford Madox
Brown, but had been discouraged by Brown's insistence on
drawing still-life objects; he was anxious now to work with Hunt
and he soon formed a third in the trio, though with him there was
never the close friendship and understanding that existed between
Hunt and Millais. Rossetti brought to their conference a restless,
romantic imagination, which added to Hunt's reforming ardour
something of the mystery of continental conspiracy and secret
societies; they decided to join themselves into a brotherhood, to

which four other foundation members were admitted, Woolner the sculptor, W. M. Rossetti and F. G. Stephens,[1] both of whom were to make their mark as critics rather than painters, and James Collinson, brought in on a wave of enthusiasm by Rossetti. The name Pre-Raphaelite[2] was decided on one evening when they had been looking through a volume of Lasinio's engravings of the frescoes in the Campo Santo at Pisa, published in 1828. It is hard for us today to imagine ourselves back into the general state of knowledge of the arts a hundred years ago. Only those who could travel abroad could hope to see the great works of European painting; the National Gallery was still but a small collection with hardly any examples of quattrocento art. There were great private collections in England, but they were not easy of access, and armies of servants expected handsome gratuities from the visitors, who were hurried through heavily curtained rooms with neither time nor light for seeing anything. For reproductions there were engravings, outline drawings, and copies in oil or water-colour of the better known works, copies in which later stylistic trends were often apparent. England had however one unique advantage, the Raphael cartoons at Hampton Court, the greatest Italian work outside Italy and a powerful influence on English historical painting; to question the supremacy of Raphael in England of all countries was an act of presumptuous temerity; and the term 'Pre-Raphaelite', whatever exact meaning the Brotherhood gave to it, might well seem an insolent challenge. Actually they do not seem to have given very close thought to its content. The aims of the movement were summarized by Hunt as (1) to have genuine ideas to express, (2) to study directly from nature, disregarding all arbitrary rules, (3) to envisage events as they must have happened rather than as the rules of design required:[3] their particular dislikes in 'the frivolous art of the day' were 'Monkeyana ideas, Books of Beauty, Chorister Boys, whose forms were those of melted wax with drapery of no tangible texture'. These were respectively

[1] See Basil Taylor, 'F. G. Stephens and the P.R.B.', *Arch. Rev.* civ (1948), 171.

[2] This is how Hunt writes it: W. M. Rossetti always wrote 'Praeraphaelite'.

[3] This is undoubtedly based on Ruskin, whose first two volumes of *Modern Painters* had appeared in 1843 and 1846: Hunt borrowed a copy (oddly enough, through a friend, from Cardinal Wiseman) and felt it was 'written expressly for him'.

Landseer's animals aping men, the luscious beauties engraved in
The Keepsake (1841–9), and popular High Church paintings such
as Henry Barraud's choristers entitled *We praise thee, O Lord*.[1]
Historical painting was indeed at a low ebb, as the competitions
for the cartoons had shown. Alfred Elmore, whose *Rienzi in the
Forum*[2] made some stir in 1844, was judiciously modifying the
Munich and Düsseldorf patterns to suit English tastes: F. R. Pickersgill was painting *Samson Betrayed* (Manchester: 1850) with reminiscences of Etty's pliant women, but a low-toned colour scheme that
was his own: John Cross, in the same exhibition, represented the
Burial of the two Sons of Edward IV in the Tower with the careful
narrative gestures of the French school, but Cross was already
nearing his early death.[3] Augustus Egg had won Associateship of
the Academy in 1848, with pleasantly handled literary or historical
scenes, less crowded than those of E. M. Ward, less empty than
those of C. W. Cope, but was happier with contemporary incidents
and at times, as in his *Travelling Companions* (Birmingham), could
treat them with real decorative effect. Alfred Rankley in 1846 had
produced one more version of *Edith finding the Body of Harold*
(untraced), but was turning to homelier subjects: his *Contentment*
(R.A. 1850) shows a young man in cap and gown ill at ease in
his family's simple cottage, an early treatment of this problem.[4]
Theodor von Holst won in 1841 the award at the British Institution,
one of the last given, for his huge *Raising of Jairus's Daughter*
(138×88 in.: untraced). To Rossetti, von Holst was 'that great
painter', and his mannerist pieces form a link between Fuseli, who
clearly much influenced him, and some aspects of Rossetti's art,
but death cut short his promise and today his oil paintings have

[1] Painted 1849: Christie's, 2 Nov. 1956. Reproduced G. M. Young, *Early Victorian
England* (1934), ii. 152. See W. M. Rossetti, *Praeraphaelite Diaries and Letters* (1860),
234. Thomas Landseer, Edwin's elder brother, published a volume of etchings entitled
Monkeyana in 1827.

[2] *I.L.N.* iv (1844), 373. Lytton's novel *Rienzi* had appeared in 1835 and presumably
created the popularity of the subject: Holman Hunt's painting (see below) has a
quotation from Lytton in the R.A. catalogue: for Elmore see *Art Journ.* iii (1857),
113.

[3] *I.L.N.* xvi (1850), 396; the *Samson* and the *Burial* are both reproduced.

[4] Ibid. The anecdotal subject was gaining fresh popularity in the colour prints of
George Baxter and of Le Blond & Co.

mostly disappeared and he is only known by a few drawings (Pl. 19 *b*).[1] Maclise in 1847 had made a new departure with his *Noah's Sacrifice* (Pl. 84 *b*).[2] Finely posed, spacious, uncrowded, it is painted in light colours, with flat, broad planes, which recall the German Nazarenes. This is the 'early Christian' style that Dyce also was following. Rossetti's painting of the *Girlhood of Mary Virgin*, the earliest picture to be exhibited with the initials P.R.B., at the Free Exhibition, Hyde Park Gallery, in 1849, has something of this flatness and light colours; Hunt had thought it Overbeckian, and he and Millais were irritated that Rossetti sent it without their knowledge to the Free Exhibition, which opened before the Academy. The public from the first associated the mysterious initials with medievalism and the German school, though Hunt strenuously denied it, and the angular solidity of his and Millais's painting in the Academy of 1849 even more convincingly rebutted the suggestion.

Hunt's *Rienzi vowing to obtain justice for the death of his young brother* (R.A. 1849) (coll. Mrs. E. M. Clarke) is hard to judge. It has the expressive faces (Millais and Rossetti both figure in it), the carefully studied drama, the exalted subject, that were Hunt's receipt for picture making; but its purchaser varnished it with some unsuitable resinous fluid, and forty years later Hunt largely re-painted it. The original verve is gone. Millais's painting, *Lorenzo and Isabella* (Pl. 86 *b*), is on the other hand in excellent condition. He and Hunt were both painting on a wet white ground, and gaining thereby a luminous brilliance of colour that has proved very lasting. From the beginning of his career Hunt was deeply interested in the materials of his art, the seasoning of panels, the weave of canvas, and the purity of paints.[3] At a time when devotion to bitumen and the growing commercialization of paints were beginning to take a heavy toll, the example was a valuable one.

[1] W. M. Rossetti, *Dante Gabriel Rossetti, Family Letters* (1895), i. 117: see also W. Bell Scott, *Autobiographical Notes* (1892), i. 162: some of his paintings may pass as Fuseli's: one, *Faust in his Study* (R.A. 1834), was in Christie's, no. 136, 6 Apr. 1955.

[2] Turner painted the rainbow into it on varnishing day: A. J. Finberg, *Turner* (1939), 416.

[3] See his lecture on 'The Present System of obtaining Materials in use by Artist Painters' in *Journ. of Royal Soc. of Arts* (1880).

Today, on going into a gallery of Pre-Raphaelite paintings, the immediate impression is the brightness of the colours, partially due to the juxtaposition of vivid patches, but also to the remarkable conservation of their original appearance.

For a boy of twenty Millais's *Isabella* is a surprising *tour de force*: the subject is from Keats and the original sketch for it was done as part of a scheme for illustrating the poem with etchings by Hunt and himself. Hunt had already done a drawing that is closely linked with Millais's picture: the dog rubbing itself against the leg of Lorenzo's desk is the one kicked by the brother in the painting; there are the same carefully awkward poses, such as Lorenzo's twisted legs, and the same daring problems in perspective.[1] Hunt's design, however, could never have achieved the unity and intensity of that of Millais; this extraordinary rhythm of heads in profile, slow and heavy on the left, quick and rippling on the right till it comes to rest in the wide circular movement of the lovers bent in on one another.

All three pictures, particularly Rossetti's, received considerable and on the whole friendly notice, though the *Athenaeum* complained of foreign and archaic mannerisms, the absence of shadow and 'the utter want of rationality' in the figure with the 'extended and unwieldy legs'. It was not long, however, before criticism took a sharper turn, and at the Academy of the following year, 1850, it broke in full violence. Shortly before the exhibition opened the meaning of the initials P.R.B., which had appeared on all three paintings, was discovered, probably through an unguarded disclosure by Rossetti, and published by the press. The *Illustrated London News* in its gossip column, 'Town Talk and Table Talk', explained 'the hieroglyphics in question'. 'To this league belong the ingenious gentlemen who profess themselves practitioners of "Early Christian Art" and who, setting aside the medieval schools of Italy, the Raffaelles, Guidos, and Titians, and all such small beer daubers—devote their energies to the reproductions of saints

---

[1] Reproduced Hunt, *Pre-Raphaelitism*, i. 143. Hunt returned to the subject in his *Isabella and the Pot of Basil* (1867: Newcastle): in that same year Rossetti did an elaborate and morbid drawing of Isabella kissing her lover's severed head (Sotheby's, 15.5.57, No. 13).

squeezed out perfectly flat . . . their appearance being further improved by their limbs being stuck akimbo, so as to produce a most interesting series of angles and finely-developed elbows.'[1] This is a fine derangement of epithets. Early Christian and flatness applies to the Nazarenes, and to some of the work of Dyce and Maclise; but to the general public the Pre-Raphaelite pictures undoubtedly did appear flat, because they lacked the deep shadows, the elaborate chiaroscuro which was so much admired. Rossetti had again exhibited his picture *The Annunciation* at another gallery: it is Pre-Raphaelite in its high tones and its unusual posing. Hunt showed at the Academy his *Christians escaping from persecuting Druids* (Oxford) which the *Athenaeum* in a severe article admitted had 'a sense of novelty in its arrangement'; but it was for Millais's 'pictorial blasphemy' that the full blast was reserved. In the catalogue the picture had no title, only the quotation from Zechariah xiii. 6, 'And one shall say unto him, What are these wounds in thine hands? Then he shall answer, Those with which I was wounded in the house of my friends.' There were ambiguities, probably more muddled than willed, in the application of these words to the scene of Christ in the carpenter's shop. This was a subject which had recently been treated, in the Academy of 1847, by J. R. Herbert, *Our Saviour, subject to his parents at Nazareth* (Pl. 87). Herbert was, under the influence of Pugin, a convert to Roman Catholicism and had turned from *Keepsake* scenes to religious, Overbeckian painting. 'Puginesque conventionalities', one critic termed his picture,[2] but that was mild condemnation compared to the outcry that awaited Millais's realism, his blistered hands and worn faces. Charles Dickens's famous leading article in his new periodical *Household Words*[3] has been repeatedly quoted: 'the kneeling woman, so horrible in her ugliness . . . that she would stand out as a Monster in the vilest cabaret in France . . . the snuffy old woman . . . waiting at the counter to be served with an ounce of her favourite mixture . . . the dirty drunkards in a high state of

---

[1] *I.L.N.* xvi (1850), 306: for comment on influence of *I.L.N.* woodcuts see A. P. Oppé in *Early Victorian England* (ed. G. M. Young, 1934), ii. 162.
[2] *Fine Arts Journ.* i (1847), 450.
[3] 'Old Lamps for New Ones', *Household Words*, i (1850), 265.

varicose veins'. It is surprising enough to find Dickens so hot against realism, but this was realism in sacred places, and the article as a whole is not as bitter as quotations from it, the juicier quotations, make it sound. What outraged Dickens was the name Pre-Raphaelite: it was an attack on progress: Raphael had taught that Beauty was an indispensable element of art, 'a delusion in which artists have continued until this present nineteenth century, when it was reserved for some bold aspirants to "put it down" ': there were soon to be Pre-Newtonian and Pre-Harveian brotherhoods and the P.G.A.P.C.B. or Pre-Gower and Pre-Chaucer Brother-hood 'for the restoration of the ancient style of spelling and the weeding out from all libraries of a person of loose character named Shakespeare'.

For the moment things looked badly for the Brotherhood: Rossetti, sensitive to all the hubbub, ceased to exhibit, and busied himself with water-colours, a medium whose rapidity better suited his impatient genius, and in which he developed a technique of strong, deep washes and intricately patterned designs to create a dream-world of moody, medieval romance entirely remote from the original Pre-Raphaelite concepts. Defence, however, was at hand, as extreme in some of its statements as had been the attack. The hanging committee of 1851, with considerable courage, accepted another group of Pre-Raphaelite pictures: Hunt's *Valentine rescuing Sylvia from Proteus* (Birmingham), Millais's *Return of the Dove to the Ark* (Oxford), *Mariana* (coll. Sir Roger Makins), the first of their Tennysonian subjects, and *The Woodman's Daughter* (Guildhall), and Charles Collins's *Convent Thoughts* (Pl. 89 *a*). The attacks began again in the press. The most popular and praised picture of the year, which Queen Victoria wanted to buy but yielded her claim to an earlier applicant, 'a Lancashire manu-facturer of taste and liberality', was E. M. Ward's *Royal Family of France in the Prison of the Temple* (Pl. 64 *b*), a piece of anecdotal history correctly set in light and shade. Then on 13 and 30 May Ruskin fulminated: letters appeared in *The Times* signed 'The Author of Modern Painters': he admitted he had no sympathy for their Tractarian views (*The Carpenter's Shop* had been linked, surprisingly, with Puseyism; Collinson was a Roman convert; the

Coombes at Oxford, long patrons of the Brotherhood, were closely associated with the Oxford Movement);[1] but Ruskin could put up with the nun in Collins's painting because he had never seen such botanically exact drawing of the flowers: he pointed out that the young artists were copying nature not the quattrocento, that their perspective was admirable and that they were 'laying in our England the foundations of a school of art nobler than the world has seen for three hundred years'.[2]

The letter marks a turning-point in the public's attitude: there was still considerable hostile criticism, but the first shock of the bright colours and bold attitudes was over.[3] In the following year Millais's two pictures, *A Huguenot refusing to shield himself from danger by wearing the Roman Catholic badge* (coll. Huntington Hartford, New York) and *Ophelia*, finally won the day. Both enjoyed great popularity, and the former begins a series of pictures of lovers in situations of dramatic tension that had an easy appeal. Then in 1856 Millais exhibited two pictures which in their depth of feeling, in their merging of scene, colour, emotion into a unity, have a unique place in British art: *The Blind Girl* and *Autumn Leaves*. In the former (Birmingham) the subject is a sentimental one: the blind girl, sitting in the brilliant sunshine, while a butterfly alights on her shawl and her younger sister turns to look at the rainbow; but the strong monumental design, the sense of space in the background, brings the narrative detail under control, and the effect is one of atmosphere not of cumulated incidents (Pl. 92 *b*). *Autumn Leaves* (Manchester) has hardly any narrative content at all: it depends largely on its strange colours, purple and brown garments, russet leaves against the brilliant, clear colours of a Scotch east coast sunset. 'By much', said Ruskin, 'the most poetical work the painter has yet conceived, and also, as far as I know, the first instance existing of a perfectly painted twilight.'[4] They were

---

[1] See J. E. Alden, *The Pre-Raphaelites at Oxford* (Oxford, 1948), and V. S. S. Coles, *S. Barnabas', Oxford* (Oxford, 1919). Collins's garden was painted from that of the Clarendon Press.   [2] *Works*, xii. 319–27.

[3] Lady Trevelyan writing in 1852 was 'petrified at the hideousness and audacity' of *The Carpenter's Shop* but 'after a long study, one is so absorbed in its depth and earnestness, that one learns to forget all its offences'. *Selections from Literary and Artistic Remains*, ed. P. Wooster (1879), 147.   [4] *Works*, xiv. 66.

generous words: in April 1854 Ruskin's wife had left him; the marriage was annulled at the instance of her family and in July 1855 she married Millais. It had been a time of great stress for all parties; it is in the period of peace, the first year of his marriage, that Millais painted his two greatest pictures.

At the end of 1853 Hunt had left for Palestine, determined to follow out his principles of painting actuality, 'making conscience of locality',[1] by using the scenery and types of the Holy Land for his representation of scriptural themes. He left completed for the Academy of 1854 two pictures, one of which was finally to establish the standing of Pre-Raphaelitism in popular estimation. *The Light of the World* in engravings was to become one of the most widely known religious pictures and was profoundly to affect the Christian visual imagination.[2] Hunt spent long nights painting in an orchard by moonlight; the clustering weeds, the light of the lantern on the robe were given most painstaking study; Ruskin wrote a famous interpretation of all the symbolic details: the barred door, the ivy, the hovering bat, the fallen apples, the leaves sprouting from the crown of thorns (Pl. 88 *b*). It remains, particularly in small-scale reproduction, a somewhat uncomfortable picture, for all the admiration it has aroused. The face has a period sentimentality which has become distasteful through much imitation; the robe conveys little of the form beneath it and has little sense of texture in itself; but in the original, in the first version which hangs now in Keble College chapel, the painting, with its deep colours, its pervasive green moonlight broken by the reddish lamplight, has an unmistakable power. Hunt's other picture, which he thought of as a pendant to *The Light of the World*, was *The Awakening Conscience* (Pl. 88 *a*),[3] which was a scene from

[1] E. Young, *Pre-Raffaelitism or A Popular Enquiry into some newly-asserted Principles* (1857), 180.

[2] The later eighteenth century saw a revival in England of the painting of large religious scenes as altar pieces: Matthew Peters's *Annunciation* (1799) in Lincoln cathedral or Richard Westall's *Ecce Homo* at Langham Place are examples. *The Light of the World* popularized a new and Protestant type of religious art, didactic rather than emotional, for the aisle rather than the altar. The original sketch is in Manchester City Art Galleries: the largest version, in St. Paul's cathedral, was painted in the years 1899 to 1904.

[3] The title was changed to *The Awakened Conscience* when Hunt later softened the

contemporary life, supported in the catalogue by quotations from Isaiah and Ecclesiasticus. It shows a kept woman with her lover suddenly roused to thoughts of her home and early life by the words of '*Oft, in the Stilly Night*'—'Fond memory brings the light of other days around me.' It is a somewhat terrifying performance: the room is too distractingly ugly; it is too full of significant details, too dependent on the narrative they convey; it is a powerful chapter from a novel, but it oversteps the dangerous boundary between visual art and didactic literature.

It was inevitable that the Pre-Raphaelites should turn to contemporary subjects. They were thinking more seriously about the purpose of art than any other group at the time, and from a considered use of romanticism they passed to experiments with realism. In the first number of *The Germ*, the Pre-Raphaelite paper, there is an article by J. L. Tupper, 'The Subject in Art'. It is not a formal manifesto of the Brotherhood, but it must have had their general approval; it argued that the subjects of High Art should be 'objects which address and excite the activity of man's rational and benevolent powers' and that 'Fine art excites in proportion to the excitor influence of the objects'.[1] Tupper's list includes scenes from *good* plays, poems, &c., the repertory of the early P.R.B. pictures, but he uses the argument that the known and familiar are most likely to excite. Millais's *The Rescue* (1855) depended for much of its effect on the everyday nature of the peril represented, and is in striking contrast to the Fuselian sensationalism of the opening years of the century (Pl. 3). The most striking application of their methods to current themes came, however, from an artist who was never a member of the Brotherhood, though in close contact with them, Ford Madox Brown. Trained in Antwerp and Paris, his early paintings such as *The Execution of Mary, Queen of Scots* (1841: Whitworth Art Gallery, Manchester),[2] were traditionally

---

expression on the woman's face. The model was Annie Miller, who later (1859) was the cause of the breach between Hunt and Rossetti. See O. Doughty, *A Victorian Romantic* (1949), 259.

[1] i (1850), 17: *The Germ* ran to four numbers and then collapsed: see W. M. Rossetti, *Facsimile Reprint of The Germ* (1901).

[2] There is a problem over this picture: the Whitworth version differs from that

posed and lit, if already slightly pungent in characterization, but in 1851 he exhibited his large canvas of *Chaucer at the Court of Edward III* (Sydney) in which there were portraits of several of the Pre-Raphaelite group and many reflections of their theories, particularly in the slightly affected gaucherie of the attitudes. The following year he began on his painting *Work* (Pl. 86 *a*), which he was not to complete till 1863. The subject grew out of some studies of navvies working on road excavations in Hampstead: 'the British excavator . . . in the full swing of his activity . . . appeared to me . . . at least as worthy of the powers of an English painter as the fisherman of the Adriatic, the peasant of the Campagna, or the Neapolitan lazzarone'.[1] Three years earlier, in 1849, Courbet had painted his *Stonebreakers*, and in 1850 the uproar in Paris over the *Funeral at Ornans* had equalled that in England over *The Carpenter's Shop*. Whereas, however, Courbet concentrated on the action and rhythm of his road-menders, Brown piles up a whole treatise of social observation which requires several pages of explanation and smothers the original impetus. Far more effective was *The Last of England* (Birmingham) painted, with full Pre-Raphaelite rigours, between 1852 and 1855. The picture originated from the farewells to Woolner, the sculptor member of the Brotherhood, when he left for Australia. It has a harsh stridency of colour and a mass of significant detail, but it is held together by the bold simplicity of the main design and its admirable adaptation to the tondo shape. It has become a familiar and unforgettable image.

While their range of painted subjects were thus expanding, the Pre-Raphaelites were conquering a new field, that of book illustration.[2] The age of the steel engraving was passing and being replaced by that of engraving on wood. Thomas Bewick's cutting of the white lines into the block, that gives such atmospheric effect to the

reproduced in F. M. Hueffer, *Ford Madox Brown* (1896), being much more realistic, almost verging in the facial expressions on caricature.

[1] F. M. Hueffer, op. cit. 189.

[2] On this large and important subject, which can receive but summary treatment here, see Gleeson White, *English Illustration: 'The Sixties'* (1906); Forrest Reid, *Illustrators of the Sixties* (1928); H. Reitlinger, *From Hogarth to Kenne* (1938); H. Hubbard, *Some Victorian Draughtsmen* (1944).

small vignettes of his *British Birds* (1797–1804), had no immediate successors.[1] It was with the coming of the popular illustrated magazine that wood engraving, from which a greater number of satisfactory impressions could be taken, began to supersede the metal medium. Thomson's *Seasons*, that still powerful work, appeared in a new edition in 1842 with 'engraved illustrations from designs drawn on wood' by Redgrave, Horsley, Cope, Webster, Townsend, Frank Stone, J. P. Knight, Creswick, and others (Pl. 95 *b*). In 1841 appeared the first volume of *Punch*. John Leech[2] was drawing for it, with a thin wiry line and a flair for the grotesque, in the tradition of Cruikshank and a little also of Henry Alken, for the hunting field provided many of his humorous incidents. Richard Doyle designed the famous cover; John Tenniel, Charles Keene, George du Maurier became contributors. A year junior to *Punch*, the *Illustrated London News* also was soon employing a considerable group of artists, Henry Corbould and John Gilbert in particular. Here there was a demand for a wide range of subjects, many of them sensational and horrific; but speed and facility were required and the slick romanticism of Gilbert, seen at its best in his illustrations to Shakespeare, is far from the pondered reflections of the Brotherhood.[3]

In 1859 the editors of *Punch* published the first volume of *Once a Week, An illustrated miscellany of Literature, Art, Science and Popular Information*.[4] It aimed at presenting illustration on as serious a level as writing, and the first volume contained the opening of Charles Reade's *A Good Fight* (the first draft of *The Cloister and the Hearth*) illustrated by Charles Keene. It also had several engravings by Millais, including the striking *Plague of Elliant*, one of his most grim and powerful works. Two earlier books mark Pre-Raphaelite progress in illustration, William Allingham's *Music Master* (1855), with designs by Arthur Hughes, Millais and Rossetti, and Moxon's edition of Tennyson's *Poems* (1857), where Millais, Hunt and

  [1] M. Weekley, *Thomas Bewick* (1953).

  [2] W. P. Frith, *John Leech*, 2 vols. (1891).

  [3] The preface to the first volume of the *I.L.N.* states that 'Art—as now fostered, and redundant in the peculiar and facile department of wood engraving—has become the bride of literature.'

  [4] J. Pennell, 'Once a Week: a great art magazine', *Bibliographica*, iii (1897), 60.

Rossetti can be compared with the older generation, Maclise, Mulready, and Horsley. In *The Music Master* Rossetti's *Maids of Elfen-Mere* (Pl. 94 *a*) is admirably done; he himself thought it had been spoilt by Dalziel in the cutting, but at Oxford Burne-Jones and Morris 'pored over it continually'.[1] If in painting the Pre-Raphaelites sometimes overworked the detail, in line they were most capably selective. The great output demanded by the illustrated journals meant that much of the actual work on the blocks was carried out by commercial firms such as Messrs. Dalziel and Messrs. Swain. The particular genius of the designers of the sixties lay in their ability to present material that was technically appropriate for these large-scale methods. It was Millais who was to put engraving to the fullest use. Rossetti, temperamental and dilatory, quarrelled with the Dalziel brothers[2] and his engravings are few. In *Once a Week*, the *Cornhill*,[3] Willmott's *Poets of the Nineteenth Century*, above all his twelve 'Parables of Our Lord' in *Good Words*,[4] Millais produced a series of designs that in the flow and economy of the line and their directness of narrative have few equals in English art (Pl. 95 *a*). It is a curious phenomenon that these potent images were being created while he was painting *My First Sermon* (Guildhall), one of his most banal pieces of child sentimentality, singled out at the Academy dinner of 1863 by the archbishop of Canterbury as a touching example of how art fulfils its 'high and noble mission'.[5]

Round Millais in the pages of the periodicals and collected books of verse a group was now working that constituted 'The Golden Period of Illustration'. Frederick Sandys and Frederic Shields[6] were

---

[1] J. W. Mackail, *William Morris* (1899), i. 87.

[2] See Forrest Reid, op. cit. 41; and G. and E. Dalziel, *The Brothers Dalziel. A Record of Fifty Years Work* (1901), 86.

[3] See *The Cornhill Gallery of Engravings from Drawings on Wood* (1865) containing Millais's illustrations to *Framley Parsonage* and *The Small House at Alington*.

[4] *Illustrations to The Parables*, by T. Guthrie (1863).

[5] J. G. Millais, *Life and Letters*, i. 378.

[6] Esther Wood, 'The Art of Frederick Sandys', Winter Number of *The Artist* (1896): *Reproductions of Woodcuts by F. Sandys 1860–1866*, ed. by and published for Mary Sandys (n.d.). E. Mills, *Life and Letters of Frederic Shields* (1912): the *Plague* woodcuts were published in *Laurie's Shilling Entertainment Library* and are exceedingly rare: the original drawings for them are in the Manchester Art Gallery.

much under the influence of Rossetti, though Shields's great series of designs for Defoe's *Journal of the Plague* (1863) have roots in the tradition of Fuseli and David Scott. A. B. Houghton, Frederick Walker, and G. J. Pinwell were more influenced by Millais. All three died young, in the same year, 1875, Houghton being thirty-nine, Walker thirty-five, and Pinwell thirty-three.[1] It was a sad and long felt deprivation to English art. Walker enjoyed also considerable repute as a painter, and his *Harbour of Refuge* (1872) combines the representational skill and the easy sentiment to which Millais had by then fallen, dragging much of English art with him. Or so it seems today. G. E. Street owned one of Walker's paintings, *The Old Gate* (1869). 'It was', his son writes, 'his most cherished possession, and I think it added permanently and distinctly to his sense of well being and happiness.'[2]

In 1862 two engravings appeared in *Good Words*, four in *Once a Week*, by a young artist, then studying in Paris, James McNeill Whistler. In the following year his *White Girl*[3] was to be the sensation of the Salon des Refusés, even with Manet's *Déjeuner sur l'herbe* as its rival. A new, powerful and controversial artist was growing up to maturity, but his art and his quarrels belong to the last quarter of the century. Another artist, working for *Cornhill*, was of a very different type. The young Frederic Leighton[4] had made a name for himself in 1855, when the Queen had purchased his *Cimabue's Madonna carried in procession through the streets of Florence*, a large pastiche of quattrocento motifs. Now in the sixties he was illustrating, with surprising force, the serial issues of George Eliot's *Romola* (Pl. 94 b). Soon, however, classical imaginings would take him from Renaissance Italy, and he and Edward Poynter, whose *Faithful unto Death* (Liverpool) made a great stir in 1867, were joining forces with Alma-Tadema to banish the

[1] For Walker see monographs by C. Phillips (1897) and C. Black (n.d.): for Houghton, L. Houseman, 'A forgotten Book-illustrator', *Bibliographica*, i (1895).

[2] *Memoirs*, 39; the painting is now in the Tate Gallery.

[3] Reproduced E. L. Cary, *Works of J. McN. Whistler* (New York, 1907). See E. R. and J. Pennell, *Life of J. McN. Whistler*, 2 vols. (1908): James Laver, *Whistler* (1930).

[4] Mrs. Russell Barrington, *Life and Letters of Lord Leighton*, 2 vols. (1906).

special Pre-Raphaelite blend of romance and realism from their polished, well-swept marble halls.[1]

A commission from *Good Words* reopened the Scottish invasion of London. In 1862 John Pettie came from Edinburgh to London, and with him came William Orchardson. Both were pupils of Robert Scott Lauder, a great teacher, whose portrait of David Scott (S.N.P.G.) is one of the most moving documents of late mid-century romanticism. In his pupils the romantic sense of horror and awe disappears, and their story telling, even if in historical trappings, is of the popular, anecdotal type. They are close in mood to their English contemporaries in the sixties, the St. John's Wood clique as they were called, a group led by Philip Calderon, Frederic Leighton, G. A. Storey, and W. F. Yeames,[2] who felt the Pre-Raphaelite influence, but soon softened its force and asperities; if sometimes morbid, as in Yeames's *Exorcising* (1867: V. and A.), a scene of flagellation, they were never terrible. When in 1857 the horrors of Delhi and Cawnpore were brought home to England by gruesome woodcuts and ghastly, not always verified, details, both of the massacres and the executions that followed,[3] serious art responded, not with some new *Massacre of Scio*, but with Frederick Goodall's *Relief of Lucknow* (Sheffield), where the Scottish lass, Jessie, in the hard-pressed entrenchment, hears the distant sound of the pipes, a triumph of anecdote over agony. Noel Paton's *In Memoriam* showed, indeed, sepoys advancing on hapless English women, but after its Academy exhibition the sepoys were painted out, and rescuing Highlanders substituted.[4] Edward Armitage essayed in his *Retribution* (Pl. 90 c) for Leeds Town Hall the allegorical monumentality of earlier times, but there is something almost grotesque, an all too apparent

---

[1] See W. Gaunt, *Victorian Olympus* (1952); Cosmo Monkhouse, 'Lord Leighton', *Scribner's Mag.* xix (1896), 399.

[2] See M. H. Stephen Smith, *Art and Anecdote* (n.d.). Another Scotsman, John Phillip, was exhibiting his scenes of Spanish life, pictorial rather than narrative, in London in the fifties and sixties: the *Spanish Contrabandistas* (1858: Royal coll.) has strong echoes of Wilkie; *La Gloria* (1864: Edinburgh) has a more individual brilliance of colour and movement.

[3] See *A Narrative of the Indian Revolt* illustrated with nearly two hundred engravings (1858).   [4] E. Chesneau, *English School of Painting* (1885), 208: untraced.

lack of conviction, in his battle between a muscular Justice and a
ferocious tiger. Passions and inspiration were dwindling and the
Pre-Raphaelites had failed to re-vivify them, despite the disciples
who now claimed their part in the movement: William Burton,
Arthur Hughes, Walter Deverell (early dead in 1854), Thomas
Seddon who went to Syria with Hunt and died on a second visit
there in 1856, R. B. Martineau, John Brett, H. Wallis, W. L.
Windus.[1] Between 1858 and 1862 these and others, amongst them
Burne-Jones, Morris, Swinburne, and the architects Burges, Street,
Webb, and Woodward, met in the Hogarth Club, with F. G.
Stephens as secretary. Then it too dissolved, and none of these
painters kept his early promise.

All important movements in the visual arts are accompanied by
theorizing, implicit or explicit, about the act of sight. Hunt and
Millais sought behind the academic tradition the actual colours of
nature; this was what they were supremely interested in; they
believed also that it was impossible to paint anything without
studying it carefully; this meant that the time factor in their
vision was a lengthy one; the whole subject was thoroughly
examined and every point in it brought into focus. The future was
to lie with a quite different moment of sight, the impression, a
future that was to be instructed in many ways by photography, an
invention whose impact in 1849 had been barely felt. In his second
course of Slade lectures in 1884, Ruskin, speaking of Hunt's
Strayed Sheep (Pl. 85 *b*), painted in 1853, said of it: 'It showed . . .
the absolutely faithful balances of colour and shade by which
actual sunshine might be transposed into a key in which the
harmonies possible with material pigments should yet produce the
same impressions upon the mind which were caused by the light
itself.'[2] To us today the hard clear outlines of Hunt's cliffs, even
though the decrease in sharpness with distance is carefully mastered,
and the almost harsh emphasis on form to the exclusion of glim-
mering surfaces seem unreal; we wonder how these men could
have been so blind to much that Constable could have taught

---

[1] The Academy of 1856 was the great year for the disciples, containing Burton's
Cavalier and Puritan (Guildhall), Windus's *Burd Helen* (Liverpool), and Wallis's *Death
of Chatterton*.   [2] *Works*, xxxiii. 272.

them: but in their day they broke a mannered tradition, and something survives of the vitality with which they did it. Neither Hunt nor Millais believed that this registration of detail was an essential feature of high art; both believed it a necessary phase.

Others were tending towards these precise renderings. John Frederick Lewis[1] in 1850 returned from ten years oriental seclusion in Cairo and became the chief purveyor of the visual claims of the Levant. In oils and water-colours he essayed, to the admiration of Ruskin, an analysis of colour in brilliant sunshine, every detail clear and sharp. *In the Bey's Garden* (1865) (Pl. 89 *b*) has the same concentration as Charles Collins's *Convent Thoughts* and shares in a somewhat similar sensual appraisement. In comparison much of Hunt and Millais is broadly painted, the row of poplars in the *Hireling Shepherd*[2] or the sloping meadow in the *Blind Girl*. These, however, were backgrounds painted out of doors to figures posed in the studio. Sticklers for accuracy in costume, demanding faces of character largely chosen from among their friends, the Pre-Raphaelites could never have grouped their historical incidents in the open countryside, and figures and backgrounds do not always coalesce. The Impressionists seized the fleeting moods of landscape, not pondered narrative scenes. Millais by the mid-fifties was advocating 'breadth', but it was coming to mean with him slacker, speedier productivity. 'His battle cry', Swinburne wrote, 'is "Philistia, be thou glad of me".'[3] His facile narrative gift led him into trivial and easily popular sentiment; his pictures though not memorable were easily remembered.

The term Pre-Raphaelite, despite and largely because of Ruskin, remained an ambiguous one. He had first of all to reconcile it with his great passion for Turner, and reconcile it he did. Turner was Pre-Raphaelite in the sincerity with which he rendered what he saw, but he saw visions withheld from other men: this is an

[1] Hugh Stokes in *Walker's Quarterly*, xxviii (1920): for Lewis's reaction to Pre-Raphaelitism see Hunt, op. cit. i. 270. A different but equally detailed vision of the East can be seen in the paintings of Richard Dadd, who, as an insane parricide, spent forty-four years in Bethlem and Broadmoor.   [2] Manchester: R.A. 1852.

[3] *Notes on the Royal Academy Exhibition, 1868*, by Wm. M. Rossetti and Algernon C. Swinburne. See also P. G. Hamerton, 'The Re-action from Pre-Raphaelitism', *The Fine Arts*, ii (1864), 255.

argument that would make the Impressionists Pre-Raphaelite also, and no doubt in that luxuriant and elusive mind, where inconsistency could always be stayed by eloquence, Ruskin could have done that also. More pertinent and as difficult, it had to include Rossetti: more, it had to include Rossetti as having 'total and, I believe, earliest, originality in the sternly materialistic, though deeply reverent, veracity, with which alone, of all schools of painters, this brotherhood of Englishmen has conceived the circumstances of the life of Christ'.[1] There was in fact a tiresome and prolonged battle as to Rossetti's rightful place in the foundation of the society; and in later years Hunt resented it and struck back with some force. Rossetti himself was in no doubt on the matter; in 1862 he wrote to the French art historian, Chesneau, that the qualities of realism, emotional but extremely minute in detail, which are the mark of the Pre-Raphaelite style, are found chiefly in all the pictures of Holman Hunt, in the greater part of those of Madox Brown, in some pieces of Hughes and in the admirable work of Millais's youth. 'C'est la camaraderie, plûtot que la collaboration réelle du style, qui a uni mon nom aux leurs dans les jours d'enthusiasme d'il y a vingt ans.'[2] This is clear and accurate. Rossetti was a great influence in English art and letters, with disciples of his own. Arthur Hughes, Val Prinsep, William Morris, and Edward Burne-Jones had in 1858 busied themselves under his direction frescoing the roof of the library in Benjamin Woodward's new polychrome building for the Oxford Union.[3] The paintings, surviving today in a blurred condition, can never have been satisfactory, and the episode is little more than a venture at undergraduate level, but it marks a new line of departure. Burne-Jones's strange blend of medievalism and classicism, dreamy, elegant, and pale, is the antithesis of early Pre-Raphaelite crudity and vigour; his aestheticism is the antithesis of Ruskin's 'stern materialism': where Hunt's details provide an easily accessible commentary on the main theme, Rossetti and Burne-Jones sought for an ideal world that could be experienced rather than understood; but

[1] Slade Lectures 1884; *Works*, xxxiii. 270.
[2] W. M. Rossetti, *Dante Gabriel Rossetti: Family Letters*, 2 vols. (1895), i. 129.
[3] See *Arch. Rev.* lxxix (1936).

Rossetti could not be dissociated from the original term, and it was constantly applied to his glowing, richly dressed, long-necked women, whom he painted in the sixties, once more in oils, and to the more sombre, cloudy-haired beauty of Jane Morris that succeeded them. However their paths diverged, each of the original trio remained a Pre-Raphaelite to the general public. The personalities were as powerful as the paintings.

It was in 1859 that William Morris,[1] then twenty-five, married Jane Burden in St. Michael's, Oxford. For the young couple, Philip Webb, who had been a fellow pupil of Morris in G. E. Street's Oxford office, designed the Red House at Bexley.[2] It was built of good quality brick, the windows and doorways slightly emphasized by patterning in the setting, the various parts of the house clearly defined by the gables (Pl. 83 b). Inside, the fireplaces were of red brick; the garden was a square hedged plot. All this is today all too familiar, but it was then regarded as a new departure, and has always been taken as a turning-point in the development of the English house, though in fact it owes something to Pugin and much to Butterfield and Street. Once again, as so often in Pre-Raphaelite history, it is the personalities involved, the house parties rather than the house, that account for its fame.

The type of furniture that went with the austere taste of the Red House was not easily found on the mid-Victorian market, and it was from the search for it that eventually came the foundation in 1861 of the firm of Morris, Marshall, Faulkner & Co., with premises at No. 8, Red Lion Square. Marshall had been brought in by Ford Madox Brown, and was the district surveyor at Tottenham; Faulkner was an Oxford man, first at Exeter and then a tutor at University College: each of them brought certain practical gifts to the creative enthusiasms of the new business. The influence of its

---

[1] See amongst many books on Morris, Aymer Vallance, *William Morris: His Art, Writings and Public Life* (1897); J. W. Mackail, *Life of William Morris*, 2 vols. (1899); G. H. Crow, *William Morris Designer* (Studio Special Number, 1934): there are two important articles on Morris as a designer by Peter Floud in *The Listener*, lii (1954), 562, 615.

[2] W. R. Lethaby, *Philip Webb and his Work* (1935); see also George Lack, 'An appreciation of Philip Webb, *Arch. Rev.* xxxviii (1915), i; J. Brandon-Jones, 'Philip Webb and Norman Shaw', *Architectural Association Journ.* lxxi (1955), 9 and 40.

products on English design lies in the years beyond 1870, though some exhibits were ready for the International Exhibition of 1862, No. 5783 'Decorated Furniture, Tapestries etc.', and No. 6734 'Stained glass windows'.[1] The details of the furniture and tapestry were commended as 'satisfactory to the archaeologist'.

'Whatever you have in your rooms', Morris said, at a much later date,[2] 'think first of the walls.' The first of the famous wall-papers issued was the Daisy Pattern (Pl. 83 a), though the Trellis Pattern had been earlier designed. In the latter the trellis simulates an actual opening in the wall, the creepers climb in and out of it in relief, and naturalistic birds, drawn by Philip Webb, perch upon it. It is an over-all design, but so large and distinct in its units as hardly to achieve an overall effect. It includes everything which Owen Jones condemned, and much that Morris would later have repudiated. In the Daisy Pattern all this is changed: the flowers are flat and stylized, the background is a flecked and dotted field. This is the essential Morris that was to create a lasting and lovely tradition, though he himself in the years ahead was to try many other experiments.

The stained glass exhibited in 1862 was mainly designed by Rossetti, and was eventually set in the east window of G. F. Bodley's church of St. Martin at Scarborough; but it was Burne-Jones who in this medium was to be the formative influence.[3] Already in 1859 he had designed for Messrs. Powell of Whitefriars the St. Frideswide window in Christ Church, Oxford. From 1861 he worked only for the Morris firm, and his elongated, mannered figures set against finely drawn foliage backgrounds that recall Morris wallpapers, green and mellow in colouring beside most Victorian windows, have a permanent place in English ecclesiastical art.

Thomas Woolner had returned from Australia in 1854, after a lively but unproductive attempt in the gold diggings[4] and a period

---

[1] *Illustrated Catalogue*: see A. Vallance, op. cit. 59.

[2] Lecture on 'The Lesser Arts' (1877): published in *Hopes and Fears for Art*.

[3] H. Wilson, 'The Work of Sir Edward Burne-Jones, more especially in decoration and design', *Arch. Rev.* i (1897), 171, 225, 273.

[4] Many of his letters from Australia are printed in his *Life and Letters* (1894) by his daughter, Amy Woolner: see also *Portfolio*, ii (1871), 97.

modelling medallions more successfully in Melbourne. He now abandoned the idealistic sculpture of his earlier phase, his *Eleanor sucking the Poison from Prince Edward's Wound* (R.A. 1843) and his *Death of Boadicea*, submitted for the Palace of Westminster competition in 1844,[1] and became a competent provider of portraits. His busts of Tennyson (Pl. 61 *c*), and of Gladstone (Ashmolean Museum, Oxford, 1868), and his statue of Lord Macaulay (1866) in the ante-chapel of Trinity College, Cambridge, are distinguished works, worthy their subjects. He also was responsible for the statues of Bacon and the Prince Consort in the Science Museum at Oxford, where he was working once more with the Pre-Raphaelite circle and where Alexander Munro, his exact contemporary, a gifted sculptor, much loved by his collaborators, supplied six of the standing figures. Munro began his career as a stonemason on the duke of Sutherland's estate, and was then employed under John Thomas on the Houses of Parliament. The *Boy with a Dolphin* fountain at the Grosvenor Gate of Hyde Park shows his pleasant, gentle art; but neither he nor Woolner could bring new inspiration to English statuary.

In 1853 Millais had become A.R.A.: three years earlier he had been elected before it was discovered that he was too young to be eligible. In 1864 he became R.A. and in the last year of his life (1896) he became President. Hunt was never a member of the Academy. He had stood for election in 1856 and failed; in 1860 Eastlake urged him to exhibit *Christ in the Temple*, offering to place a rail in front of it 'such as Mr. Frith's *Derby Day* had';[2] but Hunt declined, and never became an Academician. It is indicative of a growing breach between the Academy and much that was progressive in the arts. In its new galleries at Burlington House, designed by Sydney Smirke, the building (1867–79) partially financed by a bequest from John Gibson, the Academy began a career of more partisan selection and less certain authority. *Christ in the Temple* was sold for £5,500 to a dealer, who exhibited it at a

[1] *Literary Gazette* (1844), 483: neither is now known.

[2] In 1858; the only previous rail had been for Wilkie's *Chelsea Pensioners*: see W. P. Frith, *My Autobiography* (1887), i, chap. xxi: Frith always protested that his paintings were free of 'Pre-Raphaelite taint'.

shilling entry fee to large crowds.[1] It was sent to Windsor so that the Queen and Prince Consort might admire it at leisure. From then on many of Hunt's pictures toured not only the British Isles but America and Australia. Alone of the Brotherhood, chronicling it all in his remarkable *History of Pre-Raphaelitism*, he kept on in the original path; when he was in the sixties, toiling up the steep stair of Magdalen Tower, morning after morning, at 4 a.m. to catch the right sunrise for his May Day picture; painting every detail with care, surprisingly holding his horizontal design together as he had done in the even bolder scheme of *The Scapegoat*; softening none of the colours, drawing with a hard line so that the folds of the surplices seem rigid and moulded; but not altogether true to the canon that things should be painted as they happen; the flowers were invented for effect, to typify the spring, and, because to greet the sun is an ancient rite, a venerable Parsee, unbeknown to the college, was introduced among the Fellows (Pl. 96 *b*). Symbolism has burst the bonds of actuality; here too it is a long way from the early days and their preciseness in thinking on the event.

[1] Now in Birmingham: it is a striking example of Hunt's careful rendering of Palestinian types and settings, Protestant accuracy rather than Catholic imagination. *The Scapegoat* and *May Day* are both at Port Sunlight.

XII

MEMORIALS, PORTRAITS, AND PHOTOGRAPHY

IT had been an age much given to commemoration, and almost more given to controversy about methods and aims of commemoration. The Napoleonic heroes monumentally remembered in St. Paul's had served as a pretext to raise questions of admission and maintenance in London's cathedral and abbey. In 1831 Sydney Smith, more famous as a wit than as an archaeologist, became a canon of St. Paul's. 'There has been', said C. R. Cockerell in 1841,[1] 'no superintendence at all comparable to his': but Smith was much alarmed by the prospect of free admission, and defended an entrance fee of 2*d*. 'to see the statues'. The picture he draws of behaviour in the cathedral is a reminder that, below any experiments in aristocratic or upper middle class refinement, the people of London, ill fed, ill housed, uneducated, moved but slowly in any changing of their habits. 'The cathedral [is] constantly and shamelessly polluted with ordure, the pews are sometimes turned into cabinets d'aisance, and the prayer books torn up; the monuments are scribbled all over, and often with grossest indecency.'[2] At Westminster, behaviour seems to have been more orderly, and here the main list of damage is due to the setting up of galleries for coronations. That of George IV, lavish in its display, had brought a heavy toll of broken heads, hands and drapery: William IV's had been more carefully conducted but at that of Victoria many monuments were damaged, amongst them 'that fine one by Flaxman to Lord Mansfield'. 'What!' said a labourer to Allan Cunningham, who as Chantrey's assistant had worked much in the abbey, 'can you expect a man who has only 18*s*. a week to take

---

[1] *P.P. 1841*, vi. 474 (Report from Select Committee on National Monuments and Works of Art). A permanent ecclesiastical commission had been appointed in 1836, and the unpopularity of the Church during the Reform Bill agitations singled it out as something that must be reformed. [2] Ibid., 452.

care of sculpture.'[1] Others, notably John Britton, felt greater uneasiness about the clash between the Gothic setting and the ever-growing number of monuments. There was, following the fire of 1834, to be much discussion as to the possibility of housing some of them in the new Palace of Westminster. Britton held that free entry had a civilizing effect, and that increase in taste was the only sure way to protect works of art, a view endorsed by the Committee on Monuments appointed in 1841. It was, however, not till 1851, the year of Exhibition tourism, that the 2d. entrance fee at St. Paul's was abolished.[2]

Trafalgar and Waterloo, those twin peaks of national heroism, at once released an artistic output in verse, in painting, in sculpture, and in architecture. Statues, many in Coade stone, were rapidly raised. The Prince Regent, seeking to use Nash's Marble Arch as a Trafalgar memorial, commissioned from Flaxman a Britannia, which later, when the scheme was given up, was converted into a Minerva for the east end of the National Gallery. Liverpool in 1813 commissioned Matthew Wyatt and Richard Westmacott to erect a monument in the quadrangle behind their Town Hall, a nude figure of Nelson carried upwards by a Victory, while round the base sit chained and despondent figures, clearly inspired by Tacca's famous Leghorn prisoners. Meanwhile, no conclusion was reached as to the main national monument. The question was discussed in Parliament in 1818, but it was not till 1838 that a Nelson Memorial Committee was formed and a competition held for designs. The entries were very varied.[3] It was generally agreed that the oddest was by Benedetto Pistrucci, a Roman who had settled in London and whose design of St. George and the Dragon was long familiar on golden sovereigns. Undeterred by the miniature work of his general practice, Pistrucci proposed a colossal trident, 89 feet high, rising from a segment of the globe on which three reclining Victories were carving memorials of the hero. 'It would', said the *Art-Union*, 'be nothing more nor less than a large toasting fork.'[4]

---

[1] *P.P. 1841*, vi. 537.　　　[2] G. L. Prestige, *St. Paul's in its Glory* (1955), 67.

[3] For criticisms see *Art-Union Journ.* (1839), 18.

[4] See also *Literary Gazette* (1839), 393. Each artist had to send in a printed explanation of his design. There is a bound collection of these in the Bodleian Library, Oxford, under the press mark B.3.16 Art.

J. M. Derick produced a composition of triple columns; James Foggo a lighthouse; Thomas Hopper a circular open temple; J. G. Lough a figure of Nelson 16 feet high on a wide plinth with below him figures of sailors; Peter Hollins, returning to Flaxman's scheme, proposed a figure of Britannia, 120 feet high. The Committee awarded the first prize to William Railton, an architect who had travelled in Greece and published a supplement to Stuart's *Antiquities of Athens*, but who, characteristically of the times, had mainly been employed on Gothic buildings. His winning design, however, was entirely classical, a Corinthian column ('that order having *never* been used in England for this purpose')[1] rising from a pedestal having on its four sides bas-reliefs of Nelson's victories (St. Vincent, Copenhagen, the Nile, and Trafalgar), approached by a flight of twelve steps at the angles of which were four recumbent Egyptian lions. The second prize was given to E. H. Baily for an obelisk at the base of which stood the figure of Nelson. As so often, a compromise was decided on. Baily was selected as the sculptor of the figure to crown Railton's column.

Columns had a particular fascination for the English: *the* Monument was still that to the great fire and even the Nelson column (190 feet in the design, reduced to 160 feet) was not to over-top its 202 feet.[2] The Vendôme column in Paris, erected in 1806 in honour of Napoleon, had received much comment; the Grand Army column at Boulogne, begun in 1808, seemed to dominate the Channel; and across the Atlantic in Baltimore another foe, George Washington, was commemorated in 1821 by Robert Mills's column, then standing on a hill outside the town. Nelson himself had already by 1838 had two columns dedicated to him; those at Dublin (1808) and at Yarmouth (1817–19), both to the designs of William Wilkins, that at Yarmouth being a Doric column, 144 feet high, ending in 'a circular fane supported by caryatids and surmounted by a Britannia on a globe', the figures all being in Coade stone.[3] Anglesey had his column erected in 1816

---

[1] Railton's *Explanation* in Bodleian *Nelson Papers*.

[2] A. E. Richardson and R. R. Phillips, 'Memorials of War', *Arch. Rev.* xxxvii (1915), 63 and 96.

[3] 'A Critical Examination of the Architecture of the Nelson Column erected at Yarmouth', *Annals of the Fine Arts*, iv (1820), 511.

overlooking the Menai Straits; Picton had a short-lived basalt column at Carmarthen, designed by John Nash; Lord Hill's column at Shrewsbury, designed by John Carline (1816), rises from a base ornamented with four couchant lions; the duke of York has his column (1834) in Waterloo Place and for his duchess the old column at Seven Dials was re-erected in 1822 at Weybridge; a year before the competition Baily had completed his statue of Lord Grey to top the column at Newcastle. There was, however, at once a considerable outcry against 'one more detached column',[1] and the usual attack on the Committee, who in fact were very lacking in any experts or even well known connoisseurs: 'They don't even', exclaimed the lively writer in *The Probe*, 'invite Mr. Rogers to their deliberations.'[2] The whole position was a complex one. The Nelson Committee, a private body, had been ceded the site in Trafalgar Square for the monument by the Commissioners of Woods and Forests, and in June 1840 this was confirmed by the Lords of the Treasury, who also endorsed Barry's scheme for terracing the roadway immediately before the National Gallery. In July 1840, however, a Select Committee of the House of Commons on Trafalgar Square, having consulted various eminent architects, in whose opinions, it was admitted, 'as might be expected in a matter of taste, there is not perfect unanimity',[3] reported against the column. The National Gallery had never won much favour, but a giant column in front of it hardly seemed likely to make it any more tolerable. Work, however, had begun on the foundation for the column, and despite criticism it proceeded. In October 1843 the *Illustrated London News* published drawings of the completed column, of Baily's statue (17 feet high, cut out of stone from the duke of Buccleuch's Granton quarry) being exhibited at Charing Cross, and finally of the statue being raised into position.[4] The ingenuities required for this last act did much to establish the statue in the popularity it has always retained and, as the level of London's roof tops has steadily grown around it, it has

[1] *Art-Union Journ.* (1839), 18.
[2] *The Probe: A Review of Works of Art* (1839), 107.
[3] For a summary of their views see *Athenaeum* (1840), 653. The *Parliamentary Papers* are 1840, vols. xii, 387, and xxix, 753.   [4] *I.L.N.* iii (1843), 265, 289, 331, 340.

become more and more an essential feature at the heart of the most planned part of London. It was some time yet before the bronze reliefs were completed on the pedestal; but in 1849 J. E. Carew's scene of Nelson's death was ready and, soon after, the other three, by Watson, Woodington, and Ternouth, were in position. In 1867 Landseer's bronze lions, not without controversy nor without success, completed this great if tardy scheme.

Wellington and Waterloo were hardly less contentious. Sir Richard Westmacott carved the Waterloo Vase, now in Buckingham Palace gardens, out of blocks of marble which Napoleon had reserved to commemorate some triumph of his own;[1] and it was Sir Richard also who was responsible for the huge bronze Achilles in Hyde Park, the tribute of the women of England to the Iron Duke, 'a quaint idea', it seemed to Princess Lieven, for them to set up 'a heroic figure without a scrap of clothing'.[2] Rennie's great bridge, opened in 1817, was named after the victory, and George IV presented the colossal nude statue of Napoleon by Canova to the Duke for Apsley House, where Benjamin Wyatt was carrying out extensive and, as it proved, extravagant alterations; and there it stands, the greatest piece of neo-classical sculpture in England, imprisoned in the curve of the conqueror's staircase. It was, however, between 1838 and 1846 that the real trouble took place. A large subscription was raised for an equestrian monument of the Duke to be placed on top of Decimus Burton's arch, then in front of the entrance to Hyde Park, now at the entry to Constitution Hill. The task was committed to Matthew Cotes Wyatt, a somewhat rash step for only two years earlier many unkind things had been said of his statue of George III in Cockspur Street and it had been mysteriously damaged on the eve of the unveiling.[3] In 1839 a wooden model of the Duke's statue was put up on the arch and not well received, but the work was continued and when the large bronze, nearly 30 feet high, was put in position (Pl. 34 a), the storm burst: questions

[1] See *Gentleman's Mag.* (1836), 186, and *Naval and Military Mag.* (1828), 368.

[2] *Private Letters of Princess Lieven to Prince Metternich 1820–26*, ed. P. Quennell (1937), 165.

[3] *Burl. Mag.* xx (1912), 289; Wyatt's original design showed the King driving a chariot over the dragon of faction: sketch in *Repository of Arts*, xiii (1822), 361.

in the House, pamphlets, *Punch*, protests by the Institute of British Architects, disclaimers of responsibility by the Queen. It would be no easy task now to erect a large public monument without controversy, but our controversialists deliver their blows, as painfully perhaps, but with more civility. The Arch and the Statue stands out even in the nineteenth century as one of the greatest fine art rows. Lord Morpeth, however, the First Commissioner of Works stood firm, and the controversy gradually died down: when in 1871 Claude Monet painted a view across the Green Park (Philadelphia), it is the vast silhouette of the equestrian figure that looms across the mist; but even custom could not bring it into favour and in 1883 it was at length moved from its pedestal and banished to a small copse at Aldershot.[1]

The deaths of Peel in 1850 and of Wellington himself in 1852 were events that, in their different ways, created widespread public emotion. Peel's statue at Bury (1852) in Lancashire, where were the family mills, was by the much-employed Baily; that in Westminster Abbey, in the conventional flowing robes of the Roman forum,[2] is by John Gibson. The Duke's funeral was perhaps the greatest London ceremony of the century. Redgrave and Cole were entrusted with the design of the car, but in the end, partially through the Prince Consort's intervention, it was carried out by the German refugee architect, Gottfried Semper, who produced a recondite, classical piece that was, at least in England, to be the last example of its kind.[3] For the ceremonies £100,000 had been voted by Parliament, from which £20,000 was left for a permanent memorial in St. Paul's, and in 1857 the First Commissioner of Works, Sir Benjamin Hall, 'Big Ben', advertised premiums for a competition. From the first, the competition was criticized as being open to foreigners and as setting up yet another memorial to human triumphs in a church where such thoughts should be forgotten. There were rumours that the design was in fact to be

[1] *Country Life*, 25 May and 15 June 1951.

[2] *I.L.N.* xviii (1851), 161, and xxiii (1853), 279, 328; for other statues see *I.L.N.* xx (1852), 448, and xxi (1852), 157.

[3] See L. Ettlinger, 'The Duke of Wellington's Funeral Car', *Journ. W.C.I.* iii (1939–40), 254. The car is now in the crypt of St. Paul's. For Queen Victoria's funeral a gun carriage was used.

given to the court favourite, Marochetti.[1] There were, however, about ninety entries for the competition. Exhibited in Westminster Hall, they must have been a striking spectacle, with winged Victories, plunging horses, mourning queens and roaring lions on every side. The first prize was given to W. Calder Marshall, the second to Woodington. Alfred Stevens received a prize of £100: '(This) award', wrote the critic of the *Art Journal*, 'is unquestionably a mistake. On no possible principle of judgment can we understand how this work came to be singled out.'[2] Other criticisms were, however, more favourable, though it is clear that the architectural form of the monument, as opposed to the large statuary groups then fashionable, puzzled many of the critics. The *Illustrated London News* on the whole admired it, but its woodcut representation of it verges on a caricature. The other designs, with the exception of one by a Florentine firm, where a low arch was employed, all showed a standing or seated figure, in uniform or toga, on a pedestal surrounded by allegorical or military figures.[3] Calder Marshall's, the first prize-winner, is a very competent design along conventional lines: Edgar Papworth (third premium), Baily's pupil and son-in-law, showed an angel closing the door of a tomb, a clear reminiscence of the years he had spent studying in Rome.

The awards had been made without regard to the proposed site, and with no pledge as to the eventual commission. After thirteen months delay, it was offered to Stevens. Lord John Manners was now First Commissioner, and seems throughout to have favoured Stevens's design, which was warmly supported also by Francis Cranmer Penrose, the architect of St. Paul's cathedral. Penrose was no mean ally:[4] a distinguished athlete and traveller, he had in 1851

---

[1] *Art Journ.* iii (1857), 229; there had in fact been a preliminary select list of Baily, Foley, Marochetti, and Gibson.

[2] Ibid. 293. As unexpected as Stevens's Renaissance design is the style in which John Shaw built (1855–9) Wellington College, another of the Duke's memorials, where the high-pitched roofs owe much to France.

[3] They are reproduced *I.L.N.* xxxi (1857), 225, 277.

[4] He rowed three years for Cambridge against Oxford: his mother was 'Mrs. Markham': Matthew Arnold was his first cousin: his daughter, Emily, was successively Principal of Bedford College, Holloway College, and Somerville College.

published his *Principles of Athenian Architecture*, which had established new standards of accuracy in the study of Greek buildings. His devotion to Wren's intentions in St. Paul's naturally attracted him to a design which showed a sensitive appreciation of its surroundings. Unfortunately the commission was accompanied by the stipulation that a full-scale model of the work was to be completed and placed in St. Paul's before the final work should be begun; the site was altered to the chapel of the Bishop's Consistory Court; and the sum allotted reduced from £20,000 to £11,000. Stevens at once saw that this figure was an impossible one; he, however, undertook it for £14,000, not realizing all the problems of accommodation and material involved in producing a full-scale model 30 feet high. It is the beginning of a sorry story. Stevens already had in hand schemes for paintings in the dome of the new Reading Room at the British Museum and for his series of interior decorations at Dorchester House: while he was still working on the monument, Penrose, in his enthusiasm for St. Paul's, persuaded him to undertake designs for completing the mosaics in the dome and for sculpture groups under the spandrels. With all this work, with no convenient space for his model, with no money and with his uneasy, secretive temperament, it ended in a new Commissioner of Works, Acton Smee Ayrton, seizing the unfinished model in 1869, eleven years after the commission had been given, and proposing that another artist should finish it. The affair was, after an agonizing interval, patched up, and, when Stevens died in 1875, the monument had been erected except for the equestrian portrait which had been abandoned under protests from Dean Milman against such emblems of worldly triumph. In 1892, thanks to Lord Leighton, the monument was moved to the original position allotted to it. In 1912, D. S. MacColl[1] after a long campaign had the mounted figure cast from Stevens's model, and now it rides in place, the only extant complete example of Stevens's grand and masterly designs (Pl. 91). Dorchester House is gone, and the great caryatids of its mantelpiece, more polished than Stevens intended, are become museum pieces at the Tate Gallery; the dome of the British Museum was never undertaken; at St. Paul's only one

[1] 'The Wellington Monument of Alfred Stevens', *Arch. Rev.* xiii (1903), 87.

mosaic, the powerful figure of Isaiah, was carried out under Stevens's supervision. He lives in his figure sketches, his red chalk drawings, his small models, and only the Wellington Memorial, the bane and misery of his closing years, is a complete witness to as great an artist as any, born out of his time, High Renaissance in feeling and inspiration, but a great master who, whatever examples he recalls, need fear no depreciatory murmurs about derivative art.[1]

Gothic was a more easily acceptable style than Renaissance, and in the development of Gothic memorials it was appropriate that the commemoration of Sir Walter Scott should provide a pattern, dominating the long valley of Princes Street with its 200-feet spire. Erected between 1840 and 1846 by a local architect, Meikle Kemp,[2] its design is based on that of a market cross, and the tracery is largely taken from Melrose, where once Scott had looked over the young man's shoulder as he sketched. There was a minor battle of the styles. Cadell, the famous Edinburgh publisher, was anxious to reverse the decision and to have the scheme entrusted to Chantrey: but finally in 1840 the foundation stone was laid and six years afterwards the monument was formally inaugurated. Tragedy had intervened. On a foggy night in March 1844 Kemp missed his way returning home, fell into the Edinburgh canal and was drowned with his great work still unfinished.

Almost as famous and familiar, though much smaller in scale, is the Martyrs' Memorial at Oxford. 'At the present period', said the appeal for subscriptions, 'there seems to be a general disposition to commemorate, by national Monuments, the great achievements of our illustrious countrymen.'[3] It was certainly no overstatement, though here, with the Oxford Movement under way, the commemoration of Cranmer, Latimer, and Ridley cannot be considered entirely devoid of partisan enthusiasm. The competition, in which the design of the Eleanor Crosses was commended to the architects, was won by Gilbert Scott, still a partner in the firm of

[1] Biographies by Sir Walter Armstrong (Paris, 1881), H. Stannus (1891), K. R. Towndrow (1939); and K. R. Towndrow, *The Works of Alfred Stevens in the Tate Gallery* (1950).

[2] T. Bonnar, *Biographical Sketch of G. M. Kemp* (Edinburgh, 1892).

[3] *Address published by the Martyrs' Memorial Committee* (1838).

Scott and Moffat. This hexagonal shaft, 70 feet high, betrays its nineteenth-century origin in the flatly applied arches of its first storey and in the clumsiness of some of its carved detail. The statues were by Henry Weekes, Chantrey's assistant, and hardly match the Gothic niches in which they stand. Pugin wrote an ingenious pamphlet,[1] accusing the martyrs of a nice selection of vices, and trying to prove that by erecting it the Committee endorsed the doctrine and ritual of Cranmer's first prayer book, which 'the sort of people who are likely to subscribe to your monument will not relish'. But despite such carpings, the Martyrs' Memorial established itself in popular favour,[2] and, if youth has sometimes treated it with little reverence, it is now passing, after considerable restoration, into respectable and not unadmired antiquity.

Most famous of all is the Albert Memorial in Hyde Park,[3] which has come to stand for the final condemnation of Gothic unreality. It is in fact a summary of the period. Its polychromatic effect is everything that Pugin or Butterfield could desire, though singularly difficult to maintain in London grime. The wrought iron canopy, covered with lead, supported on bronze capitals, inlaid with 'agate, onyx, jasper, cornelian, crystal, marble, granite and other richly coloured hard substances', was the work of Messrs. Skidmore of Coventry[4] and is immensely ingenious. Sixteen electrotyped figures are included in it, typifying the sciences and virtues, designed by H. H. Armstead, J. B. Philip, and J. Redfern.[5]

---

[1] *A Letter on the Proposed Protestant Memorial to Cranmer, Ridley and Latymer* (1839).

[2] It was by 1851 copied as far afield as Tasmania, where a version of it in Hobart commemorates Sir Eardley Wilmot (*I.L.N.* xviii (1851) 4). R. C. Carpenter's Wellington memorial in St. Nicholas's, Brighton, is another version of the Eleanor Cross motif.

[3] *The National Monument to his Royal Highness, the Prince Consort* (publ. J. Murray, 1873).

[4] Francis Alexander Skidmore, inspired by John Hardman's example, took up medieval metal work in his firm at Coventry in 1847. Among his works are the wrought iron roof of Oxford Museum and the choir screens at Lichfield and Hereford cathedrals. See *Art Journ.* vi (1867), 13.

[5] For the development of the electrotype process see S. Timmins, *The Resources, Products and Industrial History of Birmingham* (1866), 516. Redfern was responsible also for many of the statues on the west front of Salisbury cathedral.

The whole is supported on four granite piers of clustered shafts. This elegantly elaborate design is curiously out of keeping with its wide base, where rows of steps ascend to a sculptured podium with large statuary groups at each of the four corners and four even larger marble groups marking the outer edge of the platform. The memorial when it was begun in 1864 had already had a chequered history. Schemes to commemorate Prince Albert's part in the Great Exhibition had been many and various; scholarships in the arts and sciences were the Prince's own wish; it was thought by others that Baron Marochetti's statue of Richard Cœur-de-Lion, one of the great successes of the Exhibition, might be usefully employed; in the end Joseph Durham was commissioned to carry out a group of Britannia presiding over the four quarters of the globe; Queen Victoria was substituted at the Prince's wish for Britannia; then on his death the figure was again changed to that of the Prince himself, and the work was erected in the gardens of the Royal Agricultural Society and later transferred to the forecourt of the Albert Hall. This was the actual memorial statue of the Exhibition. It was inadequate to meet the outburst of feeling on the Prince's premature death. The lead was taken by the lord mayor, Sir William Cubitt, brother of Thomas Cubitt the builder and himself a railway engineer of international repute, who had been knighted for the part he had taken in erecting the Crystal Palace. The original scheme was to be for a personal monument and a memorial hall, but when in 1864 Sir George Gilbert Scott's design was selected at an estimated cost of £110,000, the idea of the hall was abandoned and the Albert Hall, of which the Queen laid the foundation stone in 1867, was financed by separate subscriptions and the formation of a company of shareholders with perpetual interests in boxes and seats.[1]

The bronze statue of the Prince was not placed in its shrine till the beginning of 1876. By securing this commission J. H. Foley had established his claim to be considered the leading English sculptor. Originally that royal favourite, Baron Marochetti, had been entrusted with it, but his first model did not give satisfaction and the baron died in 1867 without completing a new design.

[1] See *Art Journ.* vi (1867), 170.

Foley himself did not live to see his figure fully cast, as he died in 1874, at the age of fifty-six. Much of his work had been sent overseas, and Calcutta has his three large bronze equestrian statues of Hardinge, Outram, and Canning. The Hardinge in particular was one of the most admired works of the time.[1] Neither the statue of Prince Albert nor his group of Asia at the south-east angle of the pediment can be considered among his happiest achievements. In proportion and general effect from a distance the gilded central statue tells well enough, but the pose is in itself a banal and uninteresting one; the fact that the Prince holds the catalogue of the Great Exhibition is hardly enough to give point and vitality to his appearance; there is competence, but the inspiration is wearing thin. The other three groups of Europe, Africa, and America were respectively by MacDowell, Theed, and Bell. Theed's is an ingeniously arranged composition with much variety within its pyramidal line (Pl. 90 *b*): it is certainly the most successful of the four, but John Bell, as always, puts much life and vigour into his personifications. On the angles of the plinth or podium were four more groups, Agriculture, Manufactures, Commerce, and Engineering by Calder Marshall, Weekes, Thornycroft, and Lawlor, and round the podium itself was a processional frieze showing the great painters, poets, musicians, sculptors, and architects of the world, carved by H. H. Armstead and J. B. Philip. Armstead had already shown in his reliefs for the Queen's Robing Room at Westminster that he had considerable inventive ability.[2] Here he and his collaborator produced a most varied range of movements throughout the design and a large repertory of poses, skilfully adapted to the varying costumes. Iconographically some of the passages in the frieze are not without interest. In a group of artists Turner sits talking to Wilkie, who stands looking down at the sketch-book on Turner's knee; Flaxman draws industriously,

---

[1] Cast by Messrs. Elkington of Birmingham from guns captured in the Afghan war: the horse alone weighed 4½ tons: S. Timmins, *Resources, Products and Industrial History of Birmingham* (1866), 515. The Outram statue was removed from its pedestal in 1957, the centenary of the Mutiny: *I.L.N.* ccxxxi (1957), 293.

[2] See J. L. Tupper in *Portfolio*, ii (1871), 130. Philip had also been employed in the later stages at Westminster. The north and west sides are by Philip, the south and east by Armstead.

ignoring the presence of Canova and Thorwaldsen immediately behind him; and Cockerell is engaged in conversation with Barry, while Pugin stands in the corner angle, detached from all around him (Pl. 90 a).

Amongst the early memorials of Waterloo was the Wellington shield, designed by Stothard and presented to the Duke by the merchants and bankers of London. Throughout the century memorial or trophy plate grew steadily in popularity and ingenuity. Centre pieces were much in vogue, and whereas two designed by Paul Storr to commemorate Peninsular victories still consist of classical wreaths and allegorical figures, a more realistic vein was coming into favour. The Latham centrepiece (Royal East Kent Regiment) displays 'frozen into perpetuity' the incident at the battle of Albuhera when Ensign Latham's left arm was completely severed as he clung to the French standard.[1] Such sensational episodes were not restricted to army mess plate. In 1851, when, stimulated by the Exhibition, Messrs. Hunt and Roskell and Messrs. Garrard[2] produced some of their most elaborate pieces, the latter's emperor of Russia vase for the Ascot races was surmounted by a sleigh pursued by wolves, and for the Goodwood races the same firm produced a stirring *Combat between Roderick Dhu and Fitz-James*. Hunt and Roskell's Tweeddale testimonial showed Scottish peasants defeating the Danes (Pl. 80 a), and the testimonial plate to Lord Ellenborough, one of the most resplendent of the exhibits, showed in its centrepiece *Asia crowning Britannia*, while below a British sepoy kept guard over Afghan and Chinese prisoners.[3] It is a relief to turn from such subjects to Garrard's table centre of 1842, designed by Prince Albert with representations of four of the Queen's dogs.[4]

The great men and great events had also their medals. It was a time of dynasties in the arts, and to the Wyatts and the Westmacotts the Wyons must be added. The family came originally from Cologne in the reign of George I, and it was Thomas Wyon

[1] See *Catalogue*, '*Tradition in Silver*', Diploma Gallery, R.A. (1956), No. 124.
[2] *Garrard's 1721–1911* (1912).
[3] *I.L.N.* xviii (1851), 375, 511, and xix (1851), 149.
[4] *Journ. of Design*, i (1849), 33.

(1792–1817) who, though but little past twenty, engraved the medal for the peace of 1815, when he also received the post of chief engraver to the Mint. After his early death Benjamin (1802–58), Joseph (1836–73) and William Wyon (1795–1851) were responsible for many fine commemorative medals, for the great seals and for much of the coinage.

In the *Athenaeum* of 1842,[1] a contributor noted 'a novel species of monumental commemoration': Dean Chandler of Chichester had placed a stained glass window in the east end of the south aisle of Chichester cathedral in memory of his sister. Memorial windows were not in fact entirely novel. They were known in the middle ages, though generally commemorating some event rather than an individual: kings, ecclesiastics, and great noblemen from time to time appeared in them as donors. But the great movement for individual commemoration of parishioners, which was in the second half of the century to fill English churches with the products of Hardman, Clayton and Bell, O'Connor, Wailes and others, was, at the time of Dean Chandler's 'innovation', comparatively unfamiliar. The restorations begun at many cathedrals and churches in the late eighteenth century had led to the provision of new glass. At St. George's, Windsor, for instance, between 1787 and 1790 the whole of the mullions and tracery of the east window of the choir were removed and a large painting on glass of the Resurrection, by Thomas Jervaise after a design by Benjamin West, was inserted.[2] In the type of transparency for which West's designs were used, Francis Eginton (d. 1805) of Birmingham was probably the best-known practitioner, painting with enamel colours, 'brown shade and yellow stain on a white base, with little or no outline and few leads'.[3] Most of his numerous works have been removed from their windows, and if not destroyed are stored away, and nothing is so inaccessible as stored windows. His work was carried on by his son, William Raphael Eginton (1778–1834), who copied

---

[1] 568.

[2] T. Willement, *An Account of the Restorations of the Collegiate Chapel of St. George, Windsor* (1844), 6.

[3] J. Hardman Powell, 'The Art of Stained Glass in Birmingham', in *Industrial History of Birmingham*, ed. S. Timmins (1866), 520. St. Alkmund, Shrewsbury, has a typical window by Eginton.

Raphael's *School of Athens*[1] for the great library window at Stour-head, and by Messrs. F. and C. Pemberton who as late as 1849 still quoted Eginton as 'the great reviver of modern glass painting'. But by that date, much was changed. Thomas Willement (1786–1871), who obtained the title of 'artist in stained glass' to Queen Victoria, was in the twenties and thirties the most popular provider of stained-glass windows for the new castles such as Penrhyn or Alton Towers, and played a large part in reviving the use of heraldic glazings. Such commissions considerably outnumbered his church windows but these steadily increased towards the mid-century. Willement's fancy was, in his own words, for 'rich and powerful colours'. These were obtained by pieces of coloured glass on which the shading only was tinted in, and they have proved very durable and lasting. In revolt against the large panes of the transparencies, Willement used Gothic tracery, frequently restoring mullions where they had been taken out. A fellow of the Society of Antiquaries, he belonged to the supporters of archaeological exactitude and aimed at reproducing medieval types. Unfortunately he and his draughtsmen had very little sense of the style they were copying, and his figures are singularly gauche and unconvincing; but his popularity and prestige were considerable and his manner was copied throughout England long after better examples were available.[2] Changing tastes may be seen in his persuasion of the canons of St. George's, Windsor, to abandon the designs by West for a Crucifixion in the west window, even though the glass had been 'considerably advanced' before the painter's death.[3] The canons eventually presented it 'as an embellishment to the cathedral church now in progress in Calcutta', where it still remains in

[1] For another Raphaelesque design compare Joseph Backler's *Transfiguration* in St. Thomas's, Dudley: reproduced pl. 64, C. Woodforde, *English Stained and Painted Glass* (Oxford, 1954); see also *Magazine of the Fine Arts*, i (1821), 187.

[2] The east window in Thomas Rickman's fine church (1826) at Hampton Lucy (Warws.) is the one Willement himself selects to reproduce as frontispiece to *A Concise Account of the Principal Works in Stained Glass . . . executed by Thomas Willement* (privately printed, 1840), a window that, in part, has survived both Scott's apsidal extension of the chancel (1858) and bomb blast in the 1940's.

[3] T. Willement, *An Account of the Restorations of the Collegiate Chapel of St. George, Windsor* (1844), 10.

position. In 1822–8 another famous replacement occurred, that of the fourteenth-century glass in Winchester College chapel by copies, very competent in their way, produced by the firm of Betton and Evans of Shrewsbury.

Willement's strong tints are shown on a drab background: the use of clear glass in the backgrounds or of very light colours, so as to achieve brilliant contrasts, is largely associated with the designs of Pugin. Pugin first worked with Willement (at Alton Towers), with Wailes of Newcastle, and with Warrington of London. Newcastle was a considerable centre of the glass trade and its firms were widely employed throughout the country. It was, however, in the Birmingham firm of John Hardman that Pugin found the true executant of his plans. There was, writes John Hardman Powell, Hardman's nephew and Pugin's son-in-law, between them 'an almost brotherly friendship, which lasted undisturbed during fifteen years of daily correspondence and frequent personal converse'.[1] The window of the Immaculate Conception at St. Chad's, Birmingham, has already been mentioned:[2] the window of the north transept of Hereford cathedral is another notable example, and in 1867 an even more splendid window was sent out by the firm to St. Patrick's cathedral in Melbourne (Pl. 77 b). Hardman made much use of a silvery stain to gain brightness and luminosity and some of his effects, particularly his light flesh tints, have not proved lasting, but there is nearly always in work by his firm a sense of rhythm, some distinction in figure drawing and some real translucency. Messrs. Clayton and Bell rival the Hardmans in the second half of the century as a firm of repute, much of whose work is now coming back into favour. They provided in 1863 the glass for Gilbert Scott's reconstruction of the east window at Windsor, when West's transparency of the Ascension was removed and Gothic mullions and tracery restored, the whole in memory of the Prince Consort and in time for the Prince of Wales's marriage. The great east window at Lincoln, the work of Ward and Hughes in 1855, is another example of the range of efficiency of Victorian glaziers.

[1] *Industrial History of Birmingham*, ed. S. Timmins (1866), 253.
[2] See above, p. 232.

While shrines, columns, statues, glass, and plate commemorated the mighty, a painted portrait remained the conventional way of transmitting a man's memory to posterity. At the opening of the century miniature portraits were still popular and there were talented practitioners of the art such as Richard Cosway, one of the essential figures of the Regency, John Smart, George Engleheart, and Ozias Humphrey.[1] As these artists, all users of an eighteenth-century tradition, disappeared, a new type of miniature came to the fore, larger, square, a further manifestation of the range of water-colour. Andrew Robertson, another of the Scottish invaders of London, was the leader in this development, rivalled by A. E. Chalon, and it was Robertson's pupil, William Charles Ross, knighted in 1842, who was its most successful exponent. Tactful in his likenesses, competent in his technique, he produced a record of early Victorian society and provided the backgrounds and poses which the photographers were to take over for their cartes-de-visite.

For larger portraits there were in the forties and fifties H. W. Pickersgill, pedestrian and accurate; Sir George Hayter; George Richmond and his son, William; John Prescott Knight, whose distinguished renderings of eminent men look down not ineffec-tively from many walls of clubs, board rooms, and civic offices; Mrs. Margaret Carpenter, who had first exhibited at the Academy in 1815, had steadily built up a considerable and deserved repu-tation and had made some notable contributions to the striking collection of 'Leaving Portraits' formed at Eton between 1756 and 1868. Of them all, Sir Francis Grant, President of the Royal Academy in succession to Eastlake, was the most fashionable. Younger son of an old Scottish family,[2] married to a niece of the duke of Rutland, he had standing that was independent of his artistic achievement, and it was almost by chance that he became a well-known painter, for he did not attempt to exhibit till he was

[1] B. S. Long, *British Miniaturists* (1930); G. Reynolds, *English Portrait Miniaturists* (1932), chaps. xiv–xvi.

[2] Grant's clientèle was largely an English one: his fellow Scots, John Watson Gordon, P.R.S.A., and John Graham Gilbert, continued, in Edinburgh and Glasgow respectively, the high standards of Scottish portraiture, though both exhibited from time to time in London.

thirty-one. Nothing could be more of a contrast with the struggling early days of most of the leading artists of the first half of the century. Grant's equestrian portraits and groups, his shooting parties and hunt breakfasts, greatly pleased. He was at ease with his subjects and his sitters, and, though lack of systematic training is at times evident, he had a genuine talent and his brushwork is often surprisingly assured and convincing. He has a breezy directness completely at variance with the suave grace and finish of Franz Xavier Winterhalter, who in occasional forays from Paris was investing the English Royal house with a vague Third Empire charm.

The greatest English portrait of the century was produced by a man whose main activities were in other fields. Alfred Stevens's portrait of Mary Ann Collmann, with its contro-posto of the head turned away from the line of the arm and its rich colouring, tells remarkably as a design, but it is as a revelation of character that it is unforgettable (Pl. 93 a). The Collmanns and Stevens were closely linked by friendship, and the portrait is an intensely personal document. He painted her husband also, a vivid sensitive study, but without the finality of the rendering of the wife. In one other unfinished painting, the sad rendering of another friend's wife, Mrs. Mitchell and her child, both to die shortly after the painting was made, Stevens shows again something of this profound interpretative power and his sense of the decorative opportunities of portraiture.

Another painter, like Stevens more often engaged in large decorative allegorical pieces, contributed a series of notable portraits to the second half of the century. G. F. Watts was essentially an eclectic genius. In his subject painting quattrocento Florence, Titian, Rubens, Flaxman, Fuseli, Etty, are all in varying degrees present. His portraits show similar borrowings. Lady Holland (Royal collection), his hostess at Casa Feroni in 1843, in her large straw hat, 'in the manner of the Chapeau de Paille',[1] recalls Reynolds's Kitty Fisher rather than Susanne Fourmet. Mrs. Nassau Senior (1858) (coll. O. N. Senior, Esq.) is painted in much stronger colours: the rich green of the background, the red of the draperies,

[1] *Catalogue*, Watts' Exhibition, Tate Gallery, 1954, No. 6.

the treatment of her accessories, the symbolic act of watering flowers 'as an allusion to her gracious and beneficent nature',[1] are in accordance with contemporary Pre-Raphaelite theories. Mrs. Louis Huth (Dublin), painted about the same year, and Lady Margaret Beaumont and her daughter (Pl. 92 *a*), painted in 1862, recall Gainsborough in the grace of the posing and the shimmer of the drapery, though there is a purposeful expression, a tilt of the smoothly coiled heads with these Victorian ladies, which is far removed from Gainsborough's sublimated elegance.

The tradition of Gainsborough and Reynolds was no longer the only rival. In 1826 Joseph Nichéphore Niepce took the first photograph, a view from his window, with an eight hours exposure.[2] Three years later he entered into partnership with Louis Jacques Mandé Daguerre, who had made considerable stir in Paris and London with his subtly lit dioramas, one of them showing a moonlit view of the ruins of Holyrood. Ten years later the process of the daguerreotype was announced to the world. 'From today', Paul Delaroche exclaimed, 'painting is dead.' In 1841 the first portrait studio was opened in London by Richard Beard, who patented a process for colouring daguerreotypes.[3] At the same time (1841) William Henry Fox Talbot[4] patented the calotype process by which prints could be made from a paper negative, and this was put to striking use by David Octavius Hill,[5] a landscape painter, working in collaboration with a chemist, Robert Adamson. In 1851 Frederick Scott Archer announced the collodion process. Photography was still for some twenty years to be a cumbersome business, in which the plates had to be exposed in a wet state and developed and fixed on the spot in a dark-room tent. Such problems, however, did not deter enthusiasts, and there was a rapid appreciation of the new possibilities that were opened up. Ruskin in 1845 was busily collecting daguerreotypes of Venetian architecture. 'Its a most

[1] Ibid., No. 21.

[2] See H. and A. Gernsheim, *The History of Photography* (1955).

[3] Some of Beard's best-known daguerreotypes are those taken of the Crystal Palace for John Tallis's *Description*: see above, p. 258, n. 1.

[4] For 'The Talbotype-sunpictures' see *Art Union Journ.* viii (1846), 143.

[5] H. Schwarz, *David Octavius Hill, Master of Photography* (1932).

blessed invention, that's what it is', he wrote to his father.[1] Roger Fenton[2] took a photographic van to the Crimea, bringing back a long series of carefully posed portraits of officers and discreet views of the terrain. In the Art Treasures Exhibition of 1857 O. G. Rejlander, a Swede who had settled in England, showed a large composition (30 in. by 15 in.) made from over thirty negatives entitled *The Two Ways of Life*. It was a complex group of classically draped men and almost nude women, and aimed at the high art of the contemporary French salons. It caused considerable sensation and was bought by Queen Victoria for the Prince Consort. H. P. Robinson in a long career reflected the changing Academy standards in his posed groups; his *Fading Away* (1858) is a pathetic, Redgrave anecdote, and his posed groups of 1862 are very close to Frederick Walker. In the sixties an eccentric and forceful lady, moving in the circles of Tennyson and G. F. Watts, Julia Margaret Cameron,[3] took up photography. It was the period when the carte-de-visite portrait, posed against some exceedingly artificial background, was enjoying huge popularity. Mrs. Cameron worked with larger plates, concentrating on the head only in a close-up view. Some of her studies, *Divine Love*, *Madonna and Child* and so forth, for which Mary Hillier, her housemaid, appropriately draped, was generally the model, have a strongly period sentiment, but her portraits of the great literary figures whom she knew are penetrating records. They are also, for all the occasional reminiscences of the poses, a new art form, using a chiaroscuro which is distinct from anything that painting could achieve, and concentrating on the head alone, in quite a new scale relationship to the pictorial surface.

If it was in the carefully posed portrait that photography had its first triumphs, it was the snapshot that was to provide the new repertoire of movements and poses. 'We thought we could add something to what is known about [the mechanism of walking]

---

[1] *Works*, iii. 210. His later views on photography were less favourable.

[2] H. and A. Gernsheim, *Roger Fenton* (1954). For his photographs of English houses cf. Pl. 15 c.

[3] See monograph by H. Gernsheim (1948); she was helped in her early work by David Wynfield, one of the St. John's Wood clique and a great-nephew of Wilkie: see M. H. Stephen-Smith, *Art and Anecdote* (n.d.), 153.

from a new source . . . namely the instantaneous photograph.' So wrote Oliver Wendell Holmes in 1863,[1] and very shortly this new vision, a new sense of varying focus and of unexpected angles, was to make its mark on the older art, and to be a component in a visual revolution as important as that created by Renaissance experiments with linear perspective. In 1870 amongst refugees from the siege and the commune in Paris were Monet, Pissarro and Sisley, and in December 1870 the French dealer, Paul Durand-Ruel exhibited some Impressionist paintings at his gallery at 168 New Bond Street.[2] It was a new world that was beginning, one to which England was for a time to contribute little, and to absorb little from it. In the first quarter of the century Europe had recognized the vitality and interest of English painting and sculpture; in the middle years Pre-Raphaelitism attracted some attention, but was never accepted as a movement of European importance. The architects of the Gothic revival had secured continental commissions; the architecture of the last quarter of the century, of which William Nesfield and Richard Norman Shaw were the protagonists, earned, for no very cogent reasons, the thoroughly English nickname of the Queen Anne Style. The much envied prosperity of England was in the period between the Crimean War and 1914 to be discounted by a not unmerited continental contempt for English taste and visual accomplishment.

Dining at Samuel Rogers's table,[3] Flaxman once criticized the Waverley novels as having 'in no respect tended to improve the moral condition of mankind'. Even amid Regency romanticism, such stricter claims were asserted, and in the mid-century the new patrons, self-made men such as Vernon, Sheepshanks, Elkanah Bicknell, and Wells of Redleaf required that the visual arts should be edifying and suited to the home. Themselves insatiate raconteurs, they liked an easy narrative content, but where the novel flourished, finding new subtleties of delineation, painting declined

[1] *Atlantic Monthly*, xi (1863), 567, quoted B. Newhall, 'Photography and the Development of Kinetic Visualization', *Journ. W.C.I.* vii (1944), 41.

[2] See Douglas Cooper, 'The French Impressionists and their Relations with England' in his important introduction to *The Courtauld Collection* (1954), 19.

[3] R. E. Roberts, *Samuel Rogers and his Circle* (1910), 171.

into illustration. 'Effect' was deeply suspect, and 'finish' was evidence of the artist's skill and industry. 'If there be one painter of our own time', wrote Lord Francis Egerton,[1] 'who deserves praise for the example of labour united with genius, it is Mr. Landseer.' Those who bought Landseer's paintings or engravings crowded the opera to hear the competent melodies of *The Bohemian Girl*. They were a vigorous stock in a time of transition and liked enjoyable pleasures. Emotional reactions, which today seem over facile, were to them praiseworthy indications of a more humane outlook, and their sentimentality was a stage in the growth of social responsibility. Much that then was prized has now been devalued and what seemed high art has become mere sociological detail. 'Not the fruit of experience, but experience itself' was soon to provide a new and more enticing end.[2] But much remains, impervious to changing taste. The dazzling light of Turner is upon the period, and the visionary Blake and the observant Constable are of this company. In the great water-colourists, in Wilkie's sense of gesture and pose, in St. George's Hall and Cockerell's buildings, in the intensity of Pugin and the competence of Barry, in the so often frustrated genius of Alfred Stevens and in the early works of the Pre-Raphaelites, the years here chronicled were richly endowed.

[1] Q.R. lxii (1838), 145.
[2] This famous passage occurs in the concluding essay of Walter Pater's *Renaissance*, dated 1868, though the essays were not published till 1873.

BIBLIOGRAPHY

THE vast output of English nineteenth-century writings on art can here be only suggested by a selection of periodical and other contemporary publications. Memoirs, novels, accounts of travels, collections of letters are all liable to break into discussions of taste and aesthetic theory, and anecdotes of artists, whom it had become fashionable to lionize. Beyond these, much information remains as yet unsifted in manuscript collections and in family accounts and papers, for which the articles on particular houses in *Country Life* often provide useful guidance. The two- or three-volume biographies of artists, generally published shortly after their death and nearly always unindexed, contain much information about the arts as a whole, and the more important of them are listed here, but recent monographs and articles on individuals and specialized subjects are given in footnotes in the text and are not repeated in the Bibliography. Catalogues of public and private collections, special exhibitions and sales, and guide books (in particular *The Buildings of England* edited by Dr. Pevsner) are important sources of information, of which again only a selection can be listed. The endless nineteenth-century pattern books for houses and for designs in all materials and branches, and the technical treatises on the practice of the arts are only represented by a few examples.

The *Architectural Review* has played such a large part in the revival of nineteenth-century studies that it must receive special mention, but references to particular articles in it and other periodicals are confined to the footnotes. The novels of the period are so closely connected to the subject matter of much of the painting that it is impossible to study one without the other: I have not listed works dealing with literature, but I am much indebted to the writings of Louis Cazamian, Humphrey House, Mario Praz, Eino Railo, Kathleen Tillotson, and D. P. Varma.

Where no name is given, the place of publication is London.

DICTIONARIES

BRYAN, M. *Dictionary of Painters and Engravers*, 1st ed., 2 vols. (1816); revised by G. Stanley (1849) and by G. C. Williamson (1903–4).
COLVIN, H. M. *A Biographical Dictionary of English Architects 1660–1840* (1954).
Dictionary of National Biography (1885–1937).
ELMES, JAMES. *A Topographical Dictionary of London and its Environs* (1831).
GUNNIS, RUPERT. *Dictionary of British Sculptors 1660–1851* (1953).

MACQUOID, P., and EDWARDS, H. C. R. *The Dictionary of English Furniture*, revised and enlarged by H. C. R. Edwards, 3 vols. (1954).

PAPWORTH, WYATT. *The Dictionary of Architecture* (Architectural Publication Society), 8 vols. (1852–92).

REDGRAVE, SAMUEL. *A Dictionary of Artists of the English School*, revised ed. (1878).

CATALOGUES

Birmingham: Museum and Art Gallery: Catalogue of Paintings (1930).

—— —— *Catalogue of Drawings* (1939).

British Portraits: Royal Academy (1955–6).

GRAVES, ALGERNON. *The Royal Academy of Arts*, 8 vols. (1905–6).

—— *The British Institution 1806–1867* (1908).

—— *A Century of Loan Exhibitions (1813–1912)*, 5 vols. (1913–15).

Manchester: Art Gallery, Handbook to the Permanent Collection, compiled by J. E. Phythian (1910).

—— *Whitworth Institute: Historical Catalogue of the Collection of Water Colour Drawings by Deceased Artists*, by Cosimo Monkhouse (1894).

National Gallery Catalogue: British School (1946), by Martin Davies.

Royal Academy: Catalogues 1769–1849: interleaved copy with notes, manuscript letters, and illustrations, compiled by A. N. Anderton, British Museum.

—— *The First Hundred Years of the*: Catalogue of Exhibition, Royal Academy (1951–2).

South Kensington Museum: A Descriptive Catalogue of the Historical Collection of Water-Colour Paintings in the South Kensington Museum, by Samuel Redgrave (1877).

Tate Gallery: British School (1947).

Victoria and Albert Museum: Catalogue of Oil Paintings, including the Sheepshanks Collection (1907).

—— *Catalogue of Water Colour Paintings by British Artists and Foreigners working in Great Britain* (1927).

GUIDE BOOKS

Murray's Architectural Guides, ed. by John Betjeman and John Piper: *Buckinghamshire* (1948) and *Berkshire* (1949) by the editors; *Lancashire* (1955) by Peter Fleetwood-Hesketh.

Shell Guides, ed. by John Betjeman (1935–).

The Buildings of England, ed. by Nikolaus Pevsner: Penguin Books (1951–).

WORKS WRITTEN BEFORE 1870

PERIODICALS

Annals of the Fine Arts, 5 vols. (1817–20).

The Architectural Magazine, ed. J. C. Loudon, 5 vols. (1834–8).

The Art-Union: A Monthly Journal of the Fine Arts, etc., 8 vols. (1844–8); continued as *The Art Journal* (1849–   ).

The Athenaeum, London Literary and Critical Journal (1828–   ).

Bell's Weekly Messenger (1795–1817).

Blackwood's *Edinburgh Magazine* (1817–   ).

The Builder (1843–   ).

The Building News (1855–   ).

The Cornhill Magazine (1860–   ).

The Ecclesiologist, published by the Cambridge Camden Society, 29 vols. (1842–68).

The Edinburgh Review (1803–   ).

The European Magazine (1782–1825; N.S. 1825–6).

The Examiner (1806–81).

The Fine Arts Journal, a weekly record of painting, sculpture, architecture, music, etc. (1846–7).

The Fine Arts Quarterly Review, 3 vols. (1863–5); N.S. (1866–   ).

Foreign Review and Continental Miscellany, 5 vols. (1828–30).

Fraser's Magazine for Town and Country, 80 vols. (1830–69).

The Gentleman's Magazine, 113 vols. (1731–1833).

The Germ, Nos. 1 and 2; continued as *Art and Poetry*, Nos. 3 and 4 (1850) (facsimile reprint of, W. M. Rossetti, 1901).

Household Words: A Weekly Journal conducted by Charles Dickens, 19 vols. (1850–9).

The Illustrated London News (1842–   ).

The Indicator, 2 vols. (1820–2).

The Journal of Design and Manufactures, 6 vols. (1849–52).

Library of the Fine Arts, or Monthly Repertory, 21 vols. (1831–2); N.S. 4 vols. (1832–3).

The Literary Gazette and Journal of Belles Lettres, Arts, Sciences etc., 42 vols. (1817–58); N.S. 8 vols. (1858–62).

The Magazine and Review of Literature, Science and the Arts, 5 nos. (1830).

The Magazine of the Fine Arts, and Monthly Review of Painting, Sculpture, Architecture, and Engraving, 1 vol. (1821).

The Monthly Magazine and British Register, 63 vols. (1796–1826); continued as *The Monthly Magazine; or British Register of Literature, Sciences and the Belles-Lettres*, 26 vols. (1826–38); continued as *The Monthly Magazine*, 9 vols. (1839–43).

The Monthly Review, or Literary Journal, Enlarged, 108 vols. 1st and 2nd ser. (1790–1825); 3rd ser. 15 vols. (1826–30); 4th ser. 45 vols. (1831–45).

The Monthly Review of Literature, Science and Art, 19 nos. (1863–5).

The New Monthly Magazine and Universal Register (1814–20); continued as *The New Monthly Magazine and Literary Journal* (1821–36); and as *The New Monthly Magazine and Humorist* (1837–71).

Once a Week (1859–79).

The Probe, a review of new publications of art etc., 1 vol. (1839).

The Quarterly Review (1809–)

The Repository of Arts, Literature, Commerce, Manufactures, Fashions and Politics, published by R. Ackermann, 2nd ser. 14 vols., 3rd ser. 12 vols., 4th ser. 9 vols. (1809–29).

Royal Institute of British Architects: Sessional Papers of (1862–6); *Transactions of* (1842–).

The Somerset House Gazette and Literary Museum, 2 vols. (1824).

GENERAL LITERATURE

ACKERMANN, R. *The Microcosm of London,* 3 vols. (1805).

ALISON, A. *Essays on the Nature and Principles of Taste* (1790).

BALLANTINE, JAMES. *The Life of David Roberts* (Edinburgh, 1866).

BARRY, A. *Memoir of the Life and Works of Sir Charles Barry, Architect* (1867).

BRAY, MRS. *Life of Thomas Stothard* (1851).

COLLINS, W. WILKIE. *Memoirs of the Life of William Collins,* 2 vols. (1848).

COOK, D. *Art in England* (1869).

COTTINGHAM, L. N. *The Smiths, Founders, and Ornamental Metal Workers Director* (2nd ed., enlarged 1824).

CUNNINGHAM, ALLAN. *Lives of the most eminent British Painters, Sculptors and Architects* (1829–33), ed. Mrs. Heaton, 3 vols. (1879–80).

—— *The Life of Sir David Wilkie,* 2 vols. (1843).

EASTLAKE, SIR CHARLES L. *Contributions to the Literature of the Fine Arts* (1848); 2nd ser. with memoir by Lady Eastlake (1870).

EASTLAKE, C. L. *Hints on Household Taste in Furniture, Upholstery and Other Details* (1868); 3rd ed., revised (1872).

EDWARDS, EDWARD. *The Fine Arts in England; their State and Prospects considered relatively to National Education.* Pt. I, *The Administrative Economics of the Fine Arts* (1840).

ELMES, JAMES. *Metropolitan Improvements; or London in the Nineteenth Century, being a series of views . . . from Drawings,* by T. H. Shepherd (1827).

FARINGTON, JOSEPH. *Diary 1793–1821,* ed. by James Greig, 8 vols. (1922–8). (A typescript of the complete diary is deposited by gracious permission of Her Majesty the Queen in the Print Room of the British Museum.)

FERGUSSON, JAMES. *An historical inquiry into the true principles of Beauty in Art, more especially with reference to Architecture* (1849)

FERGUSSON, JAMES. *History of Architecture*, 3 vols. (1862—72): Vol. III, The Modern Styles of Architecture (1872).

FERREY, B. *Recollections of A. N. W. Pugin* (1861).

FLAXMAN, JOHN. *Lectures on Sculpture* (1829); 2nd ed. enlarged (1838).

GILCHRIST, A. *Life of William Etty*, 2 vols. (1855).

—— *Life of William Blake*, 2 vols. (1863); ed. Ruthven Todd (1945).

GRANVILLE, A. B. *The Spas of England*, 2 vols. (1841).

HALL, S. C. *The Gallery of Modern Sculpture* (1858–9).

—— *The Vernon Gallery* (n.d.).

HAYDON, B. R. *Lectures on Painting and Design*, 2 vols. (1846).

—— *The Autobiography and Memoirs of*, ed. by T. Taylor, 1st and 2nd eds. (1853); new eds. by A. P. O. Penrose (1926) and by M. Elwin (1920).

HAZLITT, WILLIAM. *Centenary Edition of the Complete Works of*, ed. P. P. Howe, 21 vols. (1930–4).

KERR, ROBERT. *The Gentleman's House* (1864).

KNIGHT, R. P. *The Landscape* (1794).

—— *Analytical Inquiry into the Principles of Taste* (1805).

KNIGHT, W. *Memorials of Coleorton being letters to Sir George and Lady Beaumont 1803 to 1834*, 2 vols. (Edinburgh, 1887).

KNOWLES, J. *The Life and Writings of Henry Fuseli*, 2 vols. (1831).

LEEDS, W. H. *The Travellers Club House . . . and the Revival of the Italian Style* (1839).

LESLIE, C. R. *Memoirs of the Life of John Constable, R.A.*, 1st ed. (1845); ed. and enlarged by Hon. Andrew Shirley (1937); ed. by Jonathan Mayne (1951).

—— *Autobiographical Recollections of the Life of*, ed. Tom Taylor (1860).

London: History and Views of, including its Modern Improvements etc., 2 vols. (1837).

LOUDON, J. C. *An Encyclopaedia of Cottage, Farm and Villa Architecture and Furniture* (1833); revised ed. by Mrs. Loudon (1846).

PALGRAVE, F. T. *Essays on Art* (1866).

—— *Gems of English Art of this Century*; printed in colours (1869).

PRICE, UVEDALE. *An Essay on the Picturesque as compared with the Sublime and the Beautiful*, 2 vols. (1794–8).

—— *A Dialogue on the distinct characters of the Picturesque and the Beautiful* (Hereford, 1801).

PYE, JOHN. *Patronage of British Art* (1845).

PYNE, W. H. *The History of the Royal Residences*, 3 vols. (1819).

—— *Wine and Walnuts* (1824).

RAIMBACH, ABRAHAM. *Memoirs and Recollections of the late Abraham Raimbach Esq.*, ed. by M. T. S. Raimbach (1843).

REDGRAVE, RICHARD. *The Sheepshanks Gallery* (1870).

—— and SAMUEL. *A Century of Painters of the English School*, 2 vols. (1865); 2nd ed. abridged and continued to the present time, 1 vol. (1890); ed. Ruthven Todd as *A Century of British Painters* (1947).

RICKMAN, THOMAS. *Attempt to Discriminate the Styles of English Architecture from the Conquest to the Reformation* (1819).

SANDBY, W. *The History of the Royal Academy of Arts*, 2 vols. (1862).

SCOTT, G. G. *Remarks on Secular and Domestic Architecture* (1858).

SCOTT, W. BELL. *Half-hour Lectures on the History and Practice of the Fine and Ornamental Arts* (1867).

—— *The British School of Sculpture* (1871).

SHEE, M. A. *Life of Sir Martin Archer Shee*, 2 vols. (1860).

SHERER, JOHN. *The Gallery of British Artists*, 2 vols. (n.d., c. 1870).

SMITH, J. T. *Nollekens and his Times* (1828); ed. G. W. Stonier (1945).

STUART, JAMES, and REVETT, NICHOLAS. *The Antiquities of Athens*, 4 vols. (1762–1816).

TALLIS, JOHN. *London Street Views* (1838–40).

TATHAM, C. H. *Designs for Ornamental Plate* (1806).

TENNYSON, ALFRED. *Poems*, illustrated ed. by Edward Moxon (1857).

TREVELYAN, LADY PAULINA JERMYN. *Selections from Literary and Artistic Remains*, ed. P. Wooster (1879).

UPCOTT, WILLIAM. *A Bibliographical Account of the Principal Works relating to English Topography*, 3 vols. (1818).

UWINS, Mrs. *A Memoir of Thomas Uwins, R.A.*, 2 vols. (1851).

VARLEY, JOHN. *Landscape Design* (1816).

WAAGEN, G. F. *Works of art and artists in England*, trans. H. E. Lloyd, 3 vols. (1838).

—— *Treasures of art in Great Britain*, trans. Lady Eastlake, 4 vols. (1854–7).

—— *A Walk through the Art-Treasures Exhibition at Manchester, under the guidance of Dr. W.* (1857).

WILLIAMS, D. E. *The Life and Correspondence of Sir Thomas Lawrence, Kt.*, 2 vols. (1831).

LATER WORKS

ADDISON, W. *English Spas* (1951).

ADDLESHAW, G. W. O., and ETCHELLS, F. *The Architectural Setting of Anglican Worship* (1948).

AUBRAT, O. *La Peinture de Genre en Angleterre 1764–1850* (n.d., Paris).

BAKER, C. H. COLLINS. *British Painting* (1933).

BARMAN, C. *An Introduction to Railway Architecture* (1950).

BATE, PERCY. *The English Pre-Raphaelite Painters: their Associates and Successors* (1901).

BECKETT, R. B. *John Constable and the Fishers* (1952).

BELL, J. MUNRO, and HAYDEN, A. *Chippendale, Sheraton and Hepplewhite Furniture Designs* (1938).

BEMROSE, G. *Nineteenth Century English Pottery and Porcelain* (1952).

BETJEMAN, JOHN. *First and Last Loves* (1952).

BINYON, L. *English Water-Colours* (1933).

BØE, A. *From Gothic Revival to Functional Form* (Oslo and Oxford, 1957).

BRIGGS, M. S. *Goths and Vandals* (1952).

BRYDALL, R. *Art in Scotland* (1889).

BURCH, R. M. *Colour Printing and Colour Printers* (1910).

BURY, A. *Two Centuries of British Water-Colour Painting* (1950).

CALLOW, WILLIAM. *An Autobiography*, ed. H. M. Cundall (1908).

CHANCELLOR, E. BERESFORD. *Lives of the British Sculptors* (1911).

—— *Life in Regency and Early Victorian Times* (1926).

CHESNEAU, E. *La Peinture Anglaise* (1882): Eng. trans. by L. N. Hetherington (1888).

CLARK, K. M. *The Gothic Revival* (1923); 2nd ed. (1950).

CLARKE, B. F. L. *Church Builders of the Nineteenth Century* (1938).

CLAYDEN, P. W. *Rogers and his Contemporaries*, 2 vols. (1889).

CLUNN, H. P. *The Face of London*; revised ed. (1956).

COLE, SIR HENRY. *Fifty Years of Public Work*, 2 vols. (1884).

COOPER, T. S. *My Life* (1891).

COPE, C. H. *Reminiscences of Charles West Cope* (1891).

COX, DAVID. *Treatise on Landscape Painting and Effect in Watercolour* (1814–16); ed. A. L. Baldry (1922).

CROKER, JOHN W. *Letters, Diaries and Memoirs*, ed. L. J. Jennings, 3 vols. (1884).

CUNDALL, H. M. *A History of Water Colour Painting* (1929).

CURSITER, STANLEY. *Scottish Art* (1949).

DICKES, W. F. *The Norwich School of Painting* (1905).

DODDS, JOHN W. *The Age of Paradox: A Biography of England 1841–1851* (1952).

DUTTON, R. *The Victorian Home* (1954).

EASTLAKE, C. L. *A History of the Gothic Revival* (1872).

EASTLAKE, ELIZABETH, LADY. *Journals and Correspondence of Lady Eastlake*, ed. by C. E. Smith, 2 vols. (1895).

ESDAILE, K. A. *English Monumental Sculpture since the Renaissance* (1927).

EVANS, JOAN. *John Ruskin* (1954).

FAY, C. R. *The Palace of Industry, 1851* (Cambridge, 1951).

FINBERG, A. J. *English Water Colour Painters* (1906).

—— *The Life of J. M. W. Turner, R.A.* (1939).

FRITH, W. P. *My Autobiography and Reminiscences*, 3 vols. (1887–8).

FRY, ROGER. *Reflections on British Painting* (1934).

GAUNT, WILLIAM. *The Pre-Raphaelite Tragedy* (1942).

GEORGE, M. D. *Catalogue of Political and Personal Satires Preserved in the Department of Prints and Drawings in the British Museum*: viii, 1801–10 (1947); ix, 1811–19 (1949).

GERNSHEIM, HELMUT and ALISON. *The History of Photography* (1955).

GOODHART-RENDEL, H. S. *English Architecture since the Regency* (1953).

GOTCH, J. A. *The Growth and Work of the Royal Institute of British Architects* (1934).

GRAHAM, J. MURRAY. *An Historical View of Literature and Art in Great Britain* (1871).

GRANT, M. H. *A Chronological History of the Old English Landscape Painters*, 3 vols. (n.d.).

GRAY, BASIL. *The English Print* (1937).

GRIGSON, GEOFFREY. *The Harp of Aeolus* (1947).

GWYNN, D. *Lord Shrewsbury, Pugin and the Catholic Revival* (1946).

HALL, S. C. *Retrospect of a Long Life*, 2 vols. (1883).

HEATH, VERNON. *Recollections* (1892).

HITCHCOCK, H.-R. *Early Victorian Architecture*, 2 vols. (1954).

HODGSON, J. E., and EATON, F. A. *The Royal Academy and its Members* (1905).

HOLME, C. *The Royal Academy from Reynolds to Millais* (1904).

HORSLEY, J. C. *Recollections of a Royal Academician* (1903).

HUBBARD, H. *Some Victorian Draughtsmen* (1944).

HUDSON, O., and LUCKHURST, K. W. *The Royal Society of Arts* (1954).

HUGHES, C. E. *Early English Water Colour* (1913), ed. J. Mayne (1950).

HUNT, W. HOLMAN. *Pre-Raphaelitism and the Pre-Raphaelite Brotherhood*, 2 vols. (1905).

HUSSEY, C. *The Picturesque* (1927).

HUTCHISON, S. C. *The Homes of the Royal Academy* (1956).

INGLIS-JONES, E. *Peacocks in Paradise* (1951).

IRONSIDE, ROBIN, and GERE, JOHN. *Pre-Raphaelite Painters* (1948).

ISON, W. *The Georgian Buildings of Bath* (1948).

—— *The Georgian Buildings of Bristol* (1952).

JEWITT, L. *The Ceramic Art of Great Britain*, ii (1878).

JOURDAIN, M., and ROSE, F. *English Furniture: 1750–1830* (1953).

KLINGENDER, F. D. *Hogarth and English Caricature* (1944).

—— *Art and the Industrial Revolution* (1947).

LAMB, W. R. M. *The Royal Academy* (1951).

LAYARD, G. S. *Sir Thomas Lawrence's Letter-Bag* (1906).

LEMAITRE, HENRI. *Le Paysage anglais a l'aquarelle 1760–1851* (Paris, 1955).

LOW, DAVID. *British Cartoonists, Caricaturists and Comic Artists* (1932).

MACCOLL, D. S. *Nineteenth Century Art* (Glasgow, 1902).

MARKHAM, V. R. *Paxton and the Bachelor Duke* (1935).

MARTIN, THEODORE. *The Life of the Prince Consort*, 5 vols. (1875–80).

MEEKS, C. L. V. *The Railroad Station* (Yale University Press, 1956).

MILLAIS, J. G. *The Life and Letters of Sir John Everett Millais*, 2 vols. (1890).

MUTHER, RICHARD. *Geschichte der Englischen Malerei* (Berlin, 1903).

PENZER, N. M. *Paul Storr* (1954).

PEVSNER, NIKOLAUS. *Matthew Digby Wyatt* (Cambridge, 1950).

—— *High Victorian Design* (1951).

PILCHER, D. *The Regency Style* (1947).

PIPER, DAVID. *The English Face* (1957).

PIPER, JOHN. *British Romantic Artists* (1932).

REDGRAVE, F. M. *Richard Redgrave, A Memoir compiled from his Diary* (1891).

REILLY, P. *An Introduction to Regency Architecture* (1948).

REYNOLDS, GRAHAM. *English Portrait Miniatures* (1952).

—— *Painters of the Victorian Scene* (1953).

RICHARDSON, A. E. *Monumental Classic Architecture in Great Britain and Ireland during the eighteenth and nineteenth centuries* (1914).

—— *An Introduction to Georgian Architecture* (1949).

—— and GILL, C. LOVETT. *Regional Architecture of the West of England* (1924).

ROBERTS, R. ELLIS. *Samuel Rogers and his Circle* (1910).

ROE, F. G. *Victorian Furniture* (1952).

ROGET, J. L. *History of the Old Water Colour Society*, 2 vols. (1891).

ROWELL, G. *The Victorian Theatre* (1956).

RUSKIN, JOHN. *The Complete Works*, ed. by E. T. Cook and Alexander Wedderburn, 39 vols. (1903–12).

—— *Diaries of John Ruskin*, ed. Joan Evans, i and ii (1956–8).

SCOTT, G. G. *Personal and Professional Recollections* (1879).

SCOTT, W. BELL. *Autobiographical Notes*, 2 vols. (1892).

SITWELL, S. *Conversation Pieces* (1936).

—— *Narrative Paintings* (1937).

SIZERANNE, R. DE LA. *La Peinture anglaise contemporaine* (Paris, 1895); Eng. trans. (1898).

SMITH, H. CLIFFORD. *Buckingham Palace* (1931).

SMITH, M. H. STEPHEN. *Art and Anecdote: Recollections of W. F. Yeames, R.A. his Life and his Friends* (n.d.).

STEEGMAN, JOHN. *The Rule of Taste* (1936).

—— *Consort of Taste 1830–1870* (1950).

STEWART, C. *The Stones of Manchester* (1956).

STREET, A. E. *Memoir of G. E. Street* (1888).

SUMMERSON, JOHN. *John Nash, Architect to George IV* (1935).

—— *Georgian London* (1948).

—— *Heavenly Mansions* (1949).

—— *Architecture in Britain 1530–1830* (1953).

TEMPLE, A. G. *The Art of Painting in the Queen's Reign* (1897).

TINKER, C. B. *Painter and Poet* (Harvard, 1938).

TIPPING, H. A. *English Homes*, vol. vi (1926).

WEEKES, HENRY. *Lectures on Art* (1880).

WHIFFEN, M. *Stuart and Georgian Churches* (1947–8).

WHITLEY. *Art in England 1800–1820* (Cambridge, 1928).

—— *Art in England 1821–1837* (Cambridge, 1937).

—— Papers: 14 vols. of Notes and Cuttings in the British Museum.

WILLIAMS, I. A. *Early English Watercolours Painting* (1952).

WILLIS, R., and CLARK, J. W. *The Architectural History of the University of Cambridge*, 3 vols. (1886).

WILMOT-BUXTON, H. J. *English Painters* (1883).

YOUNG, G. M. (ed. by). *Early Victorian England*, 2 vols. (1934).

INDEX

References in **black** type are to plates

I. WILLIAM BLAKE: THE GENIUS OF SHAKESPEARE. British Museum

2. BENJAMIN WEST: DEATH ON THE PALE HORSE. Pennsylvania Academy of the Fine Arts

3. *a.* SIR JOHN EVERETT MILLAIS: THE RESCUE. National Gallery of Victoria, Melbourne

b. J. H. FUSELI: ALMANSARIS VISITS HUON IN PRISON. Kunsthaus, Zurich

4. *a.* J. H. FUSELI: HELENA AND THE COUNTESS.   Engraved by J. G. Walker
   b. JAMES GILLRAY: DIDO IN DESPAIR (DETAIL).   Colour print

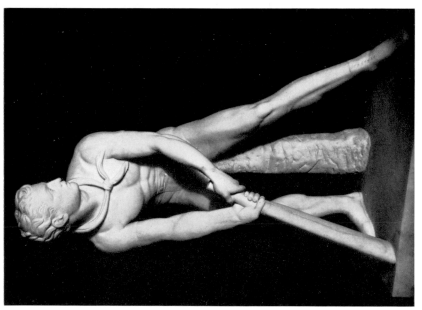

5. *a.* HENRY ROSSI: THE BATSMAN.   Coll. the Duke of Bedford

   b. JAMES LOUGH: THOMAS MIDDLETON, BISHOP OF CALCUTTA.   St. Paul's Cathedral

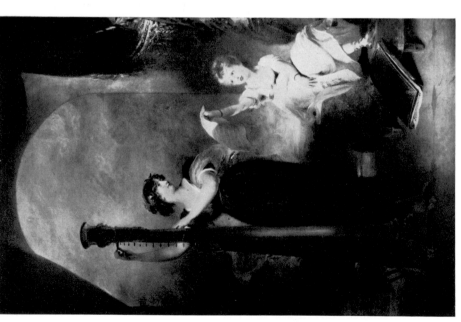

6. *a.* SIR THOMAS LAWRENCE: PRINCESS OF WALES AND PRINCESS CHARLOTTE.
Reproduced by gracious permission of Her Majesty the Queen

b. G. H. HARLOW: THE MISSES ANNE AND FANNY LEADER. Philadelphia Museum of Art

7. *a.* JAMES NORTHCOTE: ALEXANDER I OF RUSSIA RESCUING A PEASANT BOY FROM DROWNING.
Royal Society of Medicine

b. SIR THOMAS LAWRENCE: JOHN PHILIP KEMBLE AS CORIOLANUS. Guildhall Art Gallery

8. WILLIAM OWEN: LADY BEAUMONT. National Gallery of Victoria, Melbourne

9. THOMAS PHILLIPS: BERIAH BOTFIELD. Coll. the Marquess of Bath

10. *a.* J. C. IBBETSON: CONWAY CASTLE. Victoria and Albert Museum
  b. FRANCIS TOWNE: CONWAY CASTLE. Private collection

11. *a.* J. M. W. TURNER: PEMBROKE CASTLE, THUNDERSTORM APPROACHING.
Coll. W. Eustace Pitt-Millar, Esq.
b. FRANCIS DANBY: CONWAY CASTLE. British Museum.

12. *a*. JAMES WYATT: FONTHILL ABBEY. Drawn and engraved by T. Higham
b. J. M. W. TURNER: HAFOD. Lady Lever Art Gallery, Port Sunlight

13. JAMES WYATT:
a. BELVOIR CASTLE: THE SOUTH-WEST RANGE
b. ASHRIDGE PARK: VIEW FROM TERRACE GARDEN

14. THOMAS HOPPER. PENRHYN CASTLE
a. THE HEAD OF THE STAIRCASE
b. THE GREAT KEEP AND SOUTH FACE

15. *a*. SIR ROBERT SMIRKE: EASTNOR CASTLE
   b. JAMES THOMSON: GRITTLETON HOUSE: THE STAIRCASE WELL
   c. ROBERT LUGAR: MAESLLWCH CASTLE.
      From a photograph c. 1870 attributed to Roger Fenton

16. *a*. WILLIAM PAYNE: SKATING SCENE. British Museum
b. JOHN GLOVER: MILLES PLAINS, TASMANIA.
Tasmanian Museum and Art Gallery, Hobart

17. *a.* THOMAS GIRTIN: KIRKSTALL ABBEY. British Museum
   b. DAVID COX: THE NIGHT TRAIN. City Art Gallery, Birmingham

18. *a.* JOHN CROME: THE SHADOWED ROAD. Victoria and Albert Museum
b. J. S. COTMAN: CHIRK AQUEDUCT. Victoria and Albert Museum

19. *a.* JOSHUA CRISTALL: FIGURES AT WELL.   National Gallery of Victoria, Melbourne
    b. THEODOR VON HOLST: LES ADIEUX.   National Gallery of Canada, Ottawa

20. *a*. WILLIAM BLAKE: JESSEY AND THE EAGLE'S NEST. Engraving
    b. SAMUEL PROUT: MARVELS OF ANCIENT ROME. City Art Gallery, Bristol

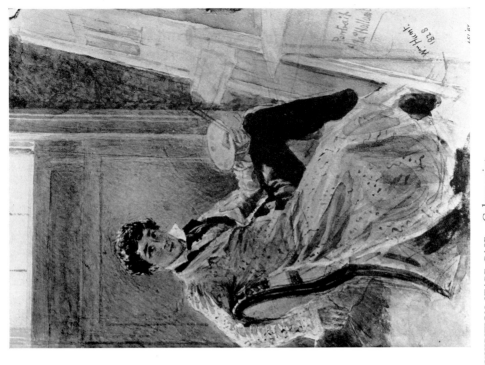

21. *a*. THOMAS ROWLANDSON: EXHIBITION STARE-CASE. Colour print
b. W. H. HUNT: JAMES HOLLAND, PAINTER, Victoria and Albert Museum

22. *a*. J. S. COTMAN: THE HARVEST FIELD, A PASTORAL.   City Art Gallery, Leeds
b. G. F. ROBSON: DURHAM CATHEDRAL.   Ashmolean Museum, Oxford

23. *a.* THOMAS STOTHARD: THE MEETING OF OTHELLO AND DESDEMONA
IN CYPRUS. Memorial Theatre, Stratford-upon-Avon

b. JAMES WARD: BULL, COW AND CALF. Castle Museum and Art Gallery,
Nottingham

24. *a*. JOHN CROME: BOULEVARD DES ITALIENS.   Coll. Q. E. Gurney, Esq.
b. ROBERT HILLS: STAGS IN KNOLE PARK.   Victoria and Albert Museum

25. SIR EDWIN LANDSEER:
a. THE HUNTING OF CHEVY CHASE. City Art Gallery, Birmingham
b. THE HUNTED STAG. Tate Gallery

26. *a*. WILLIAM BLAKE: HOMER AND THE ANCIENT POETS. Tate Gallery
    b. SAMUEL PALMER: OAK TREE, SHOREHAM, KENT. National Gallery of Canada, Ottawa

27. *a.* WILLIAM BLAKE: THE WHIRLWIND OF LOVERS: PAOLO AND FRANCESCA.
City Art Gallery, Birmingham
b. JOHN FLAXMAN: PAOLO AND FRANCESCA. Engraved by Tommaso Piroli

28. BRIGHTON:
a. WILLIAM PORDEN: THE DOME
b. JOHN NASH: THE ROYAL PAVILION, EAST FRONT

29. *a.* GEORGE DANCE: COLEORTON HALL.   Aquatint after a drawing by William Westall
   b. T. M. RICHARDSON: GRAINGER STREET, NEWCASTLE.   Laing Art Gallery, New-
       castle-upon-Tyne

30. *a.* JOHN NASH AND JAMES BURTON: WATERLOO PLACE

b. SIR JOHN RENNIE: GATEWAY TO ROYAL VICTUALLING YARD, STONEHOUSE, PLYMOUTH

31. *a.* THOMAS HARDWICK: PARISH CHURCH OF ST. MARYLEBONE

b. C. R. COCKERELL: HOLY TRINITY CHURCH, HOTWELLS, BRISTOL

32. *a.* LYPIATT TERRACE, CHELTENHAM
  b. JOHN FORBES: THE PUMP ROOM, PITTVILLE, CHELTENHAM
  c. AMON WILDS: GATEWAY TO PARK CRESCENT, WORTHING
  d. STEPHEN GEARY: EGYPTIAN COLUMNS, HIGHGATE CEMETERY

33. *a.* H. A. DARBISHIRE: COLUMBIA MARKET, BETHNAL GREEN
b. JOHN NASH AND JAMES THOMSON: CUMBERLAND TERRACE

34. *a.* HYDE PARK CORNER, *c.* 1880
b. KER STREET, DEVONPORT

35. *a.* WILLIAM WILKINS: DOWNING COLLEGE, CAMBRIDGE
b. SIR JOHN SOANE: PITZHANGER MANOR, EALING

36. *a*. JOHN FLAXMAN: THE PLEIAD STARS. Engraved by William Blake
    b. SILVER GILT VASE: DESIGNED BY JOHN FLAXMAN: MARK OF
       PAUL STORR. Reproduced by gracious permission of Her Majesty
       the Queen

37. *a.* CHAMBERLAIN WORCESTER FRUIT-DISH: *c.* 1800. Coll.
Mrs. W. E. Bassett, Melbourne
b. EDWARD CALVERT: CLASSICAL LANDSCAPE.
Ashmolean Museum, Oxford

38. *a.* P. F. POOLE: THE VISION OF EZEKIEL.   Tate Gallery
b. J. M. W. TURNER: THE DELUGE.   Tate Gallery

39. *a.* J. M. W. TURNER: SNOW STORM: HANNIBAL AND HIS ARMY CROSSING THE ALPS.
Tate Gallery

b. SLAVERS THROWING OVERBOARD THE DEAD AND DYING—TYPHON COMING ON
(DETAIL). Museum of Fine Arts, Boston

40. *a.* J. M. W. TURNER: THE PASSAGE OF THE ST. GOTHARD, FROM THE CENTRE OF THE DEVIL'S BRIDGE. Coll. Mr. and
Mrs. Esmond Morse

b. JOHN MARTIN. THE BARD. Laing Art Gallery, Newcastle-upon-Tyne

41. FRANCIS DANBY: THE DELIVERY OUT OF EGYPT: PHARAOH AND HIS HOSTS OVERWHELMED IN THE RED SEA.
Harris Museum and Art Gallery, Preston

42. J. M. W. TURNER:

a. CROSSING THE BROOK. Tate Gallery
b. MERCURY AND ARGUS. National Gallery of Canada, Ottawa

43. *a.* GEORGE JONES: THE BURNING FIERY FURNACE. Tate Gallery
    b. J. M. W. TURNER: SHADRACH, MESHACH, AND ABEDNEGO COMING FORTH FROM THE BURNING FIERY FURNACE.
    Tate Gallery

44. *a.* J. M. W. TURNER: PETWORTH HOUSE FROM THE LAKE—DEWY MORNING.
   National Trust, Petworth House
   b. JOHN CONSTABLE: THE WHITE HORSE.   Frick Collection, New York

45. *a*. J. M. W. TURNER: BRIGHTON FROM THE SEA. National Trust, Petworth House
   b. JOHN CONSTABLE: THE MARINE PARADE AND CHAIN PIER, BRIGHTON. Tate
   Gallery

46. J. M. W. TURNER: THE SHIPWRECK: FISHING BOATS ENDEAVOURING TO RESCUE THE CREW.   Tate Gallery

47. JOHN CONSTABLE: WHITEHALL STAIRS OR THE OPENING OF WATERLOO BRIDGE. Coll. Harry Ferguson, Esq.

48. *a*. THOMAS BANKS: MONUMENT TO CAPT. RICHARD BURGESS. St. Paul's
Cathedral
b. JOHN BACON THE YOUNGER: MONUMENT TO SIR JOHN MOORE.
St. Paul's Cathedral

49. *a*. WILLIAM THEED AND E. H. BAILY: MONUMENT TO SIR WILLIAM
PONSONBY. St. Paul's Cathedral

   b. JOHN FLAXMAN: MONUMENT TO LORD MANSFIELD (DETAIL).
Westminster Abbey

50. *a.* SIR FRANCIS CHANTREY: BISHOP RYDER. Lichfield Cathedral

b. JOHN FLAXMAN: LADY FITZHARRIS AND HER CHILDREN. Christchurch Priory, Hants

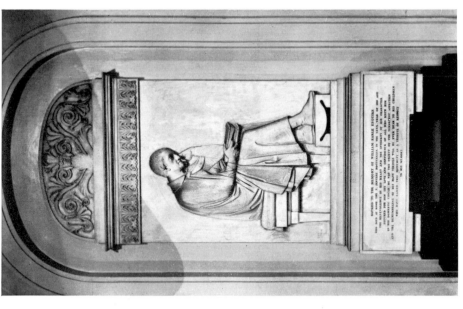

51. *a.* JOHN GIBSON: WILLIAM EARLE. St. James's Chapel, Liverpool
    b. JOHN FOSTER. St. James's Cemetery Chapel, Liverpool

52. *a.* JOHN GIBSON: QUEEN VICTORIA BETWEEN JUSTICE AND MERCY. Prince's Chamber, Palace of Westminster

b. R. J. WYATT: MONUMENT TO MRS. LEGH (DETAIL). Winwick

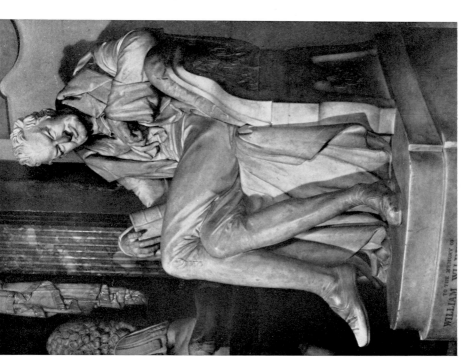

53. *a.* SAMUEL JOSEPH: WILLIAM WILBERFORCE. Westminster Abbey

b. SIR RICHARD WESTMACOTT: MONUMENT TO CHARLES JAMES FOX (DETAIL). Westminster Abbey

54. *a.* SIR FRANCIS CHANTREY: MONUMENT TO CHILDREN OF REV.
W. ROBINSON (DETAIL). Lichfield Cathedral
b. JOSEPH DURHAM: WAITING FOR HIS INNINGS.
Corporation of London, City of London School

55. M. C. WYATT: MONUMENT TO PRINCESS CHARLOTTE. St. George's Chapel, Windsor

56. GEORGE DAWE: A CHILD RESCUED BY ITS MOTHER FROM AN EAGLE'S NEST

57. SIR DAVID WILKIE: GENERAL SIR DAVID BAIRD DISCOVERING THE BODY OF THE
SULTAN TIPPOO SAIB. Edinburgh Castle

58. SIR DAVID WILKIE:

a. BLIND MAN'S BUFF. Reproduced by gracious permission of Her Majesty the Queen

b. PEEP-O'-DAY BOY'S CABIN, WEST OF IRELAND. Tate Gallery

59. SIR DAVID WILKIE:

a. GOING TO THE DRAWING-ROOM, HOLYROOD HOUSE. National Gallery of Canada, Ottawa

b. ENTRY OF GEORGE IV INTO HOLYROOD HOUSE. Scottish National Portrait Gallery

60. PORTRAITS OF WILKIE:

a. SIR WILLIAM BEECHEY: 1808. Scottish National Portrait Gallery

b. JOHN JACKSON: 1807: PENCIL DRAWING. British Museum

c. SELF PORTRAIT: 1813. National Portrait Gallery

d. THOMAS PHILLIPS: 1829. Tate Gallery

61. *a.* SIR FRANCIS CHANTREY: SIR WALTER SCOTT. Lady Lever Art Gallery, Port Sunlight
   b. SIR FRANCIS CHANTREY: MRS. JORDAN (DETAIL). Coll. the Earl of Munster
   c. THOMAS WOOLNER: LORD TENNYSON. Westminster Abbey
   d. SIR JOSEPH EDGAR BOEHM: THOMAS CARLYLE (DETAIL). Scottish National Portrait
      Gallery

62. *a*. WILLIAM ETTY: THE COMBAT. From an engraving by G. T. Doo
   b. SIR GEORGE HAYTER: CIRCASSIAN WOMEN SOLD TO BRIGANDS.
   Coll. J. Gold, Esq.

63. B. R. HAYDON:

a. NERO HARPING WHILE ROME BURNED. Coll. Sir H. Gengoult Smith, Melbourne
b. CHAIRING THE MEMBER. Tate Gallery

64. *a.* WILLIAM COLLINS: DISPOSAL OF A FAVOURITE LAMB. Messrs. Williams
   Grafton Street
   b. E. M. WARD: THE ROYAL FAMILY OF FRANCE IN THE PRISON OF THE
   TEMPLE. Harris Museum and Art Gallery, Preston

65. *a.* C. R. LESLIE: THE TWO PRINCES IN THE TOWER.   Victoria and Albert Museum
    b. SIR CHARLES EASTLAKE: THE CHAMPION.   City Art Gallery, Birmingham

66. *a.* CLARKSON STANFIELD: THE ABANDONED.   From a collotype
b. P. F. POOLE: SOLOMON EAGLE.   Mappin Art Gallery, Sheffield

67. *a.* C. R. COCKERELL: DESIGN FOR THE ROYAL EXCHANGE. Royal Institute of British
      Architects
    b. THE ASHMOLEAN MUSEUM AND TAYLOR INSTITUTION

68. *a.* SIR CHARLES BARRY: ST. PETER'S, BRIGHTON
b. JAMES SAVAGE: ST. LUKE'S, CHELSEA

69. A. W. PUGIN: ST. CHAD'S CATHEDRAL, BIRMINGHAM:
   a. EXTERIOR FROM THE NORTH
   b. SCREEN AND EAST END

70. *a*. A. W. PUGIN: ST. GILES', CHEADLE
b. R. D. CHANTRELL: ST. PETER'S, LEEDS

71. *a.* R. C. CARPENTER: TOWER OF ST. PAUL'S, BRIGHTON

b. WILLIAM BUTTERFIELD: ALL SAINTS, MARGARET STREET, LONDON: SOUTH WALL OF NAVE

c. WILLIAM BUTTERFIELD: TOWER OF ALL SAINTS, MARGARET STREET

72. *a.* SIR CHARLES BARRY: BRIDGEWATER HOUSE
b. ANTHONY SALVIN: HARLAXTON HALL

73. A. W. PUGIN:
a. WEST DOORWAY, ST. GILES', CHEADLE
b. ANGEL FROM CHAPEL IN ALTON TOWERS
c. C. R. COCKERELL: SPANDREL FIGURE, ST. GEORGE'S HALL, LIVERPOOL

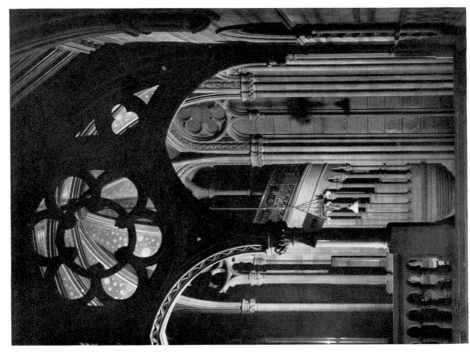

74. *a*. H. L. ELMES: INTERIOR, ST. GEORGE'S HALL, LIVERPOOL: ORGAN CASE DESIGNED BY C. R. COCKERELL

b. ALFRED WATERHOUSE: STAIRWAY IN TOWN HALL, MANCHESTER

75. *a.* J. B. BUNNING: THE COAL EXCHANGE, LOWER THAMES STREET, LONDON
b. SIR CHARLES AND E. M. BARRY: TOWN HALL, HALIFAX

76. *a*. SIR GEORGE GILBERT SCOTT: ST. PANCRAS HOTEL
b. G. E. STREET: THE GREAT HALL, THE LAW COURTS

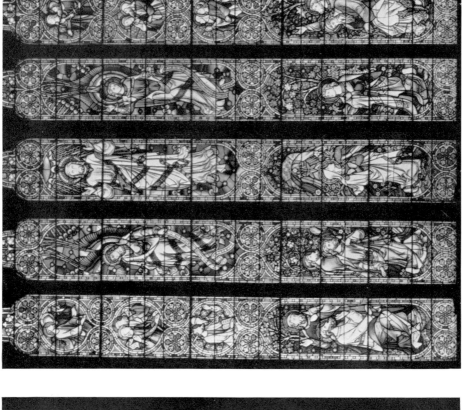

77. *a.* SIR GEORGE GILBERT SCOTT: ALL SOULS, HALIFAX: CAPITALS

b. JOHN HARDMAN & CO.: CENTRAL LIGHTS OF WEST WINDOW, ST. PATRICK'S CATHEDRAL, MELBOURNE

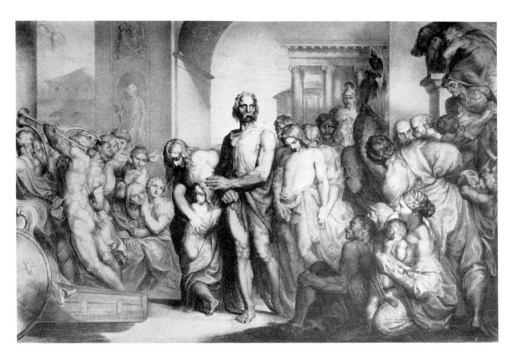

78. *a.* G. F. WATTS: CARACTACUS LED IN TRIUMPH. From a lithograph
    b. THE QUEEN'S ROBING ROOM: PALACE OF WESTMINSTER

79. DANIEL MACLISE:

a. DEATH OF NELSON (DETAIL)

b. MEETING OF WELLINGTON AND BLÜCHER (DETAIL).

Royal Gallery, Palace of Westminster

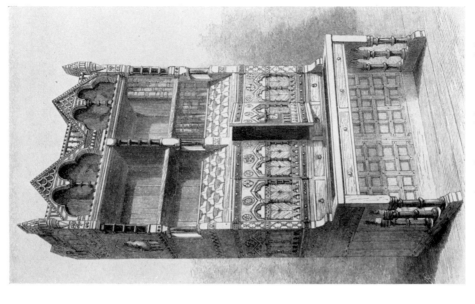

80. *a.* HUNT AND ROSKELL: TWEEDDALE MEMORIAL. From the Illustrated Catalogue of the Great Exhibition
b. R. NORMAN SHAW: OAK BOOKCASE WITH TABLE. From the Illustrated Catalogue of the International Exhibition of 1862

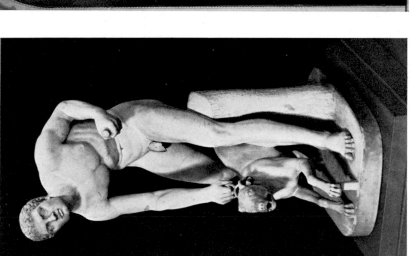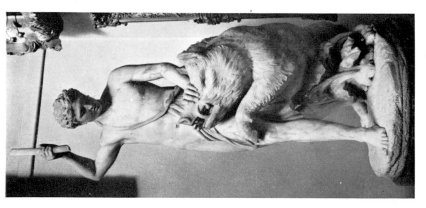

81. *a.* J. E. CAREW: ADONIS AND THE BOAR. National Trust, Petworth House

b. JOHN GIBSON: THE HUNTER AND HIS DOG. Usher Art Gallery, Lincoln

c. W. THEED: THE BARD. The Mansion House

82. *a.* PRINTED COTTON (BIRDS COPIED FROM AUDUBON). Victoria and Albert Museum
b. CRYSTAL PALACE: NORTH TRANSEPT. Engraved by R. Bibbey

83. *a*. WILLIAM MORRIS: THE DAISY PATTERN WALLPAPER
b. PHILIP WEBB: THE RED HOUSE, BEXLEY HEATH

84. *a*. WILLIAM DYCE: JOASH SHOOTING THE ARROW OF DELIVERANCE. Kunsthalle, Hamburg

b. DANIEL MACLISE: NOAH'S SACRIFICE. Temple Newsam House, Leeds

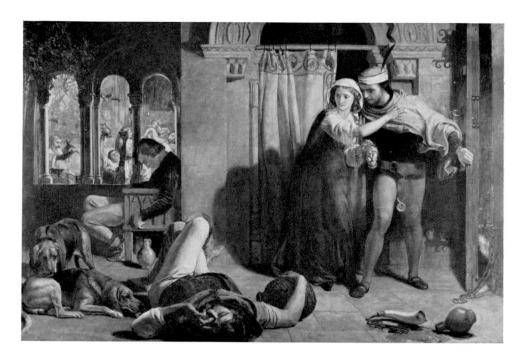

85. W. HOLMAN HUNT:
a. THE FLIGHT OF MADELINE AND PORPHYRO.   Guildhall Art Gallery
b. STRAYED SHEEP.   Tate Gallery

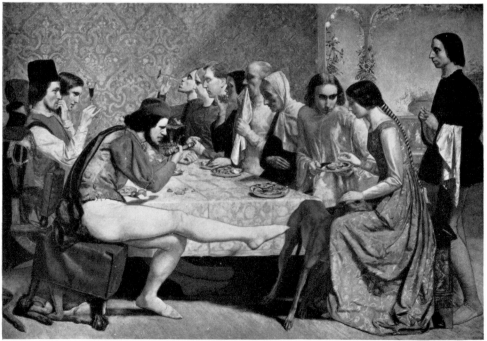

86. *a*. FORD MADOX BROWN: WORK.   City Art Galleries, Manchester

b. SIR JOHN EVERETT MILLAIS: LORENZO AND ISABELLA.   Walker Art Gallery, Liverpool

87. *a*. J. R. HERBERT: OUR SAVIOUR, SUBJECT TO HIS PARENTS AT NAZARETH.
   Guildhall Art Gallery
   b. SIR JOHN EVERETT MILLAIS: CHRIST IN THE HOUSE OF HIS PARENTS. Tate
   Gallery

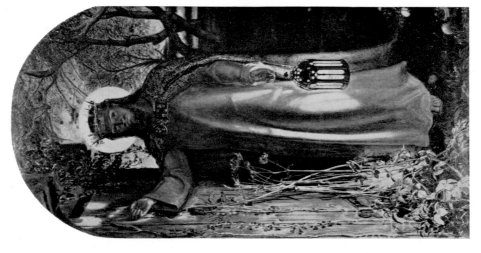

88. W. HOLMAN HUNT:

a. THE AWAKENED CONSCIENCE. Coll. Sir Colin Anderson

b. THE LIGHT OF THE WORLD. City Art Galleries, Manchester

89. *a.* C. A. COLLINS: CONVENT THOUGHTS.   Ashmolean Museum, Oxford
b. J. F. LEWIS: IN THE BEY'S GARDEN. Harris Museum and Art Gallery, Preston

90. *a*. JOHN PHILIP: PUGIN, SCOTT, COCKERELL AND BARRY FROM FRIEZE
      OF ALBERT MEMORIAL
  b. WILLIAM THEED: AFRICA: ALBERT MEMORIAL
  c. EDWARD ARMITAGE: RETRIBUTION. City Art Gallery, Leeds

91. ALFRED STEVENS: THE WELLINGTON MEMORIAL.
St. Paul's Cathedral

92. *a.* G. F. WATTS: LADY MARGARET BEAUMONT AND HER DAUGHTER.   Coll. Viscount Allendale
b. SIR JOHN EVERETT MILLAIS: THE BLIND GIRL.   City Art Gallery, Birmingham

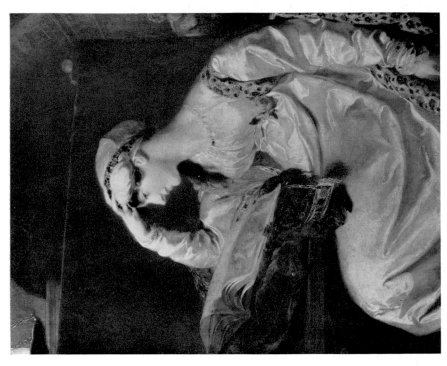

93. *a.* ALFRED STEVENS: MRS. COLLMANN. Tate Gallery
b. SIR THOMAS LAWRENCE. MRS. WOLFF. Art Institute of Chicago

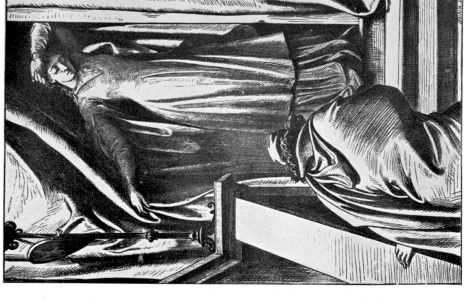

94. *a.* DANTE GABRIEL ROSSETTI: THE MAIDS OF ELFIN-MERE.   Engraved by Dalziel
b. SIR FREDERICK LEIGHTON: SCENE FROM ROMOLA.   Engraved by Joseph Swain

Tends on the little island's verdant swell,

The shepherd's sea-girt reign ; or, to the rocks

Dire-clinging, gathers his ovarious food ;

Or sweeps the fishy shore ; or treasures up

The plumage, rising full, to form the bed

Of luxury.　And here a while the muse,

High-hovering o'er the broad cerulean scene,

Sees Caledonia, in romantic view :

Her airy mountains, from the waving main,

Invested with a keen diffusive sky,

Breathing the soul acute ; her forests huge,

Incult, robust, and tall, by Nature's hand

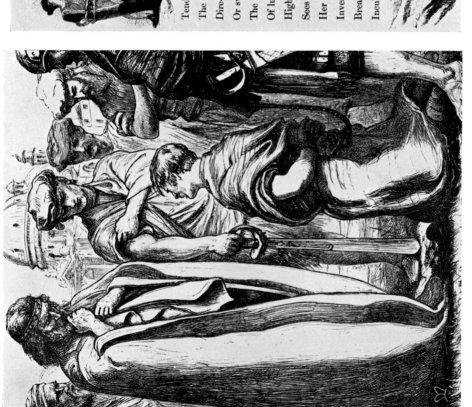

95.　*a*.　SIR JOHN EVERETT MILLAIS: THE UNMERCIFUL SERVANT.　Wood engraving
　　b.　R. REDGRAVE: ILLUSTRATION TO THOMSON'S SEASONS.　Engraved by T. Williams

96. *a.* THOMAS WEBSTER: A VILLAGE CHOIR. Victoria and Albert Museum
b. WILLIAM HOLMAN HUNT: MAY MORNING ON MAGDALEN TOWER.
Lady Lever Art Gallery, Port Sunlight